HAKUIN'S PRECIOUS MIRROR CAVE

Hakuin's Precious Mirror Cave

A ZEN MISCELLANY

EDITED AND TRANSLATED BY

Norman Waddell

COUNTERPOINT · BERKELEY

Library of Congress Cataloging-in-Publication Data

Hakuin, 1686–1769.
  [Selections. English. 2009]
  Hakuin's Precious mirror cave : a Zen miscellany / edited
and translated by Norman Waddell.
    p. cm.
  1. Rinzai (Sect)—Doctrines—Early works to 1800.
2. Hakuin, 1686–1769. I. Waddell, Norman. II. Title.

  BQ9399.E593E5 2009
  294.3'927—dc22   2008051631

ISBN 978-1-58243-497-1

Cover and interior design by Gopa & Ted2, Inc.
Printed in the United States of America

COUNTERPOINT
2560 Ninth Street, Suite 318
Berkeley, CA 94710
www.counterpointpress.com

Dedicated to Nishitani Keiji (1900–1990),

with grateful memories

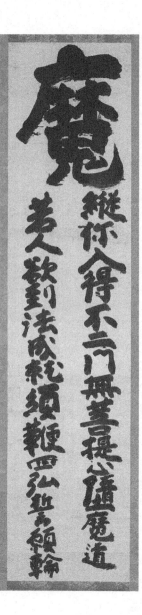

魔

縱你入得不二門　無菩提心墮魔道

若人欲識法成就　須鞭四弘堅願輪

DEVIL

Even if you enter the gate of nonduality,
if you lack the Bodhi-mind, you will sink into the
ways of the devil. If you want to bring your quest for
the great Dharma to completion, you must spur
forward the wheel of the Four Great Vows.

This fine example of Hakuin's calligraphy,
dominated by the single large character *Ma*
(Mara, the Devil or Destroyer; the enemy
of Buddhist practice), can be said to express
in a nutshell the essence of his teaching.

: Contents :

Contents

: General Introduction :

PRECIOUS MIRROR CAVE is made up of two parts.[1] The first is a collection of five works by Zen Master Hakuin (1685–1768) spanning a wide range of subjects and themes, including some that until now have been unknown in the West. The second is a chronological biography of Hakuin compiled by his chief disciple Tōrei Enji, the only such work that covers his entire life from birth to death. In the introduction that follows I will situate these works and other of Hakuin's principal publications within the teaching career he was busily engaged in over the second half of his life, with the focus on his final twenty-five years during which all the written works appeared.

Hakuin spent his entire life in the small village of Hara in Suruga province (present-day Shizuoka prefecture), a post station on the great Tōkaidō road that ran between the capital at Kyoto and the administrative center in Edo (present-day Tokyo). This stretch of the road through Suruga province, passing between Mount Fuji and Suruga Bay, was one of the busiest and also one the most beautiful in its entire three-hundred-mile length. A fascinating assortment of people and sights, together with the latest news from around the country, passed in a constant stream through the post station, creating an unusually stimulating environment that would inform young Hakuin's mind from an early age. Many of the peddlers, street entertainers, and the like that infested the road became subject matter in writings and paintings that appeared in his later years.

As the son of the proprietor of the post house Omodakaya, which stabled and provided relay packhorses to travelers, Hakuin was raised in relatively privileged circumstances. When he was ordained into the Buddhist priesthood at fourteen, the ceremony took place at Shōin-ji, the tiny Zen temple located almost adjacent to his home. And it was there at Shōin-ji, after being installed as abbot at the age of thirty-one, that he would remain for the rest of his long life. He was away from the village only when called by his religious activities—the extensive Zen pilgrimages in search of enlightenment he undertook in his youth and the countless trips he later made as a priest to conduct practice meetings around the country.

After reaching great enlightenment in his early forties, teaching Zen was Hakuin's life, and he taught indefatigably right up until his death forty years later, at the age of eighty-three. In his final decades, he turned to the written word to help spread his teaching.[2] In addition to a number of voluminous works in Chinese in the traditional Zen manner, he composed more than twenty-five works in Japanese that are distinguished by an astonishing range of subjects and themes, and an originality, immediacy, and creative exuberance that make the works of his contemporaries appear dry and pedantic by comparison. The powerful impact of their vigorous style, a direct embodiment of Hakuin's indomitable, larger-than-life personality, creates an impression similar to that we receive, often with even greater force, from his painting and calligraphy.

Another distinguishing feature of these writings—seen in *The Tale of My Childhood* (Chapter One) and *Idle Talk on a Night Boat* (Chapter Three)—is the large amount of personal history they contain, which is especially unusual in a Zen context, because priests have generally been reluctant, in books at least, to discuss their own experiences. The only other example in Japanese Zen that comes readily to mind is the great seventeenth-century Rinzai teacher Bankei Yōtaku (1622–93), whose published sermons are also dominated by stories of his religious quest. But whereas in Bankei's case the sermons were transcribed against his explicit orders and published by his disciples, Hakuin made a very deliberate and persistent effort to put his experiences before the public. This inclination is clear even in his earliest printed works,[3] and definitely increased with age, as if the older he became, the more convinced he was that his personal experiences were as significant, and inspiring, as those of the illustrious ancestors in Zen history whose words and deeds figure so prominently in his works. He obviously felt them to be a legitimate and potent teaching tool, one that, especially being firsthand, could exert great impact on his audience.

Our knowledge of Hakuin's religious career is based on three main sources. For the first half, the religious quest that began in childhood and continued up until the decisive satori he experienced in his forty-first year, the primary sources of information are the detailed autobiographical accounts in *Wild Ivy* and *The Tale of My Childhood*. They constitute a rich and fascinating personal record with few parallels in Zen literature. While *The Tale of My Childhood*, the earlier of the two, breaks off in Hakuin's twenty-fourth year with accounts of his study under the Zen master Shōju, *Wild Ivy* takes the story a few years further, into the post-satori phase of his career. And although the two narratives cover much the same ground, it is usually possible by comparing similar descriptions of an episode to get a better understanding of the event in question. The enlightenment experience that marks the end of his quest is at once the start of his long and tireless teaching career, and for this the *Chronological Biography* (Chapter Six) compiled by his disciple Tōrei remains virtually the only source we have.

Our reliance on Hakuin and his leading heir for information about his life makes it appropriate to question their accuracy. Given Hakuin's motive for writing—he clearly wanted his narratives to encourage and caution Zen students—and a self-acknowledged penchant for exaggeration, we might reasonably suspect that he would embellish or revise certain events in his life to make them agree more closely with his program for Zen study. He may even have invented some. And Tōrei could well be out to buff up his old boss's reputation, of course. Ultimately, since no independent biographies exist to corroborate or refute their version of events, forming a definitive assessment of their veracity is impossible. That said, in studying Hakuin's works over a period of many years, I have found his tales of personal history to be as reliable as most autobiography, with regard both to the events he recounts and the dates that he gives for them.

Much the same can be said of Tōrei's *Chronological Biography*. Although such a biography (called *nempu* in Japanese) was not normally compiled until after the subject's death, Hakuin seems to have directed Tōrei to begin work on his *Chronological Biography* while he was still alive, advising him and probably looking over his shoulder during much of the compilation process. As a result, there do not seem to be many conspicuous differences between Tōrei's work and Hakuin's narratives, although again, the events described can for the most part be verified only by checking them against Hakuin's own accounts.

The final part of *Wild Ivy*, describing the years following the initial satori Hakuin achieved at the age of twenty-three studying under Rinzai teacher Shōju Rōjin in the mountains of Shinano province, gives an account of the debilitating "Zen sickness" he contracted after leaving Shōju that forced him temporarily to cease his Zen practice. The fullest account of this illness, including the story of Hakuin's visit to the hermit Hakuyū in the mountains of Kyoto and descriptions of meditation techniques he learned from him, is found in *Idle Talk on a Night Boat*, his most famous and widely read work.

Evidence scattered through the records suggests that he may still have been using those techniques after he returned to Hara from his travels at the age of thirty-one and was installed as abbot at Shōin-ji. Having succeeded in vanquishing the Zen sickness, he was now attempting, apparently on his own, to deepen and broaden his realization. He would later call this the "post-satori" phase of his training.

Hakuin (he adopted the name at thirty-three, having been born Iwajirō and having been known by his ordination name Ekaku) seems to have spent the first ten years at Shōin-ji in this same way: studying sutras and Zen records by day and doing zazen through the nights. He had a small room built behind the abbot's quarters where he could devote himself quietly to zazen free from external cares. He also tells of cinching himself tightly into a derelict palanquin and sitting until dawn—"like an image of Bodhidharma."

Shōin-ji was then in an advanced state of disrepair—stars shining through the roof beams at night, floors sodden with rain and dew—and it was also extremely poor. One day in those early years, appalled at seeing how haggard his solitary monk had become, he exclaimed, "Look what's happened to you from staying here and helping me! We have no doors or panels in the halls. We can't use the lamps. Our only assets worth noting are the moonlight and sound of the wind. I have no way of making things easier even for a single monk like you!" (*Chronological Biography*). Providing support for his monks was, of course, part of a master's obligation.

The *Chronological Biography* records that in Hakuin's thirty-second year he was lecturing at Shōin-ji on a Zen text to a small group of people—the first instance of what would be an increasingly important part of his teaching duties. Before long, students began arriving, a handful at first, but in the winter of his thirty-sixth year suddenly increasing with the arrival of a group of twenty traveling monks who asked for, and reluctantly received, his permission to stay.

Meanwhile, Hakuin pressed ahead in his long quest for enlightenment, which finally culminated one autumn night in his forty-first year. He had stayed up late reading the *Lotus Sutra* by lamplight. As the churring of a cricket reached his ears, "he was suddenly one with great enlightenment." All the nagging doubts that had plagued him for years vanished, along with an uneasiness he had felt at being unable to incorporate the tranquility he experienced during zazen into his everyday life. He now knew beyond any doubt that he was ready to teach others "with the perfect, untrammeled freedom of the Bodhisattvas." Tōrei characterized this moment by saying that Hakuin "had grasped the true meaning of the Bodhi-mind, that is, he had realized that the Bodhi-mind was nothing other than carrying out the Four Universal Vows" (Sentient beings are numberless. I vow to liberate them all. Defiling passions are endless. I vow to eradicate them all. Dharma teachings are infinite. I vow to learn them all. The Buddha way is unexcelled. I vow to master it). Hakuin would often characterize this effort as working toward deeper self-attainment while striving at the same time to lead others to liberation.

From that time forward, Hakuin threw himself into his teaching without reservation. While he demanded total dedication from his monks, temple routine was relatively informal. There were no set schedules for sutra-chanting or other rituals and, if temple legend is to be believed, Hakuin would appear for *teishō*, formal Zen lectures, wearing a tattered old jacket and carrying a long *kiseru* pipe in his hand. But if the rules may have been lax, the students were not. The haiku poet Rikei (?–1762), visiting Shōin-ji some thirty years later (Hakuin was sixty-eight), left a vivid picture in his travel diary of the monks at the temple—ten in residence, the others presumably living in the vicinity by their own wits—focused singlemindedly on their practice while subsisting on extremely meager rations.[4]

Hakuin's autobiographical narratives leave off at the point when his attention shifts from his own awakening to his evolving career as a teacher. Fortunately, Tōrei's *Chronological Biography*, taking as its main theme Hakuin's dealings with his students, fills in the highlights of the remaining decades of his life. Some of these accounts are episodes of considerable length that describe the practice and attainment of some of his more gifted lay students. Most of the clerics who appear in the *Biography* are visitors to Shōin-ji, not resident monks, and the episodes in which they figure tend to be rather perfunctory. Hakuin's immediate disciples, the men who would shoulder the burden of transmitting his Zen to future generations, receive relatively little space in Tōrei's accounts.

Letters and short prose pieces from Hakuin's forties and fifties are also helpful in filling in the portrait of life at Shōin-ji during this period. The following letter, for example, serves to confirm continuing hard times at the temple, but it also shows Hakuin at age forty-four, closer in that century to old than to middle age, evincing a reluctance to undertake a lecture assignment that is totally at odds with the frenetic teaching activity that marked his sixties and seventies. He is declining an invitation he had received from another temple to lecture on the *Vimalakirti Sutra*.

I am unable to imagine how a shuffling jackass like me could hope to emulate a thoroughbred stallion. How can a crow be expected to carol like a celestial phoenix? But I am nonetheless deeply grateful to you for remembering a boorish rustic and for joining together as you have in such a kind and sincere attempt to nurture his career along. I am sure you were inspired to do this by a deep desire to advance the Zen teaching. Alas, I am equally sure that you all are aware I am not a man of superior virtue, merely the priest of an impoverished little temple engaged in a constant struggle to keep it up and running. After I had served here at Shōin-ji for eight years, we finally succeeded, after a great deal of trouble, in striking a fresh vein of water under the dried-up old well. Now, four years and much additional hardship later, we have managed to finish rethatching the leaky roofs. But I still have no monk to help me with temple affairs, and no parishioners I can turn to for help.

More to the point, on scrutinizing my heart from corner to corner, I have been unable to come up with a single utterance worthy of communicating to your audience, much less attempt to lecture on the *Vimalakirti Sutra*'s marvelous teaching of nonduality. In light of this, after repeated and agonizing self-examination, I am afraid I must decline the high honor you have sought to bestow upon me. I write this with tearful eyes, my body dripping with nervous sweat. Since there is no lack of fine veteran priests in the neighborhood, I am sure you will be able to find someone to perform the task you propose. Begging your deep forgiveness, I am most sincerely yours,   Hakuin
(*Poison Flowers in a Thicket of Thorns*)

An Informal Talk (*Shōsan*) Hakuin gave on the eve of the winter solstice, probably dating from his late forties, provides even more detail about temple life at the time, and in one or two offhand remarks reveals glimpses of the warmer, human side of Zen Master Hakuin, including the fact that he had a pet *mikei* (tricolored) cat to which he was greatly attached.

How to describe the life at Shōin-ji as we reach the winter solstice? Above all, our poverty, so dire even heroes like Meng Pen and Hsia Yu [the proverbial strong men of ancient China] would be powerless to alleviate it. If it was possible for me to show people the actual state of affairs that exist around here, I'm sure they would find them more laughable than the crazy antics of Cudapanthaka. The old woman who comes around to lend a hand and was incensed to see my lice-ridden robes is now busily boiling them in a cauldron. My trusted servant has just returned from the fields all covered with dirt to announce we can expect a fine crop of large daikon radishes this year. Brother Sa has set a trap for the tomcat who keeps sneaking in to harass my favorite *mikei* cat. In the kitchen Brother Gaku is rapping on the kettle as he boils up a batch of rice gruel that will be so thin we're sure to see our faces reflected in it.[5]

None of the monks who have assembled here, men with eyes as ravenous as crocodiles and barbs as keen as porcupines, have the slightest concern for the descendents of Vulture Peak. With their hawk-like claws and sharp owl-like beaks, they have no interest whatever in traditional temple rules and regulations like those laid down by Po-chang. They sleep in broken-down shrines or deserted old halls they've managed to locate and come here to study with me wrapped in paper kimonos to ward off the cold, sipping water to stave off hunger pangs.

When I teach them or talk to them about Zen I sometimes employ snatches of country songs and popular street jingles in the local Suruga dialect. Otherwise, their ration is nothing but harsh scolding outbursts and a steady rain of abuse. Meals are in the tradition of P'u-hua—greens and then more greens. As to the support of the fifty monks who've gathered here, I don't give two hoots for that.

Long ago, Master Tung-shan delivered an Informal Talk to his monks on the eve of the winter solstice while they were enjoying some seasonal fruit.[6] It gave me the idea of buying my students some tangerines at the local market—but there wasn't enough money for that. Still, I don't want you comparing my Informal Talk with T'ung-shan's and concluding that mine is without redeeming merit. I've got some specially-made fox slobber for you! Tomorrow morning I'm going to serve up!

(*Poison Words from a Thicket of Thorn*)

Hakuin's fifties brought another significant change in his career. His growing reputation as a teacher had started attracting a large number of students to Shōin-ji, and in 1736, a training hall (*sōdo*) was built to accommodate the new arrivals. Although he had already lectured, informally and formally, more than a score of times in his thirties and forties, at the age of fifty-five he conducted his first large and important lecture meeting at Shōin-ji. His text was the Zen records of the Sung dynasty priest Hsi-keng, and more than four hundred people attended. To set the stage for the meeting and encourage the participants, he gave a series of introductory talks (*fusetsu*) prior to the start of the lectures. They appeared three years later in a revised form as *Dharma Talks Introductory to Lectures on the Record of Hsi-keng*, his first published work.[7] Hakuin made the Dharma talks the occasion to deliver a call to arms, a public declaration of his determination to reform the Rinzai school. It included passionate tirades against contemporary teachers he felt were undermining its authentic traditions. It is also perhaps the best single work on Hakuin Zen, a lengthy treatise that incorporates virtually all his basic views on Zen teaching and training.

Tōrei wrote that as a result of this lecture meeting Hakuin's name became known throughout the country. Seasoned monks now came from all over the country seeking his instruction. Even with its new training hall, tiny Shōin-ji could not possibly deal with such numbers and most new arrivals were forced to fend for themselves. They sought lodgings with farmers, in empty dwellings or abandoned halls and shrines throughout the countryside around the temple, transforming the woods and hills into a great center for Zen practice.

The success of *Dharma Talks Introductory to Lectures on the Record of Hsi-keng* may have shown Hakuin the great possibilities inherent in the printed word. Not only was it an exceedingly efficacious way of transmitting his Zen teaching to an immediate audience, but it would also make it available to generations of Zen students still unborn. Three years later, he published another large and important work in the Chinese style. Titled *A Record of Sendai's Comments on the Poems of Cold Mountain,* it contained his commentary on the works of the semi-legendary T'ang poet Han-shan. It was one of his favorite texts, which he had been using in Zen lectures since his forties. As with other Zen works of this type, Hakuin's primary concern was to elucidate Han-shan's poems from a Zen perspective. What makes Hakuin's work a bit different from other examples of the genre is that the line-by-line notes he attaches to the poems become forums for disquisitions on his own teaching. Some of the notes extend to prodigious length, such as the one that contains the entire text of *Idle Talk on a Night Boat.* He would publish it ten years later as an independent work. Hakuin was a born storyteller, and in this relatively early publication, we find him making full use of his gift.

When Hakuin began publishing in earnest in his sixties, he had already acquired a vigorous literary style honed in the countless letters and treatises of religious instruction he had composed through the years. Many of his Japanese publications are written in a highly rhetorical prose, marked by a heavy use of Chinese characters and presented in an epistolary format. The first of these works to appear, in his sixty-third year, was *Oradegama,* a collection of letters of religious instruction regarded as among his highest achievements in this style.[8]

Generally classed as *kana hōgo* (Buddhist works written in

Japanese), they share a style of Japanese that mixes Chinese characters and Japanese syllabary, but with a heavy preponderance of characters over syllabary that makes it closely resemble the peculiar *kambun* style that Japanese use for reading Chinese texts. Hakuin uses this style with great power and skill, at times blending phrasing of great elegance with the language and rhythms of the street, to produce expressions of delightful humor that at the same time incorporate his essential Zen message without compromise or simplification.

He gave the majority of his *kana hōgo* titles taken from the names of common weeds—*Snake Strawberries, Spear Grass, Horse Thistles, Hopvines, Moxa, Goose Grass, Wild Ivy*—perhaps to suggest their humble origins, or their hardiness and tendency to proliferate. In Zen, the proliferating weeds of the mind are a time-honored theme. Hakuin's *Weed-Pulling Songs,* for example, exhorts students to engage in constant mental weeding as the means of cultivating the original mind.

Old Granny's Tea-Grinding Songs (Chapter Four) is the representative example of another of the unusual writing genres Hakuin employed during these years. These are short verse works—*A Wake Up Call for Sleepyheads* and *Popular Rhymes for the Great Way* are two other well-known titles—composed using the rhythms, and often parodying the content, of various categories of street patter used by peddlers, beggar-monks, and entertainers out on the Tōkaidō road. The way in which Hakuin adapts their voices to tout his religious agenda closely parallels his visual portrayals of these same figures in his Zen paintings. In both cases, the vital popular culture of Edo Japan becomes a vehicle for delivering his religious message to a new and largely untapped audience.[9]

Another unusual feature of these Japanese writings is the distinctive format in which they were originally printed, using woodblocks that had been engraved directly from Hakuin's own holograph copy of the text. The work is thus presented to the reader in his highly idiosyncratic calligraphy that is at times quite difficult to make out. Most of them originally appeared in temple editions or printings otherwise funded by donations from Hakuin's friends and followers. It was a costly business, and readers of Hakuin's letters frequently encounter his vigorous, not to say aggressive, efforts to solicit these funds.

His painting and calligraphy are another part of his teaching activity that cannot go unmentioned. He seems to have been producing art for people virtually nonstop throughout his sixties and seventies. Although it is impossible to know how many works he actually produced, it has been estimated that at least ten thousand examples of his *Zenga* (the modern term for Zen paintings) are still extant.

Hakuin continued to hold frequent lecture meetings at Shōin-ji and other temples in Suruga and surrounding provinces into his late seventies. A few, like the assembly on the *Record of Hsi-keng* in his mid-fifties, were large affairs, but more often they were on a smaller scale. At times they would involve long journeys lasting many days, such as the trip he made his sixty-fifth year to distant Bitchū province on the Inland Sea in western Honshū, followed by a second visit the next year to lead practice sessions in the same area.

On the way back from the second of these trips he stopped over in Kyoto. He ended up staying for three months, during which he lectured on the *Blue Cliff Record,* the most important koan collection in Rinzai Zen, at two of the great Kyoto monasteries, Myōshin-ji (to which Shōin-ji was affiliated) and Tōfuku-ji, as well as at the imperial convents Hōkyō-ji and Kōshō-in, which were also Rinzai institutions. Invited to the convents by the two young abbesses, imperial princesses still in their twenties, Hakuin was dismayed to find them wearing gorgeous robes, eating sumptuous meals, and surrounded by hosts of servants who performed all the temple chores. He was inspired to compose a long letter to them (it was later published under the title *Horse Thistles*) in which he cites examples of simplicity in the lives led by the great Zen figures of the past, suggesting that the nuns should henceforth wear ordinary cloth robes, eat simply and sparingly, and perform the temple chores themselves. Not surprisingly, these admonitions, addressed to daughters of the reigning emperor, were soon making the rounds of the capital.

Dream Words from the Land of Dreams, Hakuin's major

commentarial work in the traditional Zen style, composed in Chinese and modeled on the *Blue Cliff Record*, appeared in 1749, his sixty-fourth year. It is one of his three major works in Chinese, the other two being *A Record of Sendai's Comments on the Poems of Cold Mountain* (1746) and *Poison Flowers in a Thicket of Thorns* (1758). A supplement to *Poison Flowers,* consisting of miscellaneous works, including *Poison Words for the Heart,* his famous commentary on the *Heart Sutra,* came out several years later.[10]

But measured by the amount of writings, paintings, and calligraphies, the most productive decade of Hakuin's life was his seventies. *Goose Grass,* his longest work, a composite collection of four different titles including *The Tale of My Childhood* and *The Tale of Yūkichi of Takayama* (Chapter Two), was written between his seventy-third and seventy-sixth years.

During these years, he was also busy working out other ways to facilitate the transmission of his teachings to future generations. He assembled large donations from his lay followers to purchase the site of a ruined temple named Ryūtaku-ji for his disciple Tōrei. It was beautifully situated on the lower slopes of Mount Fuji, and "no more than a bull's roar away from the Mishima post station" (*Chronological Biography*). Ryūtaku-ji would become a major training center for the study of Hakuin Zen.

According to the *Chronological Biography,* by the spring of Hakuin's seventy-eighth year "a general debility brought on by illness and old age were increasingly evident. He had lost his former vitality and mental sharpness. Lecturing exhausted him, as though the immense energy he had been pouring into his teaching activity was now used up." By the following spring, he had recuperated to the point that he was able to conduct a long series of Zen lectures, which more than seven hundred people came to attend. Part way through, however, the burden became too much for him and he asked his Dharma heirs Ishin Eryū and Tōrei Enji to share the teaching seat with him. This general pattern continued more or less up until his death at eighty-three. He continued to instruct students, though in a greatly reduced capacity, and would often have to ask others to take his place on the lecture seat. Yet we also know, from the dates he inscribed on them, that he was producing incredibly large numbers of wonderful *Zenga* and powerful calligraphies right up until his death.

Hakuin, who left an unusually large group of talented disciples to carry on his teaching, boasted in his final years that "a finer group of men could not be found even in the assemblies of the great teachers of the past." The number of students he confirmed as his Dharma heirs will probably never be known. Although one list frequently cited includes over forty names, it could well be much larger. Despite their importance, few of these students receive more than passing mention in Tōrei's *Chronological Biography*. In conclusion I will introduce a few of these men whose combined efforts in spreading Hakuin's Zen Dharma were instrumental in enabling it to be transmitted to the present day. Although the priests selected here all enjoyed successful careers, some have now almost vanished from the historical record. What information about them remains is contained in a nineteenth century work titled *Stories from a Thicket of Thorn and Briar*, a collection of anecdotes of Hakuin and his students compiled by Myōki Sōseki (1774–1848), a priest four generations after Hakuin.[11] The remainder of this introduction consists of excerpts from this collection.

   Stories from a Thicket of Thorn and Briar, arranged more or less chronologically, begins with Ryōsai Genmyō (1706–86), the first of Hakuin's students to receive his Dharma sanction, qualifying him to teach. Ryōsai had already experienced an enlightenment under the Rinzai priest Kogetsu Zenzai (1667–1751) in Kyushu. It came as he was listening to Kogetsu lecture on the *Ten Ox-Herding Pictures*. At their first encounter Hakuin, then in his late forties, is said to have exclaimed, "Monju [Manjushri] Bodhisattva has arrived!" After leaving Shōin-ji, Ryōsai took up residence at a temple in Mikawa province. He went on to have a very successful career (a collection of his Zen records was later published). Hakuin, however, seems to have had second thoughts about Ryōsai. He told an attendant: "I was too hasty in sanctioning him. Because of that, he is now unable to make any progress. If I had only waited another three years, I don't think anyone in the country could have stood up against him." Asked why he had affirmed him, Hakuin replied with a sigh, "In those days it seemed to me as though I had never seen anyone like him. A Zen teacher should be extremely careful about giving Dharma sanction to students."

Kaigan Kotetsu (n.d.) and Daikyū Ebō (1715–74), like Ryōsai and Tōrei, came to Hakuin from Kogetsu's temple in Kyushu. Both had reached an enlightenment and were sure they had nothing left to learn. On a journey to the mountains of Kumano to "hide their virtue" and mature their attainment, they stopped over at a temple, where they happened to see an unusual Chinese inscription hanging on the wall. It was a verse comment on the koan "The precept-breaking priest does not go to hell; the student who upholds them does not enter Nirvana":

Dawdling ants struggle to carry a dragonfly's stiff wing,
A pair of young swallows stop to rest on a willow branch;
Silkworm girls are carrying baskets, faces pale and wan,
Young boys stealing bamboo shoots escape through
    a hedge.

The two monks were unable to make head or tail of the verse. They thought it was gibberish scribbled down by some foreigner. But when they learned it was the work of a priest named Hakuin, they changed their plans and proceeded to Shōin-ji to see him. Personal interviews with Hakuin convinced them that they were no match for him, and they decided to stay on, pledging that they would not leave until they had completed the "great matter" of Zen practice. Later in life, Kaigan wrote that Daikyū was much superior to him in capacity. "Daikyū knew after once crossing lances with the master that he had lost. I was unaware that he had taken me alive until my bow was broken and I'd used up all my arrows."

Not much is known about Kaigan's later career except that he served as abbot of a temple in Kai province. Daikyū ended up as abbot of the great Tōfuku-ji in Kyoto and, in that capacity, was instrumental in transmitting Hakuin's teaching to the large and important Zen monasteries in the capital.

Ishin Eryū (1720–69) studied with Hakuin for many years and is said to have inherited his Zen style, although the severity, not to say violence, of his teaching methods exceeded Hakuin's by tenfold. He kept an unsheathed sword by his side during *sanzen* (his personal sessions with students). If they showed the least hesitation in responding, he would grab the sword and chase them out of the room. Once senior monk Tō (later Reigen Etō), another Hakuin student, came to Ishin's temple. Wearing his *kesa* (a kind of surplice worn over the shoulder or around the neck) and attired in his formal Dharma robe, he was ushered to Ishin's chambers in a second-floor room. When Tō proceeded to make the proper bows, Ishin said, "Let's dispense with that. I have something I want to ask you. A giant and powerful demon grabs you by the arm and is about to toss you into the Hell of Fiery Torment. How would you extricate yourself from that danger?" Tō was unable to give an immediate response. Ishin jumped up and kicked him down the stairs. The fall to the floor below stunned Tō. Picking himself up, he went into the privy and began doing zazen. Seven days later, he experienced an enlightenment. He rushed up the stairs and set forth his understanding to Ishin. "If you understand that, you can stop doing zazen," he said, confirming Tō's enlightenment.

Not all Hakuin's followers were as fierce. Enkei Sojun (1715–74) was, like Ishin, a native of the backside of western Honshu on the Sea of Japan, but he is described as being as different from Ishin as sky from mud. Mild-mannered, Enkei always treated his students with compassion, and during his teaching career in his native Matsue, Izumo province, he earned the respect of public officials and general populace alike. This was in contrast to Ishin (who also resided at a temple in Izumo province), whose reputation seems to have suffered after his death. In the nineteenth century, when Myōki, a compiler of *Stories from a Thicket of Thorn and Briar,* asked a priest from Izumo about the two men, he replied that people still revered the memory of "Priest Enkei," but did not even bother to use the honorific title of priest when referring to Ishin. (It must be said in Ishin's defense that he was highly respected in the Zen community of his time, and despite his ferocity, prominent laymen such as the great Nanga painter Ike Taiga visited his *sanzen* room.)

Suiō Genrō (1717–89), Hakuin's successor at Shōin-ji, was perhaps the most unusual of his students. Although given pretty short shrift in most modern works on Hakuin, in the earlier records he and Tōrei are set forward as the master's two chief disciples. He is described as a "born drinker," the possessor of brilliant talent and an irrepressibly independent spirit who bucked at constraint from any quarter. When he arrived at Shōin-ji at the age of twenty-nine, Hakuin immediately discerned his extraordinary potential. Suiō always took *sanzen* from Hakuin in the middle of the night. No one knew anything about it. He reached a profound attainment during the twenty years he studied with Hakuin, yet he always hid his ability and continued to live as an ordinary monk in the Shōin-ji assembly. He built a hermitage in Ashihara, a village over seventy miles from Shōin-ji, and returned to Shōin-ji only when Hakuin was giving talks. One story, said to epitomize the adamancy of his refusal to submit to others, tells of Suiō leaving the temple as usual immediately after Hakuin finished speaking. Hakuin told his attendant to summon Suiō, but when the attendant looked for him, he was told that Suiō had already left. The attendant set out along the road looking for him, and when he finally caught up with him, he told him to return immediately to the temple because Master Hakuin had summoned him. "He may have summoned me," replied Suiō abruptly, "but I didn't summon him," and continued on his way. Uninterested in fine distinctions, Suiō neither did zazen nor recited sutras. Until he was designated head priest at Shōin-ji, he had no fixed residence and at night would just stretch out and go to sleep wherever he happened to be. His favorite pastimes seemed to be drinking sake, enjoying a game of go, and drawing pictures with his writing brush (he was a very accomplished painter of *Zenga*). People had trouble making up their minds whether he was a truly great priest or just a shiftless good-for-nothing. At the Myōshin-ji headquarters temple in Kyoto where he had gone to receive the rank of *Dai-ichiza*, he told the senior priest in charge that he would assume the name Suiō, "drunken old man." Asked why he had chosen such a name, he said, "Because I'm fond of sake." "We can't accept a name like that," the senior priest said, and he suggested that Suiō use another character for *Sui*, one that means "accomplished" or "old man who has mastered the Way." Suiō agreed.

Suiō didn't like to stay at Shōin-ji when Hakuin was in residence, so he moved to a solitary dwelling in nearby Ihara village. But when Hakuin fell ill some years later, Suiō returned and nursed him. Suiō continued to follow his own bent even after Hakuin's death. For the first seven years as abbot at Shōin-ji, whenever students requested *sanzen* or instructions for Zen training, he would reply, "I don't know anything about that. Go to Ryūtaku-ji and take *sanzen* from Tōrei." When Hakuin's important seventh death anniversary came around, former students from throughout the country, over two hundred people in all, converged on Shōin-ji. They finally were able to make Suiō agree to hold a Dharma meeting and deliver a series of Zen lectures in honor of the occasion. From that time on, large numbers of students began coming to Shōin-ji to study with Suiō. He ceased to refuse them his guidance, and he also began making teaching trips, holding practice sessions and lecture meetings at neighboring temples that were attended by hundreds of people.

Tōrei Enji (1721–92), the most important of Hakuin's Dharma successors, a highly reputed Zen master in his own right, and the compiler of Hakuin's *Chronological Biography*, deserves special mention. The following sketch of his career, focusing on the interplay between him and his teacher Hakuin, is based on *The Chronological Biography of Zen Priest Tōrei* (*Tōrei Oshō Nempu*) compiled by Tōrei's disciple Taikan Bunshu.

After becoming a monk at the age of eight, Tōrei left his home temple in eastern Ōmi province (modern Shiga prefecture) at sixteen and traveled to the far-off island of Kyushu to study with Kogetsu Zenzai. He returned to the Kansai area two years later, practicing under other Rinzai teachers and experiencing an initial satori while at Hōjō-ji in Tamba province. In autumn of his twentieth year he engaged in a lengthy solitary retreat at Rengedani in Ōmi province. He practiced zazen continuously for many days, finally becoming so exhausted that he was no longer able to keep himself from falling over. As he lamented, "I'm no longer able to seek the Way that I pledged to attain," he suddenly collapsed to the ground. As he was falling, before his head struck the earth, he experienced enlightenment.

Tōrei, having entered the post-satori phase of his training, now focused his practice on acquiring the same freedom in his everyday activity that he enjoyed when he was immersed in the tranquility of zazen. He had heard from a fellow monk about Hakuin and the strict and uncompromising methods he used when dealing with his monks, which were said to be so forbidding that most students fled after just one encounter. Overcoming the fear that he might be totally humiliated and "find himself lying on his back on the ground," he "whipped the dead ox forward once again" and proceeded to Hakuin at Shōin-ji. At their first meeting Hakuin said, "You really should have come here sooner. I've been hearing about you for some time now."

A few months after Tōrei entered the assembly at Shōin-ji he was forced to return home to recuperate from a bowel ailment he had contracted. He was able to return to the temple later the same year, but he was obliged to leave once again the following year to care for his sick mother. On this second trip, after his mother had recovered, he went on to Kyoto to engage in a solitary retreat. It ended up lasting for several years and brought him a number of additional satoris. But the austere life to which he had subjected himself took its toll on his health. He developed tuberculosis, a disease he would suffer from for the remainder of his life. His condition gradually worsened, until the physicians he consulted gave up on him. Believing that he was at the gates of death, he wrote a work titled *On the Inexhaustible Lamp of Zen* to transmit to later generations the essentials of Zen that he had grasped while studying under Hakuin. He sent it to Hakuin and the following year he received a letter from the master expressing his high praise for the work.

Continuing to pursue his practice in Kyoto, Tōrei now experienced a satori that he said enabled him "to grasp the wonderful enlightened activity that Master Hakuin enjoyed in his everyday life." From then on, his physical condition steadily improved.[12]

Another satori, during a retreat some years later that lasted for one hundred and fifty days, was affirmed by Hakuin with the words, "You have truly penetrated it." Soon after, he summoned Tōrei to his chambers and presented him with his Dharma robe, signifying that he was sanctioning Tōrei as his Dharma successor. "I have lectured on the *Blue Cliff Record* four times wearing this gold-brocade robe," he said. "I now pass it on to you. Do not let the transmission die out!"

Hakuin urged Tōrei to become the head priest of Muryō-ji, a run-down, poverty-stricken temple in nearby Hina village. Muryō-ji was, in fact, not even registered as a temple, and Tōrei, who felt just as Hakuin had before him that his own training was still his first priority, was disinclined to accept the position. He stayed up all night, musing over his dilemma: "I left my home and joined the priesthood for the sake of achieving the Dharma . . . but if I don't accept, Muryō-ji will surely fall into ruin." He decided to accede to Hakuin's request, but first he made him agree to three conditions: (1) He would not later try to persuade Tōrei to move from Muryō-ji and succeed him as abbot at Shōin-ji. (2) He would make all the decisions relating to Muryō-ji himself, and would not be obliged to take the opinions of others (i.e., Hakuin) into consideration. (3) As he had vowed never to remain tied down in one place, he would be free, if ever he so desired, to leave Muryō-ji in the care of another priest.

Three years later Hakuin tried to persuade Tōrei to receive the rank of *Dai-ichiza*—the minimum requirement for a priest to be accredited as temple abbot—from the headquarters temple of Myōshin-ji in Kyoto. Tōrei begged off. He said that he was still too young, that Muryō-ji was in any case not a real temple, and that it would make him appear ridiculous in the eyes of his fellow monks. But Hakuin's sincere and relentless entreaties—citing his advanced age and repeating how much he wanted to see Tōrei embark on his teaching career before he died—finally forced him to relent.

A year later Hakuin attempted to appoint Tōrei as his successor at Shōin-ji, breaking one of his promises, and Tōrei, after another night on his zazen cushion mulling his choices, decided:

"There's nothing I can do but leave here and go into hiding." Telling Hakuin that he was making a trip to the shrine at Mount Akiba in Tōtōmi province to pray for Hakuin's continued health and long life, he set out instead for Kyoto. When letters Hakuin sent imploring Tōrei to return failed to move him, he tried another tack that proved more successful. He purchased a ruined temple named Ryūtaku-ji not far from Shōin-ji, then he sent Tōrei a letter informing him of the purchase and requesting him to return and rebuild the temple. Two years later, Tōrei was installed as abbot of the new temple, on the lower slopes of Mount Fuji. He remained and taught at Ryūtaku-ji more or less permanently until his seventieth year, also sharing teaching duties at Shōin-ji when Hakuin's strength declined in his final decade.

Gasan Jitō (1727–97), the last of Hakuin's students introduced in Myōki's *Stories from a Thicket of Thorn and Briar*, was obviously, judging from the large number of pages allotted to him, regarded as being of particular importance. Not only was Gasan the last of Hakuin's major disciples, it was through his students Inzan Ien (1751–1814) and Takujū Kosen (1760–1833) that Hakuin Zen was able to continue as the dominant line of Japanese Zen to the present day. These men are credited with propagating Hakuin's teaching methods and organizing the koans in use into a more systematic program.

After becoming a monk under the famous priest Gessen Zenne, a Dharma heir of Kogetsu Zenzai, Gasan set out on pilgrimage at the age of fifteen, experiencing a "small satori" the same year. In the years that followed, he studied under more than thirty different Rinzai teachers around the country, but finding that none of them could "counter the sharpness and force of his Zen thrusts," he returned to Gessen, now residing at Tōki-an in Nagata (near present-day Yokohama). Gessen affirmed Gasan's enlightenment and asked him to stay on at the temple. Gasan's travels had led him to Shōin-ji on more than one occasion, but he had never requested an interview with Hakuin. He decided it was time to pay him a visit. Gessen tried to dissuade him from going, but when Gasan learned that Hakuin would be conducting a lecture meeting in Edo, he set out to attend. When Gasan entered Hakuin's chambers and attempted to present his understanding, Hakuin stopped him. "I don't know which bogus priest you've come from," Hakuin roared, "but stop winnowing those humbugger lips of yours!" He struck Gasan and drove him out of the room. Gasan, undeterred by the setback, returned two more times to Hakuin's chambers and both times he was beaten and driven from the room. "My enlightenment is surely genuine, but that old priest just doesn't want to admit it," thought Gasan. After the lecture meeting ended, he sat on his seat in the Monks' Hall and thought, "He's one of the greatest Zen teachers in the country. Maybe he has a good reason for hitting me. Maybe he knows something the other priests don't." He went to Hakuin's chambers to apologize. "I was wrong to oppose you the way I did," he said. "Please forgive me, and tell me how I should proceed." "You're still young," replied Hakuin. "Do you really want to haul that Zen of yours—and that paper-thin satori—around your whole life? You might be able to pick up a few speaking skills and they may enable you to preach with some eloquence, but when the time comes, and you are face to face with death, none of that will help you in the least. If you want to lead the kind of life that is a source of constant joy, you must hear the sound of my one hand."

Gasan, just over thirty at the time, returned to Gessen at Tōki-an to report that he had decided to stay and continue his study at Hakuin's temple. Once again Gessen attempted to dissuade him, but Gasan's mind was already made up. He returned to Shōin-ji and became a disciple of Hakuin, studying with him while serving as his attendant for four years until Hakuin's death. As Hakuin's advanced age made it more and more difficult for him to teach with his former vigor, Gasan began to seek instruction from Tōrei as well.

Gasan later served as head priest at Rinshō-in in Edo, but later, after Gessen's death in 1781, he returned to reside at Tōki-an. It was there that many talented students, including Inzan and Takujū, gathered to receive his instruction.

Once, during a series of lectures on Hakuin's *Dream Words from the Land of Dreams* that he conducted at Shōin-ji in his later years, Gasan said, "I remember when this temple was filled with many outstanding religious seekers, men who subsequently went on to become fine temple priests themselves, who taught, and greatly benefited, countless students. That second generation of priests has all passed away, and now, incredibly, an ignorant priest such as myself has ascended to the high seat at Shōin-ji and with a great sense of awe attempts to preach and uplift the Zen Dharma. Today, the former style of Zen Master Hakuin has all but fallen into the dust. You monks here today must all concentrate your efforts on reviving that vital tradition. How deeply sad and regrettable to have to watch the ancestral Zen gardens entering their final weeks of autumn."

In praising Hakuin to his assembly, Gasan said, "What I admire is not that Master Hakuin had such outstanding virtue, or that his reputation now extends through all corners of the land, or that his enlightenment far surpassed that of the patriarchal teachers of past or present, or that he had penetrated to a clear understanding of the difficult-to-pass koans one by one, without a single exception, or that when he preached the Dharma with absolute freedom and total fearlessness, it was like the roar of the lion king himself, or that when he was surrounded by three hundred, five hundred, or seven or eight hundred disciples, he seemed like a manifestation of the Buddha himself. But when all the Zen teachers that I visited in my youth were powerless to oppose me, old Hakuin alone answered me with those venomous means of his and three times administered stiff doses of his staff, rendering me powerless, unable to go either backward or forward, and thus enabled me to complete the great matter of my religious quest— it is that, and that alone, that I greatly admire. It is no easy matter for a teacher to achieve!"

AUTHOR'S NOTE

Dates throughout are given as they appear in the texts, according to the lunar calendar in use in Edo Japan. This means, for example, that Hakuin's birth is given as the twenty-fifth day of the twelfth month of 1685, not January 19, 1686, as it would be converted to the Western calendar. I have, however, used the Western method of calculating age, subtracting one year from the ages given in the original texts, which follow the Japanese system of counting a person one year old at birth.

In winding up the third of a series of Counterpoint books that has kept me occupied fairly constantly over the past eighteen months, I would like to take the opportunity to belatedly acknowledge my gratitude to Roxanna Aliaga, senior editor at Counterpoint, for helping things along and bearing with me through that period, and to Trish Hoard, for editing two long and involved manuscripts with consummate patience and painstaking care. I would also like to thank Nelson Foster for his encouragement and many valuable suggestions in the early stages of the editing process. My final and greatest debt is to my wife Yoshie, for her unfailing cheerfulness during the years it took to bring the books to completion.

HAKUIN'S PRECIOUS MIRROR CAVE

1: The Tale of My Childhood   :

THE TALE OF HOW I SPURRED MYSELF ON IN MY CHILD-
HOOD (*Sakushin Osana Monogatari*) is the first of two
lengthy autobiographical narratives Hakuin composed in his
final decade. Hakuin's somewhat unwieldy title, apparently influenced by *Spurring Zen Students Through the Barrier,* a Chinese
anthology that had snapped him out of a period of despondency
in his early years of practice, was no doubt chosen to underscore
his primary aim, which was to inspire other students to follow,
and learn from, his example.[1] I have been unable to discover his
reason for using the Japanese word *osana* (childhood), normally
referring to early childhood, in the title of a narrative that devotes
so much space to events that took place in his twenties, though
it may simply be that with advancing age the parameters of his
youthfulness had changed.[2] I follow Hakuin in using the abbreviated title *The Tale of My Childhood.*

Hakuin tells us that he published *The Tale of My Childhood* at
the request of a group of advanced lay students he had taught in
Edo. They had specifically asked for a work that would do three
things: explain the importance of the post-satori phase of Zen
training, give an account of his early religious career, and provide lists containing the names of people he had awarded certificates of enlightenment, the temples where he had held practice
assemblies and given formal lectures, and the titles of all works
he had published.

Until his seventies, Hakuin assigned beginning students the traditional Mu koan, switching then to a two-part koan of his own devising: the famous Hear the Sound of One Hand, followed by Put a Stop to All Sounds. Hakuin continually stresses the need for students to practice assiduously to reach the initial breakthrough experience known as *kenshō* (seeing into the true nature) achieved through zazen-centered koan practice. Because of this, his teaching is often referred to as "*kenshō* Zen." However, he also makes very clear that while *kenshō* is a threshold students must cross, the ultimate goal is the life of ongoing practice that commences after the initial *kenshō* is achieved.

Hakuin's program for post-satori practice is designed so that students deepen and mature their initial attainment while at the same time helping others advance to enlightenment as well. They begin by working through a series of complex, "hard-to-pass koans." (Hakuin gives different lists of these koans, and he apparently had no set system as was true in later Hakuin Zen.) Proceeding deeper into this process, students must read widely in both Buddhist and non-Buddhist literature to "accumulate a vast store of Dharma assets," the knowledge and wisdom they will need in teaching others, the next and final phase of post-satori training. Hakuin sometimes uses the term "post-satori training" in a limited sense to refer to this period preparatory to teaching, but more often it specifies the life of practice in a broader sense, beginning after *kenshō* and continuing on indefinitely. As the student continues to pursue post-satori training, maturing his enlightenment while "working unstintingly to impart the great gift of the Dharma," he will one day discover, "without being aware of it," that "the mastery of the Buddha Way," the goal he had vowed to fulfill, has been achieved. "If you work for others' salvation in fulfillment of the Four Great Vows," he wrote in his commentary on the *Blue Cliff Record*, "you are unconsciously proceeding forward toward the perfection of wisdom in yourself." Personal enlightenment is only possible within the process of working to save others.

While the basic principles of "post-satori" (*gogo* in Japanese) practice were an important element in Hakuin's teaching from the beginning, we do not begin to encounter the term in his writing until his mid-seventies, by which time he had apparently decided that it needed greater emphasis. It is the major focus of the two volumes from *Goose Grass* translated here—*The Tale of My Childhood* and *The Tale of Yūkichi*—both of which were published in his seventy-sixth year.

As Hakuin tells it, when the request for a work on post-satori practice arrived from his students, he already had a version of *The Tale of My Childhood* in manuscript; it was only their keen desire to see it published that prompted him to revise it and allow it to be printed. The lists the students requested were included in the original manuscript but were deleted prior to publication. However, we know from a surviving manuscript copy that the list contained the names of more than a hundred students whose *kenshō* or satori Hakuin had confirmed. The reason they were deleted from the text is unknown. Perhaps students in the Takayama area themselves requested their names be removed. Hakuin's teachings and his students were being sharply attacked by priests of the other Buddhist sects at the time (see page 49), and they may have thought it prudent for the time being to avoid being identified as his followers. Though the lists of temples and titles the students had requested were deleted from *The Tale of My Childhood* as well, Hakuin included them both in *Wild Ivy*, the second of his autobiographies, published two years before his death.

The Tale of My Childhood and *The Tale of Yūkichi of Takayama* (Chapter Two), two independent though related works, comprise the third and final section of a larger collection titled *Goose Grass*. (The first two sections of *Goose Grass*, not included here, are *A Story of Four Filial Sisters of Takatsuka* and *Accounts of the Miraculous Effects of the Ten Phrase Kannon Sutra for Prolonging Life*.)

A Story of Four Filial Sisters of Takatsuka, bearing a postscript stating that it was written in the seventh month of 1759, Hakuin's seventy-fourth year, purports to relate the true story of four orphaned sisters who, in hoping to advance their parents' standing in the next life, copied out over a period of three years the entire text of the *Lotus Sutra*. Hakuin states that he composed the work because he wanted other people to know about the young girls' filial devotion and the benefits to be gained from venerating the *Lotus Sutra*. The title story, however, makes up only small part of the section. It is preceded by a series of miracle tales of people who, owing to the extraordinary virtue of the *Lotus Sutra*, escaped death and the sufferings of hell and returned to give elaborate eyewitness descriptions of the terrifying sights and torments of the Buddhist hells. This places *Four Filial Sisters* in the Buddhist literary genre known as "tales of karmic cause-and-effect" (*inga monogatari*). Hakuin seems to have been the only Rinzai priest to have published such tales, though with over ten volumes of them to his credit, he more than made up for the lack.[3] What distinguishes Hakuin's tales from those compiled by priests of the other Buddhist sects is his tendency to break into the narrative to explain specific points in light of his own teaching and to deliver sharp attacks on contemporary teachers.

Accounts of the Miraculous Effects of the Ten Phrase Kannon Sutra for Prolonging Life was, according to its postscript, written in the tenth month of 1759, the same year as *The Four Filial Sisters*. It consists of a long series of stories—three thick volumes in the original woodblock edition—in the same "cause-and-effect" vein as *A Story of Four Filial Sisters*, although in this case the miracles are brought about by venerating Kannon, the Bodhisattva of compassion, and reciting the brief *Ten Phrase Kannon Sutra for Prolonging Life*.[4]

Although these four works share the omnibus title *Goose Grass*, no edition of *Goose Grass* containing them all has come to light, and it seems unlikely they were ever issued as a single collection. Hakuin adopted a similar method on other occasions. The works titled *Hopvines, Idle Talk on a Night Boat*, and *Horse Thistles* each contain two totally unrelated works. I suspect (though I cannot prove) that this strategy was connected with the rather mundane shifts he was obliged to employ in negotiating all the works into print.

Even as individual publications, the *Goose Grass* works are exceedingly rare. The editors of *The Complete Works of Zen Priest Hakuin* (1935) included only *A Story of Four Filial Sisters* of *Takatsuka* and a portion of *Accounts of the Miraculous Effects of the Ten Phrase Kannon Sutra for Prolonging Life* under that title, apparently unaware of the existence of the other sections. *The Tale of My Childhood* and *The Tale of Yūkichi* remained inaccessible until 1938, when they were published in *A Collection of Zen Master Hakuin's Writings*, a one-volume anthology of Hakuin's works edited by the Buddhist scholar Tokiwa Daijō.

PREFACE TO *THE TALE OF MY CHILDHOOD*

Zen Master Po-yun stated: "It was because I was acquainted with a great many of the words and deeds of former teachers that I was able to complete my religious quest."[5] An utterance of truly incalculable worth!

This year, the eleventh of the Hōreki era (1761), an elderly layman who had retired from active life came all the way from Edo to visit me at Shōin-ji.[6] We sat down and had a good leisurely talk, in the course of which he told me the following:

"Master, two years ago, in spring of 1759, you were in Edo for five months giving Zen lectures and Dharma talks, and in that short space of time you drove thirty superior students through the initial koan barriers into *kenshō*. When you visited Edo once again in spring of this year to renew your credentials with the government,[7] you were there for only two or three months, but forty more people passed your One Hand koans during that time.[8] That means in just two short visits you awarded Dragon Staff certificates to seventy people, confirming their entrance into enlightenment.[9] It is a tremendous achievement, even when compared to the accomplishments of other great Dharma teachers of the past.

"In former times celebrated Zen teachers from around the country came to teach in the capital and impressed its citizens, who filed in one after another to receive their instruction. But not a single one of those students is known to have actually achieved an authentic breakthrough into great enlightenment. In more recent times, Zen masters Gudō, Daigu, and Butchō taught in Edo, and they succeeded in producing students such as Lady Kasuga,

Suzuki Shōsan, and Matsuo Bashō. But with those exceptions, I have not heard of any teacher in the past several hundred years that has guided so many valiant students to achieve the strength and joy of religious attainment as you have in just these few years. It is entirely due to the great efficacy of your double-barrier One Hand koans. Certainly it is no exaggeration to say that this represents the pure and authentic tradition of Zen, such as emerges only once every five hundred years.

"This makes it all the more unfortunate that some of those students were persuaded upon receiving your certificate that they were fully enlightened and, as a result, decided to stop practicing Zen. Your other students in Edo are so concerned by this that when they learned I would be visiting you, they called at my home and confidentially told me the following:

"'We envy you your upcoming trip to Suruga province. We would follow close on your heels if our business obligations did not prevent us from going. When you meet Master Hakuin we would like you to transmit our message to him, and implore him on our behalf to lighten what we feel as a burdensome responsibility. We would like you to request, with the deepest respect, that he write some Dharma words that would rouse out of their lethargy those foolish students who have stopped halfway in their practice.

"'We would also like to ask him to compile a roster listing all the students throughout the land who have been awarded his certificates. We promise to preserve this list with the greatest care so that in the future we can use it to form a karmic link that will enable us to join together and work towards creating a Buddha-land on earth.

"'Next, we would like to ask that he have one of his personal attendants compile a list containing all the temples where he has held Dharma practice meetings, specifying which sutras and Zen texts he employed at each of them, and a list describing each of the works he himself has written and published to benefit future students with words of caution and encouragement. The words and phrases bequeathed by the great Zen teachers of the past are far beyond our limited understanding, but if we could have even a few words from our teacher, they could inspire us to carry our religious quest through to completion, in the same way that those of the ancient teachers inspired Zen Master Po-yun.

"'Finally, we have been told a sermon on the torments sinners undergo in hell that the master heard when he was seven or eight years old caused him to suffer grievously from fears of falling into hell; that these fears gave rise to a religious aspiration that eventually led to his entering the priesthood; and that following various trials and tribulations he attained *kenshō*, which instilled in him the great desire to fulfill the Four Bodhisattva Vows. We should like very much to know more of the details of this part of his career. Please, friend and fellow layman, consider how deeply we are committed to achieving our goal of having the Rōshi set forth these matters in a book. Implore him, on our behalf, to write it. If you are able to bring it back with you when you return from Suruga, it will greatly inspire us all in our practice. We want everyone to know the essential importance of post-satori practice.'"

"Hakuin Rōshi, the deep aspiration of my fellow lay students in Edo is something that cannot easily be dismissed. I appeal to your great compassion. Please take pity on them. 'Lower your cloud' for us and write something that can be read and understood by all."[10]

As the layman spoke, I [Hakuin] too was deeply touched by his kindness and compassion and the fine aspirations he expressed. I wanted to arouse those who had become indolent in their practice. I had in fact already written a manuscript of Dharma words dealing with the matter of post-satori practice that for certain reasons I was hesitant about publishing, and I had not told anyone about it. But then, quite recently, when I heard about the divine oracle that the great deity Inari of Takayama in Hida province had delivered through the mouth of young Yūkichi, the happiness I felt inspired me to commit his story to paper, in my rustic manner, and before I knew it I had scribbled off a work that ran to over a hundred sheets. I expect that practicers of the first rank will just throw it aside, perhaps spit on it, and not give it a second thought. Dismiss it as another example of old Hakuin trying to squeeze some Dharma milk from his withered old paps. But that's all right. I don't care.

I have addressed certain issues regarding the events that took place at Takayama in the postscript to *The Tale of Yūkichi. Look carefully! Look very carefully!*[11]

Summer of the sixth month of the eleventh year of Hōreki (1761). This concludes the preface to *The Tale of My Childhood.*

THE TALE OF MY CHILDHOOD

*The turbulent churning waves of samsaric existence cannot reach
   the precious clarity of the sea of emptiness.
Amid the silence that reigns within the gates of Dhyana, there is
   no difference between coming and going, past and present.*

During his lifetime, Shakyamuni Buddha preached the Dharma at three hundred and sixty different locations, expounding eighty-four thousand Dharmas, among them the Sudden and Gradual, Lesser and Greater, Esoteric and Indeterminate teachings.[12] Among them the most wonderful, most mysterious, most superlative of all is the Zen teaching, the path of enlightenment attained through the experience of *kenshō*. Buddhas who have appeared in the world one after another have all attained supreme enlightenment by means of *kenshō*. All the wise and enlightened ones of the past and present and the great assembly of Bodhisattvas as well have ascended to the stage of perfect and sudden enlightenment after first attaining *kenshō*.

Kenshō is experienced with various degrees of clarity and profundity, but none can surpass a *kenshō* in which the entrance into enlightenment occurs after great and strenuous effort and is accompanied by a feeling of immense joy.[13] When entrance into enlightenment occurs in a vague or halfway manner, students feel as though they are walking in the shadow of a lamp, and they are never able to attain complete and utter freedom in what they do. That is why the priest T'zu-ming called the great and strenuous effort expended by the ancients "a radiant light that will always shine with great vigor."

It is also said that "three essentials are necessary for the practice of Zen: a deeply rooted faith, a great and passionate doubt, and indomitable resolve. If even one of these is lacking, your practice will be as unsound as a tripod with a missing leg."[14] You must know that great doubt is the mother that gives birth to outstanding monks; that the firmly shut koan barriers are a wonderful elixir that can raise the pure and venerable traditions of the Zen school back to vigorous life. In order to enable students to fully penetrate their deep source and totally exhaust their subtle mysteries, the generations of patriarchs who have appeared in the three countries of India, China, and Japan to transmit the Dharma lamp have each of them put up ten thousand of these uplifting, firmly shut barriers, laid out impenetrable thickets of briar and bramble that extend for a thousand leagues. I refer to koans such as Su-shan's Memorial Tower, Wu-tsu's Water Buffalo Through the Window, Nan-ch'uan's Death, and The Old Woman Burns the Hut. It is all poisonous slobber of the most virulent kind—impossible to believe, impossible to understand, impossible to enter and pass beyond.[15] These koans are referred to as the claws and fangs of the Dharma cave, as divine, death-dealing amulets.

All the great teachers of the three worlds, those who become giant shade trees revered by all the world,[16] occupying the teaching seat, commanding assemblies of monks and guiding them in their practice, if they do not possess the key to unlock the barriers that lead beyond, they will be unable to produce any truly outstanding monks. The great master Huang-po was perfectly right to constantly lament the fact that the fine teacher Fa-jung of Mount Niu-t'ou could "preach circles around most other teachers but did not possess the secret key that can lead students beyond."[17] A teacher who is not in possession of the koan barriers will be unable to produce true disciples, and without true disciples the authentic Dharma cannot be transmitted to future generations, and its ancient traditions will fall into the dust.

Today's ignorant and heretical gangs of silent-illumination, withered-sitting Zennists, who have never even encountered these koan barriers in their dreams, in order to conceal the fact that they could never, until the day they die, possess the eye to understand, nor the power to penetrate, this truly great Dharma asset, are frequently heard to say: "What is called the 'claws and fangs of the Dharma cave' and 'divine, death-dealing amulets' do not represent the innermost depths of the Buddha-patriarchs.[18] They didn't appear until after the Zen sect had divided into five schools, at the time it burst into seven blossoms. They are provisional expediencies that Zen masters devised in order to better lead their disciples."[19]

Not so! Not so! If you were able to penetrate to the root, bore your way through the bottom, you would know how greatly mistaken you are. Don't you realize that each and every word that Shakyamuni spoke—from the first time he preached at Deer Park up until the very end at the river Hiranyavati—was a poison fang and talon of the Dharma cave? Each and every word a wicked death-dealing charm or amulet? It is difficult for people like you to imagine that the Hinayana sutras the Buddha preached at Deer Park could be far superior to the preachings of instantaneous attainment found in the five principal Mahayana sutras.[20] This is something impossible to believe and impossible to grasp, and until you have opened the eye that can truly read the sutras, you will be unable to grasp it even in your dreams. Who would believe that there were those even among the ancients who were unaware of this?

So you must strive with every ounce of strength you possess to open the eye that will enable you to read the sutras. Unless you possess this eye, even if you experience great enlightenment eighteen times and have numberless smaller enlightenments, they will surely be found under close scrutiny to be nothing but worthless delusions: dead, empty learning. If you still don't understand, you should penetrate the koan, "Chao-chou's Mud Buddha" in the *Blue Cliff Record*.[21] It will enable you to confirm that you have in fact opened the eye that can read the sutras.

Now, I have something of my own I wish most respectfully to relate for the sake of those superior seekers who explore the hidden depths. And don't say it's just another example of Hakuin's incurable penchant for long-winded stories.

Back when I was a young boy of seven or eight (I was called Iwaya),[22] my mother would take me with her when she went to visit a temple of one of the Teaching Schools.[23] Once while we were there we heard the priest describe, in excruciating detail, the terrible torments inflicted on victims in the Eight Fiery Hells and Eight Cold Hells. He had everyone in the hall scared half to death—their teeth were chattering, their knees quaking uncontrollably. I too was assailed by terrible fears. I came to feel as though there was nothing at all I could rely upon. The fears kept gnawing at me day and night. I moped about in a very unhappy state, my eyes red from the constant tears. Of course at such a tender young age, I wasn't able to dispel my fears by discussing them with my friends, so I would go off by myself and, sobbing loudly, cry my heart out in secret.

Once when I went into the bath with my mother, she directed the servant girl to keep stoking the fire beneath the iron bath cauldron with more and more wood. Flames shot wildly up enveloping the cauldron, and the sound of the water seething and churning in the tub terrified me. Suddenly, I began howling out great cries of distress that reverberated up and down the neighborhood, startling my whole family. They came rushing into the bath, gathered around me, and asked anxiously what in the world had happened. Hands grabbed me and lifted me out of the tub. I was crying inconsolably and kicking and waving my arms and throwing myself wildly about. "Did you burn yourself?" "Did you wrench something?" people asked, eager to discover the cause of such piteous cries of distress. They humored me and tried to coax some response out of me, but I paid no attention to them at all and continued to bawl away at full force.

An uncle who was there said, "This just isn't like him." Then he scolded me. "If you're going to carry on like this, at least tell us the reason. Why, you're worse than a spoiled little girl!"[24]

"Make all these people go away," I blubbered. "I won't tell anyone but my mother." With that, everyone beat a hasty exit, disappearing out the back. Alone with my mother, I placed both hands on the floor, bowed my head, and said in a hushed voice, "The truth of the matter is this. In the bath just now, even though you were holding me in your arms, when I saw those flames rising up around the cauldron, when I heard the sound of the water seething in the tub, it frightened me to the marrow of my bones. All I could think of was how much more terrible it would be to have to face the Eight Fiery Hells all alone, without you. What would I do? I was so scared that all my courage left me." With that, I let out another loud sob and began bawling again, but my mother put out her hand, stopping me, and said, "Is that what's bothering you? That's not something to be so frightened about."

"Is there some way I can avoid falling into hell?" I asked her.

"If there weren't," she replied, "how could anyone get a good night's sleep?"

"Mother, if you know something, please tell me what it is. Do something to save me from these terrible fears," I said.

"Why would I want to hide anything from you? But the bathroom is unclean. It isn't the proper place to discuss it. We'll have a long talk in due course and I'll tell you all about it."

Elated, I placed my palms together in supplication, though not, I must confess, without some question in my mind as to why she would leave me in such a frightened state, when she could have told me right away. Nonetheless, half weeping, half laughing in my happiness, I climbed back into the bath.

That night, I went to bed with an easy mind and slept until well past eight the next morning. I awoke to hear the voices of my friends—familiar partners in mischief—who were raising a terrible ruckus in the grove of the Tenjin Shrine behind our house.[25] Without a thought for the troubles of the previous day, I leaped out of bed and dashed outside to join them. They had pulled four or five baby crows down from their nest and were making great sport of tormenting the young creatures.

Seeing this brought me suddenly back to my problem. If only I could learn how to avoid falling into hell, I could join my friends and share the pleasures they were having. I turned and ran like a flash back into the house. My mother was talking with an elderly physician named Ichikawa Gendō, so I stood off to the side and waited for them to finish their conversation. After a while he left, and I went in to my mother.

"Please mother, my hair is all tangled and feels uncomfortable. Would you please comb it out and retie it for me."

"My, my, what has got into you, young man?" laughed my mother. "Next thing you know, the sun will be rising in the west."

She had the servant girl bring her the box with the combs and hair oil, then led me to a secluded veranda in one of the back rooms. I sat straight and upright before my mother, with my hands pressed together and my head bowed down.

"It's nice and quiet here," I said. "Now please tell me how I can avoid falling into hell, as you promised."

"I'll tell you after we fix your hair," she said.

"Tell me first. Then you can fix my hair all you want to," I insisted. As we continued to spar back and forth like that, I looked hard into my mother's eyes, and it suddenly dawned on me that she had no idea what to tell me. Because of the fuss I'd been making the previous night, she'd been offering me "yellow leaves" to get me to stop crying.[26] I readied myself for another temper tantrum.

Sensing this, my mother put her hand on me. "Wait a second, Iwaya," she said. "I'm not trying to hide anything. All right, I'll tell you. You should worship the deity of the Kitano Shrine. He will surely help you."

Overjoyed at this piece of advice, I jumped up, pressed my palms together, and performed three scrupulous bows before my mother. Then I stretched out my neck to allow her to comb out my hair. When she finished, I went directly to the shrine room of our house, gave it a good cleaning, hung up an image of Kitano Tenjin, offered flowers and incense, and recited the *Tenjin Sutra* twenty or so times.[27]

From then on I would arise every night at first cockcrow. I would purify myself by carefully rinsing out my mouth and washing my hands and face, and then proceed to the shrine room, where I would light a lamp and prepare offerings of incense and flowers. Then I would recite the sacred name of Kitano Tenjin, and twenty or so repetitions of the *Tenjin Sutra*.

Sometime after that, circumstances arose which led me to worship the Bodhisattva Kannon as well. In one or two nights I had the *Fumon-bon* memorized and was reciting it together with the *Tenjin Sutra* mornings and nights without fail.[28]

At about that time a Jōruri troupe from the Kansai region led by someone named Morioka Kunai came to our area, and a puppet play called *Pot-Wearing Nisshin Shōnin* was performed. In it, Lord Tokimune, the Regent at Kamakura, asks Nisshin Shōnin, "Does a person who practices the teachings of the *Lotus Sutra* feel the heat of a burning fire?" To this the Shōnin replies, "He can enter a fire without being burned. He can sink into the water without drowning." Lord Tokimune orders it put to the test. A large iron cauldron heated in a fire until it is red-hot is put over the Shōnin's head; a flaming plowshare is clamped around his chest under his arms. Through it all, Nisshin smiles and doesn't show the slightest sign of any discomfort. The military officials seated along the hall witnessing this are all astonished. To a man, they press their palms together toward the Shōnin in attitudes of deepest reverence.[29]

After witnessing that episode, I felt a sense of joy well up within me. "How wonderful," I thought. "If I could be like Nisshin, there would be no need for me to fear hell. I'll become a Buddhist priest like him. I'll exert myself strenuously and unremittingly, endure any austerity or hardship, until I become a genuine religious seeker equal to the Shōnin in every way."

When I turned twelve, I went to my mother in private and asked her permission to enter the Buddhist priesthood. Knowing only too well how my constant fear of falling into hell had reduced me to a state of tearful misery, she looked at me and, with tears glistening in her own eyes, nodded her agreement.

From spring of my thirteenth year, I began studying and memorizing all the sutras [I would need to know as a Buddhist monk]. I also started on the *Kuzōshi* anthology of poetical phrases.[30] Although unaware of it at the time, I began reading the anthology on the twenty-fifth of the ninth month and I finished on the twenty-fifth of the eleventh month. Only later did it occur to me that in reading through this work—which is said to take a novice monk three years to master—in only sixty days, I had received unseen help from the deity Tenjin.[31]

From that day in my twelfth year when the thought of entering the priesthood first entered my head, I began getting up every night at the first crow of the cock and going secretly outside to the well. I would take off all my clothes, grab the well-rope and, hauling up three bucketsful of well water, perform cold-water ablutions by pouring them over my head.[32] In winter, during the coldest weather, the rope would be coated white with ice, frozen stiffly into the hoop-like shape of the bucket. I would first always have to forcibly straighten the rope. After finishing my ablutions, I would press my palms together and fix my thoughts on the heavenly gods and Buddhas and make supplication to them:

"Please help me become a genuine priest, unrivaled throughout the land. If it is not possible, come immediately and stomp me into the earth."

When I finally got up and slung my clothes over my shoulder to return to the house, my body was totally numb from the freezing cold. I would be on the brink of losing consciousness. But that did nothing to dampen my ardor. I would recover my senses and head back into the shrine room. There I would hang up a lamp and begin my prostrations and sutra recitations as usual. At the time, no one was even aware that I was engaging in these rigorous austerities.

The next year, on the fifteenth day of the second month, I went to the temple and became a Buddhist monk.

In my fifteenth year I thought to myself, "I went and had my head shaved by a Buddhist priest. Put on a black robe. But I have yet to experience any sign of the Buddha Way's miraculous power. When I test myself with an acupuncture needle or burn moxa on my skin, the pain is as hard to bear as it ever was. I'm certainly still nowhere near measuring up to Nisshin Shōnin. It is said that the *Lotus Sutra* is the king among all the sutras the Buddha preached during his lifetime. It is claimed that even the spirits of the dead, even demons and devils, often request the *Lotus Sutra* be recited on their behalf."

I went [next door] to the small hermitage of Kan'e-bō, a priest of one of the Teaching schools, [to study the *Lotus Sutra*].³³ I found a copy of the text, bound sutra-style, set out before the altar, and began to peruse it, rendering it in the Japanese style. It took me two days to read through the entire text. When I finished and closed the last page, I emitted a deep sigh. "For the most part, this sutra merely preaches about cause and effect. True, there are two or three phrases such as the ones about the 'true aspect of all things,' and there being 'but one Vehicle alone.'³⁴ They have a wonderfully profound meaning, but what sutra doesn't contain some such phrases? If tales of karmic cause and effect possessed real religious merit, shouldn't works like the *Tale of Hōgen, Tale of Heiji,* and the *Tale of Heike* possess that merit too?"³⁵ From then on, when I saw a copy of the *Lotus Sutra*, I regarded it much the same as I would an ordinary Japanese storybook. Unfortunately, at that time I didn't possess the Dharma eye that would enable me to read the sutras. Had my eye been opened, that deep sigh could not have appeared.

At the age of eighteen, when I was residing in the monk's quarters at Byakuge-zan, I was studying a work titled *Praise of the True School,* in which I read a passage about the priest Yen-t'ou being set upon by bandits and murdered. It was a very discouraging discovery. Yen-t'ou was a great priest, the kind said to come along only once in five hundred years. "Oh my!" I reflected, "if someone like that could suffer such a fate, how can any ordinary person hope to avoid falling into hell and undergoing its torments?"³⁶

I was extremely disheartened. I completely lost my appetite—not a grain of rice would pass my throat. For days on end I struggled on in a state of severe mental anguish. I finally came to the following conclusion: "That story about Nisshin Shōnin is a fairy tale that Chikamatsu cooked up out of some commonplace notions he had in his mind at the time. I deeply regret allowing my belief in a senseless story like that to influence me into shaving my head and becoming a priest. Still, at this point I can't very well return to being a layman. I'll just have to let things work themselves out. Meantime I'll study poetry, literature, calligraphy, and painting and try to make a name for myself in one of those fields.[37] As for the future, there is nothing to do but to take what comes. I'll grow old and die along with everyone else, and then just accept whatever hell has to offer." Once decided in that direction, I focused my attention on artistic pursuits to the exclusion of all else. Whenever I saw a Buddhist image or a sutra, or anything else of a religious nature, I felt no more for them than I would for clods of earth at my feet.

The following year, my nineteenth, I joined the assembly of Baō Rōjin in Mino province. I arrived at his temple together with twelve other monks. Baō was an extremely harsh customer, as venomous as they come, almost impossible for a monk to endure. All my fellow monks slipped away and fled to other parts. But I decided to myself, "Sure, they call him the 'Wild Horse of Mino,' and everybody's afraid of him. But no one else in the present age can match his wide learning, not to speak of his mastery of poetry and literature. Even if I traveled to Shikoku or even as far as Kyushu, I could hardly hope to encounter another teacher like him. Besides, don't I have a great and talented friend in Onbazan?[38] Why should I allow Baō's severity to affect my decision to stay?"

So I remained on alone at Baō's temple. It was a spare and spartan existence, drawing water, gathering firewood, and cooking rice for meals. One day, Baō set out by himself for Ōgaki.[39] Left alone amid the solitude of the deserted temple, I got to thinking: "What a pitiful creature I am. I look like a monk but I'm not. I resemble a layman too, but I'm not a layman.[40] I'm not a Confucian, a Shintoist, or follower of Lao Tzu or Chuang Tzu either. Will I ever be able to confirm my 'Mind Master'? What is to become of me!" Streams of tears began cascading down my cheeks.

I happened to raise my gaze upward to the veranda of the Guest Hall, where hundreds of books—Buddhist and non-Buddhist alike—had been stacked on top of desks following the annual airing of the temple library. I lit an offering of incense before the books, performed twenty or so prostrations before them, and prayed earnestly to the gods and Buddhas for their guidance:

> I place my trust in the Buddhas of the ten directions who possess the ten perfections of wisdom, in all the great Bodhisattvas who have realized the path, in the benevolent gods in the heavens who stand guard over the Dharma and the deities enshrined in eighty thousand places throughout this land. Please take pity on me; extend me your imperceptible help. It has been four or five years now since I shaved my head, but I am still at sixes and sevens and have no idea what to do with my life. Which of the paths should I follow—Buddhism, Confucianism, Taoism? I am like someone standing at a crossroads with no idea which way to proceed.
>
> Beings of compassion and benevolence and bringers of joy and liberation throughout the ten directions, please reveal to me a path on which I may strive forward, with rigorous practice, to the end of my days, sacrificing life and limb together if need be.

I closed my eyes and slowly approached a pile of books on one of the desks. I reached out with my thumb and forefinger and fished blindly among the stacks until I had fixed on a single volume among them. I pulled it out, raised it high above my head several times in veneration. Then I opened it. What a risky gamble I had taken! I might have pulled out a book on medicine or ritual, mathematics or divination, a biography or history, or some Confucian work. Yet marvelously, from among all those volumes, I had chosen *Spurring Zen Students Through the Barrier*![41] What a wonderful stroke of luck it was for me! Eagerly scanning the page in front of me, I saw four or five lines of marginalia inscribed above the text. It read: "In the past, when the priest Tz'u-ming was studying at Fen-yang, he sat through the nights without sleep, oblivious to the bitter cold east of the river. Whenever the sleep demon tried to approach, he would tell himself, 'Who are you? You'll be worthless if you go on living, and no one will notice if you die,' and jab himself in the thigh with a needle-sharp gimlet."

The moment I read those words, joyous tears filled my eyes and spilled down my cheeks. They became engraved in my heart, and I felt a strong root of faith penetrate into my bones. I found myself dancing mindlessly about with joy. When Baō returned I went straight in to see him and told him what had occurred. I procured my own copy of *Spurring Zen Students Through the Barrier* and from that time on it never left my side day or night. Even when I was engaged in various daily activities, it was always there with me, rolled up and stuck inside my robe.[42]

Within an area of five to seven *ri* around Baō's temple in Mino were four or five Zen priests who possessed good reputations as teachers, but all of them preached nothing but the blind and ignorant tenets of Unborn Zen. People from all around, old and young, priests and laity, people of both high and low estate, came to receive their instruction. They swarmed in like ants, pushing forward in long files day after day.[43] A close friend of mine urged me to participate in one of their meetings, but I deplored the fact that their essential teaching was so much at odds with what was set forth in *Spurring Zen Students Through the Barrier*. Never once did I join them, nor would I lend my ear to a single word they spoke. With *Spurring Zen Students Through the Barrier* alone as my teacher, I kept pressing rigorously ahead, striving day and night without ever once letting up in my practice.

In spring of the following year I went to attend Zen lectures on the *Record of Hsi-keng* being given by Banri Oshō at Jōkō-ji, a large temple in Wakasa province. While I was there, I felt a spirit of great courage, pure and intense, arise unexpectedly within me. It filled me with an overwhelming sense of joy.[44]

Leaving Jōkō-ji, I traveled to Iyo province on the island of Shikoku, where I entered the monks' hall at Shōshū-ji in Matsuyama. While I was there a high-ranking councillor of the Daimyo issued an invitation to have "four or five monks of promise attending the Shōshū-ji lecture meeting" visit him at Matsuyama Castle. I was one of the monks selected.[45]

Our host came out and talked with us. He brought out a large number of scrolls, specimens of calligraphy and such by priests of the past that his ancestors had for generations collected and preserved in their storehouses. He had us read the calligraphy. Finally, he produced a scroll from a set of double paulownia-wood boxes that was further encased in a beautiful pouch of gold brocade. After our initial wonderment, we sat up straight and proper, placed our palms together in *gasshō* and performed deep bows. When the scroll was unrolled, we saw that it was a piece of calligraphy by Ungo Rōshi.[46] Examining it once or twice, I saw that as far as the nobility of the sentiments expressed in the text was concerned, or the skill and beauty of the brushwork, there was nothing, not a single word or character in this calligraphy that set it apart from any of the twenty or so other scrolls we had seen. Yet obviously this scroll had been treasured and revered in a very special way. Why? Giving the matter some thought, I concluded that it certainly had nothing to do with either the writing style or the brushwork. The reason it was so much more highly prized than all the rest was simply because of a definite strength it possessed that had its source in the *kenshō* experience and enlightenment. For the first time I realized that all the privations I had endured during those many years of practice had been completely mistaken.

When I returned to the monks' quarters, I gathered together all the calligraphy, dog-eared manuscripts, notes, and other writings I had acquired at different places over many years, rolled them up and bound them. I slipped quietly out to the egg-shaped grave stupas in the cemetery behind the temple and set fire to the lot. My behavior astounded my friends. They looked wonderingly at one another, sure I had taken leave of my senses. From that time on, I focused with total concentration on my koans alone, boring into them without a moment's letup.

In spring of the following year I was led by circumstances to hang up my traveling staff in the monks' quarters of Tenshō-ji in Fukuyama, Bingo province.[47] I didn't perform prostrations, I didn't chant sutras, I didn't so much as glance at writings of any kind, and not a mundane word passed from my lips. With

Spurring Zen Students Through the Barrier as my sole teacher, I worked doggedly at my koan and never let up.

That autumn I set out for home, traveling by land in the direction of Naniwa in Settsu province. I had been moved to tears when I had first heard the story of how the National Master Daijōshō-ō had traveled back and forth on the Tōkaidō over ten times yet had never once raised his head to look up as he passed beneath Mount Fuji.[48] The story had become etched in my mind and had engendered a deep respect and reverence for the National Master. A great resolve to achieve the goal I had vowed to reach suddenly rose within me. From then on, to the end of my journey, I did not see any of the mountains, rivers, trees, plants, castles, villages, and hamlets I passed. Though wide open, my eyes were blind to all the horses, oxen, pigs, dogs, and other animals moving this way and that along the road.

My traveling companions said, "If you stand on Kyōbashi Bridge in Okayama, Bizen province, and look up at the castle, it is as though you are gazing at the wonderful palace of Hsien-yang.[49] It is the most wonderful sight on the whole Tōkaidō." When we reached the bridge, my four companions stood in a row against the railing like stacks of brushwood, their eyes all riveted on the castle, all thought of further movement gone from their minds. I was standing there with them, but with eyes closed fast, deeply focused [on my koan]. I didn't see so much as a single tile the whole time, not an inch of the castle's famous white walls.

Later, as the five of us continued our journey, walking along in single file down the road, it seemed to me as though we had not taken a single step, but were standing in one place completely motionless, and the houses to our right and left and the various trees and plants that lined the road were all moving slowly backwards in unison. And when we were moving along in a boat we had boarded, it seemed as though the boat was not moving at all, that we remained completely stationary in one spot, and that the willows, reeds, and lotus flowers that lined the banks were flowing leisurely backward.[50]

We entered the roads of Harima, stepping along the bay of

Akashi, moving in time with the splendid sound of the waves striking the shore at Maiko's sandy beach. My thoughts roamed freely along dream-like paths; the sacred grove at Ikuta, the fields at Koyano were scenes I did not see. Someday the clouds of illusion will clear, and all things [*Naniwa*] be seen as delusions. I climbed the steep slope where the original person is encountered [Ōsaka], passed the waterwheel at the Yodo rapids [*Kawase*]. A fervent [Atsuta Shrine] and singleminded vow to cease [*Owari*] transmigrating in the realms of darkness spurred on [*Kakegawa*] my mind, which was bent solely on discovering [*Mitsuke-juku*] its original self-nature. But even with the Six Paths far behind, I still faced the sweat-drenched slope [*Shiomi-zaka*] so difficult for travelers. Once atop the summit, I could gaze below over the world of good and evil at Kuzubakama, then boot it onward down the Dharma path, where even watery rice is meager, to the station of Mariko, still firmly pledged to cross beyond [*Tegoshi*] the rising, falling seas of birth and death [*Shōji*] and cast aside [*Okitsu*] the floating world's nerve-rattling strife and thoughts of fortune good and ill [*Sumpu*]. At Yui and Kambara, the sorrows of separation and loss made me resolve to down the bitter pill and purge away impurities. Now the sacred mountain towered up, its snowy surface mirrored on the waters of the Fuji River, on whose current tears float past the size of horse-chestnuts, because of those who have renounced the world. At Yoshiwara, after a brief respite, the heart grew lighter as I bent my steps onward to Kashiwabara, whence amid the sadness of the floating world [*Ukishima*] in which meetings inevitably mean farewell, I reached Shōin-ji at last. It was the end of the fourth year of Hōei [*1707*].

I had left my home at eighteen. At twenty-two I now returned. My family and friends all gathered to greet me, but the words they spoke to me, about things long in the past, seemed only a cacophonous gabble. My eyes stared straight ahead, my mouth was shut fast, and not a word passed from my lips, not a single sight registered to my eyes. It was as though I was with people I had never seen before. They eyed me doubtfully, standing there in an empty daze as if I were someone who had taken leave of his senses.

There was a priest named Ryū Jōza from Echigo staying at a neighboring temple at the time.[51] We were the same age, and the moment I met him it was like a reunion with an old friend. In the course of a long conversation he told me, "There is a man named Shuchō Shuso at Eigan-ji in Echigo province, a veteran monk of superior ability who has studied with Rinzai, Sōtō, and Ōbaku teachers throughout the country. All of them awarded him their Dharma certification. He is without doubt an outstanding monk who has attained great spiritual power through a genuine enlightenment." The moment I heard about the monk I was eager to go and pay him a visit. I learned that by a stroke of good fortune, a lecture meeting on *The Eye of Men and Gods* was scheduled for the following spring at Eigan-ji.[52]

The day the winter meeting broke up, the fifteenth day of the first month, I left Suruga with three or four other monks and proceeded to Eigan-ji in Echigo to visit the veteran priest I had heard about. To my dismay, however, he turned out to be another of those doltish Dharma dunces who followed the silent-illumination, dead-sitting practices of Unborn Zen.[53]

Greatly discouraged and despondent, I felt ashamed of myself for having fallen unwittingly into the mistake of acting against the most fundamental aspiration of those Zen figures that appeared in the *Spurring Zen Students Through the Barrier.* I had made a difficult trip of a hundred *ri* pursuing a matter that had nothing whatever to do with me, when elucidation of the great matter must never place even a shred of reliance on anything extraneous to oneself.

With that, a fierce resolve fired within me. Setting the spirit of my great vow before everything else, I cast aside all other concerns and slipped unnoticed into the shrine room of Lord Toda. The floor of the room was covered with a layer of small, neatly arranged pebbles. There I hid myself and for several days straight sat in zazen like a dead man, like a person devoid of sense. I reached the end of reason, reached the limit of words, reached the end of all human skill or ability. Ordinary mental processes, consciousness, and emotions all ceased to function. It was as though I was encased in a sheet of ice ten thousand feet thick or sitting inside a bottle of purest crystal. My breath itself seemed to hang suspended. Then, in the middle of the night, a wonderful thing happened. As the sound of a distant bell reached my ears, I suddenly broke through into great enlightenment.[54] It was "mind and body falling away; fallen away mind and body."[55] It was "thrusting the jade pavilion over on its back," "smashing apart a thick sheet of solid ice."[56] The great void in all the ten directions ceased to exist. The great earth completely and utterly vanished. Not a particle remained.[57] I felt joy of an intensity I had never in my life experienced. Unthinkingly I shouted out, "How wonderful! Old Yen-t'ou is alive and well! Old Yen-t'ou still lives!"[58] and began clapping my hands and emitting loud hoots of laughter. My companions were completely bewildered by my behavior. They were sure I had taken leave of my senses.

From that time on, everyone I saw appeared to exist within a field of gossamer that shimmered and danced in the summer air. I thought to myself, "No one in the past two or three hundred years has ever experienced such a marvelous breakthrough." My rampant pride soared up like a banner on a mountain peak. My arrogance raced forth like an onrushing tide.

It was the fifth year of the Hōei period [1709]—the spring of my twenty-third year—several days before the opening of the lecture meeting on *The Eye of Men and Gods*.

Upwards of two hundred people had gathered to attend the meeting. They were quartered in different halls. I was placed in charge of fifty people who had been housed in the main hall of neighboring Kyūshō-ji, a Sōtō temple, that had been borrowed for use as an annex. One of my assistants at the annex was named Dan Jōza.

Dan had been over at the main hall. He suddenly came running back in a state of excitement.

"A strange monk just arrived," he said. "He's a shabby-looking old veteran between thirty and forty years old with a scruffy head of hair and grimy face. His robe is all ragged and he carries a tattered old travel pouch over his shoulder. He walked in carrying a stout oak staff six or seven feet long which he planted on the ground beside him and was balancing with his finger poised at the tip.[59] He didn't even know the proper etiquette required of newly arrived monks. He just stood there in the entranceway, straight and unmoving like a large withered tree, asking for permission to stay in a gruff Bandō voice.[60] He's the living image of a crazy monk. If a man like that is allowed to stay, he's sure to end up having an extremely disruptive influence on the meeting. We'd be far better off getting rid of him as quickly as possible."[61]

Dan, gasping for breath by the time he had finished blurting all this out, then took off again to visit the senior monks in the main temple. He soon reappeared, this time his face contorted in disgust. "Well, something highly disagreeable seems to be shaping up. I heard the officials over in the main temple discussing what to do with the new arrival. They said since they had no space for him there, they had no choice but to put him up temporarily here at Kyūshō-ji. The abbot is of the same mind, so they'll probably be coming here soon to force him on us. An extremely disagreeable turn of events, if you ask me."

Dan then turned to me. "What's your opinion, senior monk? It seems to me we should refuse him. If we agree and allow him to stay, he's sure to cause a great deal of trouble. It will affect everyone here." Before he had even finished saying this, six or seven of the other monks began adding their voices to the discussion, their brows pinched deep with furrows of concern. "We can't allow it. We can't allow it," they said. "If they're going to accept trouble-makers like him and send them all over here to foist off on us, some serious disturbance is sure to arise that we'll be unable to deal with. Even before this, people have been whispering privately about the Kyūshō-ji annex being the place where all the dubious cases are sent. If five or six of these brazen characters, known all over the country for disrupting training halls, are concentrated in one place, something serious is bound to happen before the meeting is over. Utterly deplorable. Even you will be unable to control it, senior monk. Why ask for trouble?"

Grumblings and mutterings passed quietly through the hall. "Surely the best course of action is to refuse him," they all concluded. But before the words had even left their mouths, I shook my head, and said, "Quiet down, all of you! I don't want to hear any more of your endless speculations. I'm tired of it! And as for you, Dan, you aren't doing what I told you to do. Your mind is not on your practice, so your energy is not focused where it should be. That's why when something like this comes up you have plenty of time to go running around picking up useless bits of mundane gossip about somebody else's troubles or mistakes. You insist on latching onto these rumors that have nothing to do with you. You go around retelling them to others and end up undermining not only your own religious resolve but that of your companions as well. I don't care who enters this hall, the second he makes the slightest move out of line, there won't be any questions. I'm just going to throw him out, and that will be the end of it. There's no need for any of you to discuss it anymore. When it comes down to it, brother Dan, it's the presence of people like you that is disturbing this meeting."

Just as I finished delivering this rebuke, Chō Shuso arrived at the annex, bringing the new monk with him. He announced in a sincere and obliging manner, "This is Kaku Jōza [senior monk Sōkaku], who has just arrived from Shinano province. Since both the old and new halls over at the main temple are completely full, we would be deeply obliged if you would let him stay here and afford him the benefit of your guidance."

"To begin with," I replied, "you can see we are very cramped here as well. This hall has been borrowed from the temple of another school. If you intend on quartering so many people here, you should be extremely careful to select the best-behaved students. If, on the other hand, you are going to make a point of carefully sifting out all the ruffians and hall-wreckers that assemble here from different parts and send them to us, then no one here will have a moment's peace of mind day or night. But even if that is not true, I've heard that some of the priests at the main temple are deeply concerned about the situation. They are saying, 'The meeting is proceeding exactly according to plan, but we're worried about the Kyūshō-ji annex. If you take five or six notorious hall-wreckers and misfits from around the country and throw them together in one place like that, sooner or later, before the training session is over, a serious incident—something that's going to freeze our livers—is sure to occur. All we can do is to sit here with worried looks on our faces, waiting for it to happen.' In any case, I'm afraid I have no alternative but to refuse your request."

Before I had finished speaking, Chō Jōza said, "Please don't say that. The head priest himself came to this decision because he thought he could count on you."

"If that is so," I replied, "I must apologize for what I said. In that case, it would be unseemly for me to refuse. Whichever way things turn out, good or ill, I'll do as you say. But if this man shows the least sign of any irregular behavior, I'm going to throw him out and send him back to the main temple. Is that agreed?"

"That will be perfectly acceptable to us," the head monk replied. He then turned and cautioned the new monk: "I want you to be completely clear about what we have just agreed to. Make any false step at all, and you won't be allowed to stay a moment longer. Devote yourself singlemindedly to your practice. Your mind should be focused solely on the great matter of kenshō and enlightenment. And don't forget that any unnecessary talking, loud conversation, laughter, or the like is strictly forbidden." The monk bowed to the floor in agreement.

I threw in some warnings of my own. "When wrong-headed monks with bad habits come around, initially they always appear to be obedient and well-behaved, looking to all the world like genuine seekers who have come to penetrate the secret depths. But after as little as five or ten days, when they have had time to size up their fellow monks, they start treating the temple norms as if they were dirt, the time-honored standards of Zen as though they were balls of matted filth. They pay no attention to the senior monks above them, bully the younger monks, and end up dropping out in the middle of the training session. They disappear and are seen no more. In recent years such rascals have appeared in great number in training halls around the country. You've probably heard about them yourself.

"I am Kaku from Suruga province.[62] You don't want to mix with me. You won't find another monk in Izu, Kai, Tōtōmi, or

Shinano who can stand up to me. If you start feeling free and easy and get it into your head to start something, I promise I'll deal very severely with you."

"I can see it's going to be pretty intimidating around here," the head monk laughed. "Kaku Jōza, you're going to have to devote yourself to your practice with the greatest care, as if you were living inside a cave of demons or in a tiger's den. Otherwise, you're in for some big trouble." He then returned to the main temple.

Kaku just sat there silently and circumspectly, looking a bit sheepish. The other monks in the hall viewed the new arrival with obvious contempt. No one bothered even to look at him or speak to him. He was treated like a menial servant, made to take the lowest-ranking seat in the hall, and assigned a desk in the very back of the room.

The next day the lecture meeting opened and the temple was in a general state of confusion and disorder. In the evening four or five of the senior monks from the main hall appeared in the annex. One of them tested a few of the monks regarding some passages from *The Eye of Men and Gods* that the priest had taken up in his lecture. After they left, the head monk Chō Jōza showed up. After uttering some words about how well the opening had gone, he picked up a copy of *The Eye of Men and Gods* lying nearby, flipped it open to two or three passages, and made some critical comments. Then he too left.

Kaku cautiously approached my desk and asked in a low whisper, "Was that the head monk at this temple?"

"It was. What about it?" I replied.

"Those comments he and the other monks made just now," he replied. "I'd like to say something about them."

"If you have anything to say, say it!" I answered. "If you're right, I'll confirm it for you. If you're wrong, I'll set you straight."

Kaku smiled. Then he spoke. "Now I'm not saying the remarks the head monk made didn't show some discernment. He seems to have above average ability. Once that's said, however, none of his comments went beyond the elementary stage of 'seeking advice about one's own ideas.'"[63]

I opened a copy of *The Eye of Men and Gods* that was lying

nearby. After I had carefully examined several of the passages, ones dealing with the great matter that is so difficult to understand and penetrate, I realized that Kaku Jōza was indeed a veteran monk of superior capacity. I was greatly astonished and greatly delighted. "What teacher in this day and age," I thought to myself, "could have produced such a monk?"

I asked Kaku who his teacher was. "He's a recluse of Iiyama in Shinano province named Shōju Rōjin," he replied. "He was a student of Shidō Munan, who was himself a direct heir of National Master Daien Hōkan.[64] My teacher was ordained by Zen Master Shidō Munan, who always had a special affection for him."

A thrill of delight passed through my heart when I heard those words, as I reflected, "National Master Hōkan is a figure I have deeply revered and respected for many years. He is the kind of teacher who appears only once in five hundred years. How lucky I am to encounter someone belonging to his Dharma lineage. After the retreat is over here, I'd like to go and study under Master Shōju."

The night before the lecture meeting ended, I confided my feelings to Kaku: "I'd like to go to Iiyama and request an interview with your teacher. What do you think?"

"That's just what I'd been hoping for," he replied.

The next morning, before the drums and temple bell announced the end of the meeting, Kaku and I slipped away from the temple and were soon hurrying along a deserted back trail up over the pass at Mount Tomikura. We arrived in Iiyama, and I was granted an interview with Shōju Rōjin.

The old teacher took one look at me and immediately asked, "How do you see Chao-chou's Mu?"

"No way to lay a hand or foot on it," I replied.

Shōju reached out, pushed the end of my nose with his fingers, and said, "Well, I just got a hand on it!"

I was unable to utter a single word. He had crushed my pride and arrogance as easily as if he were smashing an egg on a large rock. His blistering shouts, the furious blows that rained from his fists, shattered my spirit and struck terror into my soul. Once he picked me up and tossed me off the veranda of the temple as if I were a kitten. I landed on the ground four or five feet below, losing consciousness. I was completely dead to the world and lay there for what must have been about an hour. The old man stood above me on the veranda clapping his hands with glee and emitting loud brays of laughter. I finally recovered my senses, got up and bowed to him three times. He took pity on me and assigned me a koan—Su-shan's Memorial Tower—to work on.[65]

"Focus singlemindedly on this story," he told me. "Long ago, after Hsi-keng Rōshi had once died the Great Death, he bored into this story for four long years, and he eventually emerged as a great shade tree without equal in all of China. It is said Hsi-keng's descendents would increase daily in this country as well.[66] But even if one of these descendents were to achieve eighteen great satoris and small satoris beyond count,[67] so long as he has not penetrated this story, he cannot be recognized as a true disciple of the Japanese teacher Daiō or his disciple Daitō."

With that, I began gnawing on the koan from the front. I went at it from the sides. I forgot both food and sleep. The tremendous sense of joy I had felt on my previous enlightenment was now all transformed into a boundless agony. I pushed myself mercilessly, expending ten times more effort than I had back in the shrine room at Eigan-ji.

One day, I took my bowl and went into the village below Iiyama Castle. I stationed myself beside the gate of a house and stood there totally motionless, a lump of blank oblivion. Out of the blue, the local madman, eyes bulging menacingly out, dashed up to me brandishing a broom in his hands. He began striking me furiously about the head with the handle, leaving my sedge hat in tatters. I was given a terrible fright, taken totally by surprise. I toppled over unconscious and lay on the ground for about an hour. People who witnessed the event thought the fellow had killed me.[68] But after a while I regained my senses and picked myself up off the ground. As I did, I suddenly found that I had penetrated several koans that until that time I had been totally unable to get any grip on at all. I had bored into them right to their roots and smashed them to smithereens.

Beside myself with joy, I walked slowly and exultantly back to the hermitage. Shōju, who was standing on the veranda, took one look at me approaching in the distance and called out with a smile on his face, "Have you attained something?" I went up to him and related the particulars of my realization. He was extremely pleased. He proceeded to throw up a ten thousand–fold barrier before me. He laid out a thicket of thorns and briars a thousand-fold deep. But before the day was out, I had passed through them all without a single hitch. Scarcely able to contain his joy, Shōju came up beside me, took out his fan, and patted me with it on the back three times.

"Excellent. Excellent," he said. "But don't be satisfied with this minor attainment. The farther you proceed into enlightenment, the harder you must strive. The greater the understanding you achieve, the more effort you must exert. Do not cease striving until the day you die. Sadly, in recent times people in both the Sōtō and Rinzai schools have taken this initial attainment and made it into achievement of the ultimate, most cherished goal. They have transformed it into the final end of their school's religious training. It is true Master Lin-chi told his monks that they should wait until the yearning ceases in their mind, that this cessation of yearning is the true teaching,[69] but that is just a case of teaching through the use of expedient means. Yet today's priests insist on presenting Lin-chi's words as the great matter of the Zen school, a phrase that leads students to deeper attainment. They seem to believe that Zen consists in merely achieving a state of non-seeking or non-attachment, no-thought, or no-mind. Not one of them seems to be aware that such ideas portend the demise of the Buddha's Dharma, and are the fundamental reason the true traditions of Zen are dying out. It goes without saying that they are totally unaware of the practice that continues after satori.

"Today Zen teachers of this blind and ignorant 'silent-illumination' variety, men given such fine labels as 'good teacher' and 'eminent priest,' are quick to tell you, their faces shining with virtue, things like this:

All authentic Zen priests dislike, avoid, and endeavor to expunge at all costs the seeking, questing mind—the yearnings of the worldly passions. The desire to practice Zen is a matter of seeking, as is the quest for satori or *kenshō*. So is preaching the Dharma and teaching students. Reciting sutras or dharanis is seeking. Bowing and performing prostrations involves seeking. Writing calligraphy and studying texts is seeking. Reading and copying sutras is seeking. Koan study, the student's morning and evening visits to receive his teacher's instruction, are also seeking. What you need to do is to focus exclusively on remaining without thought, without mind, without seeking or attachment. Stay free of thinking or seeking anything at all. Be just like a block of wood in its original state, which is perfectly fine just as it comes from the woods. Everyone is born a Buddha. Why start seeking and trying to become one? Why seek to become enlightened? It's like Musō Kokushi's waka says,

> A bowl and its cover,
> plain unvarnished wood
> straight from the mountains,
> no lacquer to put on,
> no color to wear off.

So what if you don't experience satori? It doesn't mean you have to eat your food through your nose. It still goes in through your mouth. It doesn't mean when you piss, you have to do it on a millstone. You still go to the privy. When you want to move, you move. When you have an inclination to sit, you sit. You are from the very first perfectly free. There's nothing fettering any of your activities. What need is there to seek attainment beyond that of some kind of 'divine power' or 'miraculous working.'

This self is fine just as it is. It is Buddha, and for this Buddha there is no heaven or hell, no samsara or nirvana. That is why it has been said,

Living in the world,
A matter of eating, defecating,
Sleeping and getting up;
After that, all that's left
Is just dying.[70]

There are, from that perspective, no sentient beings to be saved and no Dharma to be preached.

"With that, the teachers of these false do-nothing, silent-illumination doctrines, and the ignorant students who swallow their nonsense, proceed to put their 'plain bowl and cover' Zen into practice in their daily lives, eating their fill, then going and dozing off as they sit in rows like so many lumps doing zazen, never exerting themselves in any true Zen practice at all. Immured on all four sides by darkness, unable to tell east from west, north from south—it is as if they were trussed up with ropes and suspended into the pitch darkness of a bottomless chasm. When they die, they're surely bound for the Black Rope Hell.

"It's one thing to fall into hell because you bamboozle yourself, but these fellows are also fooling large numbers of lay followers with their teachings, dragging them down into the depths with them. Their transgression is of greater gravity than the Five Cardinal Sins! They'll surely fall into the Hell of Incessant Suffering when they die and undergo endless torments.

"These false Zen teachings are truly frightening. You should never become involved with such teachers. From now on, you should focus all your effort on post-satori training, establishing a great root of faith, arousing a spirit of unfaltering diligence second to none, calling forth a mind of great courage, whipping forward the wheel of the Four Great and Universal Vows, and thus repaying your profound debt to the Buddha-patriarchs.

"What do I mean by post-satori practice? It is first of all unremitting right-mindedness, continuous devotion to your practice. It is what the *Precious Mirror Samadhi* speaks of when it says, 'essential among all other essentials is to engage without interruption in hidden practice and secret activity.'[71]

"And what are the four great and universal vows?

Sentient beings are numberless. I vow to liberate them all.
Defiling passions are endless. I vow to eradicate them all.
Dharma teachings are infinite. I vow to learn them all.
The Buddha Way is unexcelled. I vow to master it.[72]

"If you desire to master the Buddha Way, you must first of all cut off all the endlessly arising passions. If you desire to cut off the afflicting passions, you must first of all vow to liberate the countless sentient beings. If you desire to liberate sentient beings, you must first of all strive continuously to engage in the great Dharma giving. If you desire to engage in the great Dharma giving—teaching the Dharma—you must first of all be completely conversant with all the Buddhist scriptures and also familiarize yourself with the writings of the wise teachers of other traditions, so as to accumulate an immense store of Dharma assets. Hence it is said: 'The Dharma teachings are infinite. I vow to learn them all.' Without these Dharma assets, you cannot engage in the teaching of the great Dharma. It is because they teach the Dharma without possessing these assets that the blind and ignorant priests who infest the land today try to have students attain a state of no-thought or no-mind and spread pernicious ideas that deny causation and rebirth.

"Strive! Strive hard! Don't fall victim to these false teachers! Don't pretend you have attained the Dharma when you haven't! Don't talk about realization until you've attained realization! Pledge that you will never, for a thousand lives or ten thousand kalpas, slacken your efforts or cease your quest. Make a habit of repeating three times over, 'Though empty space should be exhausted, my vow will never end.'[73]

"If you want to realize the Four Universal Vows, you must first put them into practice. If you want to put the Vows into practice, you must first learn all the Dharma teachings. As you go about doing this, you will one day, without even knowing it, realize that you have reached the point where the defiling passions have been severed. You must never, to the end of your life, turn from this quest even for an instant. Without a single doubt in your mind, proceed forward until you reach the stage where no falling back or regressing can occur. I wish you a long life. I deeply hope that you will live and teach until you reach my age."

Such is the gist of the teachings Shōju Rōjin gave me.[74] I plucked up a spirit of great courage and threw myself into my practice day and night, pushing myself mercilessly, and experienced the joy of satori in a number beyond count.

This was the winter of the fifth year of the Hōei era [1709]. That same winter a letter arrived from home informing me that my old teacher, Nyoga Rōjin, who had long suffered from illness and did not have much longer to live, was alone without anyone to attend to his personal needs. I therefore left Shōju's hermitage to return to my home temple in Suruga. Shōju, staff in hand, walked along with me for about one *ri*. When we parted, he took my hand in his and gave me the following words of advice: "When you leave here, do not, even for a small interval of time, relax your efforts. Strive, and continue to strive at all times to extend the gift of the Dharma for the liberation of all beings. Work with one or two students with a capacity similar to your own. In that way, you will be able to requite the profound debt you owe the Buddha-patriarchs."

I left Shōju with tears of regret welling in my eyes and bent my steps toward Suruga. Over the next year or so, I ministered to Nyoga Rōjin's needs. At the same time, I did not neglect my practice. I sat for eight sticks of incense every night,[75] never missing a single night in either the stifling heat of summer or the piercing cold of winter.

2: The Tale of Yūkichi of Takayama　　　:

HAKUIN WROTE *The Tale of Yūkichi* just after he finished *The Tale of My Childhood*, the autobiographical narrative he refers to as his "teaching on post-satori training," clearly intending that it serve as a sequel to that work. He placed it as a supplement following *The Tale of My Childhood* in the third section of the *Goose Grass* collection, explaining that he had decided to include Yūkichi's story because it presented such a wonderful opportunity to dramatize the teachings he had focused on in *The Tale of My Childhood*. Ultimately, *The Tale of Yūkichi* can be seen as a case example illustrating the essentials of post-satori practice, with Sōsuke's troubles an object lesson on the dangers facing those who neglect that important phase of their training.

Iida Yasuemon, a samurai from Takayama in Hida province (the northern part of modern Gifu prefecture) whom Hakuin has narrate the bulk of Yūkichi's tale, begins by describing the mysterious disappearance of Kojima Sōsuke. Sōsuke, an upstanding citizen of Takayama, has apparently absconded with a consignment of valuable merchandise his fellow merchants had entrusted to him. Sōsuke was a gifted Zen student who while studying with Hakuin had experienced the breakthrough known as *kenshō* or satori. He had gone on to become a leading figure among the close-knit community of Hakuin's lay followers in the Takayama area. But being ignorant of the practice that continues after satori, he thought he had achieved final enlightenment and his training was over. Priests of the local Pure Land temples used Sōsuke's suspicious disappearance as a pretext to unleash attacks on Hakuin and his Zen teaching, causing his lay followers in the city considerable embarrassment.

While all this was taking place, a fourteen-year-old boy named Yūkichi was possessed by the deity of the large Inari Shinto Shrine in Takayama. Speaking through the young boy, the deity summons the townspeople and over a period of days delivers a series of teachings and pronouncements, in the course of which he reveals Sōsuke's whereabouts and explains the reason for his disappearance. He then goes on to give a series of impressive formal Zen talks (*teishō*) in which he stoutly defends Hakuin and the methods of koan Zen and denounces the priests who have criticized him.

Speaking through Yūkichi, the deity explains that Sōsuke's mistake was in assuming that having received a certificate of satori from Hakuin, his Zen training was over and that he was now a full-fledged Dharma heir of the master and entitled to teach others. He goes on to point out that attainment of *kenshō*, as deeply significant as it is, is merely the entrance to the Buddhist life, a gateway that students must pass through before they can begin the lifelong "post-satori" practice—deepening self-attainment and eventually teaching others.

In the sense that *The Tale of Yūkichi* clarifies the significance of the certificates Hakuin gave his lay followers and the necessity of their continuing assiduous training, this curious tale reads less as a reproof to jealous priests of other sects than as a corrective to his own teaching, and perhaps even as a roundabout solicitation of business.

The Tale of Yūkichi affords a rare glimpse into areas of Hakuin's teaching activity not found in the other writings or records. We learn that Hakuin and his teaching were being subjected to severe criticism from other Buddhist priests in the city. We are also given unique descriptions of Hakuin's practice of presenting students with Zen paintings to certify their attainment of satori or enlightenment. According to Tōrei's *Chronological Biography,* Hakuin was in Takayama in 1758 for several months of lectures

Dragon Staff Certificate

on the *Blue Cliff Record*. We learn from *The Tale of Yūkichi* that members of Takayama's lay community also attended the lectures and that during the meeting quite a number of them received these paintings from Hakuin after passing his initial two-part koan—the Sound of One Hand and Put a Stop to All Sounds. The paintings depicted a priest's staff turning into a dragon (illustration),[1] altogether different in appearance, and perhaps also in impact, from the simple written documents (*inka shōmei*) a Zen teacher traditionally awarded students. They came to be called "Dragon Staff certificates."

Although the Dragon Staff certificates appear in several different forms, most of the later ones resemble the example in the illustration shown here: a wooden priest's staff made from a stout branch in the process of turning into a dragon, symbolizing the student's achievement of enlightenment. Wrapped around the staff is a *hossu*, the ceremonial whisk carried by a Zen master, and below it, curled around the lower half, a second, smaller branch. A formula inscription gives the recipient's name, the place and date where it was awarded, and the certification that he or she had duly passed Hakuin's two koans. A large number of certificates are extant, the majority of them dating from his final decades.[2] The locations and dates inscribed on them provide valuable clues to his movements during his later teaching career.

While a few of these certificates were awarded to Buddhist priests, most of them seem to have gone to lay students. In Hida (Takayama), Mino province, Edo, the Kansai area, and no doubt in other lay communities as well, the recipients formed into groups, calling themselves *jōhotsu nakama*, "league of students who have received Master Hakuin's Dragon Staff." They assumed a leadership role in local lay Zen communities, and took it upon themselves to hold practice meetings on their own. The gifted student from Takayama, Sōsuke, even delivered Zen lectures on difficult Zen texts.

In the postscript to *Tale of Yūkichi* Hakuin mentions that some people had taken issue with portions of the story, pointing out unspecified "mistakes" therein. Not only does he concede the possibility of error—"after all, I was writing about something I heard at third hand, which had taken place in a far distant province"—but he also admits to embellishing the text in places, justifying it on the grounds that it was necessary in order to convey the essential meaning inherent in Yūkichi's story.

While it is difficult to ascertain either the precise nature or the extent of the alterations Hakuin made to the story, his confession of "mistakes" and "embellishments," combined with the fanciful, not to say incredible, nature of the tale itself, is ample reason for readers even in his own day to conclude that *The Tale of Yūkichi* was a work of fiction, invented by Hakuin to promote his Zen agenda.

Strange as it may seem, however, the curious tale was apparently based on actual events that took place in Takayama. Two letters Hakuin wrote to his student Katayama Shunnan, a highly respected physician from the village of Hagiwara near Takayama, have recently been published which confirm that in 1760 a youth named Yūkichi had indeed delivered a series of talks of the type described in Hakuin's work and that he was believed by townspeople to have been possessed by the deity of the Takayama Inari Shrine. Hakuin's astonishment at learning of the boy's possession and the various pronouncements the deity had delivered through him is evident in the letters. The letters also seem to confirm that ordinary citizens of Takayama were aware of the events and that, in response to appeals the deity had made through young Yūkichi, they had donated and sent to Hakuin a collection of money sufficient to cover the cost of publishing a manuscript on Zen practice he had completed.

These two letters (translated below) establish that, even if *The Tale of Yūkichi* does not relate events exactly as they took place (and could not, of course, be expected to reproduce Yūkichi's words verbatim), the story is not merely a product of Hakuin's fertile imagination, which is surely how *The Tale of Yūkichi* would otherwise have been viewed. The letters also provide us with glimpses of Hakuin's close relationship with his lay followers and his active involvement in the publication process.

Two Letters from Hakuin to Katayama Shunnan

Letter 1: 25th of the 5th month [1761]

I was extremely glad to learn from your letters that you are still doing well and that everyone is gathering mornings and nights and practicing diligently. Nothing could give me greater pleasure. It is something that is not seen in most other lay groups. Soon I will be going to several different places to hold practice sessions, but I often think how nice it would be to see everyone in Takayama once again—though I realize, considering the long journey and the increasing infirmities of age, that it probably will not be possible.

Last winter when Kiemon from Shimohara village stopped by Shōin-ji on his way back from Edo, he told me that you and your comrades who received Dragon Staff certificates had expressed a desire to publish my Dharma words on post-satori practice. At the same time he informed me of the amazing oracles the deity of the Inari Shrine had delivered to the citizens of Takayama. He brought me the five *ryō* you had entrusted to him. I was deeply moved and extremely pleased by everyone's kindness.

I was obliged to visit Edo at the beginning of the year in order to renew my credentials with the government, so I took the manuscript of the Dharma words on post-satori practice and the money you sent with me and discussed the matter of getting it published with a bookseller. The manuscript runs to a hundred and sixty or seventy pages, so I decided to divide it into three separate volumes. That means, according to the bookseller's estimate, that the money I assembled will not cover even half of the printing costs. I'm afraid I have to turn to you once again for help. I was extremely grateful when I read in your letter last spring that you were willing to provide additional funds should they be needed. Is it possible for you and your fellow students in Takayama to send an additional four or five *ryō*?

I had intended to turn the manuscript over to the bookseller when I went to Edo, but by last spring so many people had borrowed it to make their own copies that the original had become soiled and damaged—a few of the pages had even disappeared. Moreover, I decided, acting on the recommendation you made in your previous letter, to delete from the manuscript the list of the people to whom I have awarded my Dragon Staff certificates. Also, I wanted to add five or six pages to the text. All this has made it necessary for me to write out another fair copy of the text to send to Edo. I am busily engaged in doing that now.

I contacted a number of people here in an attempt to raise the additional funds, but I was unsuccessful. I am deeply sorry to impose on you like this once again, but if you are able to send an additional five *ryō*, I would greatly appreciate it. I am well aware that it may not be possible on such short notice. If so, could you send me a promissory note as soon as possible? I will use it to borrow the money here. I will tell the publisher to send you five or ten copies as soon as the book is printed together with a receipt for the money.

I was utterly astounded to hear from Kiemon about the oracle the Inari deity of Takayama delivered through the young boy Yūkichi. We must join together and all work diligently to carry out the deity's wishes.

Sincerely yours, Hakuin

Letter 2: 2nd day of the 11th month [1761]

I was extremely pleased to hear that you and your Dragon Staff comrades and all my other students in the Takayama area are getting on so well. I remain in good health, so there is no need to worry on that account.

I was surprised and delighted to receive the five *ryō* Mr. Iiyama brought to help cover the publishing costs of my work on post-satori practice. I have no doubt that it is yet another example of the great Takayama deity's divine intervention. I am deeply grateful for all the help you have given. I meant to write thanking you for the money as soon as I received it from Mr. Iiyama, but one thing has come up after another and only now am I able to sit down and put brush to paper.

Iiyama recounted the Yūkichi story to me from first to last, informing me of all the particulars regarding the deity's possession of the young boy. I was deeply moved, and at the same time filled with a feeling of the humblest gratitude. Just then a chance for me to post the manuscript of my work to the publisher in Edo presented itself. I was obliged to quickly check the text over and send it off, together with a letter and the money you had sent. All of this kept me so occupied that I was unable to write and thank you earlier. Please forgive me.

Not long after that, the two additional *ryō* you sent arrived. It was so totally unexpected, in my happiness I just left it lying there in its envelope for a while. Anyway, thanks to Mr. Iiyama, I now know all about the Yūkichi incident and the prodigious wonders wrought by the Takayama deity. Nothing like it has ever happened before; it is totally unprecedented. I was so pleased and stimulated that I got the idea of writing a detailed account of young Yūkichi's story, calling it *The Tale of Yūkichi*, and attaching it to my manuscript. I intend to add it as a separate section following the first part, already finished, on post-satori practice. It should help promote firm belief in the Zen teaching among future generations of students as they engage in the quest for *kenshō*. Initially I was hesitant about composing the work, knowing that it would mean adding many more pages of text and of course even greater expense. I didn't feel I should put such a burden on my students in Edo.

But then the two *ryō* you sent arrived and immediately I set about composing Yūkichi's story. It kept growing and growing until it finally reached over seventy pages, much longer than I had originally intended. A day or two ago I finally was able to finish it, and it too has now been sent, along with the two *ryō*, to Edo.

But that was not the end of it, for the priest of Sōyū-ji in Takayama then showed up, bringing yet another three *ryō* in gold pieces. That made ten *ryō* in all, easily enough to print the entire work and to ensure it will appear before the end of winter. While I had the delight at this unexpected turn of events still fresh in my mind, a large group of visitors from a distant province suddenly arrived at the temple. Attending to their needs occupied me so completely that the Sōyū-ji priest was obliged to look in at least three times during the afternoon to press me to write a receipt for the money he had brought. I wasn't able to sit down and write it until now. It is late at night, and I'm afraid I may have written some of the characters incorrectly in the darkness. You may have trouble reading some of it.

With all these distractions, my plans have fallen behind schedule. I should have written separate letters to thank each of the donors for the contributions they sent. Please tell them all how grateful I am. Thanks to them, the Dharma words will soon be published. As soon as the first batch arrives from the printer, I will send ten or twenty copies to you.

Yours sincerely, Hakuin

P.S. By virtue of their selfless act, those who contributed to the publication of my Dharma words have helped keep generations of Zen students far in the future from straying into false practices and thus saved them from the terrible misfortune of falling into the evil ways. A Dharma gift greater than many thousands of ordinary good or benevolent acts. Sitting here in far-off Suruga province, I envy the donors who have now linked themselves karmically to the wonderful wisdom of *prajñā* for a thousand lives and ten thousand kalpas. Even as I write these words I am unable to stop the tears from flowing down my old cheeks. Please convey my feelings to everyone concerned.

From an old priest of sixty-two

THE TALE OF YŪKICHI OF TAKAYAMA

Relying on people's devotion the gods increase their divine power; relying on the gods' divine power people increase their good fortune.

In winter of 1759 my lay student Iida Yasuemon Yoshizumi of the Takayama clan visited Shōin-ji[3] on his way to Edo on official business. When he learned I was away teaching at Denshū-ji in nearby Taru village, he continued on to Edo. After completing his business, he stopped on his way back home at an inn at the Mishima post station, dropped off his baggage and four or five retainers who were accompanying him, and came with two of his attendants to see me at Denshū-ji. We had hardly had time to exchange greetings before he began to relate the following story:

"Something truly extraordinary has occurred recently in Takayama, an event of such divine portent as to defy human understanding. Two years ago, during the Dharma meeting you held at Sōyū-ji in Takayama, you awarded Dragon Staff certificates to more than ten people who had passed your koan barrier.[4] Kojima Sōsuke, one of your leading lay students in Takayama, was among them. Totally sincere and honest, Sōsuke is also endowed with great natural intelligence. He seemed to have acquired deep religious understanding upon passing your twofold koan.[5] After the meeting at Sōyū-ji, his fellow students began treating him with special respect, following his lead in spiritual matters, and addressing him as 'Sensei.' At their request, Sōsuke gave talks on the *Poems of Han-shan*, then delivered formal Zen lectures on the *Blue Cliff Record*, and soon earned a reputation for preaching with great discernment and an eloquence that, surprisingly enough, was deemed by some as equal to your own.

"One day, Sōsuke's fellow students assembled to discuss his future. 'We regard this man as our teacher,' one of them said. 'Although he is the eldest son of a wealthy family, they lost everything, and he now lives in poverty. He manages somehow to care for his elderly mother, but they worry day to day if they will have enough to eat. How can we, his friends and fellow students, bear to sit by and watch them suffer like this? Why don't we see if we can assemble a hundred *ryō* and find a way to use it to improve Sōsuke's life?'[6]

"'An excellent proposal,' said another. 'But a hundred *ryō* would provide no more than temporary relief. If we made the rounds of the neighboring post stations and villages asking for donations of thread, silk, and fabrics, we should be able to assemble a horseback-load of goods worth three hundred *ryō*. If we entrusted the goods to Sōsuke and sent him to Kyoto as our agent, offering him a yearly wage, in time we could expect a hundred-fold profit. Wouldn't that be a better plan in the long run?'

"All agreed to this proposal. When they had finally succeeded in assembling three hundred *ryō* worth of merchandise, they turned it over to Sōsuke and dispatched him to Kyoto. One month passed. Two months passed, but Sōsuke failed to return. No word was received, either from him or about him. Increasingly alarmed and apprehensive at this turn of events, they sent a representative to Kyoto. He went around to all the likely shops and businesses asking about Sōsuke's whereabouts, but Sōsuke had completely vanished. No one was even aware whether he was alive or dead.

"His friends' uneasiness give rise to various speculations: 'Could Sōsuke have absconded with the funds?' 'Perhaps someone else, but not Sōsuke. He would never betray our trust, much less desert his elderly mother in such a manner.' 'He may have met with an unexpected accident.' 'Perhaps he was robbed.' 'Whatever has occurred, how terribly unfortunate it had to happen to one of the finest men in the community.' His friends and associates went around with faces puckered in frowns, some struggling to hold back tears. The entire community, stunned in disbelief, seemed completely drained of its vitality.

"There were at this time in the town below Takayama Castle six or seven temples belonging to the Pure Land sects. Their priests were hostile to any teaching different from their own. They were envious of the lay Zen students in the city who had received your certificates and never ceased disparaging them in private. But being unable to approach the students in spiritual attainment, they did not dare express their feelings in public and had been obliged to sit by, gritting their teeth and witnessing the growing popularity of the rival school. Learning of the incident involving Sōsuke, they immediately sensed a chance to turn the tables on your lay followers. They began swarming like ants from the nest, rising like hornets from the hive, reviling and disparaging them at every opportunity.

"'You only have to look at history,' they said. 'Never since the Buddhist teachings first entered Japan has there been anything even resembling this silly "Dragon Staff" Zen. Never has a false teaching of this magnitude been seen either in China or Japan. It has had an especially pernicious effect on people's young sons and daughters. It is said a superior man does not take part in praising people. Yet these priests get their hooks into ignorant and impressionable young men and women and wantonly deceive and confuse them with their flattery. Telling them, "You've heard the sound of one hand!" "You've put a stop to all sounds!" Then they award them a dubious-looking scroll—a "Dragon Staff," or some such name. Though lacking any particular gift for religious matters, these young people are taken in by the excessive praise. They get all puffed up with their own importance. Without the slightest sense of shame, they are content to lie idly about all day, their minds filled with passions and desires. With an arrogance that soars higher than Mount Fuji, a pride more forceful than the rising tide, they go about bragging to everyone they meet, "I'm enlightened! I'm home free! From now on, I can act as I please. What have I to fear from stealing, or even taking life? How amusing it will be, committing all Five Cardinal Sins and Ten Transgressions." Their time is spent in the wine shops and brothels, without a single thought for their family obligations.

"'If things are allowed to continue like this, we'll have Sōsukes sprouting up right and left. But the stink you really don't want to be downwind of is the one from those phony "certificates of enlightenment"—"Dragon Staffs" or whatever—they pass out. More worthless and loathsome than fresh-used toilet paper! Anyone with even the smallest fragment should immediately rip it into tiny shreds and feed it to the fire god.'

"The priests have diatribes like this printed up. They go singing and clapping through the market and fields to attract folks' attention, handing the leaflets out to everyone they meet and mocking the Zen students: 'Oh, how happy I am!' 'Have you seen what I've seen? Have you seen what I've seen?'

"All this deeply dispirited the students who had received your Dragon Staff certificates. They moped about looking dark and distraught. Some took to their beds, hiding inside their rooms. Others merely collapsed in blubbering heaps. Elderly men and women of the town grasped hands and attempted to console one another. Weeping despondently, they began blaming events on 'that Zen teacher Hakuin': 'What could he have been thinking, awarding all those certificates to unknowing young men and women? He's made it so they can never show their faces in public again.'

"At this same time, there lived in Takayama a man by the name of Chōzaemon, who was owner of an establishment known as Matsuya. Chōzaemon had a thirteen-year-old son named Yūkichi, an extremely good-natured and clever lad who always showed the greatest filial devotion toward his parents. One day, Yūkichi dashed into the house and suddenly announced: 'I am the great deity Inari, the guardian of Takayama city. I have come because I have something important to make known to the elders and leading citizens of the town. Have the best room in the house, the one with the finest seat, cleaned and made ready for me. I will require several layers of cushions to sit upon when I deliver my pronouncements to you.' He shrieked this out in a manner that startled everyone in the house.

"Amid the commotion, people were unable to understand why he was behaving so outrageously toward his parents. They thought he had taken leave of his senses or that some malignant spirit had possessed him. Meantime Yūkichi's mother went into the family shrine room and got an amulet pouch that was hanging there. Putting it around her son's neck, she gave him several brisk slaps on the back. Yūkichi put his hands together before him in *gasshō*. His eyes closed, and he seemed to doze off. Then he lay down and was soon sound asleep. He remained that way, dead to the world, until eight o'clock the next morning. He suddenly jumped out of bed and began running around the house as if he had no knowledge whatever of the events of the previous day. Shortly after noon he went to the neighborhood bathhouse and took a leisurely bath.

"Once he returned home, however, he was just the way he had been the previous day. He yelled in the same loud shrieking voice, 'Chōzaemon! Isn't the room cleaned and ready yet? I have something of great importance to impart to you all! When I arrived at your house yesterday, someone put an amulet pouch around my neck inscribed by the Pure Land priest Yūten with the sacred name of Amida, and a talisman written by priest Hakuin. Because of that I withdrew for a short spell, but today I have returned. Spread the word. See to it that all the elders of the town assemble here. I promise that anyone who fails to attend my summons will be visited by apparitions, and I will make it impossible for him to light his kitchen fire.' The members of the household could only stand there with stunned looks on their faces.

"But an old man who lived nearby pointed out to them that

they had nothing to fear, rather that 'they should all feel extremely grateful and fortunate that Inari Daimyōjin, the august tutelary god of Takayama, had deigned to descend from the heavens to deliver an oracle to them.' People were dispatched throughout the town to spread the news of the deity's summons. Before long, townspeople young and old could be seen hurrying to Chōzaemon's house clad in their finest clothes. Once they had all assembled there, Yūkichi made his entrance, seated himself smartly on the highly-piled cushions, and solemnly addressed them:

"'I am pleased that you have gathered here. I have come to inform you of the whereabouts of your friend Kojima Sōsuke, who has been missing these many months. Sōsuke, as you know, struggled long and hard to pass the One Hand koans. He attained satori in an unmistakable *kenshō*. I am delighted to have a man of such firm and steadfast character among my followers. He is worth more than all the others put together. It was for this very reason that his fellow Zen students, who respected and admired him, were saddened to see him leading such a difficult life and inspired to do what they could to help him. The plan they devised of sending him to Kyoto as their business representative with a horseload of valuable merchandise was excellently conceived. On his arrival in Kyoto, Sōsuke entrusted the goods to some merchants and in exchange he received most of the money that was coming to him.

"'Unfortunately, a group of swindlers got wind of the transaction, ingratiated themselves into Sōsuke's favor, and using various ruses—one was to trick him into investing in a risky speculation in the rice market—they succeeded in bilking him of everything he had. Sōsuke did not squander the money in the wine shops, nor did he fritter it away in the pleasure quarters. The most regrettable thing is that all this happened because Sōsuke left his teacher too soon after achieving an undeniably authentic satori and thus never learned about the essential matter of post-satori practice.[7] In the past eminent and distinguished priests in untold numbers have achieved the great breakthrough and experienced the joy of satori, but any of them who failed to encounter an authentic teacher, someone who could convey to them the great matter of post-satori training, ended up falling into hell. And even supposing they did not fall into hell, and thanks to great suffering and countless good deeds in their previous existence were able to be born into the human realm as persons of great wealth and power, because of the principle that previous lives are completely forgotten with each new rebirth, if they merely took advantage of the privileged circumstances they had attained to commit selfish acts and pile up evil karma, there is no way they could avoid falling into hell when they died.

"'How fortunate it is that "closed barrier" koan Zen, dormant for five hundred years, managed to survive in the hinterland of Shinano province and was secretly transmitted to Master Hakuin, and how fortunate that he devoted his efforts from the spring of his twenty-fourth year exclusively to the liberation of sentient beings! At first he taught using the Mu koan; then he erected a twofold barrier of koans—the Sound of One Hand and Put a Stop to All Sounds. He called these barriers the "claws and fangs of the Dharma cave," "divine, death-dealing amulets." But even if an authentic Zen student—a patrician of the secret depths—breaks past that double barrier, he still has ten thousand additional barriers, an endless thicket of impenetrable thorns and briars, to pass through, not to mention one final, firmly closed, tightly locked gate. Once he has succeeded in passing through all these barriers one by one, he must arouse the Bodhi-mind and devote his life to carrying out the great matter of post-satori practice.

"'Master Hakuin recently wrote a book of Dharma instruction devoted exclusively to clarifying the great matter of post-satori training. For certain reasons, it has not yet been published. I want some of you here to go to Shōin-ji—don't let the distance deter you—and request the manuscript from the master. Then have it printed, and read it carefully day and night.

"'Still, I can't help pitying poor Sōsuke, constantly worrying about the elderly mother he left alone so far away. Sōsuke has not turned into a fish in some river or ocean. He is not living in China or India or any other distant land. Nor has he fallen into the Yellow Springs or one of the three unfortunate realms of karmic rebirth.[8] He has gone into hiding in a certain place in Settsu province.[9] He lives in the residence of a wealthy merchant. If you went there now, took him into custody, and had him sliced up into small pieces, shipped off to the island of devils, or boiled in oil, it would not bring back your three hundred *ryō*. But remember that you originally devised this plan because of a compassionate feeling that arose in your hearts. And you can hardly say that you are the only ones who have sustained a loss. Just wait and see: before long something totally unexpected may happen—you may end up getting all your money back. In any case, you should forgive Sōsuke. Dispatch a runner, or send a letter, and ask him to return to Takayama. Tell him he is free to look after his mother again. Such an act would surpass any Buddha-work, any good karma you could possibly perform. Isn't it said that good causes produce good effects and bad causes bad effects? Whether the loss amounts to three hundred *ryō* or a thousand, it occurred because of the plan you devised, which had its source in the mind of compassion. I am sure you will receive a profit from it that you will find more than ample. You should never harbor any regrets or feel any distress over what happened.

"'Another matter I keenly regret is the unexpected abuse and suffering the devout men and women who received Master Hakuin's certificates have had to endure on account of Sōsuke's blunder. This has caused me much grief. It was all the work of half a dozen perverse, karma-denying priests in the Takayama area, all of them belonging to different Buddhist schools and all of them loathing koan Zen for being at odds with the ignorant, muddle-headed teachings they cherish. Incapable of criticizing koan Zen openly, they attempted to discredit it using sly innuendo. When the Sōsuke affair became public, however, they had the ammunition they needed, and they used it freely to spread their abuse. Groups of their ilk are known in Buddhism as heretical demons, slanderers of the true Dharma. The transgression they commit exceeds by far the Five Cardinal Sins. They are doomed to hell when they die, and they will probably never be able to deliver themselves from the torments they encounter there.

"'One of these priests, the abbot of Such-and-such temple, might make some slight atonement for his sins were he to sincerely repent his actions and perform good works that would gather him some merit. But no such possibility exists for Priest So-and-so of Such-and-such temple. No matter how many tens of thousands of good deeds this person performed, he would never be able to deliver himself from the horrifying tortures of hell. Nothing is more terrifying than the sin of defaming the true Dharma.

"'There is an extraordinary sutra titled the *Ten Phrase Kannon Sutra for Prolonging Life.* It is a scripture of the greatest profundity, and so whenever Master Hakuin visits other provinces to hold practice assemblies and teach the Dharma, he always urges not only his own Zen students, but all religiously minded men and women to recite it. This is something that has brought great joy to the heavenly lords that protect Buddhism and to the myriad Japanese *kami* as well. In villages where this sutra is recited, calamities are unknown, destructive fires and theft are unheard of, harvests are abundant, and all the villagers live at least to the age of a hundred.

"'But these six or seven phony Nembutsu priests and their henchmen vilify any man or woman they catch reciting the sutra, denouncing them to their face and disparaging them angrily behind their backs. As a result, for over a month now not a single person in Takayama or the surrounding areas has recited the sutra. The heavenly gods glare down in indignation, the earthly deities burn with hatred at priests who would slander such a wonderful and profound sutra and keep good men and women from placing their trust in it. Even if these men manage to escape the angry retribution of their fellow townspeople, they are certain before long to experience the terrible wrath of heaven.

"'Well, that is enough for today. I have spoken long into the night. You are all probably tired of listening to me, and acting as spokesman for the deity has wearied me. I will take a short rest now. Be sure to come here again tomorrow night. I am going to explain to you a Buddhist verse called *Treatise on the Mind King* that will enhance your faith in the Buddha's way.'[10]

"At that point it seemed that the deity had left Yūkichi. Chōzaemon, the acting host, addressed his son in a tone of great deference: 'We are greatly concerned that you have not had your nap today. You have not partaken of any food either. May we offer you something to eat?'

"'I understand your concern,' replied Yūkichi, 'but food prepared by ordinary mortals is tainted by water and fire and is not suitable for a deity. Don't worry, I can manage perfectly well without food. If it would make you feel easier, however, you might purify the cooking fire and prepare a small bowl of rice gruel.'

"The people attending the assembly rejoiced at the opportunity to be of service to the deity and quickly set about purifying the cooking fire and the water. They prepared the rice gruel with great care, and when it was brought to Yūkichi, he immediately wolfed it all down. He then summoned Chōzaemon and said, 'I will retire now for some rest. Find someone who knows how to fashion sheets of writing paper into a booklet. When he has made the booklet, place it on my desk along with an inkstone, ink, and a writing brush.' Then he stretched out on the thick cushions and was soon lost in deep slumber. Several splendid silk kimonos were placed over him, and he slept soundly until past noon the following morning. Chōzaemon, in the meantime, carried out Yūkichi's instructions to the letter, placing a booklet of writing paper on the desk together with a writing brush and a stick of ink.

"Yūkichi seemed to sleep all through the night, without waking, yet the following morning the booklet on the desk was inscribed with the entire text of the *Treatise on the Mind King*, down to the very last character. The grace and elegance of the ink, the unerring correctness of the brush strokes, were those of a master calligrapher of the highest rank—a Kōbō Daishi or a Sugawara Michizane. The entire household was ecstatic at having acquired such a priceless treasure, a family heirloom they could pass down to future generations. However, several days after the deity left Yūkichi and returned to the heavens, the book strangely disappeared. Even Chōzaemon wept over the loss.

"As evening of the following day drew near, large numbers of people began assembling before Chōzaemon's residence. They came not only from Takayama but from neighboring villages two or three leagues around it as well, all having been drawn by the news of the deity's appearance. When the hour came for the oracle to begin, they all squeezed into the room adjacent to the one occupied by Yūkichi. There they offered incense, performed *gasshō*, and recited a hundred repetitions or more of the *Ten Phrase Kannon Sutra*. Then they gently slid the wooden doors open just a crack so they could peer into Yūkichi's chambers. They saw him seated with a solemn, dignified air atop the layered cushions. He rose and went to the desk on which lay the *Treatise on the Mind King* that he had written out. He opened it, bowed his head, performed *gasshō*, and after a moment of contemplation began reading out the text in a voice of indescribable sublimity and solemnity. A great hush fell over the people in the assembly, who, overcome with joy, had all instinctively placed their palms together before them in *gasshō*.

"Yūkichi began by elucidating the title of the *Treatise on the Mind King*, starting with the first word, Sōrin, or Sala trees.[11] He explained that Fu Daishi, the author of the *Treatise*, was an incarnation of the Bodhisattva Maitreya, who manifests himself throughout the world, leading sentient beings to liberation. He described the Mind King's infinite nobility and virtue, its vastness and perfect clarity, which he said everyone should revere and cherish. He urged all the people present to concentrate their effort solely on their religious practice, even if it meant undergoing great pain and sacrifice, so they could see for themselves the Mind King's divine features in all their sublimity.

"He then turned to the main body of the text, preaching in a manner so effortless, with such fluency and persuasion, that even if the great Indian preacher Purna and eminent Japanese priests such as Gizui, Reikū, Tenkei, and Hōtan[12] returned to earth, it is doubtful that even their combined eloquence could approach him. Yūkichi continued speaking all through the night. In conclusion he said, 'It has grown very late. Return to your homes now, get some rest, and then summon up a great spirit of faith and courage and strive as hard as you possibly can so that your faces will shine this very night with the intense joy of seeing the great Mind King—the essence and working of the eight consciousnesses —that is perfect and complete in you all. Throughout the past, a spirit of dauntless courage has always been the first essential for superior Zen seekers engaged in negotiating the secret depths. Nothing is more important. Did not the Buddha himself say in the *Nirvana Sutra* that with courageous resolve sentient beings could attain Buddhahood in a single instant of thought and that those who neglected their practice would not reach Nirvana even in three long kalpas?

"'Yet sentient beings of the latter type—weak and indolent sluggards who are found in all the Buddhist sects in this degenerate age[13]—are the very ones who, in attempting to conceal their own ignorance and impotence, saddle young laymen and laywomen with teachings like this:

I want you all to listen carefully to what I have to say. Koans such as hearing the sound of one hand and stopping all sounds are much too advanced and difficult for people like us who live in the age of the Latter-Day Dharma. They are simply beyond our abilities, and for us to attempt to understand them would be like a crow aping a cormorant,[14] like a fool trying to prop a ladder in the clouds. Isn't it said that "the tortoise stamps his feet with chagrin when the goose takes flight."[15] We can no more expect to grasp those koans than to see ponies prancing out of a gourd, or a fire igniting in a water jar. Isn't it said that "the crab digs a hole to the shape of its shell."[16] For people like you and me, satori is first and foremost a matter of committing no sins. Even if we did hear the sound of one hand or put a stop to all sounds, unless we rid ourselves of sin, we fall into hell; and even if we do not hear the sound and do not attain satori, so long as we commit no sins, hell does not exist. Or if it turns out that we fall into hell whether we have sinned or not, then we may as well hold hands and take the leap into the inferno together.

"Yūkichi continued, 'By feeding devout men and women this tissue of nonsense and depriving them of the Bodhi-mind, these priests cause them to lose human existence that is so difficult to attain and set them on a course that leads directly to a very long and unfortunate sojourn in one of the three terrible realms of rebirth. The priests could create no worse karma for themselves than that. Their heresy is one that denies karmic cause and effect. Priests of their ilk cannot be sufficiently loathed. From morning until night they do nothing but pile up great loads of such evil karma. They then have the gall to talk about "creating no sins!"

"'What you must pursue with absolute diligence, through any and all difficulties, is the great goal of *kenshō* and satori. It is for this reason that Shakyamuni spent eight years in the Himalayas undergoing great austerity, that the great teacher Hui-k'o stood all night in the snow and severed his arm, that Zen Master Tz'u-ming jabbed a gimlet into his thigh to keep from dozing off.

"'Anyone who wants to achieve *kenshō* must hear the sound of one hand; anyone who wants to achieve satori must put a stop to all sounds. Zen Master Hakuin drew those Dragon Staff certificates and personally awarded them to students because he wanted to encourage them to continue exerting themselves in their practice.[17] Master Hakuin's teaching—forward striving, closed barrier Zen—is an authentic Dharma that he restored to life after it had disappeared for five hundred years.

"'There is another matter that has caused special distress to the gods of heaven and earth. Since last summer, when you people had the remarkable karmic fortune to learn of the wonderful virtues of the *Ten Phrase Kannon Sutra*, all of you—men and women, young and old—devoted yourselves assiduously to reciting it. As a result you enjoyed especially bountiful rice harvests. Did you not rejoice in having the best harvest Takayama has seen in thirty-seven years? You might have continued to be free from natural calamities, destructive fires, theft, flood damage, accidents or other misfortunes if you had continued to recite the sutra. You would have continued to enjoy prosperity—to enjoy good health until at least the age of one hundred. What were you thinking of when you ceased reciting the sutra because of some slanders you heard from a criminal gang of renegade priests? What made you stop? Do you realize how deeply concerned the gods are about this?

"'I have changed my mind about making this my final talk. Come again tomorrow night. I want to encourage you to recite the *Ten Phrase Kannon Sutra* by telling you a few of the many miraculous events people in China and Japan have experienced by virtue of reciting the text. Be sure that you attend.'

"With that, the deity's discourse ended. As the sliding doors to his chambers were shut, the audience was left in tears of gratitude. Once again, they recited the *Ten Phrase Kannon Sutra* a hundred times, then they began making their way homeward.

"At sundown the following day, people packed into the extremely cramped quarters of the room adjacent to Yūkichi's chambers and began performing the usual one hundred repetitions of the *Ten Phrase Kannon Sutra*. When they finished, the sliding doors opened and the deity began to speak: 'Well, well, I am glad to see such a large gathering. This will be the last time I address you.

"'What is to be feared above all else are the eight terrifying hells that await beings in the next existence: the unspeakable suffering of the Great Shrieking Hell, the Hells of the Red Lotus, the Great Red Lotus, the Scorching Heat, and so on.[18] If anyone here were to glimpse even from a great distance the agony victims undergo in one of these hells, it would cause such great distress, such turmoil of mind, that you would immediately start spewing up blood and faint dead away. For this reason, you must devote yourselves assiduously to the *Ten Phrase Kannon Sutra*. Repeat it over and over.

"'The most important thing you can accomplish during your sojourn on earth is to attain satori—the breakthrough known as *kenshō*. Unless you do that, it won't matter how many good deeds you perform because none of them will bring any merit or benefit at all. As useless as painting pictures in the water or cultivating flowers in the air! Even if you practice the most rigorous austerities for twenty or thirty years and experience the incalculable joy of eighteen great satoris and innumerable smaller ones, so long as you lack the Bodhi-mind because you do not encounter a true teacher and learn about the practice that goes on after satori, you will be unable to avoid falling into the horrendous torments of the hellish regions.

"'This explains why Sōsuke committed the mistake he did. It was because he left his teacher Hakuin too soon, before he learned about post-satori practice, and because of that he did not possess the Bodhi-mind. It is also this that led the great deity of the Kasuga Shrine to tell Gedatsu Shōnin: "From the time of the very first Buddha, any wise man or eminent priest who lacked the Bodhi-mind has fallen into hell."[19]

"'By Bodhi-mind I mean the mind that undertakes the practice that comes after satori, which consists of proceeding forward and deepening your own enlightenment while at the same time helping those who have been left behind to achieve awakening as well. It is the great and wonderful activity of constantly teaching the Dharma, bringing joy by relieving suffering and rejoicing at the freedom and happiness thus attained, and yet through it all remaining completely unattached.[20] This, it is said, creates the causes and conditions for a Buddha-land on earth; it is the awe-inspiring activity of the Bodhisattva.

"'The *Vimalakirti Sutra* praises the Bodhisattva's total, unflagging dedication in carrying out his vow by calling him "an inexhaustible lamp."

"'The following verse is found among the poet Han-shan's works:

An excellent, most amiable fellow,
A great, strapping figure of a man—
Though still only thirty years of age,
Too many talents and skills to count.
In fact, he has only one failing at all—
He doesn't transmit the inexhaustible lamp.[21]

"'In the fourth chapter of the *Vimalakirti Sutra*, Layman Vimalakirti says: "It is like one lamp lighting up a hundred thousand lamps. All the darkness becomes brightness, and the brightness is never exhausted. Because a single Bodhisattva arouses in a hundred thousand living beings the Bodhi-mind that seeks supreme, perfect enlightenment, the Bodhisattva-activity of spreading the Dharma is unceasing. That is the meaning of 'inexhaustible lamp.' It is also the cause and condition for creating a Buddha-land on earth, and the awe-inspiring activity of the Bodhisattva."

"'The primary objective for superior students engaged in authentic Zen practice must be to become such a lamp. To do that you must arouse a great burning desire, vowing to follow the way with dauntless courage, enduring infinite pain and suffering, grudging neither life nor limb, until you achieve a *kenshō* of such clarity that you can see it as though you are looking at it in the palm of your hand.

"'In order to attain a *kenshō* or satori of that kind, you must first of all hear the sound of one hand. Nor must you be satisfied with hearing that sound; you must go on and put a stop to all sounds. Even then you cannot relax your efforts—the deeper your enlightenment becomes, the greater the effort you must expend. You must strive vigorously, struggling this way and that way, as you press on through the vast thicket of thorns and briars you must negotiate—the final difficult-to-pass barriers such as Su-shan's Memorial Tower, The Bull Comes in the Window, Chien-feng's Three Infirmities, Nan-ch'uan's Death—koans known as the "claws and fangs of the Dharma cave," as "divine death-dealing amulets."[22] After each of these barriers has been safely passed, you must read extensively in Buddhist and non-Buddhist literature, accumulate an inexhaustible store of Dharma assets, then devote your life exclusively to the endless practice of preaching the Dharma and guiding beings to liberation. Such is the great and compassionate practice of Monju, Fugen, Kannon, Seishi, Jizō, and other great Bodhisattvas who have fully realized the great Dharma.[23] Their activity cannot be grasped by followers of the Two Vehicles or by any others of limited attainment. As for Chinese priests of the Yuan and Ming dynasties whom people praise as great Zen teachers for their "silent illumination," "withered tree" teachings, people like them couldn't even imagine it in their dreams. This is an authentic teaching of the true Dharma that lay forgotten in the dust for over five hundred years until Master Hakuin revived it.

"'Now I want you all to make a mental note before you leave here tonight. Whenever you see a Zen monk on pilgrimage, be sure that you urge him to revive the authentic Zen traditions, to raise up the inexhaustible lamp so as to ensure that it is transmitted far into the future.

"'We can say, in describing the inexhaustible lamp, that its wick is the koans, the claws and fangs of the Dharma cave that bring about true and authentic kenshō; that the base on which it stands is a benevolent heart and body that is always unwaveringly firm; that its oil is the heart of great compassion that strives to lead sentient beings to liberation, to eliminate their suffering and bring them happiness; that the flame is the body of great wisdom, whose true aspect is essentially formless and nondual; that its light is the Dharma preaching, boundlessly great, imparted unceasingly with perfect freedom and eloquence to all beings in accordance with their different capacities, even till the end of time.

"'Among these, what must be specially valued, and what must be scrupulously replenished, is the oil of great compassion that strives to lead beings to liberation by preaching the Dharma. There is no Bodhi-mind apart from this. If you were to place a thousand wicks, even ten thousand wicks, on a lamp stand, you would produce light to brilliantly illuminate the four directions. But once the oil was exhausted, you wouldn't need a wind to extinguish them, they would die out of themselves. Not a flicker of light would be left behind. The oil is the Bodhi-mind of great compassion that liberates sentient beings. Without it they would all fall into the paths of the evil ones when they died.

"'And even if they should avoid that fate, they would still be subject to the principle that everything about one's previous lives is forgotten with each new rebirth. In a previous life, the great teacher Yun-men was there among the assembly who heard the Buddha preach at Vulture Peak.[24] But he was later reborn as a king on three separate occasions, and all the spiritual powers he had possessed were completely forgotten. Wu-tsu Shih-chieh was a celebrated Buddhist teacher of the highest rank, yet after he died he is said to have been reborn mistakenly as Layman Su Tung-p'o. The Precepts teacher Tao-hsuan of Nan-yueh, revered in both China and Japan, chanced to be reborn as Lord Sanetomo, the Shōgun in Kamakura. Raichō-bō, a wise and virtuous monk who traveled the country as a pilgrim, was reborn as the Shōgun Yoritomo. A certain abbot of the Tendai school, who had jurisdiction over three thousand temples on Mount Hiei, was reborn as the Shōgun Kiyomori. An eminent priest of the Precepts school who strictly upheld all five hundred precepts throughout his life was reborn as the Emperor Sutoku-in. A celebrated priest revered to this day as founder of a large Buddhist sect was reborn as the Lord of Sanuki province. Other distinguished clerics from around the country such as the Precepts teacher Kōkoku of Kii province, a well-known priest from Ōmi province, and Kaku-gen Shōnin of Kamakura have been reborn as emperors, nobles, daimyo—situations that afforded them great wealth and privilege. The names of all these priests are known and could be given, but for certain reasons I will refrain from revealing them here. The important thing to note is that in each of these cases the rebirth occurred because the priests lacked the Bodhi-mind and thus did not transmit the inexhaustible lamp.

"'Someone might say,[25] "Anyone, I don't care if he's eminent priest or not, who regains human existence after having once lost it would rejoice like the one-eyed turtle encountering a floating log in the vast ocean, like the person who witnesses the blossoming of an *udumbara* flower.[26] And if he is reborn as a king, minister, noble or other person of high rank with wealth and power to use at will, how could he hope for any greater good fortune, even if he doesn't possess the Bodhi-mind or transmit the inexhaustible lamp?"

"'Not so. Not so,' I reply. Have you not heard of the saying, "worldly fortune is a curse in the Three Worlds"?[27] What it means is this: The wise sages and eminent priests that have just been mentioned, not to speak of numberless aspirants for the Pure Land, made countless prostrations, recited and copied out vast amounts of sutra text, engaged in endless recitations of Nembutsu, sat long sessions of zazen without sleep, besides performing untold numbers of good deeds—all in hopes of attaining Buddhahood or achieving rebirth in the Pure Land. But so long as their true Dharma-eye is not opened through satori—the experience of *kenshō*—their goal of Buddhahood will remain a dream. They'll never get even a fleeting glimpse of the Pure Land. Even supposing some of them succeed in opening the Dharma-eye by attaining *kenshō*, unless they go on to arouse the Bodhi-mind and transmit the inexhaustible lamp, they can never ascend to the higher ranks of Bodhisattvahood where backsliding no longer occurs.[28] So they falter halfway to their goal and slip back, falling victim to false teachings of one kind or another. Nonetheless, since this does nothing to diminish the many good deeds accumulated from previous existences, they may be reborn into the human realm once again, perhaps as personages of great rank and wealth.

"'How true are those words about completely forgetting past existence when reborn into a new life! When these people were born into positions of wealth and power, all the good deeds they had performed in previous lives were totally forgotten—gone as surely as the morning dew. So they exulted in their great wealth and used their privileged circumstances to the full, surrounding themselves with concubines and courtesans, treating their servants harshly, wantonly taking life by hunting for sport. With minds ruled by attachment, lust, envy, and jealousy, every word they spoke, everything they did throughout the twenty-four hours became the source of evil karma.[29] It is certain that they fell into one of the three evil realms or into one of the eight difficult places of rebirth when they died,[30] undergoing torments and harrowing more numerous than Ganges sand. This is the true significance of the words "worldly fortune is a curse in the Three Worlds."

"'That is why you must revere above all else the great matter of "pointing directly at the mind and seeing into your self-nature,"[31] why you must seek above all else to become an inexhaustible lamp. Anyone who calls himself a Buddhist priest and does not transmit that lamp is as useless as a physician ignorant of medicinal herbs, as a lute player with broken fingers—he has no right whatever to be counted among the three treasures of Buddha, Dharma, and Sangha. You must learn that everything born must perish, that worldly existence is as fleeting as a flash of lightning or the dew on a morning leaf. Strive hard and do not relax your efforts for an instant to discover that vital path that takes you beyond the cycle of birth and death! Keep repeating the *Ten Phrase Kannon Sutra* silently to yourself even as you go about the activities of everyday life.

"'I have now reached the end. I have unburdened my mind of everything I had wanted to tell you. I would only add that I still find it deeply regrettable that the work Master Hakuin recently completed on the essentials of post-satori practice still lies in manuscript among his papers because no one has come forward with the funds to have it published. I want you to see that it is printed. Then divide yourselves into groups and read it carefully. This one work covers everything you need to know about the subject. Read it in light of the advice I have given you here tonight. There is no Bodhi-mind, no post-satori practice to be found apart from the teachings in this book. For future generations of Zen students they will be like a compass pointing the way through a foggy sea, like a bright light illuminating a night road. They represent the authentic traditions of the Zen school, which have been lying in the dust for more than five hundred years. They must always be given the most profound respect.

"'This Sōsuke affair is also weighing heavily on my mind. Send a runner or a letter to him. He lives at Such-and-such, a place in Settsu province, where he works at So-and-so's store. I can't allow a man of Sōsuke's character to be ruined because of three hundred or five hundred pieces of gold. He occupies a greater place in my thoughts than any of the other thousands of devotees under my protection. It was in order to make that known that I recently descended from heaven. I had a change of heart and returned above, however, when I saw Yūkichi's mother place that amulet pouch around his neck containing Amida's sacred Name written by Yūten Shōnin and a talisman by Hakuin. By the way, tomorrow the owner of the public bathhouse will come and return that pouch to you.

"'Well, that is everything I have to say for the present. When circumstances require it, I will come and instruct you again.'

"As the doors to Yūkichi's chambers slid shut, the audience was once again sobbing in gratitude. They repeated the *Ten Phrase Kannon Sutra* one hundred times and then returned to their homes.

"Yūkichi slept like a log until after eight o'clock the next morning. He leapt out of bed, ate a large breakfast, then rushed outside and was soon running about totally immersed in his boyish pleasures. Family members who had gathered in the house called him back inside. They questioned him closely about the events of the past four or five days, but to their astonishment, he insisted that he had absolutely no recollection of what had taken place.

"Just then, the owner of the public bath appeared, bringing the amulet pouch Yūkichi had worn around his neck. 'It was the strangest thing how it happened,' he told them. 'That pouch you were looking for—it suddenly just fell from a shelf in the bathhouse.' Recalling the words the deity had spoken on the previous night, everyone was amazed. Some even began clapping.

"At about this time an elderly physician named Katayama Shunnan from a village adjacent to Takayama (a man of great virtue, widely respected in the area) had been at Shōin-ji in Suruga province for several months of intensive Zen study with Master Hakuin—successfully passing in short order both One Hand koans. He left Shōin-ji the day after he received a Dragon Staff certificate from the master and arrived at his home village in exuberant spirits. Hearing the news about Yūkichi's divine possession, he set out immediately with several others for Takayama to learn more about it. He listened in amazement as people related the content of Yūkichi's first two or three nights of talks: his Zen lecture on the *Treatise on the Mind King*, the stories of people in China and Japan miraculously escaping death through recitation of the *Ten Phrase Kannon Sutra*, and his depiction of the secrets and essential importance of post-satori practice and the inexhaustible lamp. In this way, with tears streaming down his cheeks, Katayama heard the extraordinary story from beginning to end.

Without even realizing it, he had bowed his head and placed his palms together before him in *gasshō*.

"'I had always heard that the great *kami* of the Takayama Shrine was no ordinary deity,' he said to me. 'But here he manifested himself in the form of a fully attained Bodhisattva who possessed miraculous gifts of omniscience. I say that because Master Hakuin has indeed recently completed a work on post-satori practice. He composed it at the request of students in Edo who had received his Dragon Staff certificates, in order to save future Zen students from the terrible fate of falling into the evil paths because they failed to encounter a true teacher, or left their teacher too soon and were consequently ignorant of post-satori practice. The master is anxious to have the work published so he can inform large numbers of people about these vital matters, but as yet no one has donated the funds to cover the printing costs. It remains buried away, unpublished and unread, among his old papers. Unless it is printed, it will sooner or later vanish forever into the bellies of the bookworms.

"'I asked to see the work while I was at Shōin-ji and was able to read through it several times. I can verify that its contents are exactly as Yūkichi described them. How miraculous this is! Over a hundred leagues of difficult terrain separates Hida from Suruga, yet the deity saw and described these matters taking place in far-off Suruga as though he could see them in the palm of his hand. How wonderful!

"'My friends, each of the founders of the twenty-four Zen lineages that have reached our shores braved many thousand leagues of perilous ocean to seek the true Dharma in China so they might bring it back to benefit our people. Compared to that, Suruga province is comparatively close, only a hundred leagues away, and it is not in a foreign land. Why don't we apply to the deity for assistance by drawing lots? We can write the names of all who have received Master Hakuin's Dragon Staff certificates on slips of paper. One or two of the people whose names are drawn will travel to Suruga and inform the master of everything that the deity has said. They can also borrow the manuscript of his Dharma instructions and arrange to have it printed. If we form into groups and read it as the deity instructed us to, it will be like a compass that guides mariners across a foggy sea, like a raft that carries sentient beings over the vast ocean of delusion. It will clarify the paths of delusion to Zen students for a thousand years and reveal to them the proper path of Bodhisattvahood. It will be a Dharma asset without equal, a flaming torch illuminating the darkness of the road. The time for deliberation has passed. No more time can be wasted. One of us must go to Suruga. We cannot ignore an oracle delivered by the Takayama deity. We must hurry!'

"Katayama's words inspired everyone in the assembly to voice their enthusiastic consent to the plan. One man pushed his way through the assembly, looking as though he had something important to communicate. Speaking in a rather loud voice, he said: 'Yes, it is truly wonderful, surely another example of the Takayama deity's divine working! Yet look at Iiyama, sitting there puffing on that long-handled pipe of his, completely unconcerned with these proceedings. I know something about Iiyama the rest of you don't. This morning he received orders to set out tomorrow for Edo on official clan business.'

"'This is a matter that concerns everyone in this room. We are, after all, a brotherhood of sorts. Each of us has been awarded one of Master Hakuin's Dragon Staff certificates. We possess the secret transmission Zen patriarchs have handed directly down, without change, for twenty-eight generations in India and six generations in China, a transmission that for almost five hundred years has lain forgotten in the dust. What a great and good karmic act it would be, an example of skillful means even a Bodhisattva would be hard-pressed to match, to transmit to a thousand future generations of Zen practicers the genuine Dharma treasure of post-satori practice, restoring to them a wonderful secret that can save them from the terrible misfortune of falling into the evil paths.

"'Iiyama, you shouldn't have to be prodded to step forward. You shouldn't be sitting there half asleep as if unconcerned with this discussion. You should be volunteering to visit Master Hakuin on your way through Suruga province, to borrow the manuscript of his Dharma words, and take it to Edo and have it published so that it can benefit people in the future. This is no time to be playing possum. How can the rest of us who received the Dragon Staff feel kinship with such a man? If you refuse to take part in our plan, I propose that we take your certificate from you, expel you from our brotherhood, and have nothing further to do with you!'

"The other men came and seated themselves around Iiyama. They placed their hands on the floor, bowed deeply to him, and implored him with a single voice to agree to the plan: 'This is something you could do in conjunction with your official duties,' they said. 'We know it will cause you extra time and effort, but all of us beg you do it.'

"Far from offering any objection, Iiyama compliantly nodded his agreement. 'I've been wanting very much to continue my Zen study under Master Hakuin. Receiving the order to go to Edo was a completely unexpected stroke of fortune—like a ferry appearing to a weary traveler just as he reaches the ford. Normally, I would take the Kiso Road to Edo, but this time I'll go by the Tōkaidō instead.[32] I'll go directly to Master Hakuin's temple in Suruga and request an interview. It will give me a chance to clear up some doubts about my practice as well.'

"The always quick-witted Katayama Shunnan broke in at this point and, producing five gold pieces, said, 'Take these as a small contribution toward the cost of printing the master's Dharma words. I'll arrange for the balance to be sent along later.' Iiyama happily accepted the money and set out the very next day, walking quickly along the Tōkaidō undaunted by the many miles of rugged terrain that lay before him.

"When he arrived at Shōin-ji and introduced himself, the monk in charge informed him that the master was away. At the request of students, including the monks of Shōin-ji, he was holding a lecture meeting at Denshū-ji in Taro village near the Mishima post station.[33] The news greatly disappointed Iiyama. Deliberating over what to do next, he soon realized that his official duties had to be given preference. He would proceed directly to Edo, conclude his business there, and then visit Denshū-ji on his way back.

"Iiyama stopped at the Mishima post station on his return from Edo. Leaving his followers and baggage at an inn, he continued on to Denshū-ji alone to visit the master. He had hardly dismounted from his horse before he began to hurriedly relate the story of Yūkichi's divine possession. Gradually filling in the details, he was able to make known to the master from beginning to end the events that had taken place in Takayama.

"Iiyama described something he felt was 'particularly unfortunate' that took place one night. Yūkichi was clarifying the great matter of the Bodhisattva's essential post-satori activity, relating accounts of the careers of the great teachers of China and Japan, men worshipped as great and inexhaustible lamps unrivaled for their clear-eyed discernment. He described the untold trials and tribulations they underwent as the desire to seek the Way arose in their minds and they strove to penetrate the koan barriers, how they overcame all obstacles by turning forward the wheel of the Four Universal Vows and raising the great Dharma banner to teach sentient beings and lead them to liberation. The 'unfortunate circumstance' Iiyama referred to was the audience. It was made up largely of simple, illiterate folk, men and women whose capacities were less than those of the lowliest beggar-priests. None among them could have remembered even one of the names of the illustrious Zen patriarchs whose lives Yūkichi had described to them. Iiyama said that many were tearfully lamenting the fact that this unprecedented talk had been pretty much wasted on such an audience.

"Iiyama addressed his appeal to Master Hakuin: 'Please, from the great compassion of your universal vow, agree to write down, in Yūkichi's place, the story of what transpired during those meetings in Takayama. If you appended it to your Dharma instructions when they are printed, it would undoubtedly revive and invigorate the true teaching of the Bodhi-mind and post-satori practice that has been abandoned these five hundred years. No Bodhisattva could perform a greater act than this.'

"Iiyama begged the master to allow him to see the manuscript of his Dharma words, saying he would regard a mere glance at it as ample reward for the long trip he had made. 'Of course,' the master replied, 'it will be my pleasure,' and he told his attendant to bring out the manuscript.

"Iiyama raised the manuscript over his head again and again in veneration, unable to stem the tears of gratitude running down his cheeks. 'I stayed up into the night reading it,' he said the next day. 'And too soon the dawn brought the long autumn night to an end. I could not help regretting that my official duties prevented me from staying and attending the master's remaining lectures. If I had, I am sure all the fatigue of my travels would have vanished. A great pity indeed, but as the saying goes, "no concession is allowed to those engaged in official duties."'

"A few days after Iiyama left Denshū-ji and set out for Takayama, the lecture meeting drew to a successful end. The master was in good spirits as he made his way back to Shōin-ji, though preoccupied with several concerns. One was the question of calling upon his lay followers in Edo, people who had received his Dharma certificates, to bear the expense of having the Dharma words printed. The other was which of his attendants (or perhaps one of the monks residing at Shōin-ji) to send to Edo to make the request. However, on reaching Shōin-ji he found that yet another singular coincidence was waiting for him. The haiku master Ōshima Ryōta had come to engage in koan study and was on hand at the temple to welcome him back.[34] The master was delighted and astonished at the same time by this further stroke of good fortune. He said that he attributed it to the divine intervention of the deities at the Kompira and Akiba shrines.[35]

"Mr. Ōshima concluded his *sanzen* with the master, passing both the One Hand and Stopping All Sounds koans. As the master awarded him a Dragon Staff certificate, he also handed him the manuscript of the Dharma instructions and the money Katayama had donated, asking him to undertake the responsibility of taking it to Edo and having it printed. He explained that the work still lacked four or five pages of text he intended to add at the end, but he promised to send them along as soon as he could finish them. Ōshima willingly agreed to the request and set out for Edo with the manuscript.

"Later, Ōshima sent several letters from Edo requesting the

missing pages, but the master was so busily occupied at the time—traveling first to the Kōtoku-ji in Hida village, Izu province, then to Ryūtaku-ji in Sawaji to conduct enshrinement ceremonies for a new Buddhist image—that he forgot all about the promise he had made. It was the auspicious arrival of a letter from Katayama Shunnan in Takayama containing two more *ryō* to cover the remaining printing costs that finally spurred him to complete Yūkichi's story, which he titled *The Tale of Yūkichi of Takayama*. He still wanted to add some additional pages to the work in response to a request from Iiyama that he describe the difficulties famous Zen teachers of China and Japan had experienced in their quest for enlightenment and subsequent post-satori practice. He set aside time to begin the work, but his busy schedule again intervened. One thing and then another came up and kept him from finishing it until the end of the tenth month.

"Fortunately, just at that time the priest Inryō, abbot of Shōkō-ji in Nihonmatsu in northern Ōshū,[36] stopped over at Shōin-ji on a return trip from Kyoto. Seizing the chance, which he saw as another splendid opportunity, the master persuaded Inryō to remain at Shōin-ji for four or five days. During that time he finished up the remaining pages, which Inryō then delivered to Ōshima in Edo."[37]

The accounts that follow describe the difficulties that Zen patriarchs of China and Japan underwent as they pursued their post-satori training.

The sutras tell us that Prince Siddhartha went into the forest of Uruvela beside the Neranjara River and engaged in an austere regimen of zazen meditation for six years, continuing until his body wasted away to the point that it resembled a withered tree, and that finally, while seated on a mat of *kisshō* grass under a Jambu tree, he suddenly attained great enlightenment. He thought, "The Dharma that I have attained is extremely profound and difficult to understand. Sentient beings, finding it impossible to grasp or believe, would surely slander it, and that would cause them to fall into the evil paths."

The diligence of the venerable Mahakashyapa in performing

the twelve austere disciplines reached a degree of severity none of today's students could hope to approach.[38]

The venerable Parshva, the tenth Indian Zen patriarch, entered the priesthood at the age of eighty, vowing that he would continue his religious practice without lying down until he attained complete deliverance.

Hui-k'o, the Second Chinese Zen patriarch, stood throughout the night buried to his waist in snow at Mount Shao-shih.

Zen Master Fa-ch'ang, who practiced zazen in a hut on the pinnacle of Great Plum Mountain, living on pine flowers and wearing a robe woven of lotus leaf fiber, is said to have balanced a ten-inch iron stupa on top of his head to keep from dozing off.[39]

Chao-chou's training hall was not large since he sought no donations from the lay community. When the leg of his Zen chair broke, he mended it by lashing a piece of charred wood to it with some rope. He used it that way for many years, always refusing his attendants' pleas to have it properly fixed.[40]

Zen Master Yang-ch'i lived for twenty years in a broken-down temple that offered scant protection from the elements: in winter, snow fell inside the room, covering the floor like scattered pearls.[41]

The great teacher Po-chang is famous for strictly adhering to his saying, "A day without work means a day without food."[42]

For sixty years, the Fourth Chinese patriarch Tao-hsin never laid down to sleep while engaged in Zen practice.[43]

Zen Master Hsuan-sha sat all day long, taking only enough food to keep himself alive.[44]

Zen Master Ling-yu devoted himself to the Way continuously for forty years at the summit of Mount Ta-kuei, allowing no temple buildings to be built and no temple equipment to be acquired.[45]

Tz'u-ming was a priest whose great diligence has become a true model for the Zen school: at Fen-yang he sat through the long nights oblivious of the bone-chilling cold east of the river, admonishing himself whenever the sleep demon attacked, "What am I? I'll be useless if I go on living, and no one will notice if I die," and jabbing himself in the thigh with a sharp gimlet. Tz'u-ming attained a strength of spirit that earned him the sobriquet "lion of Hsi-he." Even if you combed the entire world today you wouldn't turn up a single person anywhere like him.[46]

The priest Pao-shih sat in zazen for ten straight days.[47]

Hsueh-feng sat for seven days. A priest who in later life was honored with the title National Teacher sat for forty years without sleeping, keeping warm by covering himself with fallen leaves. One old crock of a priest lived eating nothing but mountain yams, which he baked inside piles of burning cow dung.[48]

Master Daitō concealed himself among a colony of beggars for twenty years while maturing his realization.[49]

Master Kanzan, founder of Myōshin-ji, continued his practice for many years while working as a day laborer for the peasant farmers in Ibuka.

Zen Master Bassui was known to engage in five- to ten-day sessions of uninterrupted zazen during which his breath sometimes seemed to cease, alarming his followers, who thought he had passed away. The divine strength he achieved has shined brilliantly throughout the centuries.[50]

When Zen Master Hosshin was studying in China at the monastery on Mount Ching he is said to have done zazen for three years inside a privy behind the training hall, sitting until the skin on his buttocks festered and maggots appeared in the running sores.[51]

National Master Hottō, founder of Kōkoku-ji in Yura, studied for nine years in China. He is reported to have constantly done zazen with tears in his eyes.

National Master Hōkan, founder of Daisen-ji in Mino province, worked unceasingly at his practice until suddenly "the bottom dropped out of the bucket" and he experienced great enlightenment: "The phoenix broke through the golden net. The crane flew free of its cage." In later years, even after Hōkan became a deeply venerated figure in temples throughout the land, he went to continue his practice with Zen Master Yōzan at the Shōtaku-in subtemple of Myōshin-ji. Yōzan examined him, spewed at him several doses of the most virulent slobber—claws and fangs of the Dharma cave, divine death-dealing amulets. As he wrestled with the koans, Yōzan showed him no mercy, hurling a storm of verbal abuse, dealing him countless blows with his staff. Hōkan escaped into the bamboo thicket behind Yōzan's temple and began doing zazen on top a large rock, determined to sit to the death. When night came, dense black clouds of mosquitoes descended on him, greatly distracting his practice, but they succeeding only in spurring him to greater effort. Throwing off his robe he sat completely naked all through the night. At first light, his breath seemingly having ceased altogether, he suddenly entered the Great Death, attaining a very profound realization. Looking down at his body in the early morning light, he found his body covered so completely with mosquitoes that he could not even seen his own skin. When he stood up and brushed them off, their blood-swollen bodies fell to the ground like so many crimson cherries, forming a thick carpet around him. When he went to Master Yōzan and explained what had happened, Yōzan was overjoyed, immediately confirming his enlightenment.[52]

I do not have time now to relate stories of the hardships all the enlightened Buddhist priests—incomparable Zen students of the kind that appear only once in five hundred years—experienced during their training. Every time I start thinking about these men and what they lived through, even in mid-winter my back becomes covered with beads of cold sweat.

Where, my fellow Zen students, do we belong? Isn't it strange that Zen practice was a great struggle for those in the past, while those of today find it to be an easy, undemanding endeavor? If the easy-going attitude of today is correct, the difficulties undergone by those in the past must have been mistaken. Yet if they were not mistaken, the easy-going attitude of today is wrong. Should we adopt the difficult path, or the easy one? My position in this matter goes without saying. I choose the difficult path. Why is that? It is because teachers today who advocate the easy path do so in order to justify the practice they themselves engaged in. So long as they continue doing this, taking phantoms for true reality, even the meager attainment of a Shravaka will remain beyond them. Like old polecats or foxes, they will slumber their lives away in their underground burrows, unable to save even themselves. But those in the past who chose the difficult path of rigorous practice heedless of the hardships they encountered inevitably penetrated to the deep source of the Dharma and went on to become true sages, Buddha-patriarchs who could greatly benefit sentient beings by guiding them to enlightenment. They were like venerable dragons that bring welcome rain to the world. How delightful and how gratifying it is to accomplish such wonderful things!

Teachers employ skillful means of infinite variety as they guide sentient beings. Sometimes they are refined and subtle, sometimes not. But of all their skillful means the most important by far is the preaching of the Dharma.

The Treatise on the Great Man states:[53]

Material donations such as clothing, food and drink, housing, and gems belong to the mundane world of human beings. Donations in the form of Dharma teaching belong to the realm of great compassion. Material donations help relieve the physical suffering of sentient beings; offerings of Dharma teaching are a boundless treasure of inexhaustible wisdom. Although material donations can bring physical contentment, donations of the teaching bring contentment to the heart. While sentient beings hold material donations dear, those of the world venerate donations of Dharma teaching. Material donations are esteemed by the ignorant, donations of the Dharma teaching by the wise. Material donations give pleasure in the immediate present, donations of Dharma teaching impart the indescribable joy of the Pure Land and Nirvana.

A gatha states:

Buddha's wisdom working in emptiness
Makes thick clouds of great compassion
Shower the Dharma teaching like nectar,
Filling to repletion the entire world;
It uses the Bodhisattva virtues as skillful means

To bring the peace of release from suffering. [54]
You should practice and purify the Eightfold Path
Until the ultimate fruit of Nirvana is reached.

In the *Sutra of Unprecedented Things*[55] it is written:

> The god Taishaku-ten once asked a wild fox if there was any merit in donating food or Dharma teachings to people. The fox replied that those who gave food and drink as alms helped people to live until a later day and that those who gave them precious jewels relieved their worldly poverty for a lifetime but burdened them with shackles of a different kind. Preaching the Dharma to guide them to liberation—which is called giving them the Dharma gift—creates a Dharma that will enable them to transcend the world.

There is another teaching among those bequeathed by the Buddha that states:[56]

> The Buddha preached two kinds of alms, material gifts and gifts of the Dharma, saying that the Dharma gift was the most important. Material gifts are necessarily limited; the Dharma gift is boundless. The rewards that material gifts bring belong to the realms of desire; those that accrue from Dharma gifts totally transcend the Three Worlds.[57] Material donations can never be sufficient, regardless of their size; the Dharma gift can enable sentient beings to advance to the purity of the other shore. Both the wise and the unwise engage in material donations, but Dharma giving is performed by the wise alone. Material donations may bring good fortune to the recipient, but the gift of Dharma enriches both giver and receiver. Material donations are merely beneficial in a physical sense, while the Dharma gift benefits the heart and mind as well. And while material donations increase the fundamental illness of the recipient,

the gift of the Dharma works to eliminate the source of the illness in the Three Poisons.

According to the *Great Collection Sutra*:

Rather than giving large donations, it is better to recite a single Buddhist verse in all sincerity and retain it in mind. The extreme sublimity of the Dharma gift is far greater than any gift of food or drink.

The *Sutra of Laymen's Precepts* says:

Leading sentient beings, making sure that they receive the precepts and learn the truth of Buddha wisdom, encouraging them to copy the sutras and to recite them—these are called giving them the Dharma gift. In the future, those who engage in this giving will achieve a most wonderful rebirth in the Deva realms. Why is that? Hearing the Dharma eliminates anger from sentient beings' hearts; this becomes a cause that enables them to gain rebirth in the highest of the Deva realms. Hearing the Dharma fills sentient beings' hearts with compassion such that they cease to take life; this becomes a cause that enables them to be reborn in the highest realm of desire and achieve long life. Hearing the Dharma, sentient beings cease to steal money or property from others; this becomes a cause that enables them to be reborn into circumstances of great wealth. Hearing the Dharma opens sentient beings' hearts, causing them to take pleasure in giving to others; this becomes a cause that blesses them with sound, healthy bodies in their next rebirth. Hearing the Dharma puts an end to sentient beings' selfishness; this becomes a cause that enables them to attain peace and comfort in their next rebirth. Hearing the Dharma purges sentient beings' hearts of anger and ignorance; this becomes a cause that assures them unfettered eloquence in their next rebirth. Hearing the Dharma enables sentient beings to attain the unfettered freedom of the believing mind; this becomes a cause that enables them to clarify their true nature totally in their next rebirth.

The same is true for giving sentient beings the gift of the Dharma precepts or for teaching them the truth of Buddha wisdom. It is for this reason that the gift of the Dharma, preaching the Dharma to others, is superior by far to giving them material donations.

Kokurin [Hakuin] says:[58]

I do not believe there is any work in the entire Buddhist canon that does not expound the virtues of preaching the Dharma either in its introduction, in the course of its discussion, or in the conclusions it draws. We must all regard preaching the Dharma with the greatest veneration, as a karmic cause of the highest order. Yet if a person preaches the Dharma with even the slightest thought for reputation, gain, or profit, or with the slightest sense of self-importance in his heart, then the preaching becomes impure and will generate a karmic cause that will send the preacher straight into hell instead. Because of that, preaching the Dharma must be approached with the greatest circumspection; it must be undertaken with the utmost care.

The *Vimalakirti Sutra* says that one whose mind still resides in the world of birth-and-death must not preach the Dharma. Elsewhere it is said that those who lack the true eye of wisdom, who cannot distinguish the various capacities in his listeners, should not preach the Dharma,[59] and that a person must not preach the teachings of the Lesser Vehicle to those with the capacity to receive those of the Greater Vehicle.[60] Chao-chou said that if a false teacher preaches the true Dharma, the true Dharma becomes a false Dharma.[61] All of those words are only too true.

If a person intends to hold up the inexhaustible lamp and engage in Dharma preaching, he or she must first of all resolve to subjugate the sleep demon. There are numerous examples in the past of students whose practice was hindered by sleep demons. They plagued the Buddha's cousin Aniruddha. The Buddha scolded him for sleeping, saying, "Creatures such as clams and snails that doze in the mud for a thousand years can never encounter a Tathagata when he appears in the world." His words fired Aniruddha with a tremendous resolve. He engaged in a session of zazen for seven days and seven nights without sleep, and finally he attained the all-seeing eye of enlightenment. I can think of no better examples to encourage those who would subjugate the sleep demon than Master Tz'u-ming's jabbing himself in the thigh with a gimlet or National Master Hōkan's mastering the squadrons of mosquitoes that attacked him in the bamboo grove.

As National Master Hōttō said, "There are many who have attained the Dharma, but few who have retained it." His words deserve our most scrupulous attention.

"'This concludes my talk.[62] I sincerely hope its merits will spread far and wide and reach all sentient beings, and that they will join hands and vow together to attain mastery of the Buddha Way.[63] There could be no greater inexhaustible lamp than that.'

"The audience, having listened carefully to Yūkichi's oracle, was deeply elated and profoundly moved. People began exclaiming to one another. "How wonderful." "How great and edifying!" "A Dharma teaching like this has never been heard before!" "It will bring peace to the land. It will free us all from care long into the future!"

HAKUIN'S COLOPHON
TO THE *TALE OF YŪKICHI OF TAKAYAMA*

It has been brought to my notice that people have identified mistakes of one kind of another in the story of Yūkichi as I have told it here.[64] Their criticism is perfectly understandable. However, as the saying goes, when a text is copied three times, the character "crow" can become "here" and end up as "horse."[65] The story in question happened far away, in a place that is separated from my temple by a hundred *ri* of difficult country. By the time it reached my ears it had already been transmitted several times by word of mouth. I have little doubt that my narration of the events contains mistakes. Not only that, but young Yūkichi's preaching seemed to me to offer a wonderful opportunity for encouraging large numbers of readers to believe in the Dharma, and for that reason, in some places I have helped Yūkichi in telling his story. I ask indulgence from my readers and beg them to forgive any mistakes that have crept into the text.

3: Idle Talk on a Night Boat   :

I DLE TALK ON A NIGHT BOAT, Hakuin's most popular work, is an account of his struggle against "Zen sickness" (*zen-byō*) and of the cure he achieved through techniques of meditation he learned from a cave-dwelling hermit named Hakuyū. From the time it was first published as a single volume in 1757, *Idle Talk on a Night Boat* has remained in print more or less continuously until the present day.[1] Over this span of two and a half centuries, the work has been used as a primer on therapeutic meditation, both as a cure for "Zen sickness" and as a means of preserving health, by numberless students engaged in the rigors of Zen training. Although Hakuin wrote it for his monastic community, the meditations it sets forth became popular and were used in secular circles as well. Prior to the discovery of penicillin, many sufferers of tuberculosis in Japan used the techniques, apparently with some success, to judge from the large number of books promoting its benefits that appeared from the late nineteenth century up into the early post-war period.[2]

The basic story appeared in print quite early in Hakuin's writing career, in *A Record of Sendai's Comments on the Poems of Cold Mountain* (*Kanzan-shi sendai-kimon*, 1746), his commentary on the poems of the Chinese Zen hermit Han-shan. He included it, surprisingly, in the form of an extremely long note to one of Han-shan's verses, with the comment that he had written a short work titled *Idle Talk on a Night Boat* (*Yasenkanna*) setting forth a technique—the "butter method"—for concentrating *ki*-energy in the lower abdomen.[3] Asserting that students suffering from Zen sickness would find the technique useful, he claimed that his own monks had such a high recovery rate using his method— "nine out of ten achieving complete recoveries"—that they were soon avidly copying the manuscript for their personal use.

The 1757 version is essentially the same story, but this time it is composed in Japanese, as an independent work with a long preface containing important new material. Hakuin published the story a third time in 1766, two years before his death, in his autobiography *Wild Ivy*, where it appears as a fourth and final chapter unrelated to the autobiographical narrative that precedes it, forming what is essentially an appendix to the main text.

Although the three versions closely parallel one another,[4] those in *A Record of Sendai's Comments* and *Wild Ivy* have remained largely unknown even in Japan, the main reasons no doubt being because the former was buried in a three-volume commentary and because both works were composed in a rather difficult form of Chinese *kambun*. The story that most Japanese readers are familiar with is the version given here.

Hakuin attributes the lengthy preface that accompanies this version, comprising about forty percent of the entire work, to a disciple he calls "Hunger and Cold, the Master of Poverty Hermitage," but it was obviously written by Hakuin himself.[5] In it he sets forth his reason for writing *Idle Talk*. He explains that in almost forty years as a temple priest he had witnessed many dedicated students fall victim to Zen sickness. He then describes a secret, four-step technique for concentrating *ki* in the lower body that he guarantees will cure any type of Zen sickness. This four-step meditation technique in the Preface is different from the "butter method" he described in the main text, which he says he learned from the hermit Hakuyū, and is presumably a newer meditation he had worked out that could be performed as a kind of koan practice and was thus closer to traditional Zen meditation.

The main part of *Idle Talk* opens with a brief account of the sickness Hakuin struggled against while on pilgrimage in his twenties, whose symptoms gradually grew so severe that they forced him to curtail his training. Physically and mentally exhausted and desperate for help, he traveled to Kyoto to visit the hermit Hakuyū, who was reputed to know secret techniques of meditation that might alleviate or even cure his condition. The rest of the text—three quarters of the whole—is devoted to describing the visit to Hakuyū and recording the instructions that Hakuin received from him.

These instructions include basic principles of Chinese medical theory, cited from Chinese medical literature and Taoist and Buddhist sources, which illuminate various aspects of therapeutic meditation and outline specific techniques for preserving health and attaining long life. All these quotations emphasize the concentration of *ki* in the lower body—the *tanden* or "cinnabar field" located below the navel. Finally, Hakuyū teaches Hakuin his own recipe for dealing with Zen sickness, a technique he calls the "butter method." In the final portion of the work, Hakuin reports that after leaving Hakuyū's cave he began to practice the butter method, which in time not only enabled him to completely cure his Zen sickness and remain healthy and vigorous into old age but also was instrumental in helping him to achieve satori and penetrate many previously intractable koans.

Combining a flair for colorful anecdotes and flamboyant language, in *Idle Talk* Hakuin dramatizes the tale of his visit to Hakuyū with detail, description, and dialogue that would do credit to a novelist. It is an example of the storytelling talents that would become a distinguishing feature of his later literary work (e.g., *The Tale of My Childhood* and *The Tale of Yūkichi*). The obvious exaggerations —such as saying that Hakuyū was more than two hundred years old and suggesting that he may have been immortal—must have caused many readers to doubt the truth of his story and to suspect that he had invented the colorful figure. Hakuin does not even mention Hakuyū in his lengthy autobiography *The Tale of My Childhood*.

Doubts about Hakuyū's historicity and the truth of Hakuin's story first surfaced during the second half of the eighteenth century, probably during Hakuin's own lifetime. Hakuin's disciple Tōrei, in his *Chronological Biography* of Hakuin (Chapter Six), records his concern about criticisms he was hearing that Hakuin "was given to spinning tall tales and engaging in idle talk." He even deemed it necessary, for the sake of his teacher's reputation, to undertake a fact-finding trip to the Shirakawa district of Kyoto, where he says he succeeded in locating an old man who was able to verify that a recluse named Hakuyū had indeed lived in the area.

But the doubts about Hakuyū continued, most prominently in the widely read *Lives of Eccentrics of Recent Times* (1790). At the end of a long section devoted to a description of Hakuyū and his life, author Ban Kōkei concludes that Hakuyū was a creation of Hakuin's imagination. But Kōkei corrected this statement seven years later when he published a sequel, *Further Lives of Eccentrics of Recent Times*, where he put forward new evidence that proved Hakuyū's existence to his complete satisfaction. The well-known novelist Takizawa Bakin reached the same conclusion in the late eighteenth century, stating that he had been able to verify that a hermit named Hakuyū had indeed lived in the Shirakawa district. Bakin believed, however, that Hakuin's story about visiting the man was fiction.

The old doubts resurfaced among new generations of readers, and it was not until Itō Kazuo's *Hakuyūshi: shijitsu no shin-tankyū* (*New Research into the Historicity of Hakuyū*) was published in 1960 that the issue of Hakuyū's historicity was finally laid to rest. Itō reexamined the question in considerable detail, sifting systematically through the evidence uncovered by previous writers. In addition, he uncovered a death registry (*reimei-ki*) in Jōgan-in, a Jōdo temple in the Shirakawa district not far from Hakuyū's cave, which clearly recorded the date and manner of Hakuyū's death:

> The hermit Hakuyū—about whom all that is known is that his family name was Ishikawa and he was born in the province of Musashi—fell from a cliff on the 23rd day of the seventh month, 1709, and died two days later on the 25th. He had lived in the mountains for forty-eight years, having initially gone there at the age of fifteen.

This would mean that Hakuyū died at the respectable, though not superhuman, age of sixty-three. According to Itō's research, Hakuyū's real name was Ishikawa Jishun (1646–1709). He was not the teacher of Ishikawa Jōzan, as Hakuin suggests in the text, but probably was Jōzan's student. In 1661, at the age of fifteen, Jishun entered the hills in back of Shisendō, Jōzan's villa in the Shirakawa district, and took up residence in a cave, shunning the world for the next forty-eight years. Itō also discovered an entry in the diary of the Neo-Confucian teacher Kaibara Ekken (1630–1714) recording a trip he made in 1692 to visit Hakuyū, as he was by then known, at his cave in Shirakawa.

Although Itō's book dispelled any lingering doubts about Hakuyū's historicity, the other key question—whether or not Hakuin fabricated the story of his visit to Hakuyū—has not been completely resolved. Among those who have closely studied the evidence in what turns out to be an extremely complicated question, there is fairly wide agreement that Hakuin did not visit Hakuyū but was simply using the hermit-like figure as a means of better dramatizing his story and thus ensuring that *Idle Talk* would reach a large audience. There are still those, however, including many of the rank and file in Hakuin's own Rinzai school, who are inclined to believe that the visit did take place. It is unlikely at this date that anyone could prove the contrary, but it is hard to dismiss the fact that the death registry places Hakuyū's fatal accident a year before Hakuin says he visited him. Hakuin's title for his work also hints that he was stretching the truth. *Idle Talk on a Night Boat* alludes to the popular saying *Shirakawa yobune* ("a night boat on the Shirakawa River") that was used in describing a person who pretends to have been somewhere or to have seen something that he has not.[6] Hakuin's play on this saying was probably an attempt to alert readers at the outset not to read his story literally, that he was engaging in fiction.

However, although the story of the Hakuyū visit Hakuin tells in *Idle Talk on a Night Boat* is now generally considered to be fiction, he apparently did suffer from Zen sickness and did cure himself by practicing meditation techniques similar to those he sets forth. Owing to the widely conflicting dates Hakuin assigns the ailment in his writings, it is difficult to determine when he actually contracted the ailment. The most plausible scenario, pieced together mainly from the accounts in *Wild Ivy* and in the original manuscript version of Tōrei's *Chronological Biography,* would have the first symptoms appearing in his later twenties and recurring to plague him for a number of years after that. It was probably not until his thirty-first year or later that he was finally able to overcome the malady.

Hakuin may have discovered the meditation techniques during his wide reading in Chinese medical literature and Buddhist and Taoist texts, as well as from advice he may have received from veteran teachers. In *Wild Ivy,* he appears to credit Egoku Dōmyō, the Ōbaku teacher he visited in his twenty-ninth year, with providing the guidance that led to his recovery. Egoku is quoted as warning him against wasting his life looking for someone to cure his illness—"any attempt to cure Zen sickness can only make it worse"—and advising him to seek a secluded spot and devote himself to uninterrupted zazen. Then, using words which sound like an echo of those attributed to Hakuyū in *Idle Talk*, Egoku tells him that the cure for his illness and its cause were the same: he had contracted Zen sickness from too much zazen and that practice was now his only hope for curing it.

I have used the text of *Yasenkanna* published as volume 4 in the *Hakuin Zenji Hōgo Zenshū*, edited by Yoshizawa Katsuhiro (Zen-bunka Kenkyūsho, 2000). For the annotation, I have relied heavily on this edition, as well as on two other works: *Yasenkanna hyōshaku* (*Dispelling Doubts about Yasenkanna*), the most detailed of all the many commentaries on the work, by an anonymous nineteenth-century author (Kōgakkan, 1914); and *Hyōshaku Yasenkanna* (*Detailed Commentary on Yasenkanna*), by the Hakuin scholar Rikukawa Taiun (Sankibō, 1963).[7]

Preface to *Idle Talk on a Night Boat*
Compiled by Hunger and Cold,
the Master of Poverty Hermitage[8]

In spring of the seventh year of the Hōreki era (1757), a certain Kyoto bookseller by the name of Ogawa dispatched a letter to Shōin-ji in far-off Suruga province. It was addressed to the monks who attended Master Kokurin [Hakuin].

> It has come to my attention that there is lying buried among your teacher's papers a manuscript bearing some such title as *Idle Talk on a Night Boat*. It is said to contain many secret techniques for cultivating the life essence through disciplining the *ki*,[9] keeping the defensive *ki* and nutritive blood replete,[10] and above all achieving long life. In short, it contains the ultimate essentials for "refining the elixir" that were known to the divine sages.
>
> Superior students of today, who are keenly concerned about such matters, would welcome a work like this with the same eagerness as a farmer in a parching field scanning the skies for signs of rain. Occasionally Zen monks have made copies of the manuscript, but they keep them carefully hidden away and do not show them to others. That is like concealing the celestial dipper in a box so the gods cannot use it to send the world rain.[11] To assuage the thirst of these superior religious seekers, I would like to have the manuscript printed and ensure that it will be passed on to future generations. I have heard how in his latter years your teacher takes constant pleasure in helping his fellow men. If he believed publishing his work would benefit people, surely he would not refuse my request.

My fellow attendants and I got out the box of manuscripts and took it to the master.[12] His mouth formed into a faint smile. We then opened the box, only to find that more than half of the pages were already gone, ingested into the bellies of the bookworms.

Thereupon monks from the master's assembly brought together the copies of the text that they had made, and from them we were able to piece together a fair copy. In all, it came to some fifty pages of writing. We wrapped it up and sent it off to Mr. Ogawa in Kyoto. Being slightly senior to the other monks, I was urged to write something to introduce the work to readers and explain how it came to be written. Without hesitating, I accepted the task.

It has been nearly forty years now since the master hung up his bowl pouch at Shōin-ji.[13] Ever since, monks intent on plumbing the Zen depths have been coming to him. From the moment they set foot inside the gates, they have willingly endured the venomous slobber the master spewed at them. They welcomed the stinging blows of his stick. The thought of leaving never even entered their minds. Some stayed for ten, even twenty years, totally indifferent to the possibility that they might have to lay down their lives at Shōin-ji and become dust under the temple pines.[14] They were, to a man, towering giants of the Zen forest, dauntless heroes to all mankind.

They took shelter in old houses and other abandoned dwellings, in ancient temple halls and ruined shrines. Their lodgings were spread over an area five or six *ri* around Shōin-ji. Hunger awaited them at daybreak. Freezing cold lurked after them at night. They sustained themselves on greens and wheat chaff. Their ears were assaulted by the master's deafening shouts and abuse, their bones pummeled by furious blows from his fists and stick. What they saw made their foreheads furrow in disbelief. What they heard made their bodies break out in cold sweat. There were scenes a demon would have wept to see, sights that would have made devils press their palms together in pious supplication.

When the monks first arrived at Shōin-ji, they possessed the beauty of a Sung Yu or Ho Yen, their complexions glowing in radiant health. But before long they were as thin and haggard as a Tu Fu or Chia Tao, pallid skin drawn taut over their bony cheeks. You would have thought you were witnessing Ch'u Yuan at the river's edge about to leap to his death.[15]

Would a single one of these monks have remained at Shōin-ji even a moment if he had not been totally devoted to his quest, grudging neither health nor life itself? In utter dedication to their quest, these monks cast aside all restraint, pushing themselves past the limit of human endurance. Some injured their lungs, parching them of fluid; this led to painful abdominal ailments, which became chronic and serious and difficult to cure.

The master observed their suffering with deep concern and compassion. For days, he went around with a worried look on his face. Unable to suppress his feelings any longer, he finally "made his cloud descend,"[16] and like a mother wringing the last drops of milk from her paps to nourish a beloved son, he began to impart to them the essential secrets of *Naikan* meditation.[17]

The master began, "If one of you superior religious seekers who are vigorously engaged in Zen training finds that your heart-fire is mounting upward against the natural flow, draining you physically and mentally and upsetting the proper balance of your five organs,[18] you may attempt to correct this condition by means of acupuncture, moxabustion, or medicines. But even if you could enlist the aid of a physician as illustrious as Hua T'o, P'ien Ch'ueh, or Ts'ang Kung, you would find it impossible to cure yourself.[19]

"I possess a secret technique, perfected by the divine sages, for returning the elixir to the source below the navel.[20] I want you to try this technique. If you do, you will see for yourselves its marvelous efficacy: it will appear to you like a bright sun breaking through a veil of cloud and mist.

"Once you undertake to practice this secret technique, you should, for the time being, cease your practice of zazen and set aside your koan study. First of all, it is important for you to get a good sound sleep. Before you close your eyes, lie on your back with your legs together. Stretch them out straight, pushing downward as hard as you can with the arches of your feet. Then draw all the *ki* in your body down into the *tanden* or cinnabar field so that it fills the lower body—the space below the navel, extending down through the lower back and legs to the arches of the feet. Periodically repeat the following thoughts:

1. This *tanden* of mine in the ocean of *ki*—the lower back and legs, the arches of the feet—is nothing other than my true and original face. How can that original face have nostrils?
2. This *tanden* of mine in the ocean of *ki*—the lower back and legs, the arches of the feet—is all the home and native place of my original being. What tidings could come from that native place?
3. This *tanden* of mine in the ocean of *ki*—the lower back and legs, the arches of the feet—is all the Pure Land of my own mind.[21] How could the splendors of that Pure Land exist apart from my mind?
4. This *tanden* of mine in the ocean of *ki* is all the Amida Buddha of my own self. How could Amida Buddha preach the Dharma apart from that self?

"Turn these contemplations over and over in your mind.[22] As you do, the cumulative effect of focusing your thoughts on them will gradually increase. Before you even realize it, all your primal *ki* will concentrate in your lower body, filling the space from the lower back and legs down to the arches of the feet. The abdomen below the navel will become taut and distended—as taut and full as a leather kickball that has not been used in a game.[23]

"Continue to practice the contemplations assiduously in this same way. In as little as five to seven days and in no more than two or three weeks, all the various disorders you have been suffering from—caused by congestion within the five organs and six viscera that depletes *ki* and weakens the body—will be swept totally away and cease to exist.[24] If in that time you are not totally cured, this old neck of mine is yours for the taking."[25]

The master's students bowed deeply to him, their hearts filled with joy. They began to put in practice the instructions they had received. Each one of them experienced for himself the marvelous effects of *Naikan* meditation. For some, results came quickly; for others, it took somewhat longer. It depended entirely on how assiduously they practiced the technique. Almost all experienced complete recoveries. Their praise of the meditation knew no bounds.

The master continued:

"Even when the infirmity in your hearts is completely cured, you must not rest content with that. The stronger you become, the harder you must strive in your practice. The deeper you penetrate into enlightenment, the more resolutely you must press forward.

"When I was a young man taking my first steps along the religious path, I too developed a serious illness. Cure seemed impossible. The misery I suffered was ten times greater than anything you have experienced. I was at the end of my tether. I didn't know what to do, which way to turn. One thing I was sure of. I'd be better off dying and having done with it. At least I'd be free and no longer troubled by this wretched carcass-bag of skin.[26] Anything was better than going on as I was, wallowing impotently in black despair. Yet still I suffered. How I suffered! Then I encountered a wise man who taught me the secret method of *Naikan* meditation.[27] Thanks to him, I was able to cure myself completely, just like you monks.

"According to this man, *Naikan* meditation is the secret method the divine sages employed to prolong their lives and attain immortality, enabling those of even mediocre and inferior ability to live for three hundred years. A person of superior capacity might prolong his life almost indefinitely. I could scarcely contain my joy when I heard him say that. I began to practice the meditation and continued it faithfully for some three years. Gradually, my body and mind returned to perfect health. My vital spirits revived. I felt myself grow steadily stronger and more confident.

"It became increasingly clear at this point that even if I did master the method of *Naikan* meditation and lived to be eight hundred years old like P'eng Tsu,[28] I'd still be no better than one of those disembodied, corpse-guarding spirits that cling mulishly to emptiness.[29] I'd turn into a mangy old polecat, slumbering away in a comfortable old burrow, until eventually I passed away. Why do I say this? Well, has anyone today ever caught sight of Ko Hung? Or T'ieh-kuai? How about Chang Hua or Fei Chang?[30] Or any others who are celebrated for longevity? In any event, attaining long life in itself cannot compare with establishing the Four

Great Universal Vows in your heart and constantly working to impart the great Dharma to others as you acquire the imposing comportment of the Bodhisattva.[31] It cannot compare with realizing the true and invincible Dharma-body, which, once attained, is never lost, which is as unborn and undying as the great void. It cannot compare with realizing the great, incorruptible, adamantine body of the Buddhas.

"Later, when I acquired two or three students of my own, men of superior ability who were deeply committed to penetrating the secret depths, I had them do the *Naikan* meditation along with their Zen practice—just like peasants who work their fields and fight in the militia as well. Perhaps thirty years have passed since then. My students have increased, one or two each year. Now they number almost two hundred. Over those three decades, I've had monks come from all over the country. Some of the more zealous type pushed themselves too hard in their practice and reached a state of extreme physical and mental exhaustion that rendered them feeble and fervorless. Some were pushed to the brink of madness as the heart-fire rushed upward against the natural flow. Out of concern and compassion, I took them aside and imparted to them the secret teaching of *Naikan* meditation. It returned them to health almost immediately, and the farther they advanced into satori, the more assiduously they were able to give themselves to their training.

"I'm more than seventy years of age, but even now I don't have the slightest trace of illness or infirmity. I still have a good set of sound teeth. My hearing grows more acute with each passing year. So does my sight; I often forget to put on my spectacles at all. I give my regular sermons twice each month without fail. I travel extensively to conduct Zen meetings in answer to teaching requests from all over the country. Three hundred and sometimes five hundred people attend these gatherings. They last for fifty, even seventy days at a stretch. The monks select various sutras and Zen texts, and I deliver my arbitrary views on them. I must have conducted fifty or sixty of these meetings, yet never have I missed a single lecture. I feel more fit and vigorous today, both physically and mentally, than I did when I was in my twenties or thirties. There is not a doubt in my mind that it is all due to the marvelous effects of *Naikan* meditation."

The monks came and bowed before the master, their eyes wet with tears. "Please, Master Hakuin," they said, "write down the essentials of *Naikan* meditation. By committing them to paper, you will relieve the suffering of future generations of monks like us, when they succumb to the exhaustion and lassitude brought on by Zen sickness."

Nodding his agreement, the master took up his brush and without delay began writing out a draft. In it, he set forth the following points:

The secret of sustaining life and attaining longevity is found in disciplining the body. The secret of disciplining the body is to focus the mind in the *tanden* located in the ocean of *ki*. When the mind focuses in the *tanden*, *ki* gathers there. When *ki* gathers in the *tanden*, the true elixir is produced.[32] When the elixir is produced, the physical frame is strong and firm and the life-force is full and replete. When the life-force is full and replete, longevity is assured. This corresponds to the secret method that the ancient sages perfected for "refining the elixir nine times over" and "returning it to the source."[33] You must know that the elixir is not something located apart from the self. The essential concern above all else is to make the fire or heat in your mind (heart) descend into the lower body so that it fills the *tanden* in the ocean of *ki*.

Monks of Shōin-ji, if you practice assiduously the essential teachings I have given you and are never remiss in your efforts, it will not only cure you of Zen sickness and relieve you of fatigue and spiritual torpor, it will also enable those of you burdened with the mass of years of accumulated doubt to reach the final crowning matter of Zen training, to experience a joy so intense you will find yourselves clapping your hands ecstatically and whooping in fits of laughter. Why is this?

When the moon arrives at the zenith, shadows disappear
    from the wall.[34]

Offering incense and prostrating himself, Hunger and Cold, the Master of Poverty Hermitage, respectfully composed this preface on the twenty-fifth of the first month, in the seventh year of the Hōreki era [1757].

IDLE TALK ON A NIGHT BOAT

On the day I first committed myself to a life of Zen practice, I pledged to summon all the faith and courage at my command and dedicate myself with steadfast resolve to the pursuit of the Buddha Way. I embarked on a regimen of rigorous austerities that I continued for several years, pushing myself relentlessly. One night, everything suddenly fell away. All the doubts and uncertainties that had been burdening me over the years suddenly disappeared, roots and all, just like melted ice. Karmic roots that for endless kalpas had bound me to the cycle of birth and death completely vanished, like foam on the water.[35]

It is true, I thought to myself, the Way is not far from man.[36] All those stories about the ancient masters taking twenty or even thirty years to attain it must be fabrications. For the next several months I was waltzing on air, flagging my arms and stamping my feet in mindless rapture.

Afterwards, as I began reflecting over my everyday behavior, I could see that the two aspects of my life—the active and the meditative—were totally out of balance. No matter what I was doing, I never felt free or completely at ease. I realized I would have to rekindle a fearless resolve and once again throw myself life and limb together into the Dharma struggle. With my teeth clenched tightly and eyes focused straight ahead, I began devoting myself singlemindedly to my practice, forsaking food and sleep altogether.

Before the month was out, my heart-fire began to rise upward against the natural course, parching my lungs of their essential fluid.[37] My feet and legs were ice-cold; they felt as though they were immersed in tubs of snow. There was a continuous thrumming in my ears, as though I was walking beside a raging mountain torrent. I became abnormally weak and timid, shrinking and fearful in whatever I did. I felt totally drained, physically and mentally exhausted. Strange visions appeared to me during waking and sleeping hours alike. My armpits were always wet with perspiration. My eyes watered constantly. I traveled far and wide, visiting wise Zen teachers and seeking out noted physicians, but none of the remedies they offered brought me any relief.

Then I happened to meet someone who told me about a hermit named Master Hakuyū, who lived in a cave high in the mountains of the Shirakawa district of Kyoto. He was reputed to be between a hundred and eighty and two hundred and forty years old. His cave was three or four leagues from any human habitation.[38] He didn't like having visitors and would run off and hide whenever he saw someone approach his dwelling. It was hard to tell from looking at him whether he was a man of great wisdom or a mere fool, but the people in the surrounding villages venerated him as a sage. Rumor had it that he had been the teacher of Ishikawa Jōzan,[39] that he was deeply learned in astrology, and well versed in the medical arts as well. Folks who had approached him and requested his teaching in the proper manner, observing the proprieties, had on rare occasions been known to elicit a remark or two of enigmatic import from him. After leaving and giving the words deeper thought, the people would generally discover them to be of great benefit.

In the middle of the first month in the seventh year of the Hōei era,[40] I shouldered my travel pack, slipped quietly out of the temple in eastern Mino where I was staying, and headed for Kyoto.[41] On reaching the capital I bent my steps northward, crossing over the hills at Kurodani and making my way to the small hamlet at Shirakawa. I dropped my pack off at a teahouse and went to make inquiries about Master Hakuyū's cave. One of the villagers pointed his finger to a thin thread of rushing water high above in the hills.[42]

Using the sound of the water as my guide, I struck up into the mountains, hiking on until I came to the stream. I made my way along the bank for another league or so until the stream petered out. There was not so much as a woodcutters' trail to indicate the way. At this point, I lost my bearings completely and was unable to proceed another step. Just then I spotted an old man.[43] He directed my gaze far above to a distant site up among the swirling clouds and mist at the crest of the mountains. I could just make out a small yellowish patch, not more than an inch square, appearing and disappearing in the eddying mountain vapors. He told me it was a rushwork blind that hung over the entrance to Master Hakuyū's cave. Hitching the bottom of my robe up into my sash, I began the final ascent to Hakuyū's dwelling. I clambered over jagged rocks and pushed through heavy vines and clinging underbrush, the snow and frost gnawing into my straw sandals, damp clouds and mist drenching my robe. It was very hard going, and by the time I reached the spot where I had seen the blind, I was covered with thick oily sweat.

I now stood at the entrance to the cave. It commanded a prospect of unsurpassed beauty, completely above the vulgar dust of the world. My heart trembling with fear, my skin prickling with gooseflesh, I leaned against some rocks for a while and counted several hundred breaths.[44]

After shaking off the dirt and dust and straightening my robe to make myself presentable, I bowed down, hesitantly pushing the blind aside, and peered into the cave. I could just make out the figure of Master Hakuyū in the darkness. He was sitting perfectly erect, his eyes shut. A wonderful head of black hair flecked with bits of white reached down over his knees. He had a fine, youthful complexion, ruddy in hue like a Chinese date. He was seated on a soft mat made of grasses and wore a large jacket of coarsely woven cloth. The interior of the cave was small, not more than five feet square, and except for a small desk, there was no sign of household articles or other furnishings of any kind. On top of the desk I could see three scrolls of writing, the *Doctrine of the Mean*, *Lao Tzu*, and the *Diamond Sutra*.[45]

I introduced myself as politely as I could, explained the symptoms and causes of my illness in some detail, and appealed to the master for his help. After a while, Hakuyū opened his eyes and gave me a good hard look. Then, speaking slowly and deliberately, he explained that he was only a useless, worn-out old man—"more dead than alive." He dwelled among these mountains living on the chestnuts and wild mountain fruit he gathered.[46] He passed the nights together with the mountain deer and other wild creatures. He professed to be completely ignorant of anything else and said he was acutely embarrassed that such an important Buddhist priest had made a long trip expressly to see him.

I persisted, begging repeatedly for his help. At last, he reached out and gently took my hand. He proceeded to read my nine pulses and examine my five bodily organs.[47] His fingernails, I noticed, were almost an inch long.

Furrowing his brow, he spoke with a voice tinged with pity. "Not much can be done. You have developed a serious illness. By pushing yourself too hard, you forgot the cardinal rule of religious training. You are suffering from Zen sickness, which is extremely difficult to cure by medical means. If you attempted to treat it with acupuncture, moxabustion, or medicines, even if P'ien Ch'ueh, Ts'ang Kung, and Hua T'o attended you day and night,[48] it would do you no good. You came to this grievous pass as a result of meditation. You will never regain your health unless you are able to master the techniques of *Naikan* meditation. It is just as the old saying has it: 'When a person falls to the earth, it is from the earth that he must raise himself up.'"[49]

"Please," I said, "teach me the secret technique of *Naikan* meditation. I want to practice it together with my Zen training."

With a demeanor that was now solemn and majestic, Master Hakuyū softly and quietly replied, "Ahh, I can see that you're a very determined young man. I suppose I can tell you a few things about *Naikan* meditation that I learned many years ago. It is a secret method for sustaining life known to few people. Practiced diligently, it will yield remarkable results and enable you to look forward to a long life as well.[50]

"The Great Way is divided into the two principles of yin and yang; combining, they produce human beings and all other things. *Ki*, the universal life-force, circulates silently through the body, moving along channels or conduits from one to another of the five great organs. The blood and *ki* circulate together, ascending and descending throughout the body, making fifty complete circulations in each twenty-four-hour period.[51]

"The lungs, manifesting the Metal element, are a female organ located above the diaphragm. The liver, manifesting the Wood element, is a male organ located beneath the diaphragm. The heart, manifesting the Fire element, is the major yang organ; it is located in the upper body. The kidneys, manifesting the Water element, are the major yin organ; they are located in the lower body. The five internal organs are invested with seven marvelous powers, and two each are possessed by the spleen and kidneys.[52]

"The exhaled breath issues from the heart and the lungs; the inhaled breath enters through the kidneys and liver. With each exhalation of breath the blood and *ki* move forward three inches in their conduits: they also advance three inches with each inhalation of breath. Every twenty-four hours there are thirteen thousand five hundred inhalations and expirations of breath, and the blood and *ki* make fifty complete circulations of the body.[53]

"Fire is by nature light and unsteady and always wants to mount upward, while Water is by nature heavy and settled and wants to flow downward. If a person who is ignorant of this principle strives too hard in his meditative practice, the Fire in his heart will rush violently upward, scorching his lungs and impairing their function.

"Since a mother-and-child relation exists between the lungs, representing the Metal element, and the kidneys, representing the Water element, when the lungs are afflicted and distressed, the kidneys are also weakened and debilitated. Debilitation of the lungs and kidneys saps and enfeebles the other internal organs and disrupts the proper balance within the six viscera.[54] This results in an imbalance in the function of the body's four constituent elements (Earth, Water, Fire, Wind), some of which grow too strong and some too weak. This leads in turn to a great variety of ailments and disorders in each of the four elements. Medicines have no effect in treating them, so physicians can do little but look on with folded arms.

"Sustaining life is much like protecting a country. While a wise lord and sage ruler always thinks of the common people under him, a foolish lord and mediocre ruler concerns himself exclusively with the pastimes of the upper class. When a ruler becomes engrossed in his own selfish interests, his nine ministers vaunt their power and authority, the officials under them seek special favors, and none of them gives a thought to the poverty and suffering of the people below them. The countryside fills with pale, gaunt faces, and famine stalks the land, leaving the streets of the towns and cities littered with corpses. The wise and the good retreat into hiding, the common people burn with resentment and anger, the provincial lords grow rebellious, and the enemies on the borders rise to the attack. The people are plunged into an agony of grief and suffering until finally the nation itself ceases to exist.

"On the other hand, when the ruler turns his attention below and focuses on the common people, his ministers and officials perform their duties simply and frugally, with the hardships and suffering of the common people always in their thoughts. As a result, farmers will have an abundance of grain, women will have an abundance of cloth. The good and the wise gather to the ruler to render him service, the provincial lords are respectful and submissive, the common people prosper, and the country grows strong. Each person is obedient to his superior, no enemies threaten the borders, and the sounds of battle are no longer heard in the land, the names of the weapons of war themselves come to be forgotten.

"It is the same with the human body. A person who has arrived at attainment always keeps the mind or heart below, filling the lower body. When the lower body is filled with *ki* from the mind or heart, there is nowhere within for the seven misfortunes to operate and nowhere without for the four evils to gain an entrance.[55] The blood and *ki* are replete, the mind and heart vigorous and healthy. The lips never know the bitterness of medical potions, and the body never feels the pain of moxacautery or the acupuncture needle.

"An average or mediocre person invariably allows the *ki* in the heart to rise up unchecked so that it diffuses throughout the upper body. When the *ki* is allowed to rise unchecked, Fire [heart] on the left side damages the Metal [lungs] on the right side.[56] This puts a strain on the five senses, diminishing their working, and causes harmful disturbances in the six roots.[57]

"Because of this, the *Chuang Tzu* says, 'A True Person breathes from the heels. An ordinary person breathes from his throat.'[58]

"Hsu Chun said, 'When the *ki* is in the lower heater, the breaths are long; when the *ki* is in the upper heater, the breaths are short.'[59]

"Master Shang Yang said,[60] 'In man there is a single genuine *ki*. Its descent into the lower heater signifies the return of the single yang. If a person wants to experience the occasion when the yin reaches completion and yields to the returning yang, his proof is the warmth that is generated when *ki* is concentrated in the lower body.'

"The golden rule in the art of sustaining life is always to keep the upper body cool and the lower body warm.

"There are twelve conduits along which the blood and *ki* circulate through the body. These conduits correspond to the twelve horary signs or stems, to the twelve months of the year, and to the twelve hours of the day. They also correspond to the various permutations the hexagrams in the *I Ching* undergo in the course of their yearly cycle.[61]

"Five yin lines above, one yang line below—the hexagram known as Ground Thunder Returns—corresponds seasonally to the winter solstice.[62] It is this Chuang Tzu refers to when he speaks of 'the True Person breathing from the heels.'

"Three yang lines below and three yin lines above—the hexagram Earth and Heaven at Peace[63]—corresponds seasonally to the first month, when the ten thousand things are pregnant with the *ki* of generation and the myriad buds and flowers, receiving the beneficial moisture, burst into blossom. It is the configuration of the True Person, whose lower body is filled with primal *ki*. When a person achieves this stage, the blood and *ki* are replenished and the mind is vigorous and full of courage.

"Five yin lines below and one yang line above—the hexagram known as Splitting Apart[64]—corresponds seasonally to the ninth month. When the heavens are at this point, foliage in the garden and forest drains of color, flowers droop and wither. It is the configuration of 'the ordinary person breathing from the throat.' A person who reaches this stage is thin and haggard in appearance, with teeth growing loose and falling out.

"Because of this, the *Treatise on Prolonging Life* states:[65] 'When all six yang lines are exhausted and a person is wholly yin, death may easily occur.' What you must know is that for sustaining life the key is to have primal *ki* constantly filling the lower body.

"Long ago when Wu Ch'i-ch'u went to visit Master Shih-t'ai, he first prepared himself by performing ritual purifications, then he inquired about the art of refining the elixir. Master Shih-t'ai told him, 'I possess a marvelous secret for producing the genuine and profound elixir, but only a person of superior capacity would be able to receive and transmit it.' This is the very same secret Master Kuang Ch'eng imparted to the Yellow Emperor, who received it only after he had completed a retirement and abstinence of twenty-one days.[66]

"The genuine elixir does not exist apart from the Great Way; the Great Way does not exist apart from the genuine elixir. You Buddhists have a teaching known as the five non-leakages. Once the six desires are dispelled and the working of the five senses is forgotten, primal, undifferentiated *ki* will gather to repletion before your very eyes.[67]

"This is what T'ai-pai Tao-jen meant when he spoke about 'combining the heaven within me with the Heaven whence it derives'; what Mencius called 'a vast expansive energy (*ki*).'[68] You should draw this *ki* down and store it in the *tanden*—the ocean of *ki* located below the navel. Hold it there over the months and years, preserve it singlemindedly, sustain it unwaveringly. One morning you will suddenly overturn the elixir furnace.[69] When you do, everywhere within and without the entire universe will become a single immense piece of pure elixir.

"When that happens, you will realize for the first time that you yourself are a genuine sage, as birthless as heaven and earth, as undying as empty space. It is that moment that the true and authentic elixir furnace is perfected. Your goal is not some superficial feat like raising winds or riding mists, shrinking space or walking over water, the kind of thing even a lesser sage can perform. You are out to churn the great sea into the finest butter, to transform the great earth into purest gold.[70]

"A wise man of the past said, '"Elixir" refers to the *tanden* (cinnabar field), "liquid" to the blood in the lungs. References to "reverting the Metal liquid to cinnabar (*tan*)" thus indicate the blood in the lungs returning down into the *tanden* below the navel.'"[71]

At this point I said to Master Hakuyū, "I am deeply grateful for the instruction you have given. I am going to discontinue my zazen for a while and concentrate on curing my illness with the *Naikan* meditation. One thing still bothers me, however. Wouldn't the method you teach be an example of 'overly emphasizing cooling remedies in order to bring the heart-fire down,' which the great physician Li Shih-ts'ai warned against?[72] And if I concentrate my mind in a single place, wouldn't that impede the movement of my blood and *ki*, making them stagnate?"

A flicker of a smile crossed Master Hakuyū's face. He replied, "Not at all. Don't forget that Master Li also wrote that 'the nature of Fire is to flame upward, so it must be made to descend; the nature of Water is to flow downward, so it must be made to rise. This condition of Fire descending and Water ascending is called Intermingling. The time when Intermingling is taking place is called After Completion; the time when it is not taking place is called Before Completion. Intermingling is a configuration of life. Not Intermingling is a configuration of death.'[73]

"When Master Li speaks of 'overly emphasizing cooling remedies to bring down the heart-fire,' he is attempting to save people who follow the teachings of Tan-hsi from the mistake of relying too heavily on such remedies.[74]

"One of the ancients said, 'A tendency for ministerial Fire—Fire in the liver and the kidneys—to rise occurs because some indisposition is present in the body. In such cases, Water should be replenished. That is because Water suppresses Fire.'[75] There are two kinds of Fire, one functioning like a prince, the other like a minister. The princely Fire occurs in the upper body and governs in tranquility. The ministerial Fire occurs in the lower body and governs in activity. The former is the master of the mind and heart; the latter functions as its subordinate.[76]

"Ministerial Fire is of two kinds, one found in the kidneys, the other in the liver. The kidneys correspond to the dragon, the liver to thunder. Thus it is said: 'If the dragon remains hidden in the depths of the sea, the crash of thunder is never heard. If thunder remains confined in the marshes and bogs, the dragon never soars into the skies.'[77] Inasmuch as both seas and marshes are composed of water, does not this saying refer to the suppression of ministerial Fire's tendency to rise?

"It is also said that the heart overheats when it becomes tired and depleted of *ki*. When the heart is depleted of *ki,* it can be replenished by making it descend below and intermingle with the kidneys. This activity is known as Replenishing. This is the principle of Already Completed mentioned before.

"You, young man, developed this grave illness because your heart-fire was allowed to rush upward against the natural flow. Unless you succeed in bringing the heart down into your lower body, you will never regain your health, not even if you master all the secret practices the Three Worlds have to offer.

"You probably look at my appearance and take me for some kind of Taoist. Because of that, you may think what I've been telling you has nothing to do with Buddhism. But you're wrong. This is Zen. If in the future you are able to understand this, you will smile as you recall my words.

"As for the practice of meditation, authentic meditation is no-meditation. False meditation is meditation that is diverse and unfocused. Having contracted this grave illness by engaging in diverse meditation, don't you think now that you should save yourself by means of no-meditation?[78] If you take the Fire in your heart or mind and draw it down into the region of the *tanden* and the arches of the feet, you will as a matter of course feel cool and refreshed. You will be without the slightest mental discrimination, without even a trace of delusory thought. Not the slightest conscious thought will occur to raise the waves of emotion. This is true meditation, meditation pure and undefiled.

"So don't talk about discontinuing your Zen meditation. The Buddha himself taught that we should 'cure all kinds of illness by putting the heart down into the arches of the feet.'[79] There is a method the Agama sutras teach, in which butter is used, that is unexcelled for treating debilitation of the heart.[80]

"T'ien-t'ai Chih-i's *Great Cessation and Insight* contains an exhaustive discussion of the fundamental causes of illness, and it also sets forth highly detailed methods of treating them.[81] Twelve breathing techniques are given that are effective for curing a wide range of ailments. Another technique is given that involves visualizing the mind as a bean resting on the navel.[82] Ultimately, the essence in all these methods is to bring the heart-fire down and concentrate it in the area from the *tanden* to the arches of the feet. Not only is this effective for curing illness, it is extremely beneficial for Zen meditation as well.

"I believe the *Great Cessation and Insight* also speaks of two kinds of 'cessations': cessation in relation to true emptiness and cessation in relation to phenomena. The former is a full and perfect meditation on the true aspect of things; in the latter, primary importance is placed on focusing the *ki* in your mind or heart in the *tanden* or ocean of *ki* located in the area below the navel.[83] Students can derive great benefit from practicing these meditations.

"Long ago, Dōgen, founding patriarch of Eihei-ji temple, traveled to China and studied with Zen Master Ju-ching at T'ien-t'ung monastery. One day when he went to receive instruction in Ju-ching's chambers, Ju-ching said, 'When you practice zazen, you should place your mind above the palm of your left hand.'[84] This generally corresponds to Chih-i's cessation in relation to phenomena.

"In the *Smaller Cessation and Insight* Chih-i relates how he first came to teach this cessation of thought—the secret technique of *Naikan* meditation—and how by using it he saved his elder brother, gravely ill, from the brink of death.[85]

"The priest Po-yun said, 'I always keep my mind down filling my lower belly. I'm always using it—when I'm guiding the assembly, dealing with visiting monks, encountering students in my chambers, or engaged in talks and lectures of various kinds—and

I never use it up. Since reaching old age I've found its benefits to be especially great.'[86] How praiseworthy are Po-yun's words! Do they not agree with what the *Su-wen* tells us?: 'If you remain tranquil and free of afflicting thoughts, the true primal *ki* will conform. As long as you preserve that *ki* within, there is no place for illness to enter.'

"Moreover, the way to nourishing life by refining *ki* is to keep it filling the entire body, extending to all the three hundred and sixty joints and each of the eighty-four thousand pores of the skin. You must know that this is the ultimate secret of sustaining life.

"P'eng Tsu said, 'To promote life and cultivate *ki*, close yourself up in a room where you won't be disturbed. Prepare a mat with bedding that has been warmed and a pillow about three inches high. Lie face upward with your body completely straight. Close your eyes and confine all the *ki* in your mind within your breast. Place a goose feather on your nose. When your breathing does not disturb the feather, count three hundred breaths. When you reach a state in which your ears do not hear and your eyes do not see, cold and heat will no longer be able to discomfort you; the poisonous stings of bees and scorpions will be unable to harm you. Upon attaining the age of three hundred and sixty, you will be very close to becoming a True Person.'[87]

"Su Nei-han gave the following advice:[88] 'If you are hungry, eat some food, but stop eating before you are full. Take a long leisurely stroll. When you feel your appetite return, enter a quiet room and seat yourself in an upright posture. Begin exhaling and inhaling, counting your breaths from ten to a hundred, from a hundred to a thousand. By the time you have counted a thousand breaths, your body should be as firm and steady as a rock, your heart as tranquil and motionless as the empty sky.

"'If you continue to sit like this for a long period, in time your breath will hang suspended. You will no longer inhale or exhale. Your breath will exude in clouds and rise up like mist from the eighty-four thousand pores of your skin. You will realize with perfect clarity that all the illnesses you have suffered from, each of the countless disorders you have experienced from the beginningless beginning, have vanished of themselves. You will be like a blind man suddenly regaining his sight and no longer having any need to ask others for guidance on his way.

"'What you must do is to cut back on words and devote yourself solely to sustaining your primal *ki*. Hence it is said,[89] "Those who wish to strengthen their sight keep their eyes closed. Those who wish to strengthen their hearing avoid sounds. Those who wish to sustain the *ki* in their mind maintain their silence."'"

"You mentioned a method in which butter is used," I said. "May I ask you about that?"

Master Hakuyū replied, "When a student is training and meditating and finds that he has become exhausted in body and mind because the four constituent elements of his body are in disharmony, he should gird up his spirit and perform the following visualization:[90]

"Imagine that a lump of soft butter, pure in color and fragrance and the size and shape of a duck egg, is suddenly placed on the top of your head. Slowly it begins to melt, imparting an exquisite sensation as your head becomes moistened and saturated both within and without. It continues oozing down, moistening your shoulders, elbows, and chest, permeating your lungs, diaphragm, liver, stomach, and bowels, then continuing down the spine through the hips, pelvis, and buttocks.

"At that point, all the congestions that have accumulated within the five organs and six viscera, all the aches and pains in the abdomen and other affected parts, will follow the mind as it sinks down into the lower body. You will hear this distinctly— like water trickling from a higher to a lower place. It will continue to flow down through the body, suffusing the legs with beneficial warmth, until it reaches the arches of the feet, where it stops.

"The student should then repeat the contemplation. As the flow continues downward, it will slowly fill the lower region of the body and suffuse it with penetrating warmth, making him feel as if he is sitting immersed to his navel in a hot bath filled with a decoction of rare and fragrant medicinal herbs that have been gathered and infused by a skilled physician.

"Inasmuch as all things are created by the mind, when you engage in this contemplation your nose will actually smell the marvelous scent of pure soft butter, your body will feel the exquisite sensation of its melting touch. Body and mind will be in perfect peace and harmony. You will feel better and enjoy greater health than you did as a youth of twenty or thirty. All the undesirable accumulations in your vital organs and viscera will melt away. Stomach and bowels will function perfectly. Before you know it, your skin will glow with health. If you continue to practice this contemplation unfalteringly, there is no illness that cannot be cured, no virtue that cannot be acquired, no level of sagehood that cannot be reached, no religious practice that cannot be mastered. Whether such results appear swiftly or appear slowly depends only upon how scrupulously you apply yourself.

"I was a very sickly youth. I experienced ten times the suffering you have endured. The doctors finally gave up on me. I explored hundreds of cures on my own, but none of them brought me any relief. I turned to the gods for help, praying to the deities of both heaven and earth, begging them for their imperceptible assistance. I was marvelously blessed, because they extended me their support and protection. I came upon this wonderful soft butter method of contemplation. My joy knew no bounds. I immediately set about practicing it with total and singleminded determination. Before even a month was out, my troubles had almost totally vanished. Since that time I've never been bothered the least bit by any complaint, physical or mental.

"I became like an ignoramus, mindless and utterly free of care. I was oblivious to the passage of time. I never knew what day or month it was or whether it was a leap year or not. I gradually lost interest in things the world holds dear, forgot completely about the hopes and desires and customs of ordinary men and women. In my middle years I was compelled by circumstance to leave Kyoto and take refuge in the mountains of Wakasa province.[91] I lived there nearly thirty years, unknown to my fellow men. Looking back on that period of my life, it seems as fleeting and unreal as the dream-life that flashed through Lu-sheng's slumbering brain.[92]

"Now I live here in this solitary spot in the hills of Shirakawa, far from all human habitation. I have a layer or two of clothing to wrap around my withered old carcass. But even in mid-winter, on nights when the cold bites through the thin cotton robe, I don't freeze. Even during the months when there are no mountain fruits or nuts for me to gather and I have no grain to eat, I don't starve. It is all thanks to this contemplation.

"Young man, you have just learned a secret that you could not use up in a whole lifetime. What more could I teach you?"

Master Hakuyū sat silently with his eyes closed. I thanked him profusely, my own eyes glistening with tears, and then bade him farewell. The last vestiges of light were lingering in the topmost branches of the trees when I left the cave and made my way slowly down the mountain. Suddenly I was stopped in my tracks by the sound of wooden clogs striking the stony ground and echoing up from the sides of the valley. Half in wonder, half in disbelief, I peered apprehensively around to see the figure of Master Hakuyū coming toward me in the distance.[93]

When he was near enough to speak, he said, "No one uses these mountain trails. It's easy to lose your way. You might have trouble getting back, so I'll take you partway down." A skinny wooden staff grasped in his hand, high wooden clogs on his feet, he walked on ahead of me, talking and laughing. He moved nimbly and effortlessly over rugged cliffs and steep mountainside, covering the difficult terrain with the ease of someone strolling through a well-kept garden. After a league or so we came to the mountain stream. He said if I followed it I would have no trouble finding my way back to the village of Shirakawa. With what seemed a look of sadness, he then turned and began to retrace his steps.[94]

I stood there motionless, watching as Master Hakuyū made his way up the mountain trail, marveling at the strength and vigor of his step. He moved with such light, unfettered freedom, as if he was one who had transcended this world, had sprouted wings, and was flying up to join the ranks of Immortal Sages. Gazing at him, my heart was filled with respect and with a touch of envy as well. I also felt a pang of regret because I knew that never in this lifetime would I again be able to encounter and learn from a man such as this.

I went directly back to Shōin-ji and set about practicing *Naikan* meditation over and over on my own. In less than three years, without recourse to medicine, acupuncture, or moxabustion, the illnesses that had been plaguing me for years cleared up of themselves. What is more, during the same period I experienced the immense joy of great satori six or seven times, boring through and penetrating to the root of all the hard-to-believe, hard-to-penetrate, hard-to-grasp koans that I had never before been able to get my teeth into at all. I attained countless small satoris as well, which sent me waltzing about waving my hands in the air in mindless dance. I then knew for the first time that Zen Master Ta-hui had not been deceiving me when he wrote about experiencing eighteen great satoris and countless small ones.[95]

In the past, I used to wear two and even three layers of tabi, but the arches of my feet still always felt as though they were soaking in tubs of ice. Now, even during the three coldest months of the year, I don't need even a single pair. I no longer require a brazier to keep warm.[96] I am more than seventy years old this year, but even now I never suffer from the slightest indisposition. Surely this is all due to the lingering benefits I enjoy from having practiced the wonderful secret technique of *Naikan* meditation.[97]

Don't be saying that old Hakuin, half-dead and gasping out his final breaths, has recklessly scribbled out a long tissue of groundless nonsense hoping to hoodwink superior students. What I've put down here is not intended for those who possess spiritual powers of the first order, the kind of superior seeker who is awakened at a single blow from his master's mallet. But if dull plodding oafs like me—the kind of people who will suffer from illness as I did—set eyes on this book, read it and contemplate its meaning, they should surely be able to obtain a little help from it.[98] I'm only afraid that when other people read it, they will clap their hands and break into loud peals of laughter.[99] Why is that?

A horse chomping dried bean hulls disturbs a man at his noonday nap.[100]

Supplementary Passage A (*This passage was added to the text in the final* Wild Ivy *version; see note 97*):

Even thinking about it now, the tears trickle down my leathery old cheeks—I just can't help it. Four or five years ago I had a dream. Master Hakuyū had come all the way from the hills of Shirakawa to visit me here at Shōin-ji. We spent a whole night laughing and talking together. I felt so happy that the following morning I told the monks living at the temple all about it. They bowed and pressed their palms together in attitudes of worship. "Good! Good!" they said. "Maybe it will come to pass. Perhaps the dream will become reality. If Master Hakuyū did come here, it would be a great honor for the temple.

"You turned eighty this year, master, but your mind and body are both still strong and vigorous. You teach us and extend your help to other students far and wide. Isn't it all thanks to Master Hakuyū? Let one or two of us go to Kyoto and invite him to visit Shōin-ji. He could live here at the temple. We could provide for his needs through our begging."

A feeling of elation passed through the brotherhood. Plans began to be laid. Then a monk stepped forward. "Hold on," he said, laughing. "You're making the mistake of 'marking the side of a moving boat to show where the sword fell in.' I'm sorry to have to be the one to tell you this, but Master Hakuyū, the person you are talking about, is no longer alive. He died this past summer."

The monks clapped their hands in astonishment. "You shouldn't repeat idle rumors like that!" I said, admonishing the monk. "Hakuyū is no ordinary person. He is one of the immortal sages who by chance just happens to walk the earth. How could such a man die?"

"Unfortunately, that was his undoing. It is because he walked the earth that he met his death. Last summer, it seems he was strolling in the mountains and came to the edge of a deep ravine. It was more than a hundred yards to the other side. He tried to leap across but he didn't make it. He fell to the rocks below. His death was lamented by villagers far and near." The monk, his story completed, stood there with a forlorn look on his face. I found my own eyes shedding copious tears.

SUPPLEMENTARY PASSAGE B (*Another passage added to the* Wild Ivy *version; see note 98*):

In fact, after giving the matter more consideration, I think perhaps the benefit will not necessarily be small. In any event, the main thing—what we must all cherish and revere—is the secret method of *Naikan* meditation. In the spring of the seventh year of the Hōreki era [1757], I composed a work in Japanese that I called *Idle Talk on a Night Boat*, in which I set forth the essential principles of the meditation. Ever since then people of all kinds— monks, nuns, laymen, laywomen—have told me how, when the odds were stacked ten to one against them, they were saved from the misery of grave and incurable illness owing to the wonderful benefits of *Naikan* meditation. In numbers I cannot even count they have come to me here at Shōin-ji to thank me in person. Two or three years ago, a young man—he must have been about twenty-two or twenty-three—showed up at the temple asking to see me. When I stepped out to greet him, I was taken aback by the great bundle of presents including several gold coins that he had brought for me. He bowed his head to the ground. "I am So-and-so from Matsuzaka in Ise Province," he said. "About six years ago I came down with a serious ailment that I found impossible to cure. I tried all the secret remedies I knew, but none of them had any effect whatever. All the physicians I consulted wrote me off as a hopeless case. It seemed that there was nothing left for me to do except await the end. Then a wonderful thing happened; I chanced to read *Idle Talk on a Night Boat*. As best I could with my meager abilities, I began to practice the secret technique of *Naikan* meditation on my own. What a blessing it was! Little by little my energy began to return, and today I am restored to perfect health. I can't tell you how happy and thankful I felt. Why, I was dancing on air! It was all owing to the powerful influence of *Idle Talk on a Night Boat*, but there was nowhere I could go, no physician or healer to whom I could express my gratitude. Fortunately, as I was mulling what I should do, I heard a vague rumor that you, Master Hakuin, were the author of *Idle Talk on a Night Boat*. Immediately, I wanted to see your revered countenance so that I could express my profound gratitude to you in person. On the pretext of transacting some business in Edo, I traveled all the way from Ise province to see you. This is the happiest moment of my entire life. Nothing could exceed it."

As I listened to him relate the particulars of his story, can you imagine the happiness this old monk also felt?

4: Old Granny's Tea-Grinding Songs   :

ACCORDING TO THE COLOPHON Hakuin attached to it, *Old Granny's Tea-Grinding Songs* (*Obaba dono kohiki uta*) was completed in the winter of 1760, his seventy-fifth year. It was printed as a horizontal scroll—a unique format among Hakuin's publications—and was accompanied by two illustrations which depict the "prostitute Otafuku" and "Old Granny," the two characters whose songs make up the main body of the work.

The use of these two folksy figures and the style of the work —an exuberant sort of simple, colloquial Japanese verse—apparently led people to regard the *Tea-Grinding Songs* as simple ditties Hakuin had written in order to convey his Zen message to "illiterate common people." However, anyone who takes the trouble to read the *Songs* soon finds that, like Hakuin's other songs in this genre, they are anything but easy, being made up for the most part of difficult material obviously intended for advanced Zen students.[1]

The songs are composed of 121 lines in the alternating 7-7-7-5 syllable phrasing common in the popular songs of the day. The prostitute Otafuku is introduced in the opening lines (by an unnamed narrator as well as by Otafuku herself), which serve as an introduction to the main text of Old Granny's songs that follows.

Otafuku, whose name means literally "Much Good Fortune," is a plump, bulbous-nosed, moon-faced woman (also known as

Ofuku) who was a popular folk figure in the vibrant popular culture of the Edo period (1600–1868). Her likeness was depicted in literally countless paintings and sculptures, and she appeared frequently in the performing arts as a comic figure, the paragon of female ugliness. Her good-natured personality is usually emphasized as well, along with her eponymous role as a bringer of good fortune.

Although Otafuku is a frequent subject of Hakuin's *Zenga*,[2] this is her sole appearance in his writings. Her paradoxical role as a "homely beauty" expresses a specific Zen message, one that represents the fundamental nondualistic standpoint of Mahayana Buddhism. Ofuku—happiness and good fortune—is possible only where ordinary worldly distinctions of beauty and ugliness are transcended.

The depiction of Ofuku (to use her shorter, more popular name) as a prostitute is consistent with perceptions of her in Edo Japan. In teahouses along the Tōkaidō, maidservants occasionally serving as prostitutes were known as Okame (another of Ofuku's names). Hakuin's illustration of Ofuku in the introductory section of *Old Granny's Songs* (see below) shows her turning a stone hand-mill. The tea bowl and bamboo whisk beside her suggest the mill was used to grind tea leaves for the powdered green tea she served to customers. Her kimono, as well as her pipe and tobacco pouch, is decorated with the plum flower design that in Hakuin's *Zenga* symbolizes the Shinto deity Tenjin and identifies the wearer as someone seriously dedicated to religious pursuits, even as an exponent of Hakuin Zen. Hakuin tells us that the great happiness and good fortune that Otafuku embodies are only truly attainable through practice of the Buddhist Way and the breakthrough known as *kenshō*.

But the central character of the *Songs* is Old Granny, who is clearly a mouthpiece for Hakuin. Hakuin's illustration of her shows an old woman—her face suspiciously resembles Hakuin—wearing a kimono decorated with the same telltale plum blossom design we saw on Otafuku's robe. Well into the long series of songs in which Old Granny sets forth her teaching, she identifies herself as "Old Granny Mind Master" (*Shushin obaba*), the personification of the ultimate principle of Mind, the true or original self, the Buddha-mind or Buddha-nature inherent in all people.

Old Granny's songs are basically a series of appeals and exhortations elucidating the core of Hakuin's Zen teaching. For example, she cautions students against stopping their practice after the initial *kenshō* and settling for a limited attainment, urging them to devote themselves with even greater intensity to what Hakuin calls the "post-satori" phase of their training—a theme familiar from his other writings (see Chapters One and Two). Old Granny also attacks contemporary Zen teachers for straying from what she presents as the original traditions of koan Zen. She stresses the need for people of all classes of society—samurai, farmers, artisans, and shopkeepers—to discover the "Mind Master," but she focuses her special attention on the "samurai, Buddhist priests, and wise men" in the upper social ranks, declaring that unless such men possess the Mind Master, they are themselves "common people." As for the priests, many of them preach about ignorance and enlightenment but fail to "live in the Mind Master." They may "appear quite splendid in their fine surplices and robes, but they are in fact a truly sorry-looking lot."

OLD GRANNY'S TEA-GRINDING SONGS

Shinbe San, an Ofuku
from the shady part of town,
with her flat knobby nose
her nice big puffy cheeks—
she's really quite a doll!
Yet whatever you say,
she's pretty or she's not,
it's totally uncalled for!

"Resign yourself," people tell me,
"Your looks are Heaven's will."
I'd hate to bring on Heaven's wrath.
I get lots of love letters; have crushes too,

But don't think I'm some passing fling,
I'm not your "flower for the night"!
Scary, those notions in most men's minds,
As for good looks, that's no blessing,
Always hearing "what a pretty face";
Men aren't my cup of tea; I sleep alone.
They may whisper I'm a "man-killer,"
But I'm not one who'd take your life.
Nasuno Yoichi killed with an arrow;[3]
Otafuku, she slays you with a glance.
While admirers I count by the dozen,
There's really only one man in my life.
Enjoy Old Granny's tea-grinding songs,
Even if Ofuku's message is beyond you;
I like to sing them with understanding men,[4]
All you other riffraff *should stay away*!

Sing them old crone!
Sing us your ditties!

How merciful the blessings of heaven and earth!
They provide us with the heat and cold,
They create the nights and days for us.
We can work in the daytime and sleep at night.
Blessings of rain and dew ripen the five grains,
Nourish grasses and plants in the hills and fields.
Our debt to our ruler exceeds the highest mountain,[5]
His benefits reach down to the smallest dwelling,
And so may it continue till the end of time.
As the plants and grasses all bend to the wind,[6]
So must we never forget our debt to our lord,
It extends into the next life—far in the future.
Your debt to your parents is deeper than the sea.

If you forget it, you're lower than a dog or cat.
One filial act, even one's descendents prosper;
Parents are a field of fortune in an unsure world.

An impetuous fellow of uncertain temper,
Breaks and runs when his lord's in a pinch.
Take a good look at the character "fidelity";
A mind that doesn't waver from the center.
Though you may stand over five feet tall,
Lacking Mind Master, you're still a kid.
Even the martial arts must come second,
Mind Master comes first, before all else;
Without it, you're merely a vacant house,
Foxes and badgers move in and take over.
T'ai Kung who served kings Wen and Wu,
Bequeathed some well-known words to us:
"A soldier's great concern," says *San-lueh*,
"Is ungovernable arising of fear in the mind."[7]
If a samurai's Mind Master is unconfirmed,
He must train himself rigorously until it is.

Hachirō of Chinzei was first among archers.
It was Sanada for the lance, Kyūrō for the sword.[8]
Even a person who surpasses stalwarts like them,
When his lord enters into a desperate scrape,
If he lacks Mind Master will be worthless with fear.
Mind Master is the Confucianist's Ultimate Good,[9]
It's the mind that's unwaveringly straight and true.
Before any learned teacher of China or Japan
Is the person whose Mind Master has been confirmed.
A warrior you've maintained in greatest luxury
Stands ready at your side in your direst need.[10]
So set aside for the present your martial calling,
And learn how Mind Master can be confirmed.
Once Mind Master settles in Ultimate Good,
All precepts and rituals can be chucked aside.
So wonderful is Mind Master's virtue,

No sword on earth has a chance against it,
No bow or musket can hope to reach it—
The word *enemy* itself no longer exists!

The sky, sun, moon, the hills and seas,
Soil, grass and trees are all the Mind Master,
Even Takamagahara, the abode of the gods,
Becomes a place devoid of poisons and desires.[11]
When the *Great Learning* says "Renew the people,"[12]
It's the same as saying, "realize Ultimate Good."
High priests, people of rank, even wise sages too,
Lacking the Mind Master, are quite ordinary souls.
A palace is a straw hut, a straw hut is a palace,
It all depends on the way Mind Master works.
If everyone had Mind Master firmly in hand,
The world without governing would be a happy
    place.

How marvelous is the Mind Master's virtue—
Able to hear the sound of the single hand!
Priests blabber on about illusion and satori,
But *living* the Mind Master's the essential thing;
Cassock and surplice may make you look splendid,
But won't really fit you if Mind Master's not there;
Making the pilgrim circuit's commendable, too,
But without Mind Master the walking's in vain.

Fill the Cinnabar Field with your Mind Master,
The elixir produced will assure you long life;
No cauldron is needed to form this compound,
Just keep primal *ki* down in the Cinnabar Field.[13]
Those seeking the cinnabar elixir of timeless life
Should just keep their mind in the ocean of *ki.*
There's one graybeard who's outlived even the Void:
Mind Master who resides in the Cinnabar Field.
When Mind Master dwells in the Cinnabar Field,
The four hundred and four ailments never arise.[14]

"Old Granny Mind Master, how old are you now?"
"Me? I've lived just as long as the empty Void.[15]
Old man Empty Space might pop off any time,
But I'll always be just as I am right now;
The mountains, rivers, and great earth itself
Are my children, I'll never lack a single thing."

For a samurai, steadfast resolve is the key,
So he'd better die once while he's still alive.
Dying into life is easy as pie. Just contact
Granny Mind Master, she'll show you how.

Samurai are maintained at their lord's favor,
Quarrelling with him is an unpardonable offense.
Their loyalty may even require showing weakness,
Once their life is placed in the hands of their lord,
It's no longer theirs to employ as they please:
They must be prudent, must protect it with care,
Must limit their friendship with fellow retainers,
Must stifle their anger though called a "loyal dog."[16]
If need be, for their lord's sake, must walk the floors
Of the Interminable, Shura, or Red Lotus hells.
The sole aim of their life is protecting their lord—
Such is the brave samurai's unalterable role.

Old Granny Mind Master, where is she found?
She's taken a small house in the Cinnabar Field.
Where is the Cinnabar Field? the Ocean of *Ki*?
It's two blocks south of the Navel Crossing.[17]
Once *ki*-energy collects around the navel,
The Cinnabar elixir is as good as refined.
Cinnabar refined has power beyond price,
It smashes Mount Sumeru and the void to dust.[18]

The true formless form of the Dharma universe,
Is neither a subject that sees nor the objects seen,
Both samsara and nirvana are last night's dream;[19]

No trace of evil passions or enlightenment either,
No hell to fall into or endless suffering to endure,
No Pure Land to enter or pleasures to enjoy.

There is one great matter in your life on earth:[20]
Locating a genuinely enlightened teacher.
Today there are numerous Buddhist students
Who practice rigorously twenty, thirty years;
Perhaps they chance to reach some attainment,
Think "I'm home free! The final goal's reached!
From here on out, I'm free to act just as I please.
I can kill living beings, can even rob and steal,
Misdeeds are merely amusements to me.[21]
For me, karmic retribution no longer applies."
False, self-centered satori, denying rebirth,[22]
It's terrifying for an onlooker even to watch!
The Dharma that urges on students to *kenshō*
Now becomes a cause that lands them in hell.[23]
The inherent Mind Master is lost and forgotten,
Demons and longnosed goblins thrive in its place;
All good karmic roots having lost their effect,
A clear-eyed teacher must somehow be found.
Not knowing the secrets of post-satori training,
Old ignorant ways quicken and grow apace.
We're now in the degenerate Latter-Day Law,
A time when false views and teachings appear.
The true Zen traditions in all three countries[24]
Have fallen into the dust and are trod underfoot.
In their place a particularly dubious Dharma
Is taught in Sōtō, Rinzai, and Ōbaku schools
By priests calling themselves your "good friend"—[25]
Just look at the teaching they'd foist off on you:

"The genuine upward striving path of Zen
Doesn't require that you sit and do zazen,
Much less read sutras or patriarchs' words.
You're Buddhas already right where you stand.

By seeking the Buddha you only delude him,
By seeking the Dharma you clap it in irons.
Buddha and Bodhisattva—dreams within dreams,
Samsara, Nirvana—tracks birds leave in flight.
Have no dealings at all with 'good' and 'bad,'
Just remain at the unfurnished original ground.
Meddling muddies the clear mountain stream,
So no asking or learning, no meddling at all.[26]
This is the true, authentic teaching of Zen—
Not-seeing is Buddha, not-knowing divine."

Then these idle, impotent, lunkheaded ninnies,
After filling your ears with nonsense like this,
Calling it a "superlative way to salvation,"
Say, "Look, could anyone have believed?
We're living Buddhas from this time on!"
Then they eat and shit, sit seated in sleep,
With profiles exactly like dozing boatmen,
Chins nodding constantly over their oars.[27]
What possible good can come from that?
They are dire portents of the Dharma's ruin.

"And what then is post-satori training?
If you know, old lady, sing the answer for us."

"The question you ask is a serious one,
The Dharma's been fading for 500 years;
Though most teachers don't even know it,
Post-satori practice is the Bodhi-mind.
Long ago the great *kami* of Kasuga Shrine
Delivered this oracle to Gedatsu Shōnin:
'Ever since the first Buddha Kuruson,
Even the wisest and most eminent priests
Who lacked the Bodhi-mind fell into hell.'[28]
And what, you will ask, is the Bodhi-mind?
Even the prostitute Yamamba got it right:[29]
'Seeking Bodhi above, saving others below,

Whipping on the wheel of the Four Great Vows—
It is simply a lifetime of helping folks out.'[30]
The best way to do that is preaching the Dharma,
Preaching and piling up countless good acts.
How wonderful is the power of preaching!
All the Buddhas together can't use it all up.
Though for Dharma-preaching *kenshō* is vital,
It doesn't provide you with big enough paps.
You can't rear strong kids with inadequate dugs,
And without good offspring, the line will die out.
Hear the sound of one hand, put a stop to all sounds,
But quitting there marks you out as a heretic;[31]
Next a thousand thickets of thorn and briar—
Pass through them all! Don't leave any out!"

"Where do you go when you die, old girl?"
"Stop that boat sailing in the sea out there!"[32]
"Make your way down a twisting mountain trail,
All forty-nine turns, in less than a minute!"
"What color is the wind? How does it smell?"
"The meaning of him coming east in a dream?"
Finally, a thousand more Barriers, closed up tight,
Grave problems to afflict all students of Zen,
But without them, Zen would wither and die.
Pass them all, grudging neither life nor limb.
The great Zen master Huang-po years ago
Continually lamented with deepest regret
That the great teacher at Mount Niu-t'ou,
Who preached with such effortless freedom,
Remained ignorant of the uplifting Barriers.[33]
Without these Barriers, Zen is simply not Zen.
Carp leap countless barriers at Dragon Gate;
Foxes leap the high *torii* at Inari Shrines.[34]
Given Zen provides you with the rice you eat,
Your job isn't done till the Barriers are passed:
Su-shan's Memorial Tower, the Rhinoceros Fan,
Chien-feng's Three Lights, Nan-ch'uan's Death,

Po-yun's Not Yet There, The Lady Burns the Hut,
Ch'ien and Her Spirit Apart, Wu-tsu's Buffalo.[35]
These are the Dharma cave's claws and fangs,
Divine charms ready to divest you of your life.
After you pass through them all, one by one,
Read extensively in the inner and outer texts,
Lay up inexhaustible stores of Dharma wealth.
In responding to your students' differing needs,[36]
It's essential you locate a true Dharma seedling,
And a true Dharma seedling will want the real truth.
But the Dharma cave's talons and death-dealing charms,
Are like the two wings a bird needs to take flight:
Without them Dharma seedlings will never take root.
This is how a Buddha-land is established on earth,
It's the great work Bodhisattvas all take on themselves.
Even if empty space itself should be exhausted,
The Bodhisattva's universal vow will never end.
It's my earnest hope that a thousand ages hence,
Our school will have at least one seedling left.
If you can bore through into this old lady's mind,
The patriarchs' original spirit will never die out—
Only please, make sure that your efforts don't flag;
And now Old Granny must bid you farewell.

*Written in winter on the day the Buddha attained enlightenment
[the 8th of the 12th month], the 10th year of Hōreki [1760],
by the Old Monk Under the Sala Tree.*[37]

5: An Account
of the Precious Mirror Cave   :

A N ACCOUNT OF THE PRECIOUS MIRROR CAVE (*Hōkyōkutsu
no ki*) dates from Hakuin's mid-sixties. The original woodblock edition is extremely rare, and the text was little known until
it was republished in the *Complete Works of Zen Priest Hakuin* in
1934.[1] Like many of his writings, it was initially printed as a fac-
simile of his calligraphic manuscript. The earliest surviving copies date from the mid-nineteenth century, although the carved
wooden blocks for an edition dated 1791 were recently discovered
in a Zen temple in southern Izu, not far from the sea cavern that
Hakuin called "Precious Mirror Cave." Temple printings were
probably made down through the years for pilgrims who came to
visit the cave.

Hakuin himself may have made the trip to visit the remarkable
cave in the rocky cliffs at the southern tip of Izu peninsula, which
juts far out into the Pacific from the foothills around Mount Fuji.
To inhabitants of the area, the cave was, and is, known as Amida-
kutsu, Amida Cavern. The name derives from an old legend
which tells of shining figures of Amida Buddha and two attendant Bodhisattvas appearing to fishermen who had entered the
grotto.

According to *A History of Amida Cave, an Ancient Site in Southern Izu* (*Nanzu koseki Amida-kutsu engi*), a brief pamphlet probably dating from the late Edo period, the cave was known to the

Shingon priest Mongaku Shōnin (twelfth century), as well as to Shin Sect founder Shinran Shōnin. It later became a sacred site for devotees of Pure Land Buddhism, who believed that anyone who could enter the cave and was fortunate enough to see the Amida Triad was assured of attaining rebirth in Amida's Pure Land of Bliss. In the Edo period (1600–1868), the well-known Jōdo evangelist Yūten Shōnin (1636–1718) used the hills around the cave as a center for religious practice, and it was probably because of his association with the spot that it became a popular pilgrim site during the second half of the Edo period.

The narrator of *An Account of the Precious Mirror Cave* states that he visited the cave, and his descriptions of its interior certainly suggest firsthand knowledge. We have no way of confirming that Hakuin entered the cave himself, but he would have had ample opportunity to do so, since he made frequent trips down the Izu peninsula, traveling both by boat and on foot, to conduct religious meetings and visit temples and lay followers in the area.

The wealthy Kyoto merchant Momoi Tōu (d. 1795) describes a visit he made to the cave a few years after Hakuin's death in an essay titled *Kyūai zuihitsu* ("Dust from My Travel Satchel"). It was mid-winter when Tōu reached the port of Shimoda on the eastern side of the Izu peninsula. Greeted by the strong winds and rough seas prevalent at that time of year, he was forced to wait fifteen days until conditions improved. Then he set out for the cave:

> After the small fishing boat had been sculled out into the open sea about twenty *chō*, the mouth of the cave gradually came into view. The sea, which from the land had appeared smooth and calm, was now rising and falling outside the cave entrance with a considerable swell, making the boat heave and roll in the broken seas. There being only a light wind, however, my mind remained perfectly calm.
>
> As we drew near the cliffside, the boatman quickly cast his fishing net over a small pine tree growing over the mouth of the cave. He used it to pull the boat toward the entrance, then skillfully worked the prow forward into the

narrow opening in the cliff. After we advanced six or seven yards into the cave, light could still be seen coming from the entrance. Then the boat went farther inside, sideways to the left, where the light no longer penetrated. It was as though we had suddenly plunged into the pitch blackness of night . . . After we had moved two boat-lengths or so into the cave, we came to a rocky shelf rising high out of the water and were unable to proceed any farther. The sharp rise and fall of the swell within the cave was jolting the boat up and down and bathing our faces in watery mist. We were terrified, unable to speak. Then everyone began reciting loud choruses of Nembutsu.

Suddenly, at the far end of the cave, we saw a radiant light shining in the darkness, illuminating the cavern like a bright sun and transforming everything with a golden light. Even the water around and under the boat was permeated with a brilliant radiance as if emanating from scattered gems. We emitted cries of astonishment. But once again we were submerged in darkness and to our great dismay could see nothing whatever.

Then, suddenly, the radiant light reappeared, as dazzling as before. I was able this time to maintain more presence of mind, and I could see Amida Buddha and his two attendant Bodhisattvas on the rocky face of the far wall as if on a folding screen. About each of their heads was a bright aureole, and they were mounted on clouds. The figure of Amida Buddha was about a foot and a half in height. Kannon Bodhisattva, standing slightly in front of the Buddha, was about one foot, and Seishi Bodhisattva, standing slightly in front of and slightly apart from Kannon, appeared to be less than eight inches in height. I saw very clearly their venerable images standing in what is generally called the welcoming-aspirants form of the Amida Triad.

The Buddha's wonderful appearance, surely without precedence, moved us to tears of gratitude, the experience engraved forever in our hearts. No words of mine could be in any way adequate to describe it.

The narrator of the *Account of the Precious Mirror Cave* is a Nembutsu practitioner and seeker of rebirth in Amida Buddha's Pure Land who, it soon becomes clear, is also deeply versed in the intricacies of the Buddhist teaching. After recounting the story of a fisherman who had entered the cave and seen the images, he explains that the fisherman was able to see the figures because he had repeated Amida's name with such singleness of mind that he had attained the state of Nembutsu samadhi in which oneness with Amida's Dharma-body is achieved. The narrator goes on to elucidate the meaning of Amida's appearance, equating attainment of rebirth in the Pure Land with the Zen experience of *kenshō* or satori and citing examples of the marvelous ability that Buddhas and Bodhisattvas have shown in the past to manifest themselves in various forms and guises in order to lead sentient beings to liberation.

The name Hakuin gave to the Amida Cave, one of many Zen metaphors for the essential mind, or Buddha-mind, likens it to a mirror of perfect clarity that reflects all things as they truly are. "Precious Mirror Cave" thus evinces the message Hakuin wants his story to convey to readers, namely that the sudden appearance of the Buddhist figures illuminating the darkness of the cave replicates the experience of *kenshō*, the abrupt realization in which a Zen student sees into the true nature of self, or Mind, the Tathagata's Dharma-body. Hakuin often describes a Zen student's struggle with koans, especially those of the difficult *nantō* type, as taking place within the "darkness of the Dharma cave" (the student's mind). He sometimes explains this cave-like darkness in *An Account of the Precious Mirror Cave* using terms of Buddhist philosophy, as the "immense blackness" of the "storehouse" consciousness, the fundamental consciousness that lies at the deepest ground of the mind and is the basic source of the afflicting passions. When a student achieves the breakthrough into enlightenment, this storehouse consciousness is said to be abruptly "inverted," instantaneously becoming the "great perfect mirror wisdom [of enlightenment], suddenly flashing out and illuminating all things with blinding brightness."

This storehouse consciousness is the eighth of the "consciousnesses" (*vijnanas*) posited by the "Consciousness Only" tradition of Buddhism, which together encompass all aspects of the conscious and unconscious mind. Hakuin summarizes his understanding of the eight consciousnesses in a passage from *Poison Flowers in a Thicket of Thorns*:

Each of us is endowed with eight consciousnesses. The first five—the sensory faculties of sight, hearing, smell, taste, and touch—are able to receive data from the objective world but are unable to distinguish good and bad, beauty and ugliness. The sixth consciousness functions in response to various stimuli thus received; it moves freely within the first five consciousnesses and conceals itself within the eighth consciousness, appearing and reappearing with great freedom, moving forward here, shrinking back there. This activity is something even a Buddha is unable to control. It is owing to the working of the sixth consciousness that one is reborn as an animal, also owing to the working of the sixth consciousness that one attains Buddhahood. The seventh consciousness lies hidden in the dark areas between the sixth and eighth consciousnesses. The eighth or "storehouse" consciousness exists in a passive state of utter blankness, dull and unknowing, like a vast pool of still clear water, without any movement whatever. In it are stored, without exception, each of the passions— love, hate, sadness, compassion—you have experienced in the past. But if a student pursues his religious practice diligently and is able to break through this dark cavern of the mind, it suddenly transforms into the great perfect mirror wisdom shining forth with perfect brilliance in the attainment of enlightenment.

The "inversion" or "turning" of the storehouse consciousness was also the subject of an inscription Hakuin wrote for a wealthy farmer and Zen student named Akiyama explaining the meaning of the lay Buddhist name—Kokan, "Old Mirror"—that he had conferred upon him:

Each and every sentient being is possessed of an old mirror that reflects all things just as they are, without any distortion or lack whatever. . . . All the immense variety of things in the universe—heaven and hell, the Pure Land and the impure world, the realms of the Buddhas and of the demons, birth-and-death and Nirvana—are each of them appearances reflected on this mirror. Being the source of all of these things, this old mirror is called the "storehouse" consciousness. Since it reflects faithfully all existences without exception, it is called the Great Perfect Mirror Wisdom. . . . If you take a mallet and deliver a decisive blow to the mirror, shattering it so you see through to its root source, you are then able to use the light of the Great Perfect Mirror Wisdom at will and with total freedom to lead other living beings to deliverance. Those who do this are called Bodhisattvas, beings who embody the highest and deepest reaches of the Mahayana.

I visited the Amida Cave in 2001 with two other Hakuin scholars, thanks to the kindness of a local fisherman who placed his small boat at our disposal. Conditions being favorable, we left the protection of the small port, entered the open sea and followed the coastline for a short distance. The opening in the cliff face, now at low tide, soon came into view. The captain slowly approached the entrance, gingerly edging the small boat up to the narrow opening in the cliff and then very slowly into the interior of the cave. The boat inched forward, the darkness growing more intense until it was impossible to make out your hand in front of your face. We could sense the boat moving left, then stopping, unable to go any farther. It was then, *mirabile dictu*, that we saw what appeared to be three small figures arranged in the form of the Amida Triad shining in the darkness against the far wall. We were unable to see the images clearly enough to give precise measurements as Tōu did, yet everything we experienced, the approach to the cave, the threading through the entrance, the boat's route inside the cave, and of course the sudden appearance of the images, closely matched the description in Hakuin's narrative. We have no way of knowing whether he visited the cave or not, but the descriptions he gives of it in the story and the fact that he made numerous trips to teach at various temples on the Izu peninsula seem to suggest firsthand knowledge.

AN ACCOUNT OF THE PRECIOUS MIRROR CAVE

The Buddha preached in the *Flower Garland Sutra* that a Buddha's body fills the entire universe. He said that it is constantly being revealed to living beings.[2] If that is so, then everything the eye sees without exception should be the Tathagata's pure Dharma-body. Yet we are unable to see this Dharma-body anywhere because the eye of wisdom remains unopened in us.

Another sutra states that the Buddha is always "residing right here, preaching the Dharma and leading the countless sentient beings to the path of liberation."[3] If that is the case, everything our ears hear without exception should be the incomprehensibly deep and essential teaching preached by the Buddhas. Yet we are unable to hear that teaching, because the wondrous ear that hears all things remains unopened in us as well.

Back in the beginning years of the Kan'ei era (1624–44), there was an old fisherman who lived in a village called Teishi in Kamo county in the province of Izu. Constantly lamenting the wretchedness of the work in which he was engaged and deeply fearing the retribution that awaited him in the next life,[4] he was always reciting the Nembutsu, never neglecting it day or night. He told himself that although he was obliged to catch fish for a living, his real vocation was the Nembutsu. He recited it constantly, even when he was out on the ocean in his boat, and he would continue reciting it through the long nights, oblivious of all else, frequently forgetting to attend to his nets.

At times the old fisherman would see in the distance an uncanny radiance that seemed to float just above the surface of the waves. The strange light puzzled him, and one night he sculled his boat toward it. As he drew closer, he could make out the mouth of a sea cave among the rocky cliffs. The entrance was about twenty feet across. He steered his boat as close as he could and tried to peer inside, but the darkness was so intense that it was impossible for him to determine how far back the cave extended. The entrance closed and opened with the rising and falling of the tide and at high tide the sea rushed in, filling the cave completely.

The fisherman waited for a day when the tide was low and sculled his boat to the cave entrance. Using his oar he poled his way slowly and apprehensively through the opening in the rocky cliff. Once inside, he was able by pushing and fending against the sides of the cave to work the boat twenty feet or more into the darkness. The deeper he went, the blacker it became. In spite of himself, his knees began to quake, his blood ran cold, and he was thrown into a state of panic. On the point of fainting away, he suddenly knelt down, put his palms together in *gasshō*, and began reciting the Nembutsu. After ten repetitions, his fear gradually subsided, and he experienced a calmness and tranquility in both body and mind. Presently, he slowly opened his eyes. The inside of the cave was glowing in radiant, golden light that seemed to penetrate the very depths of his being. He noticed a strange fragrance that seemed to be wafting through the cavern.

Gazing intently into the light, he could see the ineffably marvelous form of the Buddha of Infinite Light standing solemnly and serenely with his two attendant Bodhisattvas at his sides.[5] They were figures of pure gold arrayed in inexpressible majesty. The narrow confines of the cave had been transformed into the vast infinitude of the universe itself, and within it, the Buddha's body seemed to tower up for thousands upon thousands of feet.[6]

The old fisherman began to intone the Nembutsu, tears of joy pouring down his cheeks. His body and mind both seemed to vanish, and before he knew it several hours had passed. He was suddenly aware of the waves breaking angrily against the rocky cliffs outside the cave. Afraid that the inflowing tide would block the mouth of the cave, he paid a tearful farewell to the figure of Amida Buddha and poled his boat out through the cave entrance into the ocean, all the while repeating the Nembutsu.

When he returned, he astonished his fellow villagers with the story of what had transpired, sending a wave of excitement through the surrounding area. Soon endless throngs of people were making their way to the cliffside eager to enter the cave. They would wait there until the low tide revealed the opening in the rocks, then pole their way inside to pay homage to the Buddha. No sooner were they inside than they would fling themselves down in obeisance, weeping loudly in gratitude, their faces glistening with sweat. Some would prostrate themselves and begin reciting the Nembutsu with palms pressed together in *gasshō*, weeping and emitting inarticulate cries of thanks. Some would only peer forward, looks of disappointment written on their faces. Others would survey the goings-on around them dubiously, gazing around with mouths turned in derisive smiles. Their reactions were different owing to the differences in what they saw, and those differences were in turn the result of the amount of faith they possessed and the comparative depth of their delusion.

Those who wept loud and profuse tears of gratitude did so because they were worshipping the majestic figure of a Tathagata, rising three to five feet or ten to twenty feet into the cave's pure golden light. They were the superior practicers. Those who prostrated themselves and fervently repeated the Nembutsu worshipped a sacred golden figure of six or seven inches in height emitting a radiant glittering light. These were average, ordinary devotees.[7]

Those who looked around them with expressions of disappointment on their faces did not see any golden radiance to worship, nor could they smell the precious fragrance. They moved about self-importantly, telling the others that there was nothing in the cave but three blackened pieces of burnt-out wood three to five inches high standing in a row in the darkness, with no eyes or noses or other distinguishable features. They attempted to discourage the enthusiasm in the others, directing accusations at the old fisherman. "It's his fault," they said, "deceiving people with those stories of his, getting them all worked up over nothing at all." These were the inferior practicers.

The ones who gazed around them uncertainly with derisive smiles on their lips were dull and ignorant men and women who know nothing of the Buddhist principle of cause and effect in the Three Worlds. Those who gather bits of information from popular works on Buddhism, throw in a lot of nonsense they hear from others, and make a pretense of being well informed. In fact, they are no different from non-Buddhist types who believe neither in existence after death nor in karmic retribution.

Eshin Sōzu, a priest who was not only embraced by the compassion of the Buddhas but was esteemed by the Japanese *kami* as well, used to say that people of great faith see a great Buddha, while people of little faith see a small Buddha.[8] This is a thought that I, for one, have never ceased to cherish. There is not the least difference between what Eshin said and these people entering the cave and seeing things differently according to the strength of their faith and the weight of their karmic burden. It is as though they are standing before a bright mirror, totally unable to avoid having all their goodness or evilness, beauty or ugliness, and everything else reflected just exactly as it is. That is why I would like to name the cavern in the sea-cliff "Cave of the Precious Mirror," or "Mirror Rock Cavern." It has in recent times become popularly known as the Amida Cave.

Someone said, "I have heard that Buddhas are endowed with three different bodies. Should a Tathagata such as the one that appeared in the Cave of the Precious Mirror be regarded as a Dharma-body, a Recompense-body, or a Transformation-body? Inasmuch as the reason Tathagatas appear in the world is to benefit sentient beings, one would assume that they would manifest themselves in some well-inhabited place, a village, or town, or large city. Why would a Tathagata choose to appear here, in a spot so remote from human habitation, inside a dangerous sea-cave, where you have to brave the elements, waiting for good weather and a favorable tide, before you can worship him?

"I have also heard that Tathagatas have appeared in the world one after another for the fundamental purpose of making people aware of the path of the Buddha and awakening them to his wisdom. If so, why is the Venerable One of Infinite Life the only Buddha that teaches we should 'go and be reborn in the Pure Land'?"

"It is true," I answered.[9] "Buddhas have three bodies. The Dharma-body is their essential substance, the Recompense- and Transformation-bodies their essential activity. A Tathagata such as the one who appears in the Cave of the Precious Mirror may be called a Dharma-body, a Recompense-body, or a Transformation-body. Every place and every thing—the realms of heaven and hell, the lands of purity and impurity, the mountains and rivers, the great earth, the world of Buddhas and the court of Mara, plants and grasses, groves and thickets—is without exception the true Dharma-body of the Buddha. The Dharma-body is always calm and tranquil. It is never apart from you for an instant, no matter where you are. But unless you are one of the superior seekers who have attained *kenshō*, you are unable to see it. For that reason the Buddhas manifest a Recompense-body or Transformation-body to help sentient beings reach deliverance.

"If, in accordance with your personal ability and karmic circumstances, you diligently practice seated meditation, recite sutras, repeat the Nembutsu, and undertake to live according to the precepts until discriminations cease and illusory thoughts are exhausted, you will reach the field of absolute singlemindedness and enter into the full and perfect freedom of samadhi where you will suddenly be one with the Tathagatas' true Dharma-body.[10] This is what is called *kenshō*, seeing into your true nature.

"When this happens, the Fivefold Eye suddenly opens, allowing you to see all things with perfect clarity; the Four Wisdoms are all immediately attained. This, in and of itself, is the way of enlightenment, the opening up of Buddha-wisdom that the Buddhas proclaim as their fundamental purpose—the instant when you attain the ultimate truth and discern your true nature.

"'Going' [in the words of the Pure Land tradition about 'going and being reborn' in the Pure Land] refers to the point at which thoughts and discriminations cease in the mind. 'Being reborn' refers to attainment of the ground of ultimate singlemindedness. 'Arriving' in the phrase ['Amida arrives to welcome your rebirth in his Pure Land'] refers to the ultimate truth of the Buddha described above manifesting itself, to the great matter of the 'one vehicle alone' becoming perfectly clear right before your eyes.[11]

'Welcoming' refers to the moment when the mind and environment of the aspirant are no longer two, but a perfect oneness of wisdom and ultimate truth. Seen in this way, isn't Amida's coming to welcome the devotee and offer rebirth in the Pure Land ultimately the same as the awakening of Buddha wisdom, the experience of *kenshō*?

"You should know that zazen, observance of precepts, Nembutsu, and sutra recitation are all methods that facilitate attainment of *kenshō*; that the three Buddha-bodies are nondual; that nonduality in itself is the three Buddha-bodies; and that there has never been a single Buddha or patriarch in the Three Worlds or a single wise saint who has not experienced *kenshō*.

"A person who clings to yellow sutra-scrolls with their red handles in the belief that it is the Buddha's teaching or who imagines that a clay image of the Buddha is the Buddha-body—such a person could never, even in a dream, see the true Buddha, much less talk about Buddhas manifesting themselves in towns or villages.

"The Bodhisattva Kannon manifested himself in the shell of a clam. He appeared inside a gourd. He appeared as the young wife of Mr. Ma at a place called Golden Sand Shoal.[12]

"Once on a remote and isolated south sea island, where the inhabitants were illiterate and totally ignorant of the Buddha's honored name, a place where they did nothing but gather mornings and evenings to cast their nets, Amida Buddha manifested himself as a Nembutsu fish. At some point, groups of people started the practice of forming on the beach to intone the Nembutsu in loud voices. When they attained a state of total single-mindedness in their recitation, fish would float to the surface of the waves in great numbers. All people had to do was to set out their nets and they would soon be brimming with fish of all sizes and shapes. But the number of fish that accumulated in a net would vary in proportion to the amount of Nembutsu the fisherman repeated and the loudness of his intonations.[13]

"In this way, for the inhabitants of the island the recitation of the Nembutsu became a family occupation and a central part of their lives. When one of them died, the rest would assemble and repeat the Nembutsu, and the same auspicious signs would always appear that were seen when they summoned the fish. A strange and wonderful fragrance would fill the air, and five-colored clouds would drift from the western skies to welcome the departed soul and lead it to the Pure Land. The fish were said to be manifestations of Amida, employing his skillful means in a world devoid of Buddhas to lead sentient beings to salvation.

"Ah, how far beyond the comprehension of ordinary unen-lightened mortals is the great compassion and wonderful means employed by Buddhas and Bodhisattvas. The Tathagata's appear-ance in the Cave of the Precious Mirror is an example of him man-ifesting himself differently to aspirants according to the depth of their karma and the purity of their faith. Is there any difference between the way Amida Buddha manifested himself in the cave and the way the fish appeared in response to the islanders' recita-tion of the Nembutsu? Anyone who reflects deeply on this must be inspired with a sense of awe so great as to make his hair rise on his flesh and tears of gratitude flow down his cheeks in endless streams.

"Although I am a foolish old man living here in a remote prov-ince far removed from the place where the events in the story took place, the news of the Buddha's appearance in the Precious Mirror Cave reached my ears. It moved me so deeply I could think of nothing but seizing this marvelous opportunity and somehow making my way to Kamo county in Izu province and availing myself of Amida Buddha's marvelous power—to pros-trate myself before his august figure and pray for rebirth in his Pure Land.

"Dressing in pilgrim's guise and accompanied by four or five others, I was finally able to make my way here.[14] Hiring a dubi-ous little boat from a fisherman, we poled our way into the cave. Once inside, we bowed deeply in obeisance and recited the Nem-butsu. One of the men burst into tears the instant he saw the fig-ure, prostrating himself and repeating the Buddha's name over and over. Another man pressed his palms together in *gasshō* and began sobbing out loud repetitions of the Nembutsu upon seeing the sacred form, his eyes filled with tears of gratitude. Another moved about the cave despondently, a look of disappointment on his face. 'What have you seen that makes you sob like that?' he asked. 'I can't make out a single shape in this darkness. I wish I could see something, even if it was only a paper cutout, so I could share in the joy all of you seem to experience.' He kept stretching his neck forward into the darkness and straining to see, scratching his head and looking nervously in all directions.

"Meantime, worshipping in the darkness, I could see only the flickering light caused by the movement of the waves. I could not make out the Buddha's full-moon face or blue-lotus eyes, although I did see something that looked like Buddha figures standing in a row. Sitting in the boat worshipping them, I felt a slight awakening of faith stir within me. Whatever it was I was seeing, I was sure it was a rare and wonderful thing, and I prostrated myself and continued repeating the Nembutsu.

"When I returned home, at first I felt a certain sense of regret that a seventy-year-old man like me had traveled such a distance to worship Amida without really achieving my objective. Upon greater reflection, however, I realized that the heart of Amida Buddha would not harbor feelings of like or dislike, that any such discriminations were the result of my own lack of faith. I felt ashamed at having felt such regrets, and I decided that I would repent my past karma that hindered me, fear the suffering awaiting in the next life, and devote myself with total sincerity to singleminded repetition of the Nembutsu.

"When half a year had passed, I made another trip to the Amida Cave. This time, it was entirely different. I succeeded in worshipping the Buddha in splendid fashion and found myself drenched in tears of gratitude. It made me realize that someone like me, living in this degenerate age of the Latter-Day Dharma and immersed in the cycle of rebirth, could not hope for a better teacher than Amida. Why should I leave him and go somewhere else? I decided to stay right where I was and exert myself for the rest of my days on Amida's behalf. If I should die in doing this, I could hope for no better karma [linking me to rebirth in the Pure Land]. And so I gave up my aspiration to live as a pilgrim, traveling and worshipping at sacred sites around the country.

Instead, I threw myself body and soul into the single practice of the Nembutsu.

"Meanwhile, people from all over the country were coming to worship at the Amida Cave. Sometimes unfavorable sea conditions prevented them from entering the cave, and they would be obliged to wait on the shore for long periods until conditions improved. Watching them sitting around, growing weary with the tedium of waiting, I felt sorry for them. Soliciting contributions from various sources, I built a small hut, had an image of Amida painted just as he appears in the cave, and enshrined it inside.[15]

"It is my fervent hope and prayer that the favorable karmic link I have achieved will enable me to break through the devilish net of birth-and-death hand in hand with all other beings and achieve forthwith the realm of unshakable singlemindedness, creating a Pure Land and encountering the Amida that exists in the mind alone."[16]

This was written on the Day of One Vehicle Alone, the Month of the Full Moon of Suchness, the First Year of Perfectly Integrated Formlessness (Buddha's Birthday, the second year of our Kan'en era [1749]), in the village of Tranquility, Incomprehensible County, the Dharma Realm of Interpenetrating Form and Principle, by Priest Flowers of Emptiness, disciple of Elder Priest Lightning Flash Morning Dew, incumbent of the Dream Vision Subtemple of All Dharmas Are Forms of Truth Monastery on Great Wisdom of Self-Identity Mountain.

Corrected by Absolute Purity, Disciple of the Very Reverend Perfect Unity, Abbot of Begrudging Neither Life nor Limb for the Dharma Temple.

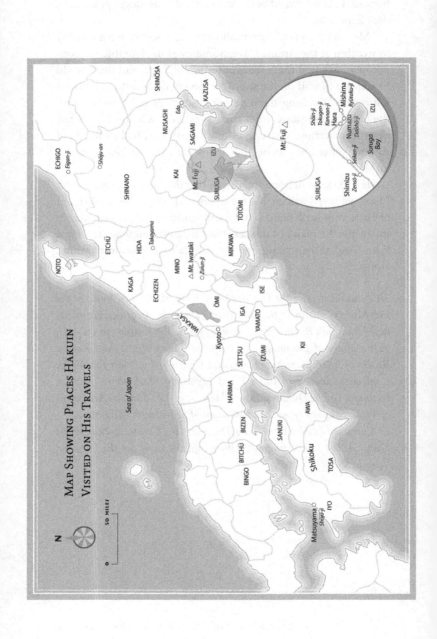

MAP SHOWING PLACES HAKUIN
VISITED ON HIS TRAVELS

6: The Chronological Biography of Zen Master Hakuin :

BY TŌREI ENJI

THE *CHRONOLOGICAL BIOGRAPHY OF ZEN MASTER HAKUIN*[1], compiled during Hakuin's lifetime by his successor Tōrei Enji, is the only translation in this book that is about, and not by, Hakuin, though as will be seen he did have a hand in producing it. It is one of the three principal sources for Hakuin's life, the only one that covers it from birth to death and provides an extensive account of the teaching career that dominated his final forty years.

Tōrei's *Chronological Biography of Zen Master Hakuin* is certainly one of the livelier examples of the traditional chronological biography (called *nempu* in Japanese) genre, which are not biographies in the sense that word is used in the West, rather collections of significant events, anecdotes, and experiences arranged under successive years. Chronological biographies in China had been compiled for distinguished Confucian figures and Zen priests as far back as the Sung dynasty. They are uncritical and reverential biographical treatments of the individual's achievements, designed for posterity and normally consisting of a good deal of rather dry narrations of what he did and when and where he did it. They are largely accurate, though they generally manage to include at least one or two stories or legends of an inspirational nature as well.[2]

Tōrei's *Chronological Biography* follows this general example, recording Hakuin's movements throughout his career in year-by-year segments. Still, one senses that the underlying intent is to use this as a means of propagating Hakuin's Zen teaching, which was probably his motive for wanting the work written in the first place. In that sense, the *Chronological Biography* corresponds rather closely to Hakuin's own works, in which he is constantly using his personal experiences as a means not only of relating his history but of conveying his religious message.

Tōrei uses his considerable literary skills to blend a wealth of unique and fascinating information into the traditional *nempu* format. He relies heavily on borrowings from the lively narratives in Hakuin's published works for the first part, covering the period of the religious quest, and fills the latter half, dealing with the teaching years, with equally fascinating information—vividly told dreams, encounters with samurai, sketches of bold lay disciples, notably women, as well as telling little incidents of daily life—most of which is not found anywhere else.

The circumstances under which Tōrei compiled the biography are only vaguely known. A letter he wrote Hakuin in 1757 (he was thirty-six, Hakuin seventy-two) shows him, six years after receiving Hakuin's Dharma transmission, already engaged in the compilation process.

My esteemed teacher, I am now engaged in composing the chronological record of your life, so as to elucidate the great hardships you encountered over your long career—the adversities you endured in Echigo and Shinano provinces and later in Izumi and Mino provinces that enabled you ultimately to penetrate both the absolute and relative principles, Dharma and everyday practice. It is something no one today could hope to equal. This is not even to mention the more than twenty years after you became head priest at Shōin-ji when you spurred yourself on day and night until the profound secret the Buddha revealed on Vulture Peak opened up to you, or the months and years during which you have concealed your virtue while engaging students with the wonderful means of Master Daitō. (*Complete Works*, Vol. 7, p. 40)

Assuming the *Chronological Biography* was compiled largely during Hakuin's lifetime, and given Tōrei's relative youth when he started it, it is natural to assume that the project was conceived by Hakuin himself and that he played some role in its composition, providing valuable information and guidance and perhaps even writing portions of the text. This and the fact that normally a teacher's disciples initiated such religious biographies postmortem means that Tōrei was placed in a somewhat novel, and at times one suspects a bit ticklish, situation.

Hakuin, as we saw in the General Introduction, was enormously pleased to have acquired such a talented and dedicated young disciple to carry on his Zen teaching. He quickly appointed him as a special attendant and assigned him a teaching role as well as literary tasks. But we also saw evidence that Tōrei was less than eager to go along with some of Hakuin's proposals. While of course deeply respecting his teacher, he apparently felt that completing his training was the first order of business. So it is not hard to imagine the interplay between the two men on the issue of the biography: the teacher cajoling the student to accept the formidable assignment, and the student, perhaps with reservations, accepting. Then the teacher, whose hands-on approach to almost everything is well substantiated, looking over the student's shoulder, so to speak, as the work progressed, and rallying him on with words of encouragement and supplies of fresh information.

Since Tōrei began his study at Shōin-ji when Hakuin was fifty-eight, he would have been in a position to have had a more or less first-hand acquaintance with many of the events that took place over the last twenty-five years of his teacher's life. However, having no direct knowledge of the first fifty-eight years covered by the chronicle, he would have been obliged to work pretty much from scratch, although we know that he filled in much of that period with narrative descriptions from Hakuin's published works. Much additional information no doubt came from his fellow monks, and from lay students and friends of the master.

Conspicuous in the early part of Tōrei's treatment of the teaching career are a number of quite lengthy, detailed, and extremely interesting episodes describing the practice and realization of Hakuin's lay followers, who for most of this period seem to have outnumbered the resident monks. However, for some reason Tōrei includes relatively few stories about his fellow priests, even important Dharma successors who were entrusted with carrying on Hakuin's teaching line. While I am unable to suggest a reason to explain this, it may have had something to do with the timing of the project and the manner in which Hakuin went about promoting it. He was still teaching when he entrusted the project to Tōrei, and some of his senior monks were still engaged in their training, while others had already left and assumed positions in other parts of the country. Even assuming that accounts of the private encounters these senior priests had with Hakuin were available to Tōrei, he may been hesitant about inserting them in the biography out of deference to the older men. It probably would have been easier to approach the lay followers, most of whom were residents of Hara and nearby villages, and get them to agree to include their experiences in the public record.

The Chronological Biography of Zen Master Hakuin was first published in 1820, fifty years after Hakuin's death, by Taikan Bunshu, Tōrei's disciple and successor at Ryūtaku-ji, and issued under the Ryūtaku-ji imprint. In the final year of his life Tōrei entrusted Taikan with his manuscript of the work with instructions that he see it into print. Taikan, only twenty-six at the time, describes the circumstances in his postscript to the printed edition:

> One day when I was serving under Master Tōrei, he brought out a religious biography of Master Hakuin to show me. He asked me to arrange to have it printed, but before I was able to do this, he passed away. I let matters rest after that, doing nothing about it until the fiftieth anniversary of Hakuin's death, which fell in the fourteenth year of the Bunka era (1817), came around. A commemorative assembly was held at Ryūtaku-ji that year at which I was asked to

deliver lectures on Master Hakuin's *Dharma Talks Introductory to Lectures on the Record of Hsi-keng*. Priests and laymen who attended the meeting made earnest requests to me to proceed with the publishing of the biography. Recalling the instructions I had received from my teacher many years before, I began, despite my native ignorance and lack of qualifications for the task, to prepare the work for the printer. I went through it and gave the text a thorough revision. I then divided it into two parts, the first covering the period of the master's practice leading to his enlightenment; the second the period of his teaching career. I did this simply to make as clear as possible the circumstances of his progress to enlightenment. Because I lacked various bits of information and had no personal knowledge of the events, many omissions and other faults have no doubt crept into the work. I nonetheless send it off to have the blocks carved so that it can be shared with the world and I can at last carry out my responsibility to my teacher.

Pressing my palms together in *gasshō* and offering incense, I respectfully inscribe this on the day of the Buddha's entrance into enlightenment, in the third year of the Bunsei era (1819).

Taikan Bunshu, priest of Daibai-ji in Tamba province.

I have followed the text in Katō Shōshun's edition of the work, *Hakuin Oshō Nempu* (Shibunkaku, 1985), with constant reference to Rikugawa Taiun's *Hakuin Oshō Shōden* (Sankibō, 1963). The latter work includes a fairly complete version of Tōrei's draft manuscript.

I have limited my own notes as far as possible to material that provides information I thought would be of interest to the reader. There are a number of parenthetical notes in the original text; some of the longer ones have been marked with asterisks and moved to the end of the yearly section in which they appear.

A few passages containing additional material of interest from other sources are given in Appendix A and Appendix B at the end of the work. Following the style of the original text, each of the yearly entries is preceded by the date in traditional year period (*nengō*) fashion and Hakuin's age at the time; modern equivalents are given in parentheses: e.g., *Genroku 9 (1696) Age 11*. Dates throughout are given as they appear in the text, but I have subtracted one year from people's ages to make them conform to Western usage.

A Chronological Biography
of Zen Master Hakuin

Part 1: Practice Leading To Enlightenment

Second Year of Jōkyō (1685) Reign of Emperor Reigen
In this year, on the night of the twenty-fifth day of the twelfth month, the master was born at Ukishima-ga-Hara, Suntō gun, in the province of Suruga. His father's surname was originally Sugiyama. The Sugiyamas were descendents of the Suzuki clan, a line of samurai that had an outstanding reputation for bravery and valor.

(Suzuki Saburō Shigeie was a vassal of Minamoto Yoshitsune [1159–93]. When Shigeie learned that Yoshitsune had escaped the forces of his brother Yoritomo and made his way into the domain of Fujiwara Hidehira in Ōshū far in the north, he realized it would no longer be possible for him to join his master. He led seven warriors who were kinsmen of his to the village of Enashi in Izu province, where they settled and lived quiet lives concealed from the world. The Sugiyamas descended from this branch of the Suzuki clan. Tracing the family roots further back, we find that even at the time the great deities of Kumano returned from India by way of China, the men of the Suzuki clan were already known far and wide as the warriors of Kumano.)[3]

The master's mother was a daughter of the Nagasawa family, who served as heads of the Hara poststation on the Tōkaidō. The Nagasawas had for generations devoted themselves to cultivating the seeds of Buddhahood through various religious activities. The master's mother was a simple, good-natured woman who took pleasure in spontaneous acts of kindness and compassion.

One night his mother dreamed she saw a figure fly toward the house from the direction of southern Ise. It alighted on the roof, holding out on a silken cloth a divine amulet from the great shrine at Ise. The grave solemnity of its appearance made her tremble with awe. When she woke, she had conceived a child. Because of this the Ise Shrine always held a special place in her heart. On the night of the master's birth the dream recurred, and when it was over she was filled with an overwhelming joy. She was thereupon delivered of a male child. The birth took place in the Hour of the Ox.

(The Nagasawas had five children, three boys and two girls. The master was their third [and youngest] son.[4])

Jōkyō 4 (1687) Age 2
Emperor Higashiyama ascends the throne.
The master felt ashamed because he was unable to stand by himself. One day, after trying again and again, he finally succeeded. Seeing his beaming face, a man exclaimed, "He's done it! Master Iwa can stand!" (Iwajirō was his childhood name.) Recalling the incident years later, the master related it to his fellow priests.

Jōkyō 5/Genroku 1 (1688) Age 3
The master had an excellent memory. He memorized a popular song of more than three hundred words that was sung in the village of Nakayama in the Sayo district. He sang it wherever he went, never forgetting or mistaking a single word. People remarked on his cleverness and quickness of mind.

Genroku 2 (1689) Age 4
One day a young family servant took the master along with her when she went down to the beach with the other servant girls to play. The master wandered off, found a quiet spot by himself to sit, and sat there gazing southward out to sea. His attention fixed on the clouds endlessly changing as they moved across the sky. "How strange and deceptive," he thought. He had by chance experienced for the first time the sad condition of life's impermanence. He suddenly burst into tears and continued to wail inconsolably. No one could understand why.

Genroku 4 (1691) Age 6

The master enjoyed visiting temples and listening to the Dharma. One day he memorized a talk he heard a temple priest give on the Devadatta chapter of the Lotus Sutra.[5] When he returned home he repeated what the priest had said for the elderly members of the household. By the time he had finished, one old man had tears in his eyes.

Living in the village was a practitioner of the Nembutsu by the name of Kyūshinbō.* No one seemed to know anything about his origins, but he had a noble and upright character and was credited with having performed superhuman feats on various occasions. The master's father often invited Kyūshinbō to the family home and entertained him with food and drink. When Kyūshinbō visited, he would seat the young boy beside him in the place of honor, and never allow ordinary laymen to occupy a better seat than the young boy.[6]

Kyūshinbō would give the master a pat on the back and say, "Your face has unusual bone structure. When you grow up you will surely become a man of great virtue and benefit the world." He would tell him, "Shakyamuni spent six years in the Himalayas. Bodhidharma spent nine years at Shao-lin. You must maintain that tradition."[7] On another occasion he told him, "One time alone. One place alone." (*jigiri, bagiri:* fix the mind in one place at all times.)

He imparted three secrets to the master:

1. "After you have eaten, consume all particles of food that remain in your bowl by adding hot water and drinking it.

2. "Always assume a crouching position when you urinate; never while standing.

3. "Exercise great care with regard to the northern quarter. Never face north when you relieve yourself. Never sleep with your feet pointing north.

"Follow these three instructions religiously. It will prolong your life and enable you to reach a ripe old age."

Up until the time of his death the master faithfully observed the directives, even when he was sick.

* (According to one legend, Kyūshinbō had initially resided at Enjō-ji in Kamiya for a hundred years, then went to study with the Ōbaku teacher Tetsugyū [1628–1700] at Mount Chōkō. When he left Tetsugyū, he did it by walking through the air. Another account has him residing first in the village of Yamanaka for twenty or thirty years, where he played constantly on a shaku-hachi, regarded by one and all as a crazy monk, and paying visits to Hara for rest and relaxation. He was said to be Hitachibō Kaison, a retainer of Mina-moto Yoshitsune, who following Yoshitsune's defeat at Takadachi had acquired secret arts from a sage he encountered and spent the rest of his life in seclu-sion from the world.)

Genroku 8 (1695) Age 10

Unusually large for his age, the master was strong and absolutely fearless. He never backed away from anything once he had started it. One day his mother took him to the Shōgenkyō-ji, a village temple, to hear Nichigon Shōnin from Kubogane deliver a ser-mon on Chih-i's *Great Cessation and Insight*.[8] Nichigon warned his listeners in no uncertain terms about the portents of divine punishment and described the terrible forms of retribution awaiting them in hell.

The sermon made the master's flesh creep, his hair rose up on end, and he trembled from head to foot. "I've always been fond of killing living things," he reflected. "I'm wild and unruly, and forever making mischief. What chance will I have to avoid falling into hell and undergoing those endless torments?" Do what he would, he was unable to banish these thoughts from his mind.

One day his mother took him into the bath. She directed one of the servant girls to stoke the fire under the tub to heat the water. Soon angry sounds came snarling up from the fire under the iron bath-cauldron. Fierce flames licked up and around the sides. The steam pricked against his skin with growing force like a rain of arrows. Suddenly, remembering the priest's descriptions of the torments that were inflicted on sinners in hell, he burst into loud bawling tears. No one could get him to stop. Finally, his mother's features hardened. "What a little sissy you are," she said sternly. "Acting like a baby girl."

Choking back tears, the master blubbered, "But mother, I'm afraid of the awful torments that await me in hell. It terrifies me just to go into the bath with you. What will become of me if I fall into the dark, burning hell pits all alone, without you? Who would come and save me?"

"So that's your problem, is it? I'm sure we can find a solution and dispel those fears of yours," she said consolingly.

"We can?"

"Yes," she said.

"Then we must find it," he declared, and ran out of the house to resume his games as if nothing had happened. He was back absorbed in his play the next morning when he suddenly remembered the resolution he had made the previous day. He decided to make some inquiries on his own. He went up to a man who happened to be staying at the posthouse at the time and pressed him for some advice. But the man was unable to offer any.

Hoping to enlist his mother's help, he went and asked her to comb out his hair. "What an odd request," she said with a laugh. "Next thing you know the sun will be setting in the west." She took him into the house, put some oil on his hair, and started combing it out. He grabbed her hand.

"Not yet," he said. "Please, first you must tell me how I can keep from falling into hell."

"First your hair," she said. "Then I'll tell you."

"No, not till you tell me, mother. I'll never let you. I'll die first."

His mother seemed at a loss for an answer. This angered him. "If you try to fool me," he warned, "I'll throw another tantrum . . ."

In an attempt to pacify him, she said, "The divine spirit of Tenmangu Shrine is enshrined in the Sainen-ji.[9] He is a deity of great power and virtue. He can save people from any suffering that karmic retribution may bring. Why don't you go to Tenjin and make a sincere appeal to him?"

The master clapped his hands together with delight. From then on he entrusted himself singlemindedly to Tenjin's divine power. Every morning, he poured three buckets of cold water over his head, offered fervent prayers to the deity, and awaited some sign of response.

Genroku 9 (1696) Age 11

One day the master hung an image of Tenjin on the wall. He lit a stick of incense, made two bows, touching his head to the floor each time, and addressed the deity:

"If I have any chance of achieving my goal, please make the smoke from this incense rise in a straight line."

He sat there for a long time in silent prayer, then opened his eyes. A thread of smoke rose straight up to the ceiling. Then a draft of air came in—the smoke billowed and scattered in all directions. The fear that he would be unable to escape Mara's evil clutches remained undispelled.

Hearing that the Bodhisattva Kannon possessed great spiritual potency and that the wondrous power of the *Fumon-bon* and the *Daihi-shu* surpassed all other religious texts, he memorized them both and began to recite them diligently.

Among the amusements at the annual festival held at the Tenjin Shrine was a skit played out by village youths on the interrogation and torture of Nisshin Shōnin at the hands of government officials in Kamakura. In questioning Nisshin, the officials ask, "Is it true what is said about practicers of the *Lotus Sutra* being able to enter a fire without being harmed, that they can be submerged under water without drowning?" When Nisshin avows that it is, the officials have a red-hot iron cauldron placed over his head. But thanks to the divine power of the *Lotus*, he remains perfectly cool and composed throughout the terrible ordeal.[10]

Watching the play, the master felt more than a touch of envy. He went home and spent the next several days reciting the *Fumon-bon* and *Daihi-shu*. He then tested himself by heating an iron tong and touching it against his thigh. The result was the same as it would have been before all the sutra-chanting—a painful burn.

Again his spirits plunged. His distress and fear grew even more acute.

"Unless I leave home and family and enter the undefiled and emancipated realm of the priesthood, how can I ever hope to attain a free and unobstructed mind like Nisshin had?" He implored his parents on bended knees to allow him to become a priest. But doting on him as they did, they refused even to consider it.

One day a mounted official being led by a hostler to the tethering post at the front of the posthouse happened to pass beneath the window of the upstairs room where the master was deeply absorbed in chanting the *Diamond Sutra*. The official motioned the hostler to pause so he could listen to the sound of the recitation. Profoundly moved, he walked away marveling at the remarkable serenity of the master's voice.

Genroku 10 (1697) Age 12

Having reached the conclusion that the confusion and defilements of worldly life were not congenial to religious practice, the master climbed Mount Yanagizawa to seek a spot more favorable to self-discipline. He came upon a flat rock, a foot or so in width, in the middle of a mountain stream. A tall cliff with unusual rock formation rose sheer behind it; below it the stream tumbled down the steep slope. It was totally removed from the world and its dust. He took a chisel and carved a likeness of Kannon Bodhisattva into the face of the cliff. Seating himself quietly before the image, he began a recitation of the *Diamond* and *Kannon* sutras and the *Daihi-shu*. After repeating them several times each and praying fervently to Kannon for assistance, he returned home. He continued this practice every day without fail, visiting the spot in the morning and not leaving until nightfall.

One day while on his way home from visiting a relative several miles distant, he found that several days of heavy rainfall had flooded the road. His path was blocked. "If I just stand here wasting time like this," he told himself, "the religious resolve I've been cultivating so diligently will surely weaken. I must cross the water and hurry back."

He shed his robe, bundled it up and slung it over his shoulder. Brandishing his sword high above his head in his right hand, he then waded across the perilous current. Upon someone later asking why he had held his sword aloft as he crossed the flood, he replied, "I've heard floodwaters are infested with huge fish and monstrous turtles, who lurk there to assault innocent people. If one of them had attacked, I would have cut it in two!"

Genroku 11 (1698) Age 13
Under the guidance of Kin Shuso of Tokugen-ji, the master learned to read Chinese texts. He had the entire *Kuzōshi*, a Zen phrase anthology, by heart in just three months. Once he had something memorized, he never forgot it. Afterwards, when he took part in Zen-type dialogues and engaged in koan study, when he composed linked verses or impromptu poems, he was able to do it without giving much thought to it. It came easily to him, like producing articles at will from his pocket.

He went to his parents and once again declared his desire to enter the priesthood. Again they refused. But this time, they realized he was not to be deterred. They began to accept the idea they would eventually be forced to part with their beloved son.

Genroku 12 (1699) Age 14
His parents finally relented. On the twenty-fifth of the second month, they took him to Tanrei Soden, the resident priest at Shōin-ji. Tanrei was a broad-minded man and an especially capable priest. He performed the tonsure ceremony making the young boy a Buddhist monk, and gave him the name Ekaku, "Wise Crane."

After Tanrei had shaved his head, he patted him on the back and said, "Always uphold the dignity of the priesthood." He gave him a piece of paper on which he had inscribed the characters for his new name. Tōhō Sokin of the Tokugen-ji wrote a congratulatory verse for the occasion:

A priest of true worth is a wonderful thing,
A joy to the Buddhas, the despair of demons,

If you hope to master the Way of the Buddhas,
Never forget the three pats of self-reflection.[11]

The master then made a vow to his teacher. "Although I may never gain the strength to keep myself from being burned by fire or swallowed by the waves, I will never abandon my quest, even if I should die in the attempt." He began to practice diligently, reciting sutras and performing bows day and night.

Soon after the ordination, Tanrei sent his young disciple to Daishō-ji in Numazu, where he was made an attendant of the abbot, Sokudō Fueki.

Genroku 13 (1700) Age 15

One morning, the master heaved a deep sigh and said, "In deciding to become a monk I turned my back on the obligation I had to my dear parents. Yet I haven't seen any glimpse of progress. People say the *Lotus* is the king among all the sutras the Buddha preached during his lifetime. Even evil demons and malignant spirits are said to revere it. It can save you from samsaric torments even when someone else recites it on your behalf. How much more effective it must be when you recite it yourself! Surely such a sutra, with its unsurpassed profundity, should be able to help me fulfill the vow I have made.

He borrowed a copy of the *Lotus Sutra* from the priest Kan'ebō and read it carefully from cover to cover.[12] But except for phrases like "There is only One Vehicle," and "All dharmas exist in perfect tranquility," he found it was merely devoted to teachings of cause and effect couched in the form of parables. He closed the book with a deep sigh. "If there is any religious merit in this sutra, it must also be found in the Chinese histories, the ancient philosophers, Noh chants, even geisha songs."

The disappointment of this discovery threw him into great mental unrest. He began to doubt the means employed in Zen's "special transmission apart from the scriptures."

Sokudō cherished the indomitable spirit of his young disciple. He could not have shown him more favor had he been his own son.

Genroku 14 (1701) Age 16
On the tenth of the first month, Tanrei Soden, the priest who had ordained the master, died. Tanrei had imparted his Zen transmission to Tōrin Soshō, the master's elder brother in the Dharma.

Genroku 16 (1703) Age 18
Spring. Leaving Daishō-ji, the master went to the village of Shimizu in his home province of Suruga and hung up his traveling staff in the training hall of the Zensō-ji. Since the monks at the temple spent all their time engaged in the study of texts, the master resolved that in the interest of pursuing the Way he would devote his efforts to performing prostrations and reciting sutras. The head priest at Zensō-ji, Sen'ei Soen, was lecturing to the brotherhood on *The Wind and Moon Collection of Zen Poetry*. One day, the subject turned to Zen Master Yen-t'ou, known as the Ferryman Monk. From a biographical note attached to the text he was reading the master learned that Yen-t'ou had been murdered by bandits. When they cut off his head, his death cry was heard for miles around. This bit of news dealt the master's hopes a heavy blow. If Yen-t'ou could not protect his own life from bandits in this world, he felt that his own prospects of avoiding hell in the next were slim indeed.

Master Yen-t'ou was praised as a "phoenix of the patriarchal groves," a "dragon of the Buddha seas." "If that is the best such a great Zen master can do," he reflected, "what chance does someone like me have escaping the tortures of hell? If I am to judge from his story, it is hard to see what is to be gained from studying Zen at all. Ahh! How can I entrust myself to a teaching that is so false and unreliable?"

He sank into despair once again. Food lost all taste for him. "Now that I've left my home and family for the priesthood," he thought, brooding to himself, "I can't just turn around and become a layman again. It would be too humiliating. I'm trapped. I can't go forward. I can't turn back. But if I do end up in hell, at least I'll be down there enduring the torments together with Tanrei, Sokudō, and all those other Buddhist teachers who have lived before me. I'll be better off just enjoying life, giving free rein to my inclinations and desires."

The master immersed himself in the pleasures of literature and the study of painting. Non-Buddhist ideas dominated his thoughts. Every time he saw a sutra or a Buddhist image, his disgust for them only increased.

When the lecture meeting ended, he stayed on at Zensō-ji.

Genroku 17/Hōei 1 (1704) Age 19

In spring, the master traveled to Zuiun-ji in the village of Hinoki, Mino province, to study with a teacher named Baō. The monk On Jōza was residing at Zuiun-ji at the time. He was the son of the Confucian teacher Kumazawa Ryūkai [Banzan], who had served the lord of Okayama in Bizen province. On Jōza and the master found they shared a similar outlook on things and soon formed a fast bond of friendship. Together they pursued the study of literature.

However, one day it dawned on the master that even if he succeeded in becoming a writer of surpassing skill, it still would not bring him peace of mind. That same day, the books in the temple library had been brought out and placed outside one of the halls for the annual airing. Climbing the steps to the hall, the master saw books of all kinds, Buddhist and non-Buddhist alike, stacked in piles on top of some tables. He approached, bowed reverently before them, and prayed:

> Confucius. Buddha. Lao Tzu. Chuang Tzu. Which one of you should I take as my teacher? I beg the heavenly Naga Kings who guard the Dharma to please indicate the right path to me.

Praying silently, he closed his eyes, reached out his hand, and picked a small volume from among the piles of books. It was *Spurring Zen Students Through the Barrier.* After holding it up in an attitude of reverence, he opened it, randomly, to a section entitled "Tz'u-ming Jabs a Gimlet in his Thigh."

In a note that someone had inscribed above the text, he read, "Long ago Tz'u-ming was practicing with Master Fen-yang, devoting himself to the study of the Way with Ta-yu, Lang-yeh and four or five others. The bitter cold east of the river kept other students away. Tz'u-ming sat alone without sleeping through the long cold nights. To spur himself to greater effort, he told himself: 'The ancients applied themselves with arduous devotion and attained a purity and radiance that could not help but spread and prosper. Look at me. What am I? I'll be useless if I go on living, and no one will notice if I die. What good am I to the Dharma?'"

When the master read the passage, wisdom that had accumulated from his past lives began to stir within him once again. Once more a deep and determined faith in the Buddha's Dharma formed in his heart. Casting aside all his previous views and notions, he now took as his guiding principle these words of Tz'u-ming.

On the twenty-seventh of the fifth month word reached him of his mother's death. His grief was inconsolable.

There was a mean streak in Baō's nature and most people steered clear of him. But the master thought, "He may be ill-natured, he may be hard on his students, yet where could I find another person with such learning?"

On the fifteenth of the seventh month the summer retreat ended and students began to leave the temple. The master alone remained. One day, Baō saw him washing daikon by the well and went over to speak to him.

"Kaku [Crane]," he said with an affectionate look in his eye. "The young birds are flying off in fine feather, aren't they?"

Hōei 2 (1705) Age 20
In spring the master left Zuiun-ji for Hōfuku-ji in Horado, Mino province, to participate in a summer retreat under head priest Nanzen Keryū. Also attending were Masaki Ryōkō and Tarumaru Sokai, two priests who were vigorously expounding the merits of "ordinary, everyday Zen." Priests and laymen throughout eastern and western Mino province had been converted to their teaching. Someone urged the master to join them. He rebuked him, saying, "Should someone who is devoted to pursuing the Way set store on what he hears people say, and not on what he sees with his own eyes?"

In autumn the master left Hōfuku-ji to pay a visit to Bankyū Echō at Reishō-in. He then went on to take part in the winter *rōhatsu* training under Daigyō Eryū at the Tōkō-ji in Ijira.[13]

Hōei 3 (1706) Age 21

Spring. Leaving Tōkō-ji, the master went to Jōkō-ji, a temple in Wakasa province, to attend Priest Banri's lectures on the *Record of Hsu-t'ang*. While there, he chanced to read a line of verse the Chinese priest Yun-chu Hsiao-shun had written when he had returned to resume the abbotship of Ch'i-hsien temple: "How often I rejoice; how often I grow angry." Tears filled his eyes, as he experienced something he had never known before.[14]

In summer the master learned that Shō Zōsu, a Dharma brother of his, was in Mino province on pilgrimage. He sought him out and persuaded him to make a trip to Shōshū-ji in Matsuyama, Iyo province, where the priest Itsuzen was lecturing on *Three Teachings of the Buddha-patriarchs*. He came upon a passage in *The Sutra of Forty-two Sections*: "A person who follows the Way is like a log floating down a river. Moving along in the current, if it touches neither bank, is not taken up by men, is not obstructed by gods or demons, is not held back in the swirls and eddies, and is not corrupted by rot and decay along the way, it will surely flow into the great sea."[15]

He was ecstatic with joy. Although he had pursued his practice with firm, unwavering faith, he had always been somewhat uncertain whether the wonderful, unsurpassed Way of the Buddhas was within the grasp of a person with his small understanding and merit. Reading these golden words had swept all lingering doubts completely away. He had not yet achieved his goal, yet his mind at that moment was perfectly clear. He felt like someone who, having traveled thousands of miles, had at long last crossed the border into his native land. From this time forth, he kept *Three Teachings of the Buddha-patriarchs* and *Spurring Zen Students Through the Barrier* with him as his constant companions.

Winter. During his visit to the Shōshū-ji, he transcribed a copy of *Three Teachings of the Buddha-patriarchs* that he found at the temple. He was invited to a Buddhist memorial feast at the residence of a high-ranking official of the local clan. The host brought out a number of scrolls of calligraphy to show the guests. He particularly treasured one scroll, which was carefully wrapped in silk. When it was unrolled, the master saw it was an inscription by Daigu Sōchiku.[16] The brushwork was unstudied, almost offhand in manner, and showed no signs of any great or unusual skill. But the master was elated as he realized that the merit of the calligraphy, the quality that commanded such respect, had nothing to do with the skillfulness with which it was written. After that he gave literature, painting, and calligraphy a wide berth and focused his energies solely on the practice of the Way.

Hōei 4 (1707) Age 22
Spring. The master left Shōshū-ji, crossing the Inland Sea to Fukuyama in Bingo province, where he attended lectures at the Shōju-ji on *Praise of the True School*. When the meeting ended, he joined a group of other monks and headed eastward toward his home in Suruga province. As he walked along, he worked with each step he took on the story of the dog and the Buddha-nature.[17] Their route took them past Okayama castle in Bizen province. The master's companions vied with each other in describing the beauties of the castle and surrounding landscape. But the master would have no part of it. "I haven't attained the Way yet," he told himself. "How can I spend time sight-seeing." He kept his eyes tightly shut until the castle was out of sight.

Upon entering Harima province, they put up at a mountain temple. The sight of a rushing mountain stream moved the master to compose a verse:

At the foot of the mountain
The stream flows without end.
If the mind of Zen is thus
How can *kenshō* be far off!

Soon after they resumed their journey one of the monks in the party fell sick. The master helped him by carrying his traveling pack for him. "I'm having a hard time too," one of the others remarked. "I'm not sure I'll be able to make it. You have a sturdy body and seem to have plenty of strength left. Would you mind carrying my pack too?"

Without a sign of reluctance, the master bundled both the monks' travel packs together with his own and threw them onto his shoulders, thinking as he did, "Maybe a good turn like this, trifling as it is, will bring me more quickly to my long-cherished goal of *kenshō*." With each step he took, he struck the ground with his staff, working his way deeper into the Mu koan.

When they reached the city of Hyōgo, they sought passage on a boat. The moon hung overhead as the master's companions, laughing and chatting with the other passengers, settled down to enjoy the trip. The master, taking off his heavy load, lay back to rest. After a short, pleasant nap, he opened his eyes to see the boat was at the harbor entrance.

"Haven't we started yet?" he called to the boatman. "How long are we going to stay here?"

"What are you babbling about, you lead-head," jeered the boatman. "Ten boats went out last night. Most were capsized in the storm. We were the only ones lucky enough to come through it alive. Everyone in the boat was begging the gods and Buddhas for help. I cut off my topknot and pledged a solemn vow to the gods of the sea. You slept and snored through it all. Snorting like a horse. I've spent a good many years at sea but in all my days I've never seen a damnable shavepate with half your piss and vinegar."

The master jumped up with a start and looked around him. His shipmates were sprawled all over the boat. They had towels wrapped around their heads, their faces were the color of dull clay. Some were gasping for breath. Others breathed feebly. The whole boat was so thickly covered with vomit there was no place to set a hand or foot. To express his regret he immediately pressed his palms together and said: "Last night, thanks to the benevolent protection of the guardian sages, it was our good fortune to escape the storm."

They disembarked and found lodging at an inn, where the master administered medicine to his incapacitated companions to help ease their discomfort. Later he offered them these words of caution, "It is said that hidden virtue is requited openly, where all can see it. What happened last night has shown me the truth of those words."

When they entered Ise province, the master heard that Baō had fallen seriously ill and had no one to care for him. "Go on home without me," he told his companions. "I must travel to Mino and take care of Baō." When they began to voice reservations, the master just turned and left. He arrived at Baō's temple and went directly to the old priest's bedside. He spent the next three months nursing Baō and attending to his needs. During the daytime hours he tried pursuing his practice amid the activities of everyday life. The nights he passed in the stillness of samadhi, doing zazen.

One night as he was doing zazen, an oval shape the size of a cat's head appeared above his hands. It recurred several nights running. At first it bothered him, but when he paid no heed to it, it disappeared. The experience made him realize that the obstacles the Evil One creates for a practicer do not come from without but are the products of his own mind.

Another time, as he was sitting through the night in a near-lifeless state, he felt himself suddenly rise into the air and rapidly sail off in a southerly direction. After he had covered several tens of leagues, passing over Toba Castle in southern Ise and seeing the shoreline of the Kii peninsula below him, he suddenly thought, "I'm a Buddhist priest. I can't allow this to continue." He gave a loud shout and found himself sitting back on his zazen cushion as before. Baō, startled by the noise, called out from his sickroom, "Kaku, what are you shouting for?"

By the tenth month, Baō had recovered from his sickness and the master left for home.

That winter, flames were seen burning brightly inside the crater of Mount Fuji.[18] For several days fires belched out and spread down along the central slopes. Rumblings were heard from deep in the earth, and were accompanied by tremors. Thick clouds of smoke and dust blotted out the light of the sun and moon and cast a dark and ominous black pall over the surrounding countryside.

Suddenly, there was a great explosion, and the mountain erupted violently, sending an avalanche of molten lava pouring in fiery streams down the mountain's eastern side. At the same instant, the ground suddenly collapsed, creating a bottomless crater that filled with an incandescent mass of fire. Great squalls of smoke and ash mushroomed out with incredible speed, enveloping the countryside with tremendous blasts of searing heat that sent flashes of lightning forking and darting down from the sky. A hail of red-hot sand and ash flew through the air and rained to earth in a deluge. A series of violent quakes rolled over the earth like giant waves in a raging sea. All the villages and hamlets within range of the newly formed crater—and they were countless in number—were completely inundated, buried under a tremendous onslaught of mud and rocky debris.

Sharp earthquakes rocked the Shōin-ji to its foundations. Temple buildings convulsed and groaned. The master's Dharma brother Tōrin Soshō, the young kitchen attendants, and the servant fled and sought safety outside the village, crouching down in fear. The master remained inside the hall of the temple all alone, sitting straight and erect doing zazen. He pledged to himself, "If I open the eye of *kenshō*, the protection of the Buddhas surely will keep me from harm. If I don't, I'll be crushed beneath the wreckage and destruction."

His elder brother Kokan came and pleaded with him to leave.[19] "How can you stay so calm?" he asked. "This building could be destroyed any second now!" "My fate is in heaven's hands," the master replied, without a trace of fear. Kokan tried several more times to make him change his mind but the master refused to budge. Instead, he used the threat of the imminent peril to gain an even greater concentration in his meditation. When the rumbling and quaking eventually subsided, the master, sitting straight and upright as before, had not suffered so much as a scratch.

Chō Shuso, a disciple of the Ōbaku teacher Egoku Dōmyō, came and stayed for a time at nearby Tokugen-ji. Kin Shuso and two other monks, Genryū and Chiei, were receiving instruction from him. The master paid Chō a visit but did not come away with a favorable impression of him.

Hōei 5 (1708) Age 23

Spring. The master accompanied Chō Shuso and two of his comrades to Eigan-ji in Takada to attend Priest Shōtetsu's lectures on *The Eye of Men and Gods*. Behind the temple was an ancestral shrine dedicated to the daimyos of the local clan. When he wasn't at the lectures, the master would retire to the shrine room and do zazen. He sat day and night, almost forgetting food and sleep.

When he took his seat in the hall to listen to the lecture, his ears did not hear the sound of the priest's voice. When he went into the hall for his meals, his eyes did not take in the things around him. Everyone he saw was floating in a shimmering haze, and his own body was enveloped in white cloud. The external world seemed to be made of purest crystal, all its various shapes perfectly transparent, without the slightest flaw or blemish. He did not attach to any of those appearances, however, and continued to spur himself forward. He felt as though he was moving slowly and surely up a precipitous mountainside carrying a heavy burden on his shoulders.

Through all the hours of day and night, whether he was sitting, lying, moving, or standing still, he was focused doggedly on his koan. This went on for ten days and nights (from the beginning of the second month to the night of the sixteenth). When dawn broke on the seventeenth, he was still sitting totally absorbed in his koan. Suddenly, he heard the echo of a bell ringing in a distant temple. The sound was faint, but the instant it reached his ears the bottom was penetrated, all objects and sensations stripped completely away—it was as if an enormous bell had boomed out right beside his ear. At that instant he achieved a great enlightenment.

He bellowed out at the top of his lungs, "*Ahhh!* Yen-t'ou! Yen-t'ou! You're all right after all! You're all right after all!" and tore down the path to the temple to request an interview with Shōtetsu. He set forth his realization, but when Shōtetsu offered what he thought was only a lame response, the master cuffed him with his hand and stalked off. He sought out [a visiting priest named] Buttō, and spoke to Chō Shuso as well. But he found the responses they made to be wanting too, and left them in a huff, shaking his sleeves.

After that, the master carried his personal views around on his shoulders for all to see, swallowing whole everyone he encountered, telling himself, "No one in the past three hundred years could have penetrated to such a glorious realization. No one in the whole world could parry my Zen thrusts."

Just at that time a monk appeared at the temple requesting permission to stay and attend the lectures. He had a cold, severe look about him, and had a disconcerting way of scrutinizing people by glaring at them over his shoulder. To the senior priests in charge of the meeting he appeared one of those fearless types of monk who might prove difficult to handle. The guestmaster led the new arrival to the annex for visiting monks, where the master had been placed in charge.

"Whenever you have one of these no-account ruffians on your hands, you palm him off on us," said the master. "This isn't a dumping ground for misfits. Why must we accept all these worthless rascals?"

"We don't think he'll respect anything but physical strength," the guestmaster explained. "If that's the case," the master smiled, "I'll take him."

The guestmaster introduced the monk, whose name was Sōkaku, and the two men sat down facing one another.[20]

"I'm Ekaku from southern Suruga," said the master. "I have a mean temper. I like nothing better than giving monks a hard time. If you step out of line, you'll be out of here before you know what's happened."

Sōkaku replied with a deep bow, his forehead touching the floor. The master assigned him a place at the back of the hall and put him to work sweeping and cleaning.

Every day the master and three or four other senior monks would gather in the hall and exchange views on the koans and other matters that the teacher had brought up in the course of the lectures. On one occasion, after the others had left, the master saw Sōkaku approach him.

"He's going to start something after all," he thought.

"Aren't those the senior monks at this meeting?" asked Sōkaku.

"What if they are?" retorted the master.

"I heard you commenting on some old koans," said Sōkaku.

"What about it?" answered the master.

Sōkaku's features turned solemn. "The lecturer was mistaken about that first koan," he said. "You people grasped the meaning. On the other koan, you were mistaken, but his understanding was quite good. All of you missed the essential point on the last one."

"What about your own understanding!" barked the master, taken aback by Sōkaku's remarks.

Sōkaku thereupon presented his own grasp of two or three of the koans. As the master listened attentively, he realized from the penetrating comments Sōkaku made that his understanding was far deeper than his or the other monks'. Mystified, he asked Sōkaku about himself.

"I'm originally from Shinano province," he said. "There's a priest there named Shōju Etan Shuso. He lives in a small hermitage in a remote village named Iiyama. He was a personal student and heir of Shidō Munan in Edo, and a grandson in the Dharma of Gudō Tōshoku. He is a totally dedicated teacher who employs the vital means of the Zen school to instruct students and guide them to higher attainment. I was in his poisonous grasp for many years."

By the time Sōkaku had finished speaking, the master was eager to visit Shōju. He wanted to set right out for Iiyama. "I agree," said Sōkaku. "I think you have the capacity and insight to enter his forge and undergo the refining blows of his hammer. His approach to teaching is clear, however. He wants only authentic seekers—young seeds and saplings that promise to grow up strong and straight. He has a great aversion to large numbers of students and the noise and commotion they bring. When we go, we must go alone. You won't be able to take those companions of yours along."

The master waited until the meeting was over, then he slipped away from the temple and set out at Sōkaku's side for Iiyama.

Until this point in his career, the master had believed confidently that the negotiation of the Way was a relatively easy matter.

Sōkaku admonished him about this, and urged him to read about the lives of the Zen teachers in the *Records of the Transmission of the Lamp*. Following Sōkaku's advice, the master read a section that dealt with the life of the great teacher Bodhidharma. He learned how Bodhidharma had left home to become a monk at the age of six, and had served as an attendant to his teacher Prajnatara for twenty years before he had been able to fully master the secrets of Prajnatara's Zen.[21] The discovery helped to diminish somewhat the rampant pride welling in the master's heart, and this also led to a deepening of wisdom.

The two men arrived at the Shōju-an hermitage in the hamlet of Kamikura below Iiyama castle in the fourth month. There they met Tekiō Etan Anju, the master of Shōju-an hermitage.

(One of the general talks [*fusetsu*] in *Poison Flowers in a Thicket of Thorns* describes Shōju's hermitage as being located deep in the forests surrounding Narasawa village, only a hedgerow removed from the village itself. The master of Shōju-an was known by the priestly names Etan and Dōkyō; Tekiō was his posthumous name. Many years later, in the second month of the second year of the Bunsei era [1819], he was awarded the rank of Dai-ichiza, or First Monk, at Myōshin-ji in Kyoto and became known as Zen Master Dōkyō Etan.)

Shōju was cutting firewood when they arrived. Sōkaku extended a greeting. Shōju glanced around. "This is Kaku Jōza from Suruga," said Sōkaku. "He would like to have an interview with you."

Shōju glanced up again, then grunted a response.

Sōkaku took the master on ahead to the hermitage. "He's an arrogant old gaffer," the master said to Sōkaku. "Sure doesn't seem to think much of me. Tomorrow I want to confront him face to face."

Sōkaku went to Shōju. "Kaku is a friend of mine. Please grant him an interview," said Sōkaku. Shōju agreed to receive the master in his chambers.

The next day when the master went to Shōju's quarters, he took along a verse he had composed to express his understanding. He presented it to Shōju. Shōju grabbed it in his left hand.

"This is what you've been able to learn," he said. He held up his right hand. "Now show me what you can see!"

"If I had any insight to show you, I'd vomit it up right now," the master replied. He made gagging sounds.

Shōju pressed the attack. "What about Chao-chou's Mu? What's your understanding of that?" he said.

"Chao-chou's Mu?" said the master. "No place at all to lay a hand or leg on it!"

Shōju reached out abruptly and seized the master by the nose. "Well," he said, "I just got a real good hand on it."

The master's whole body broke out in cold sweat. His rampant self-esteem was twisted completely away in Shōju's fingers.

"You cave-dwelling Zen corpse!" shouted Shōju, howling with laughter.

The master was unable to offer any response at all.

"Are you really satisfied being like this?" Shōju asked.

"Why shouldn't I be?" countered the master.

Shōju then brought up the story of Nan-ch'uan's Death.

The master put his hands over his ears and rose abruptly to leave the room.

"Honorable monk," called out Shōju.

The master looked back.

"Cave-dwelling Zen corpse!" jeered Shōju.

After that, whenever Shōju caught sight of the master, he just laughed and taunted him with the same words, "Cave-dwelling Zen corpse!"

Each time the master entered his chambers for an interview, Shōju would look at him and say, "Ahh! You're down in a hole. A deep deep pit. It's like I'm standing at the railing of a high pavilion looking down at someone at the bottom of a well."

During an interview in his chambers, he said, "Secretary Ch'en was standing on the top story of a pavilion with a group of government officials.[22] They saw some monks approaching in the distance. 'Zen monks on pilgrimage,' observed one of the officials.

"'No, they aren't Zen monks,' Secretary Ch'en replied. 'Wait till they come closer. I'll test them.'

"Waiting until the monks were directly below them, the

Secretary shouted down, 'Monks!' The monks looked up. The secretary turned to the officials and said, 'You see what I mean?'"

Shōju pressed his attack. "Say something in place of the official!" he demanded. "Make the secretary happy! Give me a word that shows you to be a good and understanding friend!"

The master wrestled with these turning words. Each time he came to Shōju's chambers for an interview, Shōju would lash out at him with great vehemence the moment he crossed the threshold.

When he attempted to speak, Shōju would silence him with deafening shouts.

Next Shōju brought up a verse from Case Fifty-one of the *Blue Cliff Record*: "It says, 'Living the same life makes us understanding friends.' But I don't want to know about that. I want to know what's being revealed in the words 'Dying the same death separates us completely.'"

Shōju continued, "It also says, 'South, north, east, west—we set out for home. In the dead of the night, the same snow-capped peaks, row upon row.' Those lines contain an essential Zen function. Show me how you understand them! Say it! SAY SOMETHING!"

The master thought to himself, "The old man treats me so shabbily because he doesn't know what a splendid enlightenment I've had. I'll need to muster all my strength and confront him in a struggle to the death."

The next time he entered Shōju's room and began his interview, Shōju again scolded him severely. But the master stuck defiantly to his position. Shōju grabbed him by the collar and delivered a score of blows with his fist, knocking the master down. He rolled off the veranda onto the ground and lay there unconscious. When he came to, he saw Shōju glaring down at him, roaring with laughter. His body pouring sweat, he suddenly realized how mistaken he had been. He clambered quickly back onto the veranda and prostrated himself before Shōju.

"You cave-dwelling Zen corpse!" Shōju shouted at him.

The master now threw himself into the koan of Nan-ch'uan's Death with even greater determination. Once he thought he had penetrated it, and went to Shōju's chambers to present his understanding. But Shōju refused to accept it. He chased him out with more abuse—"*Cave-dwelling Zen corpse!!*"

For days, the master labored hard over the koan. He went to the village on a begging round and took up a position beside the entrance to a house. An old woman came out and told him to leave, but the master remained where he was with a stupid look on his face. Angered, the old woman grabbed a bamboo broom. "Didn't you hear me?" she said, brandishing it over her head. "I told you to go somewhere else!" She gave him a hard swat with the broom. At that instant, the meaning of the ancient Zen masters was his. Ta-hui's verse about the round round lotus leaf.[23] Su-shan's Memorial Tower. Nan-ch'uan's Death. And all the other profound, hard-to-penetrate principles he had struggled over—that until now he had been unable to make any dent in whatever—they were all at once clear and distinct before his eyes.

He hurried back to the hermitage in an ecstasy of joy.

Before he was through the gate, Shōju saw from the look on his face what had happened and welcomed him with delight. "You have come through!" he said, confirming the master's realization.

(That same night the master's mother Myōjun appeared to him in a dream. "Thanks to your religious efforts," she said, "I will be able to rise free of the realm of suffering and attain birth in the inner palace of the Bodhisattva Maitreya." "Where are you now?" he asked. "With the King of the Northern Quarter," she said. "Have you suffered?" he asked. "Not in the least," she replied. "I simply reside here in the palace." The master asked her to stretch out her feet so he could see them. When she did this, he saw the soles of her feet were smooth, showing no trace of injury. "It's true," said the master joyfully, "there are no signs of suffering at all." She bade him farewell and was gone. A white light appeared in the sky and marvelous fragrance filled the room; then, rising upward, they vanished into the clear night sky.)[24]

The fifth month. The master told Shōju of his desire to go to Ekōzen-ji in Matsumoto to receive the full precepts. Shōju explained, and then imparted to him, the secrets of the form-less Mind precepts.[25] The master received them with tears of gratitude.

One day the master asked Shōju to instruct him in the Sōtō school's Five Ranks of Apparent and Real. Shōju replied by ask-ing the master to set forth his own understanding of the Five Ranks. When he had finished, Shōju said with a laugh, "Is that it? Nothing more?" The master was silent. "Tung-shan's Five Ranks is most useful for clarifying post-enlightenment training. Its prin-ciple is exceedingly profound," said Shōju, cautioning the master. "If there was nothing more to it than what you have understood, it would simply be a useless piece of temple furniture. Why do you suppose Tung-shan formulated the number of ranks he did?"

Later, Shōju transmitted the secrets of the Five Ranks to the master. But he stopped abruptly at the passage that says, "A dou-ble *Li* hexagram, Apparent and Real totally integrated; Putting one on the other, there are three . . ." The master begged Shōju to continue on and explain the next passage: "Completely trans-formed, there are five."[26]

"You can't expect to get it all in just one sitting," Shōju replied. "Have a look at Tung-shan's verses on the Five Ranks. Don't read anything else. Don't pay any attention to the comments and the-ories others have offered. If you do, you'll find yourself down in that old hole together with the other polecats."

One day Shōju took the master to a memorial service and meal at the house of a temple patron. Their path took them along the edge of a steep cliff. As they made their way along, walking in single file, Shōju suddenly turned and grabbed the master. "'I have the treasure of the right Dharma eye, the wondrous mind of Nirvana, the true Dharma gate of formlessness. This I entrust to you, Mahakashyapa.'[27] What's that about!" he demanded.

The master looked Shōju straight in the eye and gave him a hard slap. Shōju abandoned the exchange.

The master served at Shōju's side for over eight months, receiv-ing his instruction constantly day and night, until at last he pen-etrated the profound core of Shōju's Zen.

As a teacher, Shōju's sole concern was to produce a genuine heir, someone who would be capable of stirring up the winds of the true Zen tradition once again. He often said, "This Zen school of ours began to decline in the Sung dynasty. By the Ming, there wasn't a breath of life left in it. What poison that remains was transmitted to our country, but even here it's like looking for stars in broad daylight. A truly distressing state of affairs."

He also said, "If you scoured the entire world right now, you wouldn't come up with anything but dead men. Imposters with plausible theories. Teachers who can't even extricate themselves from their own opinions. As for final, essential, and ineffable secrets the Buddha-patriarchs have passed down from one to another, why that is something these modern-day priests haven't even glimpsed, not in their fondest dreams."

In later years the master told people, "Whenever I heard Shōju deliver judgments on other Zen teachers, I used to think, 'Why does the old fellow do that? Why does he get so riled up about respected temple priests, men whose eminence is recognized throughout the country?' I even wondered if it might not be because they belonged to a rival teaching line. After I left him, though, I traveled the length and breadth of the land and was able to visit many Zen teachers. Not once, however, did I encounter an authentic master—not a single person who possessed the true and absolute Dharma eye. It wasn't until then I could truly understand how far Shōju's Zen surpassed all the others."

Once, following a heart-to-heart talk with the master, Shōju opened his fan and began fanning the master's back. "You should succeed me and reside here at the hermitage," he said.

"You have Sōkaku," replied the master.

"He won't be able to accomplish any great undertaking," said Shōju. "He doesn't know how to conserve his vital energy."

Another time Shōju looked at the master and said, "By the time you reach my age, I believe you will have achieved great things."

In the eleventh month several of the monks the master had accompanied to Echigo the previous spring showed up at the hermitage. They had traced him there all the way from Takada. Thus far the master had been providing for his own needs by begging so as not to draw on the hermitage's meager store of provisions. The new arrivals, being less fully dedicated to true Buddhist practice, were not so scrupulous about such matters. The master feared their presence might hinder other students practicing at the hermitage. To avoid the possibility of that happening, he decided it would be best to accompany the monks back to their home province. He figured it would always be possible to return later by himself and finish his study under Shōju.

When the morning of departure arrived, Shōju, wearing wooden *geta*, accompanied them along the path for over two leagues. The master's companions began to complain about the slow pace, saying it was causing them to lose valuable time. The master asked Fuhaku,[28] a lay student of Shōju's, to take him back to the hermitage.

"We should be turning back now, master," said Fuhaku. "We could keep going on like this another ten leagues, but it still wouldn't make parting any easier."

"Where is Kaku Zōsu?" said Shōju, looking around. The master stepped forward. Shōju took his hand, gripping it tightly. "I want you to devote all your effort to turning out one or two real monks. Don't try for a large number. If you do, it will be hard to produce a superior student. If you can manage to bring up one or two authentic seedlings, the ancient Zen winds will rise once again."

After a long silence, Shōju at last released the master's hand. Turning to Ryū Zōsu (he later adopted the name Shōgan), he said, "Stay with Kaku Zōsu. He will make sure that your Dharma eye opens."

The master listened intently to Shōju's instructions, tears forming in his eyes. He thanked him and then departed.

He spent the winter retreat at Shōin-ji.

Hōei 6 (1709) Age 24

In spring, the master traveled to Nōman-ji in Koyama, Tōtōmi province, to attend lectures on the *Diamond Sutra* being given by the priest Dankai. In summer, he attended a lecture meeting on

Praise of the True School conducted by Chōmon Zen'a at Bodaiju-in in Sumpu. His Dharma brother Sōkaku came from Shōju-an in Iiyama to attend. When the meeting broke up and the master bid farewell to Sōkaku, he made a request. "Shōju is advanced in years," he said. "Brother Kaku, it may not be possible for me to visit him again. I'd like you to have him teach you the secret of the 'completely transformed, they become five,' phrase of the Five Ranks, so that you can pass it on to me." Sōkaku agreed, and the two men set out on their separate ways.

In examining his everyday behavior, the master could see an inconsistency between the active and meditative aspects of his life. When active he was never able to experience a true sense of freedom. As far as the realization he had attained was concerned and his grasp of the words of the ancients, he was sure both were exceedingly sharp and clear. To his regret, however, he realized that in the daily affairs of life he was not complete master of his mind and body. When working on a koan during zazen his mind would be calm and focused, yet this same composure was lacking when he returned to the busy world of everyday life.

Although he formulated ideas and principles with a high-minded determination and resolve, when he set about trying to apply those ideas, the influence of his former delusive mental habits would invariably intrude and prevail over the principles he had determined upon. He saw in observing the workings of his mind that in favorable circumstances feelings of attachment would appear in great number, while in unfavorable circumstances feelings of aversion would invariably arise. Under his very gaze, joy and anger, love and hate, worries and anxieties, compassion and fear would come and go, appearing and reappearing. He was unable to correct this tendency through ordinary intellectual means, and lacked the power to transform external conditions through the vital Zen function of "going beyond."

"Could it be," he reflected, "that the way of *kenshō* is just another of those words devoid of truth and substance? When the Zen patriarchs of old achieved their great transformation, weren't they like the dragon who obtains lasting and unrestricted freedom the instant he reaches a drop of water?

"The difference between the teachings of greater and lesser vehicles is a difference in the depth of the teachings that students are given to dispel their illusions. Shravakas reach a state of non-defilement by meditating on the Fourfold Truth. Pratyeka-buddhas attain Nirvana by contemplating and realizing the twelve-fold chain of dependent co-origination. Bodhisattvas develop extraordinary powers by realizing the true emptiness of all things. Zen monks turn directly within themselves to eliminate attachments to Buddha-wisdom above even as they dispel the influence of delusory mental habits below.

"I feel like a physician who possesses a wonderful knowledge of medicine but who has no effective means of curing an actual illness. I already know the remedy for discrimination. I have grasped the secrets our school has for 'going beyond'. Yet here I am still suffering from illness myself. How can I possibly hope to cure other sentient beings of their afflictions?

"There is no doubt where the cause of my problem lies. Having achieved *kenshō*, I have penetrated the nature of discrimination. But because my ties to life are still not completely severed, and because the power I might derive from samadhi is also not yet mature, I still have trouble integrating the Dharma truth I have grasped into my daily life."

The master now took the whip in hand and with his jaw set firmly and eyes open wide he once again "spurred the dead ox forward." While engaged in the affairs of every day, he pursued practice within activity; while doing zazen, he immersed himself in the tranquility of samadhi. Sleeping and eating were virtually forgotten.

In winter he went to Hōun-ji in Suruga and helped Priest Keirin instruct students.

Hōei 7 (1710) Age 25

When spring came the master left Hōun-ji and returned directly to Shōin-ji. He then joined a group that included Daigi, Shōgan, and Rokuin and went to Hōdai-ji in Sumpu, Suruga province, to attend Jōsui's lectures on the *Blue Cliff Record*. Once they entered the temple gates, sake would not be allowed, so they decided to stop off for a few cups somewhere along the way. At the Iwabu-chi post station they made for a drinking establishment. There, after drinking their fill, they chanted out a pledge in the form of a mantra: "*Sakasaraba, Sakasaraba*," Farewell to sake! Fare-well to sake!

Sōkaku arrived from Shōju-an during the lecture meeting, as he had promised. The master asked him for the secret of the "completely transformed" passage of the Five Ranks.

"It's not easy," said Sōkaku.

"Sōkaku," said the master. "Would it make it any easier if we enlisted the aid of some liquid Prajna (sake)?"

Denryū, Kyōsui, Shōgan, Rokuin, and others went and tracked down a flask of sake. Sōkaku's cup was filled, but as he raised it to his lips the master caught his hand.

"You can drink after you give me the secret," he said.

"No," Sōkaku said, "let go of my hand."

"If I let you drink all that sake," explained the master, "you won't be in any shape to explain anything."

Unable to come up with any reason to refuse, Sōkaku finally began to explain the passage. He had hardly begun, having uttered only the words, "completely transformed, they become five," when the master suddenly penetrated the meaning.

"Stop!" he cried out. "I've got it! I understand it now!"

"Don't stop him!" said the others indignantly. "We don't understand it yet."

"You can always get it from me," Hakuin replied.

By then, Sōkaku had finished off several cups of sake and they all had a good laugh.

The next day when the master found time to be alone with Sōkaku he explained the meaning he had grasped. Not a word he spoke was inconsistent with the teaching Shōju had entrusted to Sōkaku.

But the master's lack of freedom in his everyday activity still showed no sign of improvement. Weakened by long years of ardu-ous training, he was set upon by the demons of sickness. The heat in his heart began to mount upward into the area of his neck and head, parching and drying out his lungs. He consulted physicians but they were unable to help him. Twelve morbid symptoms appeared.

(1. Fire-like burning in the head. 2. Loins and legs cold as ice. 3. Eyes constantly watering. 4. Ringing in the ears. 5. Instinctive shrinking from sunlight. 6. Irrepressible sadness in darkness or shade. 7. Thinking an intolerable burden. 8. Recurrent bad dreams sapping the strength. 9. Emission of semen during sleep. 10. Restlessness and nervousness during waking hours. 11. Difficulty digesting food. 12. Cold chills unrelieved by heavy clothing.)

He became just like a confirmed invalid, losing all interest in the concerns of the world and his fellow men. But he decided that instead of just sitting back and letting himself rot away, he might as well try to find a physician who could cure him. He set out from Shōin-ji, traveling westward. When he reached Reishō-in in Mino province someone told him about a man called Hakuyū who lived in a cave in the hills of Shirakawa in the eastern part of Kyoto.

(Hakuyū's family name is unknown. In his youth he served Ishikawa Jōzan, but upon falling ill he left him to seek a means of regaining his health. At the age of twenty he encountered a mysterious stranger from whom he learned a meditation technique called the "soft butter method," as well as the art of "refining the cinnabar center." He then went into the mountains and lived a reclusive life without any fixed abode. At the age of seventy or thereabouts he lived for a time at Shisendō, the residence of Ishikawa Jōzan. Finally, he chose as a place of retirement a small plot of land among the hills of Shirakawa and lived there for over twenty years. It is not known where he died. Later, there was a rumor that someone had met him in the mountains of Wakasa province.

In Shirakawa I [Tōrei] heard from a stone-cutter that Hakuyū had once mentioned to his father that he was looking for a cave to live in. The stone-cutter's father told Hakuyū, "There's a cliff near my quarry that has a deep cave-like opening. You can live there if you find it to your liking. Hakuyū went and made the cave his residence. People would occasionally invite him for meals, or bring him fruits of the season. He had a constant stream of visitors. He was around ninety years old when he died. Examples of his calligraphy are sometimes seen.

When my late teacher [Hakuin] wrote in *Idle Talk on a Night Boat* that Hakuyū had taught Ishikawa Jōzan and that he had lived to be three hundred years old, I believe it was a case of his memory playing tricks on him. Because of that, some people have criticized him as a man who indulged in idle talk. In years past when I was living in Kyoto, I scoured around seeking information about Hakuyū. That is how I uncovered these facts about his life from the stone-cutter of Shirakawa.)

The person said, "This Hakuyū is well versed in the medical arts. He has grasped the secrets of the Way of the Sages as well. His behavior makes him appear to the world as an ignoramus, a man who cannot even speak without stuttering. He always keeps his virtue to himself and conceals his wisdom, so when people come to see him, his only response is, "I don't know." Or he answers in such a thick country accent that people can only smile at him. Unless you can convince him of your sincerity, he'll probably just treat you as he does any other passerby."

Greatly bolstered by this news, the master left Reishō-in at once and headed for Shirakawa. When he reached Kyoto he continued on without stopping, asking directions along the way. At the eastern edge of the city, he trekked several *ri* up into the mountains, and came at last to a cave hidden among the cliffs. A bamboo blind hung down over the entrance. Lifting it up, he performed a deep bow and introduced himself. "I am one who is devoted to the practice of the Way," he said. "I have been plagued for some time now by an incurable illness. Master Hakuyū, people have told me you are deeply versed in the Way of the ancient sages. They say you only pretend to be ignorant and feign a speaking impediment. I beg you to help me. Please, use the secret knowledge you possess to cure me of my affliction."

Hakuyū made a perfunctory gesture with his hand as if to dismiss the master's words. "You heard wrong," he said. "I'm no physician. Not a sage, either. Just someone who has distanced himself from the world because of illness. I'm embarrassed to have a holy monk like yourself making a long trip to pay me a visit."

But the master, not to be put off, continued to beg Hakuyū earnestly for his help. Finally, with a casual movement of his hand, Hakuyū took the master's wrist. He examined his pulses at the nine pulse points to check the working of his internal organs. His brow furrowed into a dark frown. "Not good," he said. "You have become ill because you pushed yourself too hard in your pursuit of the Way. When someone has depleted the vital *ki* in his internal organs as you have, it is very difficult to replenish it. Curing such a condition is a formidable undertaking.

"Acupuncture, moxacautery, or medicines bring no relief. Meditation caused your problem and you will never get back on your feet unless you accumulate some merit through Introspective Meditation (*Naikan*). As the saying goes, 'When you fall to the earth, it is from the earth that you must raise yourself up.'"

"Please, teach me the essentials of Introspective Meditation," said the master.

Hakuyū solemnly proceeded to explain to him the secret method of Introspective Meditation.

(The oral transmission Hakuyū gave the master is found in *Idle Talk on a Night Boat.*)

When the master came to know the secret ways of the immortal sages, he realized for the first time that the exhalation samadhi and inhalation samadhi, as well as Tathagata Zen and Patriarchal Zen, were father and mother to both the unimpeded activity of the Buddha-patriarchs and the Sages' ultimate attainment of non-defilement.

It was with reluctance that he parted from Hakuyū and returned to Shōin-ji. There he devoted himself singlemindedly to cultivating the meditation techniques he had learned. But before long the heat in his heart was mounting upward into the region of his neck and head. It continued to grow in intensity until it was almost unbearable. He found he could obtain some relief by discontinuing the meditation and doing nothing at all. But as soon as he resumed the practice and made the slightest exertion to control his mind, the heat would start to rise. Recalling having heard that when a morbid upward flow of primal *ki* such as this continued unchecked, it inevitably ended in death, he decided to put it to the test.

He went through his belongings, assembling notes and manuscripts he had accumulated during his years of koan study, and committed them to the fire. He made sure he had enough money for his funeral expenses, then he sat down and began meditating, detached and aloof, determined to sit his way through to the end. Soon *ki* energy, moving against the natural flow, began rising into the area of his upper chest. It gradually increased in intensity, pulsating up through his throat and into his jaw. As it continued moving upward, he felt a throbbing inside his nose, and reaching into his eyes. A pair of ball-shaped objects suddenly seemed to pop out from his eye-sockets. Catching at them, he felt an intense, stabbing pain in his brain. He held on desperately to the two objects, but they broke free, soaring quickly upward like a pair of skylarks and disappearing into the sky. Immediately his heart felt lighter. His sharpness and alertness returned. He had succeeded at last in severing himself from the illness that had been oppressing him for so many years.

He devoted the summer months to zazen, practicing together with Sōkaku and several other monks of his acquaintance. When autumn arrived, the senior priest Setsu Jōza of Ketsujō-ji came to Shōin-ji and lectured on the *Record of Lin-chi* at the temple's request.

Shōtoku 1 (1711) Age 26

Spring. While visiting Ryōkoku-ji in Tōtōmi province the master read the following passage in *Collection of Sand and Pebbles*:[29] "The deity of Kasuga Shrine addressed Gedatsu Shōnin of Kasagi, declaring, 'Since the time of the first Buddha Kuruson, those wise men and eminent priests who have lacked the Bodhi-mind have all fallen into the realm of demons.'" The words struck terror into the master's heart; he was covered with gooseflesh and the hair rose up all over his body.

In the second month he set out with a group of monks that included Shōgan and Rokuin. They visited Yōgen-in in the town of Sakura, Shimōsa province, and stayed on in the training hall, which was run by a priest of the Myōshin-ji line named Daiga. The head monk at Yōgen-in was Tettsū Shuso. During a discussion one day, Tettsū held up his pipe and pointing to the neck of the pipe bowl, said, "This doesn't look like a goose. Why is it called a goose neck?"

The master grabbed the pipe from Tettsū's hand, held it up by the mouth-piece (*suikuchi*) and said, "This isn't sour (*sui*). Why is it called a mouth-piece?"

A monk witnessing the exchange said, "You didn't answer the senior monk's question." The master struck him.

From Yōgen-in, the master went to Sōen-ji in Shimōsa to received instruction from head priest Tetsuzui. While he was there he met a strange monk by the name of Chōshu Dōnin who was residing at Sōen-ji at the time.

Winter, the eleventh month. News reached the master that his teacher Sokudō was ill. He left immediately for Daishō-ji to care for him. When he wasn't looking after Sokudō, he spent all his spare time doing zazen, never sitting for less than eight sticks of incense a night.

Shōtoku 2 (1712) Age 27
The master used his free hours during the day to "illuminate his mind with the teachings of the ancients." At night, when he was not busy preparing food or medicine for his teacher, he devoted himself to zazen. One day during his reading he happened upon a verse by Master Hsu-t'ang: "When I saw you off, there was a tall bamboo at the gate; / Its leaves, moving in the pure breeze, joined me in waving farewell."[30] He felt like someone moving along a dark night trail who had suddenly obtained a bright lamp. The meaning of the old saying about the ancients achieving a "samadhi of words and letters" when they reached this stage in their training was now perfectly clear to him.

Summer. He returned to Shōin-ji and lectured on *Bodhidharma's Six Gates*.

Autumn. On the twenty-fourth day of the eighth month, he received word of Sokudō's death. He went and collected his remains and brought them back to Shōin-ji.

Shōtoku 3 (1713) Age 28

The death anniversary of his teacher Tanrei fell during the first month. He burned incense at the altar, performed bows, and offered a verse:

A wind blows east over India, China and Japan,
Filling branches with flowers of different kinds;
In all those pleasant springtime shapes and colors
I see the features of my late master's ugly face.

The master heard that Jakuji of Bungo province had been appointed Shuso at Kenkoku-ji in Ise province (Jakuji later took the name Jōsan and resided at Kōfuku-ji in Shimōsa) and was making a name for himself at lecture meetings being held there. He put on his traveling gear and set out for Ise to pay Jakuji a visit. As he was passing the post station at Yui, he was accosted by a young boy selling candy.

"Please buy some of these," the boy said. "Buy them, whether you want them or not!"

"How truly he speaks," the master reflected with a sigh. "If someone has truly dedicated his life to the practice of the Way, he must continue forward, no matter what, whether he sees results or not, until he reaches his ultimate goal."

From Yui he proceeded directly to Kenkoku-ji, where he took part in a lecture meeting on the *Record of Hsu-t'ang* conducted by the priest Gikai. He also attended supplementary talks given by the senior monk Jakuji Shuso, but nothing either man said inspired him in any way.

He had heard that the eminent priest Kogetsu Zenzai had attained deep understanding after wrestling for many years with Master Ta-hui's verse about the round round lotus leaves. Kogetsu was widely acclaimed as the most virtuous priest in all Kyushu. The master was eager to visit him, hoping that with Kogetsu's help, he might be able to clear up his own doubts about Ta-hui's verse.[31]

After leaving Kenkoku-ji he headed west over the Suzuka range. He encountered a rain-swollen mountain torrent that had overflowed its banks, inundating the road. He hitched up his robe and began wading across. After slogging several hundred feet, he came to a broad expanse of water. At that instant, he suddenly penetrated into the infinite vastness of Ta-hui's verse. Beside himself with joy, he lost his footing and toppled over into the water. Some travelers came along and tried to help him up. But when he just lay back in the mud, roaring with laughter, they backed away from him, thinking he had taken leave of his senses.

Upon arriving in southern Kyoto, he took lodgings at a temple. There he overheard some monks talking about some of the marvelous incidents people ascribed to Master Kogetsu.

"Once when Priest Kogetsu prostrated himself before a statue of Manjushri Bodhisattva, he saw Manjushri bow in response. Kogetsu mentioned this to Master Gakuō, founder of his temple, during an intimate conversation they were having."[32]

"One morning, the god of the mountain appeared to Kogetsu in a dream, seeking his help in liberating some lost spirits that had been appearing in the night."

"Kogetsu is truly an old Buddha—a teacher like him rarely appears in the world."

The monks' interest in Kogetsu did not go beyond such discussions of strange and marvelous events that had been attributed to him. Nothing the master heard from them would have enabled him to get a true picture of Kogetsu's Zen teaching. Hence he could only furrow his brow and think, "If that's the kind of priest Kogetsu is, there would be nothing to gain by visiting him." He changed his plans and struck out northward for Wakasa province.

While he was stopping to rest at a roadside teashop in Shirakawa, he saw a young boy of aristocratic bearing pass by. The boy was carrying a bush warbler in a cage. The shopkeeper bowed to the boy and said, "Where are you going, young sir?"

"Lord So-and-so has a warbler that is universally praised for the elegant beauty of its song," the boy replied. "I am going to visit his residence. I want to put my bird near his, so it will learn to sing with the same beautiful voice."

"Even that young boy knows what he's about," thought the master mournfully. "Can I, a Buddhist priest, do less?"

He heard about a priest in Wakasa province named Tetsudō, who had studied under Sekiin Sōon for many years and was reputed to be an outstanding teacher. He went to Tetsudō's temple, Enshō-ji, and stayed with him through the end of the summer practice session. He then traveled to Hōun-ji in Kawachi province, hoping to receive instruction from the incumbent, Egoku Dōmyō.

The master introduced himself to Egoku. "I'm confident I have grasped the essentials of the Way," he said. "But in my everyday life I'm still unable to reach the realm of great peace and tranquility, great emancipation. Please tell me what to do."

Egoku said, "A person in your situation should live in the mountains. Remain until you wither away together with the plants and trees."

Following Egoku's advice, the master proceeded to nearby Mount Makino-o to find a hermitage where he could live and engage in solitary practice. He was forced to give up the idea and leave when the abbot of the temple that owned the mountain refused to grant him permission to stay.[33]

He had heard about a Sōtō priest named Tesshin at the nearby Inryō-ji. Tesshin had died some years before but the master was confident that if he visited Inryō-ji he would be able to learn something about Tesshin and his Zen from the people and traditions he found there. He went to Izumi province and hung his traveling staff up in Inryō-ji's training hall. Although the temple was governed by an extremely strict set of regulations, he found that almost all trace of Tesshin's influence had vanished.[34]

One day, as the master was with the other monks sweeping and cleaning in the garden behind the temple, he noticed a tiny rundown hut. Inside, he saw a copy of the *Nirvana Sutra* lying on a desk. His interest stimulated, he asked who lived in the hermitage. A monk told him it was a man named Jukaku Dōnin. "He served as Tesshin's attendant for many years. He had great aspirations but was held back by a certain carelessness in his make-up. Now he keeps pretty much to himself."

The master sought Jukaku out. He came upon an elderly man with an unsightly face and a robe hanging in tatters from his body.

He looked to be half-demented, and ran off when he saw the master approach. The master went after the old man and was finally able to corner him. He caught hold of his robe to keep him from running away again, and said, "Wait a moment, elder brother. I've traveled a long way because I wanted to learn something about Master Tesshin's Zen. I'd be much obliged if you could tell me how he taught the monks here at Inryō-ji."[35]

Jukaku stared at the master in amazement. "Wherever you go," he said, "you see the true style and traditions of our school lying in the dust, totally forgotten. Nobody's ever come here asking about my teacher. You're the first. Why are you interested in him?"

After that, when time permitted, Jukaku would talk to the master about Tesshin's religious style and the ways and methods he employed in the instruction of his monks.

One night the master sat on into the early hours of the morning. In the gathering light he heard the sound of snow falling from the trees outside the room. Suddenly he penetrated the koan, The Young Woman Comes out of Samadhi. He composed a waka:

If only I could
make you hear
the sound of snow
falling late at night
at the old temple
in the forest of Shinoda!

Shōtoku 4 (1714) Age 29

In spring the master left Inryō-ji and made his way back to Mino province, where he once again visited Priest Nanzen at Hōfuku-ji. He remained there through the summer. While he was at Hōfuku-ji he began to read the *Record of Daitō*. One of the monks said, "Long ago, there was an old temple priest who told his assembly, "I used to regard the utterances in Daitō's records as steep and unapproachable. They seemed like lightning bolts striking at a granite cliff and tearing it apart. Why didn't I realize they were merely verbal Zen—nothing but idle talk and needless speech?"

"Ah! I know just what he means," thought the master. "Chinese masters from the Yuan and Ming dynasties and continuing on right up till the present have left any number of records. But there is not one among them I can even bear to look at. How could Daitō be an exception?" That is why until now the master had put Daitō's records aside and given them no thought. He lectured on them for the first time years later, and then only because his students had requested it. In time he would come to keenly regret the error he had made in accepting unthinkingly the false views current among such wrongheaded monks. Because of that error he had for many years remained ignorant of the timeless and unmatched wisdom contained in Daitō's utterances

In autumn he left Hōfuku-ji and returned to Bankyū at Reishō-in. He stayed until winter and took part in the *rōhatsu* training session. One day, as he was doing *kinhin*, everything heretofore attained suddenly fell away, and he "roamed totally free and unrestricted beyond the mundane world."

Shōtoku 5 (1715) Age 30

Spring. The third month. The master left Reishō-in to seek a remote spot away from the world where he could devote himself single-handedly to the cultivation of the Way. He resolved to continue his quest until he achieved his goal, vowing not to stop even if it cost him his life. He headed east in the direction of the monastery at Mount Kokei. On the way, a man told him of a mountain called Iwataki, which was "cut off on all sides from worldly intrusion. There's nothing there but a tiny hut, but you couldn't ask for a better place to devote yourself quietly to zazen."

The master turned and headed for Iwataki. As he began to climb up into the mountain, he saw an old shaven-headed priest in a field harvesting wheat with some farmers. The priest had a strange glint in his eye and there was something about his appearance that struck the master as being out of the ordinary. He glanced up as the master passed and their eyes met. That night the priest paid a visit to the master's hut. The master took the opportunity to ask the priest—whose name was Sōjun Dōnin—about himself. Sōjun became a frequent visitor to the hut and passed many hours with the master.

One day, the master was out walking on the mountain. He sat down to meditate at the edge of a precipitous cliff. It was a wonderful spot, affording a splendid prospect on all sides. Suddenly, from far below, he heard a man's voice yelling up to him. "Honorable priest! You shouldn't be sitting on that rock!" He immediately climbed down from his perch.

That evening the master continued sitting late into the night. Around midnight, he heard the crunch of feet on the ground outside the hut. There was the creak of a door opening. Someone entered the hut and stood inside. He was huge, at least eight or nine feet in height, with the rough appearance of a mountain ascetic. A loud voice boomed out, "Master Kaku!"

The master did not look around or make any reply. After what seemed a long time, the figure disappeared. The master got up and surveyed the room. The door was secured just as it had been. There was no sign of anyone having entered. He then realized that the visitor who had come to test his mettle was no ordinary being.

The next day someone came to the hut and asked the master, "Did anything unusual happen last night?"

"What do you mean?" the master said.

"That big flat rock you were sitting on yesterday—it's the abode of the god of this mountain," he explained. "Anyone who climbs up there is sure to incur his wrath."

Every day the master chanted sutras and dharanis while beating a small *mokugyo*, endeavoring to deepen his concentration and promote the working of *prajñā* wisdom. One night he heard in the sky above him strains of wonderful celestial music. As he listened, the sounds grew ever more pleasing to his ears. But he simply paid them no heed and focused on contemplating the principle that all forms and appearances are false and empty. The sounds continued for six or seven nights in succession until, suddenly, in the midst of samadhi, he realized they were only figments of his own mind.

Living amid the deep mountain stillness, cut off from intrusions of external sound, with his mind perfectly tranquil and sense of hearing quiet and undisturbed, he found the least exertion of *ki* energy would immediately produce a faint ringing inside his ears. Even the slightest thought was enough to sustain the noise, which resonated deep inside his ears and gave rise to various other sounds. Later the master told his monks, "Those who engage in zazen should just be aware that such things will occur. If you live deep in the mountains practicing by yourself, you will experience Mara's seductions in many forms. They can easily distract you from your training. This is what the sutras mean, 'When the demons are at work within, the demons without gain a foothold.'"

One night as he was doing zazen, a sudden fear took hold in his heart. He could not bring himself to venture outside his hut. "What am I afraid of?" he asked himself. "I'm afraid the goblin will suddenly thrust his loathsome face up in front of me," he answered. "But, after all, what is that face? If a goblin does appear, become a goblin yourself. Confront the goblin with a goblin. What is there to fear? If you are a Buddha, it will be a Buddha as well—one Buddha confronting another Buddha. There is nothing to fear on that account either. When your own mind appears in true suchness, all things in the Dharma universe are seen in their fundamental oneness. Goblins and Buddhas have the same nature. False and true are identical. Where in all this universe can you set up a 'self' or 'other'?"

As he was contemplating these thoughts, all obstructions and impediments, physical and mental, suddenly vanished, and he experienced a state of absolute fearlessness. He later told people, "From that time on, it was the same to me whether things went smoothly or not. Now, even in the presence of those of exalted rank, I am as easy and relaxed as I am in my own sleeping quarters. Even when I am immersed in the noise and myriad appearances of the world, it is as though I am alone by myself meditating in the training hall."

One night that winter he was inspired by a snowfall to compose a waka:

Forget the thought
"how cold it is"—
There once was a man
too busy to sweep
the snow from his floor.[36]

Kyōhō 1 (1716) Age 31

The master continued to practice arduously in the hut on Mount Iwataki. Layman Shikano Tokugen arranged for his son to bring food to the master. But the master recalled those of the past who in pursuing the Way had either abstained from food or else partaken of very little. Their food and clothing were always of the poorest kind. One priest sat for a hundred days, subsisting on half of a dried persimmon twice a day. Others boiled bracken and baked wild yams to sustain their bodies and nourish their *ki* energy.[37] He thought, "Who am I to idly consume these precious offerings?" From then on, he set himself a daily ration of half a handful of rice.

One day, while he was out begging, the master heard a story about National Master Kanzan, who had lived in the neighboring mountains centuries ago.

"When Kanzan received a summons from the emperor and was about to leave the mountains of Ibuka for the capital,[38] an elderly couple approached him with tears in their eyes. 'We are ignorant people,' they said. 'But we have talked it over and come to the conclusion that we have been trespassing against the Buddha's Law. As we approach the end of our days we know we cannot hope to be absolved from the transgressions we have committed. Nevertheless we would be deeply grateful to receive a word from you. Something that would help us as we proceed into the evil paths.'

"'Come closer,' said Kanzan.

"When they did, he had them sit facing each other, one to his left and one to his right. Putting his hands on the backs of their necks, he lowered their heads in front of him until they touched. Then, after a brief pause, he suddenly knocked their heads together, and released them. Although neither the man nor his wife could comprehend the meaning of Kanzan's action, they thanked him with a deep sense of gratitude. Kanzan then set out for the capital."

The master was deeply moved as he listened to the story, realizing the profundity of Kanzan's sincerity and compassion for the old couple.

The master's father Sōi, now bedridden with illness, was deeply concerned about the fate of the family temple. "Our Shōin-ji was founded by Uncle Daizui," he said. "The two of us put a great deal of time and work into building it up. Now it is furnished with all the requisite halls and structures. It is even blessed with splendid tall trees. None of that would have been possible without Daizui's laborious efforts. Unless we take steps now to protect the temple it will before long become a field for the foxes and rabbits. My son Ekaku still hasn't returned. Oh, what are we to do?"

An old family servant (his name was Yake Shichibei) said to Sōi, "If it's Ekaku you want, I'll track him down for you and get him to come back." "But it would be very difficult to find him, no matter how hard you searched," said Sōi.

"Well, he can't have flown off to another world," Shichibei said. "I'll just comb the entire country, search everywhere under heaven, until I find him."

Taking some traveling money, Shichibei started out at once in the direction of the capital. He scoured each of the provinces he passed through—Tōtōmi, Mikawa, and Owari—one after another. Finally, at a small village in the mountains of Mino province, he heard talk of a solitary monk who was living on Mount Iwataki engaged in a severe regimen of religious practice. Shichibei went directly to Iwataki, made his way up the mountain, and sought the monk out.

The master could scarcely believe his eyes. "Shichibei, what are you doing here?" he asked in astonishment.

"Reverend priest," said Shichibei, "while you conceal yourself here like this, enjoying your spiritual exercises, Shōin-ji is without a priest. Not to mention your father, who is very ill—no one can say how much longer he has left. Don't you think you have an obligation to return home and repay some of the debt you owe him?"

Unable to defend himself against the sharp censure from the faithful old servant, the master gave in. He returned home around the final week of the eleventh month. His father was overjoyed to see him and immediately had the priest's quarters at Shōin-ji cleaned so that the master could move in and rest up from his trip.

The master came twice daily, morning and evening, to see how his father was doing. Yet he still harbored hopes, given the chance, of going back and resuming his practice at Iwataki. His father issued instructions to his brothers, children, and the senior lay members of Shōin-ji: they were to make a concerted effort to keep the master at the temple.

Kyōhō 2 (1717) Age 32

Parishioners of Shōin-ji, in league with the abbot of Seiken-ji (his priestly name was Shudaku; his *gō* was Yōshun) and other senior Rinzai priests belonging to the same teaching line as the master, devised a plan of action.[39] Assembling on the tenth day of the first month at the special feast held on the death anniversary of the master's teacher Tanrei Soden, they peremptorily performed a ceremony installing the master as the resident priest at Shōin-ji.

At the time, Shōin-ji was in an almost indescribable state of disrepair. At night, the stars shone through the roofs. The *tokonoma* was sodden with rain and dew. It was necessary for the master to wear a sedge hat as he moved about the temple attending to his duties. He had to wear wooden sandals when he was in the main hall to conduct memorial ceremonies. The assets of the temple had passed into the hands of creditors. Ceremonial equipment and other temple furnishings had all been pawned. There was an old servant named Kakuzaemon (posthumous religious name Jitsujō Dōkyū) who gathered wood for fuel, collected vegetables, and managed to produce two meals morning and night. Another monk who showed up was made an attendant of the master and was able to help supply the kitchen through daily begging rounds. One day, the master, taking a look at the monk's haggard face, exclaimed dolefully, "Oh my, look what's happened to you from staying and helping me. The halls haven't any door-panels in them. We can't use the room lamps. About the only assets around here worth noting are the moonlight and the sound of the wind. I have no way whatever of making things easier even for a single monk like you!" To show his gratitude he gave the monk some personal instruction using *Ta-hui's Letters* as a text.

As he looked back over the time he had spent in the mountains of Iwataki, he was moved to compose a waka.

> Good times, hard times too
> both fade far away,
> So happy am I now
> I'll never want to seek
> another mountain again.

A citizen of Hara named Shōji turned up at the temple one day bringing a sack of rice slung over his shoulder.

In autumn Ehatsu Zōsu came to stay and began serving as the master's attendant.

In winter the master lectured on *Precious Lessons of the Zen School*.

On the twenty-first day of the twelfth month the master's father passed away.[40]

Kyōhō 3 (1718) Age 33

In spring the master set out with Shōgan Genryū to attend a memorial feast at Chōkō-ji in Hara. On the way, as they were walking along a narrow trail, the master suddenly penetrated the heart of Nan-ch'uan's Death, achieving a far deeper understanding than before. He was ecstatic and began striking the ground again and again with his staff. Shōgan marveled uncomprehendingly at his behavior.

Tetsuzui came all the way from Sōen-ji in Shimōsa to seek the master's personal instruction. He was one hundred and three years old at the time. The master arranged for him to stay at the Funi-an in nearby Matsunaga. In the course of his study at Shōin-ji he and the master formed a fast friendship.

Summer. The master lectured on Bodhidharma's *Breaking Through Form*.[41]

The master's lay student Shōji Yūsai had a brother who went by the studio name Yūtetsu. Yūtetsu possessed an unusually keen intellect. Once as he was about to leave to attend to some business in Edo the master told him, "Birth and death is the one great matter; change comes swiftly. When you arrive at your final hour, what kind of utterance will you make?" Yūtetsu did not know what to answer. The master assigned him Daitō's waka about "seeing with the ears, hearing with the eyes" to work on. (It is found in Daitō's *Ox-herding Poems for Leisurely Humming*: "When the ear sees / And the eye hears / One has no doubts; / How naturally the rain drips / From the eaves!")

Once, when they were together in the garden, the master tested Yūtetsu by asking, "'When you grab Mount Sumeru and smash it to smithereens, the empty void shatters into two, three, four.' What is the principle of that?" Yūtetsu bent down, picked up a lump of dirt, and threw it to the ground. The master abandoned the exchange.

In autumn the master lectured on the *Record of Lin-chi*.

In the eleventh month, Myōshin-ji, the headquarters temple in Kyoto, awarded him the rank of First Monk (*Dai-ichiza*). He adopted the name Hakuin at this time and became an heir of Tōrin Soshō, who was his elder brother in the Dharma.

Kyōhō 4 (1719) Age 34

In spring, two monks came and asked Hakuin to lecture on *Praise of the True School*. He agreed. (This marked the first time he lectured on a text at the request of monks.)

In summer Sōnin from Mino province and Genshin from Kai came and became the master's attendants.

Unzan of Kongō-ji and the master were longtime friends, having known each other since they were seven or eight years old. Unzan came regularly to study with the master, and later achieved a realization. Whenever Hakuin left Shōin-ji to travel Unzan always accompanied him.[42]

Kyōhō 5 (1720) Age 35

Spring (the third month). While Hakuin was in Izu enjoying the hotspring at Yoshina he was visited by Priest Batei.*

Autumn. Hakuin went and spent a day at Seiken-ji, where Yōshun Shudaku was lecturing on the *Blue Cliff Record*. The next day, after Hakuin had left, Yōshun told the assembly, "I had trouble lecturing yesterday with the priest from Shōin-ji in attendance." This confession greatly perplexed the monk Gedatsu from Muryō-an, who was attending the meeting. "How strange for a priest of Yōshun's stature to feel that way," he mused. "Now that I know who he is, I must go and see him face to face." After the meeting ended, Gedatsu went to Shōin-ji and began to study under the master. (He was the first monk Hakuin formally accepted as a student.)

* (It is not known where Batei was from or to what teaching line he belonged. He practiced with the Ming priest Hsin-yueh Hsing-t'ao in the city of Mito and served as head monk [*Shuso*] under him. Batei's stock answer, when people asked his age, was to tell them he was seventy years old. Hakuin chaffed him about it. "You became head monk when you were a child. As an old man, you served as attendant. Is that the way they do things in Ming China?"

"What do you mean!" retorted Batei.

"Well," replied Hakuin. "I've heard that when you served as head monk at one of Hsin-yueh's practice sessions, Mokushitsu was his personal attendant. Judging from Mokushitsu's present age, you couldn't have been more than about fifteen at the time."

"Impertinent priest," chided Batei. "Pulling people's legs like that."

"On the contrary," said Hakuin. "You're the one's been pulling my leg." Batei gave a hearty laugh.)

Kyōhō 6 (1721) Age 36

The monk Ekyū of Rinsen-ji in Shimizu came to study and underwent the ceremony making him a disciple of the master. During the winter a group of twenty traveling monks arrived and sought permission to stay and study at Shōin-ji. The master refused them with great firmness, but they were not to be deterred. They sat down in a row in the garden and remained there for several days until finally and reluctantly the master relented. He held a lecture meeting for them on the *Letters of Ta-hui*. Tetsuzui came from Funi-an to help.

At the start of the tenth month, on the sixth day, word reached him that Shōju Rōjin had died.

Kyōhō 7 (1722) Age 37

In summer the master lectured on the *Treatise on the Original Man*.

Kyōhō 8 (1723) Age 38

The quality of the provisions in the temple larder grew steadily worse. The monks made the rounds of nearby shops begging for *shōyu* that had gone rancid and was about to be thrown out. Once at mealtime the temple cook, Teki Zōsu, served some cold soup. The surface was alive with wriggling maggots.

"Pay more attention to your work," scolded Hakuin.

"Maggots breed in rancid *shōyu*," said Teki. "I couldn't bring myself to kill them, so I just poured it all into the stock and made the soup without heating it."

"You mean that's all there is?" asked the master with a laugh.

"We never have extra provisions," said Teki. "We beg what others are about to discard and use it for the morning and evening meals. Why don't we set the soup aside and wait until the maggots have all hatched. Then we can ladle them out."

One day Tetsuzui came to Shōin-ji and stayed the night. The master opened up his heart as they talked and exchanged views about matters of past and present. During the night, Jizō Bodhisattva appeared to the master in a dream. His body was of infinite magnitude, filling all space. The master sat in attendance at the Bodhisattva's side, and asked him, "How do I incorporate the attainment I've achieved into my everyday life?" The Bodhisattva looked around at him and said, "As if sitting inside a thicket of razor-sharp thorns and briars." Cold shivers passed up and down the master's spine. His hair stood on end.

When dawn came, he described his dream to Tetsuzui.

"Don't let it worry you," advised Tetsuzui. But the master told someone, "It was a place Tetsuzui has yet to experience."

Kyōhō 9 (1724) Age 39
During the summer the master lectured on *Po-shan's Cautionary Words*. About twenty monks attended the meeting.

Kyōhō 10 (1725) Age 40
Hakuin had resided at Shōin-ji for ten years. During that time he had given himself singlemindedly to his practice and had endured great difficulty and privation without ever deviating from a spare, simple way of life. He followed no fixed schedule for sutra-chanting or other rituals. When darkness fell he would climb inside a derelict old palanquin and seat himself on a thick cushion he placed on the floorboard. The young boys studying at Shōin-ji would then come, wrap a futon around the master's body, and cinch him tightly into this position with a rope. There he would remain, without moving, looking just like a painting of Bodhidharma, until the following day, when the boys would come and untie him so he could relieve his bowels and take some food. The same routine was repeated every night.

Neither did he neglect the words and sayings of the Buddhas and patriarchs. They never left his side. He used them to verify the meaning of the ancient worthies' injunction "to illuminate the old teachings with the mind, to illuminate the mind with the old teachings."

He had a room built a hundred paces or so behind the abbot's quarters where he could devote himself quietly to zazen, free from all outside cares. Once he entered the room, no one except the monks permitted to receive his personal instruction dared to approach him.

He observed this same rigor and scrupulousness throughout his residence at Shōin-ji.

One night he dreamed that his mother Myōjun came and presented him with a robe of purple silk. When he accepted the garment, he felt heavy weights in both of the sleeves. On examining the sleeves, he found in each one an old mirror about five or six inches in diameter. The mirror in the right sleeve shone with a brilliance that pierced deeply into his heart. His body and everything else—mountains, rivers, the great earth itself—were like a clear and bottomless pool. He was unable to discern even a flicker of light from the mirror in the left sleeve. But no sooner did he make that observation than he suddenly realized with blinding clarity that the mirror on the left shone with a brilliance millions of times brighter than the one on the right. From that time forth, whatever he saw, it was as though he was looking at his own face. He now grasped for the first time the meaning of the words about a Tathagata seeing the Buddha-nature in his own eye.

Kyōhō 11 (1726) Age 41

Autumn. Hakuin hung up the schedule for sutra-chanting on the announcement board. At the suggestion of Tōhō Sokin of Tokugen-ji he read the *Lotus Sutra*. One night, as he was reading in the Chapter on Parables, a cricket began shrilling at the foundation stones of the temple. The instant the sound reached his ears the deep principle of the *Lotus* was suddenly his. The doubts and uncertainties that had arisen at the beginning of his religious quest and remained with him all this time now suddenly dissolved and ceased to exist. He realized the understanding he had gained in all his many satoris had been greatly mistaken. He could see with perfect clarity the reason for the *Lotus*'s reputation as the king of sutras. He let out an involuntary shout and began weeping uncontrollably. He was able to see for the first time the enlightened words and deeds that had marked Shōju's everyday life, and to understand that when the World-honored One spoke, his tongue lacked all sinew and muscle and moved with perfect freedom.

From this moment on Hakuin lived in a state of great emancipation. The enlightening activity of the Buddha-patriarchs, the Dharma eye that can grasp the sutras—they were now decisively his, without any lack whatever.[43]

The progress of the master's religious life may be divided into three general periods—the first period (from his 15th to his 23rd years) beginning when religious doubts first arose in his mind and ending with his penetration of the fundamental ground; the second period (from his 23rd to his 27th year), starting with his investigation under Shōju Rōjin of the profundities of the ultimate principle; and the third period (from his 27th to his 41st year), when he continued refining his attainment and experienced the contradictions in the aspects of activity and non-activity, phenomena and ultimate truth. I have for this reason titled the first part of this biography Practice Leading To Enlightenment.

PART 2: THE PRACTICE RESULTING FROM ATTAINMENT

Kyōhō 12 (1727) Age 42

Mr. Shōji had a fifteen-year-old daughter named Satsu.[44] She was sharp as a tack and possessed extraordinary powers of insight. Whenever her father went to practice at Shōin-ji Satsu would accompany him. She would sit from evening until dawn in a state of total absorption. Before long she experienced an enlightenment. Once her father, seeing her doing zazen on top of a bamboo chest, scolded her.

"What are you doing!" he said. "Don't you know there's an image of Buddha in that chest!"

Satsu's reply astounded him: "Then please allow me to sit where there's no Buddha!"[45]

One day a person named Rimpen ("Completely Encompassed") came for an interview with the master. After he expressed the understanding he had achieved, the master tested him: "Have you completely encompassed the great void?"[46]

Rimpen inscribed a circle in the air with his finger.

"That's still only about half," said the master.

Satsu was sitting off to the side. She said, "Only a moment ago it was completely encompassed."

The master nodded his agreement.

A monk asked Satsu, "What is the meaning of the words, 'Breaking up white rock inside a poppy seed!'"[47]

Satsu immediately threw her teacup to the floor, smashing it.

Another time the master gave her a koan and asked, "What is your understanding?"

"Excuse me master, could you go over that once more?" she said.

The master began to repeat the koan but before he had finished, she suddenly placed her hands before her on the floor in a deep bow, said, "Thank you for your trouble," and left the room.

"I'll have to watch myself," declared the master. "I've been caught short by a snotnosed little girl!"

Kyōhō 13 (1728) Age 43

Laymen Ishii Gentoku and Sugisawa Sōshin came to the master for instruction.[48]

Kyōhō 14 (1729) Age 44

Datsu Jōza brought Furugōri Kentsū to see the master. "This gentleman would like to study Zen," said Datsu.[49] "Please give him a koan."

"Why bother with giving or taking at all?" replied the master. "This very moment it's all here, right under his nose. Nothing's lacking."

"He's just a beginner," said Datsu. "Use some of your skillful means on him."

The master picked up his brush and wrote out the words: "What is the nature that sees, hears, thinks, and knows?"

Kentsū received the inscription with a bow and left. About a year later he penetrated the meaning of the words. He composed a verse to express his understanding and presented it to the master.

I pushed over a cliff that soared ten thousand feet high,
Fire flashed from my mattock, consuming the universe;
Reduced to ash myself, I now survey the four quarters,
Seeing, as before, heavy rice-tassels ripening in the fields.

After that, Kentsū's attainment was further tempered and refined by uplifting blows from the master's invincible iron hammer.

It was at about this time that the monk Gedatsu, laymen Kentsū, Gentoku, and Sōshin, formed a practice group to study under the master. They became known around Shōin-ji as "the Earl and Three Dukes of Hina village."

In autumn the master lectured on the *Kannon Sutra*.

Kyōhō 15 (1730) Age 45

In spring the master lectured on a collection of texts he had compiled for his students titled *Redolence from the Cold Forest*.[50]

Winter. On the eighth of the eleventh month, Shōju Rōjin's student Sōkaku Shuso died.[51]

A woman named Masa, the widow of a Mr. Sugiyama of Hina village, came to study at the prompting of Datsu Jōza. She threw herself into her practice with such singlemindedness that she was totally oblivious of everything else. She became so absorbed in her koan that when her young son would return from his daily calligraphy lessons he would find that his mother had completely forgotten to prepare his lunch. Feeling sorry for him, the neighbors would give him something to eat. One day as he returned from his lessons, Masa looked at him and said, "Whose little boy are you?"

"Momma, what are you saying!" the boy cried out. With that she recognized him, but before long she was deeply immersed in samadhi once again. Her strange behavior continued for several more days until, suddenly, she crossed the threshold into enlightenment. She went to the master and set forth her understanding to him. He gave her some koans to test her. She passed them without the slightest trouble.

One day, the priest Unzan was lying behind the master taking a nap when Masa came to the door of his chambers and requested an interview. Unzan got up to leave but the master motioned for him to stay. When Masa entered the room, the master asked her, "What is the meaning of a dream about Bodhidharma coming from the west?"

After Masa set forth her understanding, the master ended the interview. She bowed and left the room.

"Who was that?" asked Unzan.

The master told him about the woman.

"I've never seen anyone that pure and forthright. Yet she didn't offer the slightest opening," exclaimed Unzan in amazement.[52]

Kyōhō 16 (1731) Age 46

During the summer the master gave lectures on the *Four Part Collection*, followed with lectures on the *Poems of Cold Mountain*. Twenty-five people attended the meeting. During the spring and autumn months, whenever the master could find time he sequestered himself at a retirement retreat owned by the physician Ishii Gentoku.

Kyōhō 17 (1732) Age 47

In spring the master lectured on the *Record of Lin-chi* and the *Blue Cliff Record*. Forty people participated in the meeting. There were more than a score of monks residing and practicing at Shōin-ji.

Kyōhō 18 (1733) Age 48

In spring a priest named Kaishun of the Shingon sect came for an interview. The master took a fire iron and held it up in front of Kaishun's face. "If you feel the slightest hesitation before this piece of iron," he said, "you are not yet a truly enlightened man." Kaishun was dumbfounded. Later when the master told his colleague Yōshun Shudaku about the exchange, Yōshun remarked, "Against you, even one of the foremost teachers of the esoteric school was at a loss."

In autumn, the master lectured on *Precious Lessons of the Zen School* to over thirty monks. He read Hayashi Razan's *Study of Our Shinto Shrines*.[53]

Kyōhō 19 (1734) Age 49

In spring the priest Shōzan of Taikō-an, a subtemple of Tōfuku-ji, came to study with the master accompanied by the monk Ryōsai from Mikawa.

During the summer, for Shōzan's benefit, the master gave talks on the *Blue Cliff Record*. Over twenty people attended. Senior monks Ryōsai and Ekyū made especially significant progress, penetrating to a deep understanding of the master's words.

Kyōhō 20 (1735) Age 50
In spring the master lectured on Shōzan's behalf on the *Record of Hsu-t'ang*. After the talks, Shōzan returned to Tōfuku-ji. In summer the master lectured on *Precious Lessons of the Zen School*. In autumn (the ninth month) he sent verses to Sempo Zenju and Kōgoku Genshu congratulating them on becoming temple priests.

Gembun 1 (1736) Age 51
In spring Etsu Shuso came to study. The master gave lectures on the *Vimalakirti Sutra* that were attended by more than thirty people. There were now eight monks residing at Shōin-ji.

In summer the master lectured on the *Blue Cliff Record*.

In autumn, thanks largely to the efforts of Chō of Tango and Tan of Bungo, the construction of a new Monks' Hall was completed at Shōin-ji. The master composed a verse to express his gratitude.[54]

At the annual ceremony commemorating Bodhidharma's death, the master offered incense and read out a verse he had composed:

Having no room for the monks, we built a brand new hall,
We'd been like beggars trying to hold a sumptuous banquet.
North of the river six men became great Dharma vessels;
Five bridges went up at five fords on Mount Shao-lin.[55]

The master often told his monks, "For the last three hundred and sixty years not one real person has passed by on the Tōkaidō."

During the winter the master's lay student Uematsu Suetsuna had a small Zen Hall and kitchen constructed on the site of a former temple in Hara, and established it as a new temple named Kannonzen-ji.[56] He asked the master to conduct services to consecrate the Buddhist images in the temple. The master wrote some Dharma instructions and a memorial inscription for the occasion, both of which still exist.[57]

Gembun 2 (1737) Age 52

In spring, the master lectured on the *Blue Cliff Record* at the request of Rinzai-ji in Izu. (This marked the first time the master responded to such an invitation from another temple.) Over two hundred people attended.

During the meeting, the master overheard the monks Ryōsai and Ekyū discussing the lectures. They felt some of the interpretations he had offered on the text were different from those he had given at previous lectures. He told them, "The Dharma is like climbing a mountain or entering the sea; the higher and farther you go, the deeper you get. On some points, I felt differently this time." His words spurred the two monks to even greater effort.

Gembun 3 (1738) Age 53

Bunchū of Bizen province arrived and began to study with the master. He would later tell the other monks, "If that old teacher of ours were lecturing from the high seat at a great and important temple, the whole world would be beating a path to his door."[58]

Gembun 4 (1739) Age 54

Autumn. In the eighth month the master acceded to a request from Layman Kokan (Mr. Akiyama) and gave talks at the layman's residence on the *Letters of Ta-hui*.[59] During the meeting Tetsu of Kai, Jun of Izumo, and Kō of Bitchū served as attendants. Monks arrived one after another, among them Kyū of Rinsen-ji, Chū of Bizen, Sha of Bungo, Ro of Kai, and Totsu. The lectures, attended by more than thirty people, continued for over a month.

Following the meal commemorating the death anniversary of Bodhidharma, the monks at Shōin-ji got together and decided to make preparations for a lecture meeting on the *Record of Hsu-t'ang* the following spring. At first the master was strongly opposed to the idea, but the monks went ahead with the work anyway. As he watched how eagerly and diligently they strove toward their goal, and realized the strength of their commitment, his opposition softened.

Taking his attendants Jun and Kō with him he left the temple and sought refuge in Kashima. He later went on to Takikawa, and after that was in Hina for a time. At Shōin-ji, the monks made good use of his absence. Taku, Tetsu, Sha, and Sū repaired the old temple roofs and sank a new well shaft. Kyū and Chū made the rounds of lay parishioners to lay in a store of beans and wheat and begged vegetables to stock the kitchen. All the monks worked ceaselessly and selflessly, mending gaps and cracks in the walls and making other repairs where they were needed. Meantime, Chū, Jun, and Kō staked off an area outside the temple and rehearsed the ceremonies for the upcoming meeting so they would be ready to advise the master as to the correct procedures to follow.[60]

Gembun 5 (1740) Age 55

The lectures at Shōin-ji on the *Record of Hsu-t'ang* were held in the spring and were attended by over four hundred people. The master gave a series of introductory talks (*fusetsu*) at the opening of the lectures [a printed edition of his text was later published]. Tsū of Ryōtan-ji acted as head monk, Taku of An'yō-ji as steward, and Sai of Mikawa as senior monk. Yaku of Bungo, Tō and Ryū also took part.

Opening the lectures the master remarked, "If you wish to experience for yourselves all the different poisons in Master Hsi-keng's Dharma ocean, you should study the koan Su-shan's Memorial Tower. It is indeed wonderful the way Hsi-keng's gold lies scattered and spread over the ten temples where he served. It's like throwing down one coin, getting two in return."[61]

Then he said, "I know that compared with the great teachers of our school I'm just a humble country parson, but none of you young monks should have any doubts: if you step out of line and disturb the meeting, you'll have to deal with this staff of mine. The monks in charge have been instructed to keep close watch on you."

This meeting established the master's reputation as the foremost Zen teacher in the land.

Kampō 1 (1741) Age 56

Seasoned monks—men with "brows of steel and skulls of bronze —now began filing in from all over the country. They stayed in lodgings spread over a radius of three or four leagues around Shōin-ji, transforming the surrounding woods and hills into a great Zen practice center. Among those who came was Jun of Dewa.

Spring. On the thirteenth of the first month there was a disturbance in the kitchen. Asking the cause, the master learned it was a quarrel involving funds for an upcoming trip to Kai province where he had been invited to lecture. After personally investigating the matter, he was moved to write a verse:

We were packing and bundling things up for our tour,
How shameful, troubling such large numbers of men.
If you happen to run into historian Ssu-ma on the way,
Tell him lecturing isn't a teacher's most onerous task.

He gave talks on the *Blue Cliff Record* at Keirin-ji in Kai province that were attended by over two hundred people. Jun, Betsu, Ryū, and Tō went along to supervise the meeting. One day the senior monk Reigaku Zogen appeared for an interview.

"Where do you come from when you're born! Where do you go after you die?" asked the master.[62]

Reigaku made no reply.

When a monk from Kyushu arrived and performed his greeting, the master said, "I heard you were back. They say you've been rambling extensively beyond the barrier. What do you have to show for it?"

"You didn't hear?" said the monk. "I've studied with a number of eminent teachers. My awakening came as I was working on Pacifying the Mind—the koan barrier raised by the Second Patriarch.[63] I no longer have any doubts whatever. Everything is splendid. I'm vim and vigor from head to foot. 'Great peace and happiness.' 'Great emancipation.' 'Fire is hot. Water is cool.' What more is there to do? What more to seek? I have no ambition to lecture on the Zen records, or to amuse myself writing verses, as you do."

"What about the Second Patriarch's Pacification of Mind?" asked the master.

"As long as you seek mind, it's ungettable," said the monk.

"Scratching yourself behind the ear, your hand touches a Buddha's head—it can't be anyone but you. When will you be able to stop bending your left elbow and touching a dog's head?" said the master.

The monk sat dumbfounded.

"Fa-yen said, 'a water buffalo comes in through the window. Head, horns, four hooves all make it through. Why doesn't the tail?'[64] What does that mean?" asked the master.

The monk sat dumbfounded.

"A moment ago you told me 'fire is hot and water is cool,' but one of the ancients also said, 'Willows are not green, flowers are not red.' Look!!"

The monk sat dumbfounded.

Kampō 2 (1742) Age 57

In spring a Zen monk named Bonji came and requested an interview. He asked the master for a religious name and underwent the ceremony making him a disciple.

In the fourth month Reigaku Zogen returned to resume his study. Again the master asked, "Where do you come from when you're born! Where do you go when you die?"

Reigaku raised a finger.

"You aren't there yet," said the master. "Say something else."

"Where do you come from when you're born! Where do you go when you die?" said Reigaku.

The master wrote a verse confirming Reigaku's realization.[65]

During the summer the master acceded to a request from Ryōtan-ji in Tōtōmi province and went there to lecture on *Precious Lessons of the Zen School*.

When the master was on his way back to Shōin-ji that autumn, Yaku Jōza came to meet his palanquin. He had achieved a breakthrough and was anxious to show the master a statement he had written setting forth his understanding. The master took one look at it and berated him severely.

Kampō 3 (1743) Age 58

Spring. In the second month Tōrei Enji arrived and began his study with the master. He was appointed as a special unassigned attendant. In the third month the master lectured on *Ta-hui's Arsenal*. A monk who was residing temporarily at Shōin-ji asked him, "It's said that with a seasoned Zen teacher, 'there's no pecking in and no pecking out. Pecking in and pecking out are equally mistaken.' What principle does that elucidate?"[66]

"The chick inside the egg wants to peck but doesn't, so the mother hen pecks," the master replied. "It's important to be aware when you've failed to respond to a student satisfactorily."

The monk performed a bow.

"Peck!" said the master.

The monk gave a loud shout.

"Awakened!" said the master.

This exchange prompted the master to give a general talk to the brotherhood.[67]

Gōun of Shinano province came to study with the master. As a former student of the Sōtō priest Daibai, Gōun had penetrated to an unusually deep realization. The master ended up assigning him several koans. In the back and forth accompanying the master's subsequent examination of Gōun, he subjected him to the most penetrating scrutiny. Gōun did not display the slightest uncertainty or hesitation. The master presented him with a verse:

Divine life-taking amulets, poison fangs of the Dharma cave
Drained the color from the universe; smashed the Big
    Dipper;
Deep personal commitment, half a lifetime of devoted
    effort,
Has erected a long-lasting nine-tiger barrier in Shinano.[68]

Datsu of Ōmi province came to study.

In the ninth month the master's *Dharma Talks Introductory to Lectures on the Records of Hsi-keng* was published. In autumn monks at Shōin-ji and lay students of the master began renovating the temple kitchen. On the 25th day of the twelfth month work was completed and the cook moved into his new quarters.

Kampō 4 / Enkyō 1 (1744) Age 59

Spring, the second month. The master saw the newly published *Dharma Talks Introductory to Lectures on the Records of Hsi-keng* for the first time. In the spring he conducted belated ceremonies in observance of Bodhidharma's death anniversary (usually held in the tenth month) and Shakyamuni's enlightenment (held in the twelfth month), which had not been observed at Shōin-ji the previous year.

In winter, while he was visiting Jishō-ji in Kai province, donations were gathered and a printing was made of the *Heart Sutra*. On the way home he lectured at Rinsen-an in Shimizu on *Ch'uan-lao's Comments for the Diamond Sutra*. Since the hall at Rinsen-an was small, with room for only six students, it was not possible for a large number of people to take part. During the meeting the master instructed students with a story of a starving man at a teashop.[69]

Enkyō 2 (1745) Age 60

Spring. In the second month the master went to Jitoku-ji in Kai in answer to their request for lectures on the *Vimalakirti Sutra*. The lectures were attended by over three hundred people. Monks Chū and Yaku were put in charge of the meeting. In honor of Buddha's birthday, and also to commemorate the opening of the assembly, the master composed a verse:

> The true transmission flowed forth daily from Amra's gardens;
> Hanging up a poison drum, his true nature pierced the heavens;

True samadhi was present, clearly manifesting true
    emancipation—
A single blossom flowering the universe into absolute
    perfection.[70]

During the meeting, on the third day of the third month, Zen Master Rempō held a maigre feast to commemorate the death anniversary of his teacher Ranshitsu.

Inoue Hyōma was a samurai in the service of a high official in Edo who was deeply devoted to the *Ten Phrase Kannon Sutra*. He had a printing of the sutra made to distribute to the populace. Hyōma fell into a lifeless swoon, during which he descended into the realm of the dead and encountered Emma, the King of Hell. Emma said to him, "Your attempts to make the *Ten Phrase Kannon Sutra* known to your fellow men have been unsuccessful because you lack sufficient spiritual power. At this very moment, however, there is in your world a priest by the name of Hakuin. He lives in your own country, in Suruga province. If this Hakuin were to propagate the sutra, he would achieve far greater success than you could hope for. I want you to get him to do this."

The order had come directly from the mouth of Emma himself, so when Hyōma regained his senses he wasted no time. He immediately wrote a letter to Master Hakuin requesting his help and had it carried to Shōin-ji. This is how the master first began propagating the *Ten Phrase Kannon Sutra*. Later Hyōma paid a visit to Shōin-ji and told Hakuin about the vision he had seen.[71]

Enkyō 3 (1746) Age 61

Spring. In the second month Hakuin conducted a lecture meeting on the *Lotus Sutra* at the request of Genryū-ji in Suruga province. He gave an introductory talk (*fusetsu*) prior to the lectures.[72] A letter arrived from Tōrei, who was then residing in the eastern outskirts of Kyoto, informing the master of his acceptance of the Dharma transmission the master had offered him. The master responded with a verse:

A golden carp tailing through the weeds of the vast Ōmi
    waters,
Has surmounted countless perils and passed beyond the
    Dragon Gate;
He is free at last to sport among the poison waves of the
    Buddha Ocean
And begin performing the true charity—by giving not
    a drop to others.[73]

When the master expressed a desire to make his sanction of
Tōrei public, several of his senior disciples tried to dissuade him.
"If you can't bring yourself to believe in the man from reading
what he writes," he told them, "how are you going to understand
what is written in the books about the ancient Zen masters?"
None of those present dared make a reply.

In autumn printing was completed of the master's commentary on the *Poems of Cold Mountain*. Hakuin first saw a copy of
the work when he visited the Hōrin-ji in Kai to conduct a lecture meeting. While he was there he did a painting of the sixteen
arhats which he presented to the abbot, Zen Master Sesshū.[74] In
a verse he inscribed above the painting, he wrote:

Sixteen superior arhats, shining like jewels among men,
A waterfall plunging thousands of feet, colder than ice.
Who said the universal vow of salvation is ocean deep?
Once your worldly ties are cut it's easy going all the way.

Eboku of Shimotsuke came to study. The first time he laid eyes
on Eboku the master knew that he was no ordinary student. Layman Shōjō Dōmu also came to study. He arrived riding on an ox.
He sought the master's instruction regularly after that.

When the meeting ended, Hakuin proceeded to Sekirin-ji in
Kai province and lectured on the *Lotus Sutra*. On the way back to
Shōin-ji he stopped over at Nōjō-ji.

Enkyō 4 (1747) Age 62

Spring. A vassal of the Daimyo of Owari named Oda Heishirō Nobushige, who was accompanying his lord on one of his periodic trips to Edo, slipped away from the procession when it reached Hara to seek an interview with the master. When the master asked Nobushige about his previous study, Nobushige replied, "I enjoy visiting Buddhist teachers and receiving religious instruction from them," he answered. "But as a result of those visits, I seem to have contracted an intractable malady."

"What malady would that be?" asked the master.

"Well I first went to a Zen teacher. He had me investigate my Mind-nature. Next I went to a Precepts teacher to inquire into the secrets of the esoteric school. He introduced me to the essentials of that tradition. I started having doubts about the two teachings. Now when I engage in the Contemplation on the Letter A, my mind immediately fills with terrifying visions of hell. If I attempt to suppress them using the principle of the Mind-nature, the two standpoints clash and cause me considerable distress. When I sleep, I'm plagued by bad dreams. When I'm awake, my mind is in constant turmoil."

"Why don't you find out who it is that fears hell so much!" scolded the master.

"But my trouble is, I'm stuck in a state of emptiness," he replied.

The master uttered a series of loud shouts. "Halfbaked wretch!" he said. "A samurai is supposed to be totally devoted to his master. No hesitating in the face of fire or other dangers. He entrusts his life to the sword and spear without so much as stopping to scratch an itch or blink an eye. How could a samurai fear emptiness! Go down into the evil paths, right now. Take a good close look at all the different hells you see while you're there."

"Is it proper for a Buddhist teacher to tell a student to enter the realm of hell?" asked Nobushige.

The master laughed. "I've been there myself, many times. Seen all eighty-four thousand hells. I haven't missed a single one!"

Overjoyed, Nobushige prostrated himself before the master.

"Please," he said. "Write something to show me how I can illuminate my mind."

"What I've got to offer is so infinitely vast," replied the master, "you couldn't possibly take it all in."

"But how can you refuse me just a word or two?" said Nobushige. "Even ten thousand volumes, if I requested them?"

The master paused, then said: "Look! Go out that gate. Observe the endless procession of people passing up and down the street. Take in the inns along the sides of the road, the public lavatories, the teahouses. Look at the great pine trees lining the approach to the post station. Look at the horses and donkeys moving up and down the road. Go on to Numazu . . . or even on to Shinagawa, or into Edo itself. Watch the busy traffic moving over the Ryōgoku Bridge, the great commotion of activity of the hordes of people milling around Sensō-ji Temple. Day or night, the turmoil and confusion never let up. Yet would there be any time, as you were doing that, when you forgot yourself? Or any time when you did not forget yourself?"

Nobushige left, fully convinced of the master's teaching.

There was a serious famine this year, obliging the monks living in and around Shōin-ji to disperse. At services for the death anniversary of Bodhidharma, the master wrote a verse:

Winds sweep by like angry seas, blasting field and garden,
Scattering my idle spirits and wild demons far and wide;
Twenty worthy men, monks with vitals sheathed in iron,
Chew on vegetable stalks, keenly savoring the adversity.

Enkyō 5 / Kan'en 1 (1748) Age 63

In spring Yamanashi Harushige came to study with the master.[75*]

During the summer the master suddenly penetrated the inner meaning of the Reciprocal Interpenetration Between Apparent and Real.[76] On the fifth of the eleventh month the master took the monks living at Shōin-ji to a ceremony at Rinzai-ji commemorating the two-hundredth death anniversary of National Master Honkō.[77] At the request of the abbot Kanjū Sōtetsu he delivered comments on the religious verses in the *Record of Hsi-keng.*

After the meeting, a monk came seeking the master's instruction. During the interview he said, "I've kicked Lin-chi's Three Barriers over on their back.[78] I've gone seven steps beyond Hsuansha."

"Those aren't your words!" said Hakuin. "Where did you get them?"

"I found them in a discourse National Master Honkō delivered when he was installed as temple abbot," confessed the monk. Without thinking, the master prostrated himself, then lifted his arms up in reverence. "It's like talking about salted plums and finding your mouth watering, or like knowing the taste of a certain food by sampling a morsel from the cooking pot. It's a pity you're unable to see everything that's in that pot!"

---

* (Harushige, also known as Heishirō, was from the village of Ihara in Suruga province. Avaricious by nature and a confirmed womanizer, he had few redeeming qualities. One day when he was visiting his family temple the retired abbot said to him, "Yamanashi, you should have an image of Fudō Myōō carved in stone. It would benefit people and inspire practicers with a spirit of courage and fearlessness."

Harushige was agreeable to the idea and commissioned a stone carver to carve a statue of Fudō. He had it enshrined beside a waterfall at Mount Yoshiwara. One fine spring day he took his children to visit the spot. There wasn't a cloud in the sky and the bright green leaves sparkled in the warm sun. The children wandered off gathering flowers, leaving Harushige alone at the edge of the waterfall. As he sat there watching the foam forming on the surface of the pool, the world's transience and the brevity of human life were suddenly revealed to him. He saw some of the bubbles vanish under the falling water even as they formed, others floated a foot or two before disappearing, and some remained intact, moving over the water, for fifty yards or more. "Human life is just like that," mused Harushige. He had experienced the Buddhist principle that all is suffering and that all suffering originates from human ignorance. He rose, his body trembling uncontrollably with fear, and returned by himself. When he arrived home he saw an old man sitting at the back of the house reading *The Dharma Words of Zen Priest Takusui.*[79] Glancing at the book, Harushige's eyes came to rest on a passage that said: "A true practicer of the Way makes enlightenment alone his standard. Sometimes, a brave and courageous practicer is able to realize enlightenment in several days or weeks. Such is the meaning of the Buddha's saying about brave and fearless practicers reaching attainment in a single thought-instant, but lax and indolent ones being unable to even with the passage of three kalpas."

With that, Harushige plucked up his courage, thinking to himself, "I'm certainly capable of making it through a week or two of Zen training."

He entered the bath quarters of his house and sat in a posture of meditation. In spite of his steadfast resolve, it wasn't long before his mind was conjuring up thoughts and discriminations of various kinds; his arms and legs were aching; he was haunted by a relentless uneasiness. But when midnight came he was finally able to forget his body and mind. At first light, his eyeballs seemed suddenly to burst from their sockets and fall to the floor. Soon after that he felt searing pain in the tips of his fingers. But he clenched his teeth tightly, determined to sit his way through, and gradually seemed to return to normal. When he rose and looked around him, he was unable to perceive any noticeable change from the previous day. He left the room and began his daily routine. At day's end he returned to the bath quarters and resumed his practice, sitting as resolutely the second night as he had the first. He soon entered a deep state of samadhi and remained that way throughout the night. He sat through a third night in the same manner. At dawn on the morning of the third day, upon returning to his work, he noticed a change had taken place. Now everything he saw and heard and experienced seemed totally different. He went to the priest of a small nearby temple and told him what had happened. The priest, unable to offer any help himself, advised him to visit Master Hakuin.

Harushige hired a palanquin and set out for Shōin-ji. When the palanquin came to the summit of Satta Pass, a vast shining stretch of ocean came into view far below. At that moment, gazing out over the broad expanse, Nobushige suddenly grasped the true aspect of things in the suchness of their particularity, and penetrated for the first time the meaning of the Buddha's words, "plants and trees and the great earth itself all attain Buddhahood."

Reaching Shōin-ji, he described to Hakuin what had happened. Hakuin confirmed his realization. Harushige continued his study of Zen under Priest Kan'e Anjū, further deepening and refining his understanding.

One day he encountered a nun named Eshō, who said, "I'm an old lady. Could you please help me up without using your hands?" Harushige didn't know what to say. "You said you practice Zen," she said, scolding him. "Is that the best you can do?" The next day he grasped her meaning and she acknowledged his understanding. After that Harushige studied with several other priests, and successfully passed a number of koan barriers.[80])

Kan'en 2 (1749) Age 64

At the end of the spring training session, monks studying at Shōin-ji requested that the master lecture on the Zen records of Daitō Kokushi. He refused. "Thirty years ago, when I was in Mino province, I accepted at face value some groundless remarks I heard someone make about the *Record of Daitō*, and because of that I was led completely astray. Later on, a single word or phrase from the *Record* was enough to set my teeth chattering and my knees quaking. I would like to oblige you, if only to stop you from pestering me, but the sea is so vast, the waves so high, I'd have trouble even making out the shore. It would be foolish to attempt such a task."

Encouraged by the master's response, brothers Daku, Kun, Ju, Gyō, I, Rō, Ryū, and Jitsu got hold of a printed edition of the *Record of Daitō*. Working together, they managed to formulate a general plan for the master's lectures and to work out readings for the more difficult passages. When they took the results of their labor to the master and begged him earnestly to reconsider, he was no longer able to refuse them. He proceeded to compose verse commentaries on the work after the manner of the *Blue Cliff Record*, and wrote instructive prose comments modeled on those in the *"Sanshō-gōyō"* (*"Essential Words for Careful Study"*) section of *Daitō's Record*. He titled the finished work *Dream Words from the Land of Dreams*.[81] A strong appeal from Yūzan Zen'ichi, the priest of Ankoku-ji, persuaded him to allow a printing of the work to be made.

In spring the master gave lectures on the *Record of Lin-chi* at the Monju-dō in Tadehara.

At the summer training session he lectured on the *Blue Cliff Record*. The Ōbaku priest Kakujū came and received instruction in the Sōtō sect's Five Ranks. Kakujū later became abbot of the Ōbaku headquarters temple at Mampuku-ji, and through him Hakuin's Zen spread to the Ōbaku sect.[82]

Winter. In the eleventh month Tōrei returned to Shōin-ji to resume his study with the master. On the 25th day of the twelfth month the master presented Tōrei with a certificate of transmission and his gold brocade Dharma robe. A ceremonial feast was held, after which Tōrei departed for the Ummon-an in Iwatsuki, Musashi province. He was accompanied by the priest Gekkyū of Kai province.

Kan'en 3 (1750) Age 65

In spring Hakuin went in response to an invitation from Daijo-ji in nearby Ihara village and lectured on the *Blue Cliff Record*. In autumn he went to Jōei-ji in Tōtōmi province; while he was there he got his first look at the newly published *Dream Words from the Land of Dreams*.

In winter he was invited by Ryōkoku-ji in Harima province to deliver comments on the *Record of Hsi-keng*. One of the men attending the meeting posed a question: "Does life end when we die? Or does it go on?"

"Does what just asked that question end?" replied the master. "Does it keep going on?" The man could make no reply.

Eboku returned from Kumano to resume his study at Shōin-ji. The master's face flushed with anger as he reproached Eboku. "The noise around here bothered you so you ran off into the mountains and spent your time with the rocks and trees. You said you needed peace and quiet. Where did it get you?" He gave a loud shout.

Yotsugi Masayuki came from Kyoto to study with the master.

Kan'en 4 / Hōreki 1 (1751) Age 66

In spring Hakuin went to Bizen province in response to an invitation from Shōrin-ji in Okayama and lectured on *Ch'uan-lao's Comments on the Diamond Sutra*. From Shōrin-ji he traveled to Hōfuku-ji in Iyama for lectures on the *Four Part Collection*. He returned home by way of Kyoto, where he stayed at the residence of Yotsugi Masayuki. While he was there the painter Ike Taiga and the courtesan Ōhashi-jo came to receive his instruction.[83*]

He gave lectures on the *Blue Cliff Record* at the Yōgen-in sub-temple of Myōshin-ji.[84] The lectures were attended secretly by the abbesses of the imperial temples Hōkyō-ji and Kōshō-ji, and by Seijōkō-in, a daughter of the emperor. They were accompanied to the lectures by two high-ranking courtiers, Hamuro Yoritane and Reizei Muneie.

In winter Hakuin traveled to Daijo-ji in Ihara to continue lectures on the *Blue Cliff Record* he had started on a previous visit.

While he was there he drafted a short composition on the secrets of the Five Ranks.

One day he told the assembly of monks, "The Buddha's Dharma is like climbing a mountain: the farther you go, the higher you get. The important thing is not to retreat, not just remain where you are. From the time I entered Shōju's chambers and began to receive his instruction my mind was always disturbed and uneasy. Waking or sleeping, I couldn't shake that feeling. This winter I have reached my sixty-sixth year. Now, I often feel as if I'm strolling through the Dharma groves with Master Yun-men." His words made a deep impression on all those present.

During the meeting the master was bothered by a carbuncle. It was treated by Gisei, a physician from Ejiri.

Hakuin visited Kōrin-ji, where he had been invited to lecture on the *Blue Cliff Record*. The priest Sōhō of the Zakke-in subtemple at Myōshin-ji attended. When he set forth his understanding of Zen, Hakuin refuted him point by point. Sōhō was unable to accept the master's views.

*(Ōhashi-jo was a daughter of a high official in the service of the Daimyo of Kōfu. He received a stipend in excess of one thousand *koku*, but circumstances arose that forced him to leave his post and live as a rōnin or masterless samurai. He went with his family and youngest brother to Kyoto, where they had no fixed residence but moved from place to place until their money ran out. Finally, Ōhashi could no longer bear seeing her parents' thin and haggard appearance. "Sell me to a brothel," she said. "In the future, if things work out, we may be able to come together again." "Any parent who would sell his child to benefit himself is no better than an animal," they replied. "We would rather starve to death."

"You must think of it as a temporary expedient," Ōhashi told them. "If we don't do this, we must all die. Expedient means is not the same as true wisdom, but if it can help us out of our present difficulty, perhaps it is a kind of wisdom after all." Ōhashi's parents reluctantly agreed. She was sold to a Kyoto brothel, where she became a skilled calligrapher and took pleasure in the composition of waka poetry. Although she served her master diligently, thoughts of her former life remained to plague her: "I was born into a good family. I was raised in a splendid residence, surrounded by fine silken hangings, with maidservants at my beck and call. Now look at me, reduced to this ignominious existence."

These sad thoughts weighed heavily on her mind over the passing days and months, until finally symptoms of serious illness began to appear. Physicians who were consulted were powerless to help her.

Then one day she had a customer from the noble classes. Seeing how deeply troubled the young woman looked, he asked what was bothering her. She told him her story. "I can understand the cause of your suffering," he said. "Unless you can come up with a thousand in gold, it will be difficult to remedy your condition. However, it so happens that I am aware of a way that will enable you to free yourself completely from your troubles. You probably don't believe me, do you?"

"Why shouldn't I, if it's true?" she replied. "Please, tell me what I should do."

"It's simply a matter of detaching yourself from your seeing, hearing, feeling, and knowing," he said. "Those four faculties are all ruled by the same master. If you concentrate yourself constantly, singlemindedly, on two questions: Who is it that sees! Who is it that hears! even when you are engaged in your daily activities, your true inborn Buddha-nature will suddenly manifest itself before your very eyes. The only way you can free yourself from this world of suffering is to strive diligently and reach the point where you discern your true inborn nature."

She humbly accepted the advice and immediately began doing her best to put it into practice.

During the Enkyō era [1744–48] a series of violent storms swept the capital. In one twenty-four-hour period lightning strikes were reported at twenty-eight different places. Ōhashi, who was deathly afraid of lightning, had all the doors and curtains secured and surrounded herself with young servants. She then assumed the lotus posture and with a fierce determination began doing zazen. The house was shaken by a sudden bolt of lightning that struck with a bright flash in the garden outside. Terrified, Ōhashi toppled over in a swoon.

Minutes later when she regained her senses she found that her seeing and hearing were completely different. She wanted very much to visit a Zen teacher and have him confirm the experience she had attained, but it was not possible for her in her present situation to leave the pleasure quarters.

Later, she met a man who purchased her from the brothel and made her his wife. The man died and she remarried, this time to Layman Issō. Issō always took Ōhashi with him when he came to study with Master Hakuin. Some years later Issō permitted Ōhashi to receive ordination as a nun. She assumed the religious name Erin.

After Erin died Layman Issō came and asked me [Tōrei] to make an offering of incense. As I approached the altar I could see no mortuary tablet for her, only a statue of the Bodhisattva Kannon. When I asked about the tablet, Layman Issō replied, "Erin attained enlightenment in a woman's form. In the form of a woman she preached the Dharma. I am sure she was an incarnation of Kannon. Hence I have enshrined a statue of the Bodhisattva here. I don't think there's anything wrong with that, do you?"

Without another word, I offered the incense.)

Hōreki 2 (1752) Age 67

In spring Hakuin lectured on the *Blue Cliff Record* at Shōin-ji, completing talks he had started previously. The hall filled with all four types of Buddhist disciples—monks, nuns, laymen and -women.

On the eighth day of the fourth month the new Muryō-ji was completed and the master was welcomed to celebrations that installed him as founder of the temple.* He appointed Tōrei as abbot.

Autumn. Hakuin to Kiitsu-ji in Izu province to lecture at that temple's request on the *Record of Bukkō*.[85] Tsutsumi Yukimori traveled all the way from Kyoto to attend. While he was there Yukimori informed Hakuin about efforts Yotsugi Masayuki had made to relieve starving peasants in northern Kyoto. As an expression of his approval, the master took up his brush and painted a picture illustrating the events, adding an inscription above the painting.[86]

Winter. To celebrate the completion of the Muryō-ji, Layman Chikan (Yotsugi Masayuki) gave Tōrei seven Buddha relics for enshrinement in the temple. He requested that Master Hakuin deliver talks on the *Sutra of the Bequeathed Teaching*.

At the request of Gyokurin-ji in Matsuzaki, southern Izu, the master conducted a ceremony to commemorate the casting of a large new temple bell.

* (The elderly priest Dokuon Genri of Shinano province had restored the temple in the past, and his student Datsu Shuso had later lived there. During the Enkyō era, Hakuin's student Kairyū conceived the idea of rebuilding the temple and installing the master as its founder, but Kairyū died before the plan could be realized. A hundred pieces of gold that had been collected for the undertaking were entrusted to laymen Ishii Gentoku, Furugōri Heishichi, and Sugisawa Sōzaemon, and in time the three of them, working together, were able to carry the project through to completion.)

Hōreki 3 (1753) Age 68

Spring. In the second month Hakuin went to view the relics that had been enshrined at Muryō-ji. At the request of Nōjō-ji in Kōfu he lectured on *The Eye of Men and Gods* to more than three hundred people. During the meeting he explained the essentials of the Five Chinese Zen Schools and had students concentrate their practice on points he had indicated during his talks.

From Nōjō-ji he proceeded to Tōkō-ji in Kai province and lectured on *Poison Words for the Heart,* his commentary on the *Heart Sutra.*[87] During the meeting at Tōkō-ji a ceremony and maigre feast were held to commemorate the thirty-third death anniversary of Hakuin's teacher Shōju Rōjin. The master painted a portrait of Shōju and inscribed it with a verse:

> Holding up a trickling drop from the celestial source;
>   throwing it down,
> He caused much grief and suffering deep in the mountains
>   of Iiyama;
> Fed up with the flames of jealousy kindled among his children,
> He put an end to all his giving and became their mortal foe.

On the way home from Tōkō-ji the master stopped to give talks at Fukuō-ji, Nanshō-in, and Jigen-ji. He was back at Shōin-ji for the winter *rōhatsu* training session.

Hōreki 4 (1754) Age 69
Students and disciples presented the master with congratulatory verses in celebration of his seventieth year.

Hōreki 5 (1755) Age 70
Spring. Acceding to a request from Ryōshin-ji (in Kojima village west of Hara) the master conducted a lecture meeting on the *Vimalakirti Sutra.* Lord Matsudaira, Awa-no-kami, chief patron of the temple, attended daily. He was completely won over by the master's teaching.[88] The master returned to Shōin-ji in the fifth month.

Autumn. In the ninth month Uematsu Suetsuna presented a carved figure of Akiba Gongen to Kannon-ji and asked the master to perform consecration rites for it.

Hōreki 6 (1756) Age 71

In spring the master lectured on the *Shurangama Sutra* at Shōin-ji. Preparatory to the lectures he delivered instructions to the assembly.[89]

Summer. In the fourth month a ceremony and maigre feast was held at Kōrin-ji, near the city of Sumpu, to commemorate the 450th death anniversary of National Master Daiō; over two hundred people attended. The master was asked to offer incense and deliver a Zen commentary on Daiō's recorded sayings. Offering the incense, he said:

> When National Master Daiō made an offering of incense at a memorial service for his teacher Hsu-t'ang, he remarked, "During the many years I served as old Hsu-t'ang's attendant, we were together constantly—face to face, eye to eye. So once each year in his memory I burn a stick of incense like this and offer him a cup of tea. I don't perform a woman's bow like Master Yang-ch'i. These white turnips have always been associated with the master's native Chen-chou. To my mind they are the perfect offering in memory of the patriarch. Yet one thing I bitterly regret: he was not pleased when the round pillar shook its head. Why? Every wheel that turns leaves tracks, yet leaving tracks is not the true and vital function of a wheel."

After the assembly the master went to Jiun-ji in Shimizu where he delivered comments on the *Precious Mirror Samadhi*. He then went to Ihara and lectured on *Poison Words for the Heart,* his commentary on the *Heart Sutra*.

He returned to Shōin-ji in the sixth month. A messenger arrived from the far-off Ryukyu Islands with a letter from the priest Tōgan Gen. Tōgan had sent the man all the way to Shōin-ji in order to request a certificate of enlightenment from the master.

In autumn the master lectured on *Ta-hui's Arsenal* at the request of Jishu-in in Kai. At the start of the meeting he gave some Dharma talks. During the talks, he was troubled once again by an inflamed carbuncle. The physician Gisei treated it and in several days the inflammation subsided.

A manuscript compilation of the master's writings and sayings made by his attendant Zenjo fell into the hands of a layman from Osaka named Kida Genshō. Kida secretly took the manuscript with him when he returned to Osaka and had it printed there.[90] The work is titled *Poison Flowers in a Thicket of Thorns*.

Hōreki 7 (1757) Age 72

In spring, responding to teaching requests, the master set out for Kōzen-ji in Shinano and Nanshō-in in Kai. After stopping at Nambu in Kai province to instruct students at Kenchū-ji, he proceeded directly to Nanshō-in, where he delivered a Dharma talk and lectured on *Dream Words from the Land of Dreams*. From there he went to Hōju-an in Kai for several days of teaching, and then proceeded to Kōzen-ji, where he lectured on the *Lotus Sutra* to an assembly of over three hundred people. The meeting was sponsored by Mr. Yamamura, the local magistrate, who was chief patron of the temple. After the lectures the master responded to yet more teaching requests and made visits to Kaizen-ji and Ryōshō-ji in the city of Iida, and Enryō-ji in Mikawa province. He then returned to Shōin-ji.

Hōreki 8 (1758) Age 73

In spring the master was invited to lecture at Rurikō-ji in Mino province. He decided to use the meeting to celebrate in advance the 100th death anniversary of National Master Gudō by giving a series of lectures on the *Blue Cliff Record*. The monks living at Shōin-ji showed scant enthusiasm for the idea, but that made the master all the more determined to proceed. He placed Kanjū of Rinsen-ji and Eboku in charge of the meeting. Eventually the other monks came around and lent their support as well.

On his way to Mino province the master stopped over for several days to deliver talks at Shōrin-ji. Upon arriving at Rurikō-ji he composed a letter which he had distributed to temples far and wide. He wrote: "As we have reached the one hundredth anniversary of Master Gudō's death, I propose to deliver a series of lectures on the *Blue Cliff Record*. Anyone who feels a debt of Dharma gratitude to the National Master should come to Rurikō-ji, where they may offer incense and make their bows to him."

Senior priests Ryōsai, Tekkan, Reigen, Kuin, and Tenzui responded to the master's letter and came to take part in the meeting. The master shared the teaching seat with his disciple Tōrei, who also delivered lectures. The master sent letters to senior priests in Gudō's teaching line urging them to arrange for an edition of Master Gudō's Zen records to be published. Discussions were held and various opinions were voiced, but in the end they were unable to reach any decision on the matter. Their lack of enthusiasm incensed the master.[91]

At the end of the Rurikō-ji meeting, he received invitations from Kakurin-ji, Zui'ō-ji, Seitai-ji, and Bairyū-ji in Mino province. After visiting each of those temples, he headed for Sōyu-ji in Takayama for talks on the *Blue Cliff Record*, stopping off along the way at Saigen-ji and Gyokuryū-ji. On route to Sōyu-ji his exasperation at the failure of his fellow priests to support a printing of Gudō's records prompted him to compose a work titled *Gudō's Lingering Radiance*. When he arrived at Sōyu-ji he wrote out a fair copy of the text and showed it to the monks.

On the way back to Shōin-ji he responded to teaching requests from Ryōmon-ji, Rinsen-ji, and Myōraku-ji, then traveled south by small boat to Kuwana Castle and from there headed straight to Ryōgen-ji in Shiroko. He lectured there for over a month on the *Treatise of the Precious Storehouse*,[92] and returned to Kuwana for several days of lectures at Tenshō-ji. More teaching requests arrived. He visited the training halls of Ryūtaku-ji and Hakurin-ji in Owari province for several days, and also lectured at Chizō-in in Tōtōmi on *Hsu-t'ang's Verse Comments on Old Koans*. In winter he was back at Shōin-ji.

Not far from the Mishima post station—less than a bull's roar away—was a ruined temple named Ryūtaku-ji. It was under the jurisdiction of the Mishima temple Shingyō-ji. A group of laymen and priests who had studied under the master raised funds and purchased the site with the idea of rebuilding the temple and installing the master as its founder.

Hōreki 9 (1759) Age 74

During the New Year holiday a group including the priests Kanjū of Rinsen-an, Reisen of Kezō-ji, and Kanzui of Denshū-ji came with Mr. Ōhito to offer their respects to the master. During their conversation with him they noted that plans for Ryūtaku-ji were nearly ready and suggested that Tōrei be appointed as abbot of the new temple. The master agreed. It was decided that Layman Jōsan would travel to Kyoto and formally escort Tōrei back to Shōin-ji. The monk Dōgi was dispatched in advance to inform Tōrei of the plans.

In the second month the master received an invitation from a physician named Handa to visit Edo. Handa wanted him to give the priests and lay community in Edo a taste of the Zen school's unique and marvelous working.

The third month. Shibata Gikyō, a student of the master, obtained a manuscript containing some unpublished writings that he had been collecting in hopes they might later be added to his Zen records, *Poison Flowers in a Thicket of Thorns*, published some years before. Shibata had the manuscript printed as a one-volume supplement to the work.

In the seventh month the master traveled to Edo and stayed at Rinsen-ji. People living around the temple composed a playful verse.

> A Zen bonze of great virtue
> Is here in the neighborhood,
> Ensnared by our own Rinsen-ji;
> Even from a country thicket
> A fine aroma strikes the nose.[93]

On the twenty-fourth day of the seventh month the master opened a lecture meeting on the *Blue Cliff Record*. In the address he made to the assembly at the start of the lectures, he said: "Whatever I hold up to elucidate for you—be it only a shard or pebble—is transformed into a piece of pure gold. Where I am now, even when I'm sitting and joking and chatting informally with people, I am turning the great Dharma wheel. *Look!! Look!!*"

He then began to lecture on the *Blue Cliff Record*, the foremost text of Rinzai Zen. An outstanding group of Zen monks was in attendance, as well as a large contingent of high-ranking samurai. Crowded shoulder to shoulder into the hall, they sat trembling as they listened to the master's words. After the assembly the master went on to Tōen-ji to complete lectures he had left unfinished at an earlier meeting.

Before leaving Edo to return to Shōin-ji in the twelfth month, the master acquired ownership of Shidō-an, the hermitage in Edo where the Zen teacher Shidō Munan had formerly resided.

Hōreki 10 (1760) Age 75

Spring, the second month. The master lectured on his *Talks Introductory to Lectures on the Record of Hsi-keng* at the site of the new Ryūtaku-ji training hall. A ceremony was conducted during the meeting installing the master as temple founder. Over a hundred people attended. Ryūzan Dai-oshō of Kongōō-in on Mount Hakone donated the funds to cover the expense of the meeting.

As soon as Tōrei returned from Kyoto in the fourth month Hakuin appointed him as his successor at Ryūtaku-ji. In autumn Tōrei undertook to have the registry of Ryūtaku-ji transferred to the new site. Mr. Kamiyama raised the funds for the transaction, Oba Harushige handled the negotiations with the government officials, and Kanzui Hōin, the temple steward at Kongōō-in, came with Mr. Oba to fix the boundaries.

Hōreki 11 (1761) Age 76

In spring (the first month) the land transfer was completed, and Ryūzan, the abbot of Kongōō-in, came and certified the transaction. Many of those who had benefited from the master's teaching now began arriving. They came from Suruga province and from the surrounding provinces of Izu, Tōtōmi, and Sagami. They set to work moving rocks and hauling earth to clear the land in preparation for the laying of the foundations. Each person brought his own supply of food to avoid drawing on the temple stores. Thanks to their concerted effort the work was successfully carried to completion.

In the ninth month the master was invited to lecture at Ryūtaku-ji. When he ascended to the teaching seat, Tōrei came forward, performed a bow, and read out a verse:

Shariputra built the first temple among the groves of Gion,
His descendents, striving together, erected the house
    of Zen.
Our teacher now stands here as the Shakyamuni of his age,
May his Dharma-thunder jolt the blind and ignorant
    of today.

With more than a hundred people in attendance, Hakuin lectured on *Hsueh-feng's Memorial Inscription*.[94] Each person contributed a congratulatory verse for the occasion. Den Jōza of Ise province presented the master with a statue of the deity Idaten. The master celebrated the occasion with a verse:

To the north Prince Bishamon stoutly defends the Dharma,
Idaten stands stern guard over the other three quarters;
There is nothing much left for this feeble old monk to do,
Just turn the two wheels forward, and keep an eye on you.[95]

After the meeting ended the master remained at Ryūtaku-ji for an extended stay. One day as he was walking in the temple garden, he remarked, "How firm and solid the ground here is. How beautiful the mountains and forests!" Taking his brush he wrote out the words, "I'd like my body to be buried right here at this spot a hundred years from now."

The master took a statue of Akiba Gongen that he owned and personally enshrined it at Ryūtaku-ji. He wanted to ensure the temple would be protected against fire long into the future.

Hōreki 12 (1762) Age 77
Autumn. In the eighth month the master spent several days at Daichū-ji in Numazu helping Tōrei conduct a lecture meeting on the *Heart Sutra*. Afterwards, responding to a request for lectures on the *Record of Hsu-t'ang*, he paid a visit to Seiryō-ji.

The monks decided to hold a final lecture meeting for the master at Shōin-ji. They scheduled it for the spring of his eightieth year, the fourteenth year of Hōreki.

Hōreki 13 (1763) Age 78

Spring. The master was slightly indisposed over the New Year but he soon recovered. In the second month he lectured on the *Blue Cliff Record* at the request of Shōkō-ji in Numazu. Following that he gave talks over a period of days at five other Numazu temples: Ryōun-ji, Igen-ji, Eishō-ji, Jōin-ji, and Senryū-ji. He also visited Kōhō-in in nearby Enashi to complete some unfinished lectures on the *Blue Cliff Record*.

In the third month he lectured to over two hundred people on the *Record of Sung-yuan* at the request of Jiun-ji in Ejiri. From spring onward a general debility, brought on by old age and illness, was increasingly evident. The master had lost his former vitality and alertness. Lecturing left him extremely tired, as though the immense energy he had been pouring into his teaching activity was now used up. By mid-winter the decline was even more pronounced. The monks feared that he might be unable to conduct the final lecture meeting they had planned the following spring.

The eleventh of the twelfth month. In the middle of the night the master summoned all the monks to him. "Come close," he told them. "I have just had the most remarkable dream. It has completely restored my spirits. I now feel just the way I used to.

"I was sitting in a newly built temple, in the right-hand wing where the retired abbot lives. Setsu Shuso of Ketsujō-ji and other old friends were sitting around me. Seated in a row opposite us were the distinguished priests Gudō, Daigu, Munan, and Shōju. Yōshun, Kogetsu, Haryō, and Jōzan were there too. One of the friends sitting near me sighed and said, 'It's not right for priests of inferior capacity like us, who have trouble bringing our everyday lives into harmony with our religious understanding, to be sitting here opposite these eminent priests.' Setsu made a wry smile and said, 'You only feel that way because of the two words we lack.' All those present, even the senior priests sitting across from us, were eager to know the two words. When he told them—'Bravery and valor'—the whole room broke into applause. As I was reflecting on this it suddenly dawned on me that the people I was with were all deceased. I declared loudly, 'How can I agree to remain with you here!' and that's when I woke up. I want you all to fix this story in your minds. And you can stop worrying about me being able to complete that lecture meeting next spring!"

The master was keen and alert after that, and hardly ever had to rely on others for help of any kind.

Hōreki 14 / Meiwa 1 (1764) Age 79

Disciples of the master presented him with congratulatory verses in commemoration of his eightieth birthday. On the fifteenth of the second month he lectured on the *Record of Daiō*. He acclaimed the great prescience of Daiō's teacher Hsu-t'ang when he had declared that his "descendents would increase day by day in the land beyond the eastern seas [Japan]."[96] The meeting, attended by over seven hundred people, was supervised by the abbots of Daijō-ji, Ryūshin-ji, and Bodaiju-in, as well as by Priests Daichū, Ishin, Tōrei, and Eboku. The discipline was rigorous and the session was an unprecedented success. As it progressed, near the end of the month, the master became extremely tired and asked Ishin to share the teaching duties. Tōrei also helped, giving supplementary lectures on *Daiō's Memorial Inscription*.

In the third month when the meeting ended Eboku left for Kyoto to receive the rank of First Monk (*Dai-ichiza*) at Myōshin-ji. At this time his priest's name was officially changed to Genro; he adopted the studio name Suiō. He returned to Shōin-ji in the seventh month. The master formally retired as abbot of Shōin-ji, turning the position over to Suiō.[97]

Meiwa 2 (1765) Age 80

Spring, the first month. The master conducted a *shari* ceremony at Ryūtaku-ji.[98] He and Suiō had a falling-out. Suiō left Shōin-ji and went to stay at Kannon-ji. The master's compassionate old heart was much troubled by this turn of events. Efforts by the senior priest at Fumon-ji to console him helped ease the pain.

In the third month the master fell ill and was confined to his bed at Shōin-ji. Tōrei traveled to Edo where, in collaboration with others, he was rebuilding Shidō-an, the temple where Shidō Munan had resided. In the sixth month he returned to Shōin-ji so that he could escort the master to Edo to show him the new temple. Some of the monks at Shōin-ji blocked the way and prevented the master's palanquin from leaving. That winter Tōrei sent a letter to the monks remonstrating with them for their behavior, but their opposition to the master's trip did not weaken. On the contrary, certain malicious members of the brotherhood used Tōrei's letter to stir up further ill-will.

Meiwa 3 (1766) Age 81

At the New Year the master hung out a notice announcing that he would no longer receive students for instruction. However, the monks did not disperse.

Toward the end of the first month Tōrei sent his disciple Bunkyō from Edo to escort the master to Shido-an. They set out on the road over Mount Hakone, planning to stop over at the residence of Mr. Amano. Four of the Shōin-ji monks who had led the opposition to the master's departure came after them, surrounding the master's palanquin and forcing it to stop. They attempted to make the porters return to Shōin-ji. It was a reenactment of the scene that had taken place in China centuries ago when Senior Monk Ming followed the Sixth Patriarch to Mount Ta-yu.[99]

Bunkyō stepped forward and addressed them, "Brother monks, what possible justification could you have for such behavior?"

"Our teacher is old and weak from his long illness," they said. "You and these others come and try to carry him off to Edo. It is sure to make his condition worse. As his students, how can we stand by and let you, or anyone else, take him away?"

"The master's infirmity is only temporary," replied Bunkyō. "Besides, he himself has expressed a growing desire to go. Don't you realize that if you insist on defying his wishes in this way, you will be destroying the affection and good will that has built up over many years! We will never allow you to turn this palanquin around. If you had the strength to yank these mountains up by their roots, the strength we would muster against you would be still greater by far."

With bowed heads, the four monks silently turned and left.

The master's party proceeded to Edo. Their first stop was a guesthouse owned by Mr. Iwanami. From there they went to stay with the nun Hōjuin-ni, and then moved into Tōhoku-ji. On the eleventh day of the second month, the master entered the gates of Shidō-an hermitage. He was delighted to find that the reconstruction work was almost completed. He stayed at Shidō-an, teaching daily, for almost six months. Tōrei occasionally helped by giving supplemental talks. The monks and lay followers at Shidō-an made daily progress in their study. A large number of high-ranking officials, among them Morikawa Hyōbu (Layman Zennō) and Ozeki Shinano-no-kami, came and received instruction from the master.

The sixth month. The master transcribed the notations inscribed in a copy of the *Blue Cliff Record* that Zen Master Sekkō Sōshin had presented to his student Tōyō Eichō.[100] He made these notations the subject of lectures he delivered at the Chōju-ji in Edo.

In the seventh month he received a request for lectures from the Fukuju-in in Mishima. Before leaving Edo, responding to an invitation from that temple and from Laymen Aoki and Ōmura, he lectured at Tōhoku-ji.[101] On his way back to Suruga province he stopped over at Seiun-ji in Sagami and then proceeded to Fukuju-in, where he gave lectures on Shakyamuni's three preachings of the *Lotus Sutra*.[102] From there he went to Gyokusei-ji to complete some lectures he had left unfinished at a previous meeting.

In winter he was back at Shōin-ji.

Meiwa 4 (1767) Age 82

Spring. A proposal to have the master conduct the winter practice session at Ryūtaku-ji that year was discussed; disagreements came to the fore, leading to heated arguments.

During the spring and summer months the master spent time relaxing and enjoying the waters at Kona hot springs on the Izu peninsula.

Winter. In the tenth month the master lectured at Ryūtaku-ji on *Poison Flowers in a Thicket of Thorns*. More than two hundred and fifty outstanding monks from all over the country converged on the temple to take part. The rigorous training schedule and a strict observance of regulations enabled the monks and laity to concentrate on their practice with great intensity. The master became extremely fatigued by his teaching duties and asked Tōrei to share the teaching seat. Tōrei gave supplementary lectures on the master's *Dharma Talks Introductory to Lectures on the Record of Hsi-keng*.

Meiwa 5 (1768) Age 83

The master saw in the New Year at Ryūtaku-ji (Dragon Marsh Temple). On the first day, he offered a celebratory verse:

> Sauntering freely through the highest peaks of Dragon's Marsh,
> Old face uncommonly thick-skinned this New Year's morning,
> An elder monk of eighty-four welcomes in yet one more year;
> He owes it all—everything—to the Sound of One Hand koan.

When he finished the formal reading of the Chinese verse, he reverted to colloquial speech and declared in a loud voice, "I'm eighty-four this year. I've never had such a wonderful New Year. It's all thanks to Tōrei. I am truly, truly grateful."

Tōrei brought some New Year rice cakes for the master. He took two or three bites and left the rest for his students. Tōrei received them with reverence and withdrew.

At the end of the winter training session the master took once again to his sick bed. The physician who examined him said, "You are too addicted to sugar. Your illness is caused by the harmful effect of all the sweets you eat. We'll have to purge the sugar from your system." He gave the master a purgative and, after several visits to the privy, he seemed to feel better. The master's physician Sugiyama Yōsen had him sequestered in a room and forbade him to have visitors.[103] With the aid of unstinted sleep he was able to regain his strength.

In response to a request for lectures from nearby Tokuraku-ji he went and spoke on the *Supplement to Poison Flowers in a Thicket of Thorns*.

In the sixth month a mortuary tablet for the Emperor Reigen-in was brought and placed in Ryūtaku-ji.[104] The master conducted rites to enshrine the tablet the following month. He read out a verse:

I bow deeply to honor His majesty the tonsured emperor
     Reigen;
Who could have foreseen a jade tablet shining in this rustic
     hall?
The lotus in the garden proclaim the Buddhas' unimpeded
     virtues,
Pine trees at the gate breathe forth the Bodhisattvas' time-
     less age.

On the sixteenth of the seventh month he returned to Shōin-ji.

In winter, he made excursions to Daijō-ji in Kawanishi and Jōen-ji in Yui. For three days at the former and five days at the latter he gave talks and taught on whatever moved his fancy. While he was at Jōen-ji, he became extremely fatigued. One of the monks said, "Wouldn't it be best to suspend your teaching activity until you feel stronger?"

"What is my fatigue, compared with the famine my monks and laymen are suffering from?" the master replied.

A woman came forward and said, "If you stopped the flow of sweet dew from your lips, it would indeed be like taking food from the mouths of the starving. It would be like depriving a sick person of his physician. He would be confused, not knowing where to turn for help. However, in your present condition, if by any chance you did suffer a reverse tomorrow, and entered Nir-vana, to whom could we, your followers, turn for guidance? Even though we may not hear you preach the Dharma with words, if we can just gaze on your countenance and know that you are safe, what greater happiness could there be for us?" A faint smile formed on the master's lips.

In the eleventh month the master returned to Shōin-ji. It was evident that his condition was growing more serious.

On the sixth of the twelfth month the area was swept by a freak storm that sent lightning bolts crashing violently to earth. The next day the physician Furugōri came and examined the master's pulses.[105]

"What do you think?" asked the master.

"Nothing out of the ordinary," he replied.

"Can someone be called a skilled physician," the master chided, "when he can't even tell that his patient has only three more days to live."

Furugōri just sat with his head bowed.

Old Mr. Yamanashi was allowed to visit. A go board was brought out, but after two or three moves, the master was forced to stop.

On the tenth day, the master called Suiō to his sickbed and entrusted him with his personal affairs after his death.

At daybreak on the eleventh, the master was sleeping very peacefully, lying on his right side. He made a single loud groan, "*UNN!*" and passed away.[106]

The funeral was held on the fifteenth. A violent storm made it impossible to carry the master's body to the funeral pyre, so the cremation was postponed until the following day. Afterwards, a great many relics were found among the ashes. Most of them were discovered where oil had been poured on the fire. Resembling particles of sand or tiny pebbles, they were the color of precious blue gems. They were the true fruits of the master's meditation and wisdom. People flocked to the cremation site, more than a few behaving like the demons that thronged to the Buddha's cremation hoping to acquire precious relics from his remains. Because of this, the relics were divided into three lots and enshrined in stupas at the master's three temples: Shōin-ji, Muryō-ji, and Ryūtaku-ji.

Epilogue by Tōrei

My teacher Hakuin was a very imposing man. He combined the gaze of a tiger and the walk and movements of an ox. The extreme sharpness of his Zen activity made it difficult to approach him. Virtually tireless, he brought the same degree of care and compassion to whatever he did. In settling troubles, in rectifying wrongs, he worked with silent persuasion, private discipline. His actions, whether he was moving, standing, sitting, or lying down, were such that they could not be fathomed by either demons or non-Buddhists. The manner in which his teaching activity prospered recalled the days of the great Chinese master Ma-tsu. The adversity under which he lived and taught was reminiscent of the hardships faced by Master Ta-hui.

I have recorded in this biography a great many of the talks and lectures the master gave on Zen records, sutras, and other texts in answer to requests from temples throughout the country. There are yet others, still talked about even today, whose dates I was unable to ascertain. The general talk he gave at the Chōkō-ji in Kai province on the *Four Part Collection* is one example; another is the lecture meeting at Chōfuku-ji in Izu province on his commentary on the *Poems of Cold Mountain*. Also the meeting supervised by Chō of Tango and Kyū of Rinsen-ji that was held at the request of Layman Kokan. Or the lecture at Hōun-ji in Imaizumi on the *Record of Wu-tsu*. Wherever he went to conduct these meetings, he never allowed participants to draw upon the temple's stores; provisions were obtained entirely through begging expeditions. Indeed, the standards observed throughout were those of the great Buddhist communities of old, an exemplary model to hold up for future generations.

Once an outbreak of smallpox ravaged the area, taking a heavy toll of human life. When the illness was at its height, an elderly man approached him as he was sitting against a phoenix tree after an afternoon nap. The man got down on his knees, made a deep bow, and asked the master to write a charm or talisman for use against the smallpox.

"What kind of charm do you mean?" asked the master.

"Please write down the words Tokoura Daimyōjin," [the great deity of Tokoura] said the man. The master took up his brush, wrote out the inscription the man had requested, and gave it to him.

"No one who comes and venerates this inscription," said the old man, "will ever suffer from the smallpox." He then suddenly disappeared.

It was like that with the master, whose life was lived in the "sportive samadhi" of the perfectly enlightened person, constantly ministering to the needs and suffering of sentient beings. A great many other strange and unusual occurrences took place that I have not recorded.

His final utterance—"*Unn*"—was in every way comparable to the great death cry of old Zen Master Yen-t'ou.[107] Ordinary people, upon hearing that the master did not compose a death verse, might mistakenly think, "Master Hakuin lost a fine opportunity to make a final Zen utterance." Wrong! Wrong! That "*Unn*" was perfectly appropriate. It penetrated straight through the Heavens above; it pierced through the Yellow Springs below. I believe that it was superior by ten times to the final instructions and death verses Zen monks usually leave behind them. Ahh! When he declared that he was the kind of man who appears only once in five hundred years, it certainly was no exaggeration.

Four heirs received the master's Dharma transmission: Kairyū Ishō, Tōrei Enji, Suiō Genro, and Tōgan Gen.[108] His lay students are too numerous to list. Indeed, among priests presently engaged in teaching Zen there can be hardly a single one in all the land who did not once pass through the master's fiery forge.

APPENDIX A: SATSU (see Age 42)

The following anecdotes about Satsu are found in *Stories from a Thicket of Thorn and Briar*, an anecdotal collection of stories about Hakuin and his disciples compiled by Myōki, a priest three generations after Hakuin.

"O-Satsu was the daughter of one of Hakuin's cousins. When

she reached the age of fifteen, she thought to herself, 'I'm certainly not much to look at, but fortunately I have no physical defects. I don't think it'll be long now before I find a suitable husband and am married.' She proceeded in secret to the Akeno Kannon in nearby Yanagizawa and prayed to the Bodhisattva for help. Mornings and evenings she recited the *Kannon Sutra for Prolonging Life* and soon was reciting it constantly, even when she was sewing, washing, or cleaning. After a few days she suddenly experienced a realization."

According to the account of the story given above in the *Chronological Biography* (page 199), Satsu was squatting on top of some volumes of the *Lotus Sutra* in her bedroom. In response to her father's reproach she said: "What difference is there between the *Lotus Sutra* and my derrière?" Her father, not knowing what to make of this, went to Hakuin. Hakuin assured him that he could help her. He wrote out a waka poem: "If you can hear the voice of a crow that doesn't caw in the darkness of night, you'll welcome the father before you were born," and told the father to hang the inscription up on the wall somewhere in his house where Satsu would be sure to notice it. When Satsu saw it she said, "Priest Hakuin's handwriting. I'd expect something a bit better from him." When this was reported to Hakuin, he told Satsu's father to bring her to the temple. Hakuin asked some questions. She responded easily with no hesitation. He gave her some koans. She pondered them, and a few days later penetrated their meaning. Hakuin then tried to assign her some additional koans, but she said she was no longer interested, and when she stood firm in the face of Hakuin's entreaties, he struck her with his bamboo stick (*shippei*). Similar encounters took place in the following weeks and months, but six months later, Satsu had passed all the additional koan barriers the master had given her.

One time Satsu's father decided to find her a husband, but she was not interested just then. Her father enlisted Hakuin's help. Summoning Satsu, he said, "You have penetrated the Buddha's Dharma. Why are you so opposed to the world's Dharma? Marriage is a very important matter between men and women. You should follow your father's wishes." Satsu bowed her head in agreement and was married soon after.

Later in life, Satsu's granddaughter died, and she was suffering extreme grief over the loss. An old man who lived next door came over and admonished her for weeping and wailing. "People in the neighboring village are talking about you," he said. "They say, 'She practiced under Master Hakuin. She achieved *kenshō* and satori.' This grief over the loss of your granddaughter is excessive. Don't you think you should reflect over your actions." Satsu glared at the man. "You confounded old codger!" she said, reviling him. "What do you know? My tears and sorrow are far better than offering her incense and flowers or lighting candles for her. You don't know anything, you old crock!" The man left without another word.

That outburst was more or less characteristic of Satsu's severe and biting comments. The monks who resided at Shōin-ji and took their questions to her, thinking she was just an old woman, invariably came away looking very miserable indeed.

When Satsu passed away, Hakuin's disciple Suiō remarked to the assembly: "During the old master's lifetime, many people were able to attain a clear and unmistakable enlightenment. Of them all, O-Satsu stood preeminent. Even veteran monks, men who had practiced many years, could not approach her."

Appendix B: Disturbance in the Kitchen *(See Age 56)*

Hearing a commotion in the kitchen, I (Hakuin) inquired about it and found that a trusted servant was getting ready for an upcoming trip to Kai province where I had been invited for talks. He was preparing to go on ahead with my baggage. The noise had been caused by men gathering things together and bundling them up. Surprised to see how much was being taken, I said, "It's a long trip, think how tired you're going to be carrying all that stuff. Let's see if we can lighten the load. Then it will be 'not as much as Hua-yen, but more than Yun-feng.'" We untied the bundles and went through them looking for articles that could be left behind. In the end we were unable to dispense with a single thing.

We were packing and bundling things up for our trip,
How shameful, troubling such large numbers of men.
If you happen to run into historian Ssu-ma on the way,
Tell him lecturing isn't a teacher's most onerous task.

(*Poison Flowers, kan 9*)

The allusions to Hua-yen, Ssu-ma, and Yun-feng derive from two Zen anecdotes having to do with the baggage priests carry on their travels. The first is from *Ta-hui's Arsenal*:

"Hua-yen achieved a realization when he spilled a drink he was carrying. He wrote a verse:

This single mistake I made, this single mishap,
Has more value to me than ten thousand in gold;
Donning a sedge hat, travel pouch round my waist,
At the tip of my staff, the pure breeze and bright moon!

Minister Fu-cheng constantly mulled the meaning of this verse. Then, when he saw Hua-yen ascend to the high seat and glance to the right and the left, he experienced a sudden enlightenment. He composed a verse and presented it to Yuan-chao.

A glance at Master Hua brought deep enlightenment,
Teachers' minds can transmit conditions and causes;
Though distant by a thousand leagues of rivers and hills,
Your wondrous light and voice are before my very eyes.

After Fu-cheng had retired from his post as minister and was living in the capital, he remembered Hua-yen's verse-teaching and invited him to come and stay at his residence. On learning that Hua-yen had crossed the border of the province, he set out to meet him. As he was getting into his carriage, Ssu-ma Kuang happened by and asked where he was going. Fu-cheng replied that he had invited Zen Master Hua-yen to stay at his home and was going to meet him. Ssu-ma asked if he could go along. They rode together to the post station where they awaited Hua-yen's arrival. Presently, they saw ten cartloads of baggage pass suddenly by. Upon Ssu-ma asking the porters who the baggage belonged to, they replied that it belonged to Hua-yen. Ssu-ma mounted his horse and began to ride off. "Why are you leaving?" asked Cheng. "Didn't you want to see Hua-yen?" "I've seen altogether enough of him," replied Ssu-ma as he left.

The second story, concerning Zen priest Yung-feng, is from *Precious Lessons of the Zen School*: Huang-lung said, "Years back, when I was traveling in Hunan together with Wen-yueh, we saw a Zen monk on pilgrimage carrying a large basket. When he made a face to express his disapproval, I scolded him. 'Instead of ridding yourself of the baggage you carry in your own mind,' I said, 'you extend your worries to include even what others are carrying. Don't you find that extremely burdensome?'"

Notes

NOTES TO THE INTRODUCTION

1. Precious Mirror Cave (the title is taken from the work translated in Chapter 5) is a metaphor for the deepest level of mind where the Zen quest takes place and enlightenment occurs in the instantaneous transformation of the darkness of the eighth consciousness into the perfect clarity and brilliance of the Precious Mirror or Buddha-mind.

2. There is still no complete edition containing all the principal published works. *The Collected Works of Zen Priest Hakuin,* published in eight volumes in 1935 and running to some 2,500 pages, omitted some important works and gave incomplete texts of others. The more recent *Zen Master Hakuin's Complete Dharma Writings,* published in fourteen volumes between the years 1999 and 2003, offers for the first time excellent and annotated editions of almost all the Japanese works. Of the principal works he wrote in Chinese, only *Dream Words from the Land of Dreams,* a difficult but major commentary modeled on the *Blue Cliff Record,* has appeared in a well-annotated edition (Dōmae Sōkan, Zen-bunka Kenkyūsho, 2003). Similar editions of *Talks Introductory to Lectures on the Record of Hsi-keng* and *Poison Flowers in a Thicket of Thorns* are still needed.

3. Biographical episodes are scattered through his early works such as *A Record of Sendai's Comments on the Poems of Cold Mountain* (1746), *Talks Introductory to Lectures on the Record of Hsi-keng* (1743), and *Oradegama* (1749–51).

4. *The Religious Art of Zen Master Hakuin,* pp. 115–16.

5. Literally, *medama-gayu* or "eyeball gruel," also called "ceiling gruel," because it is so thin one's eyes (or the ceiling) can be seen reflected in it.

6. On the eve of the winter solstice, as the monks were enjoying some fruit, Tung-shan said to head monk Tai, "There is something black as lacquer that supports the heavens above and the earth below. It is always active yet activity cannot completely describe it. Tell me, where does it fail?" "Its

activity is its failing," answered Tai. T'ung-shan gave a loud shout and had the fruit taken away.

7. The work, translated in my *Essential Teachings of Zen Master Hakuin,* contains descriptions of the extensive renovations undertaken by Hakuin's monks in preparing the temple for the meeting.

8. Translated by Philip Yampolsky, *The Zen Master Hakuin: Selected Writings.*

9. For a discussion of the way Hakuin used Edo street life in his paintings, see *The Religious Art of Zen Master Hakuin.*

10. See my translation of this work, *Zen Words for the Heart.*

11. *Keikyoku-sōdan.* Completed in 1829, and published thirteen years later.

12. Although there is no mention of this in the records, it seems a safe guess that Tōrei was using the therapeutic meditations to cure himself that Hakuin had used before him. The original version of the *Idle Talk* story had been published slightly before this time.

NOTES TO CHAPTER 1

1. The Japanese title might also be translated as *The Tale of My Childhood to Spur On Others,* which would make that motive clearer.

2. The translation is based on the text in *Hakuin Zenji Hōgo Zenshū,* vol. 7.

3. His earliest known work in the genre, *Cloth Drum (Nunotsuzumi),* a collection of tales of cause and effect recounting the misfortunes that befell various unfilial sons and daughters, dates from his twenty-ninth year. He wrote it while he was staying at Inryō-ji, a Sōtō temple in Izumi province, as a letter to reproach a childhood friend named Watanabe Heizaemon for his profligate ways. A revised and greatly expanded version of the work was published in 1753, when he was in his seventies, under the title *A New Drumhead for the Cloth Drum (Saiben nunotsuzumi).*

4. Robert Aitken translates this brief text, Japanese title *Emmei Jikku Kannon-gyō,* as follows: "Kanzeon! I venerate the Buddha, with the Buddha I have my source, with the Buddha I have affinity—affinity with Buddha, Dharma, Sangha, constancy, ease, assurance, purity. Mornings my thought is Kanzeon, evenings my thought is Kanzeon, thought-after-thought arises in mind, thought after thought is not separate from mind" (*The Morning Star,* Shoemaker & Hoard, 2003). He translates the title *The Ten Verse Kannon Sūtra for Timeless Life,* interpreting the Japanese *Emmei,* which I have translated "Prolonging Life," in a way that Hakuin would no doubt have accepted.

5. This appears in a Sung collection of Zen anecdotes titled *Precious Lessons of the Zen School:*

> Zen Master Yuan-wu K'o-ch'in said to Fo-chien, "My old master Po-yun always considered the sayings and actions of former masters in whatever he did. He was always saying, 'What is not referred to in the ancient records is not in accord with the Buddhist Dharma. It was because I knew many of the words and

deeds of the past teachers that I was able to complete my religious quest.'"

6. Tōrei's holograph manuscript identifies this person as Toda Kyūemon Mitsusūke.

7. The first visit mentioned here is confirmed in the *Chronological Biography*: "In winter of 1759 the master spent the seventh month to the twelfth month in Edo." The second visit is not recorded in the *Biography*, but is mentioned in a letter to Katayama Shunnan (see Introduction to Chapter Two, pp. 43–44). When a new Shōgun was installed in Edo, Buddhist priests were required to re-register with the Magistrate for Temples and Shrines. Such a succession had occurred in 1760 when Tokugawa Ienori succeeded the previous Shōgun Ieshige. Hakuin went to Edo in spring of the following year.

8. The text describes a two-part koan, "*sekishu onjō ryōjū*," "the double-barrier of the sound of one hand." Until recently this has been mistakenly read to mean "the *difficult* barrier of the Sound of One Hand koan." From Hakuin's writings and calligraphy, however, it is clear that this refers to a two-part koan, one that he used for beginning students: after passing the Sound of One Hand koan, the student was given a second koan, Put a Stop to All Sounds.

9. An illustration of one of these Dragon Staff certificates is found on p. 41.

10. The phrase "lower your cloud" (*untō o ange shi*) was originally a Taoist expression describing the manner in which cloud-riding immortals lowered their vehicles to walk the earth (it appears frequently in the classic Chinese novel *Hsi-yu-chi*). Hakuin uses the expression to describe a teacher leaving the realm of the absolute, where verbal explanation is impossible, and descending to the relative plane to make his teaching accessible by employing expedient means.

11. This translates a short emphatic injunction, pronounced *kokani-i* in Japanese, that Master Yun-men used to end addresses to his monks.

12. These are the Hinayana and Mahayana teachings and the teachings of sudden and gradual enlightenment; esoteric and indeterminate are among four modes into which the Tendai sect classifies the Buddha's teaching.

13. In his commentary on the *Blue Cliff Record*, Hakuin says of "entrance into enlightenment" (*nyūsho*), "it is not sudden great enlightenment but a small or minor enlightenment."

14. A saying of the Yuan dynasty priest Kao-feng Yuan-miao, found in the *Record of Kao-feng* and *Son-ga kyui-gam*, a Korean work known in Japan as *Zenke-kikan*.

15. "Poisonous slobber" (*rōdoku-en*) is apparently a variation of "poisonous (wild) fox slobber" (*koen* or *yako-enda*), a metaphor for the "poisonous words" used by Zen teachers. Since the wild fox commonly appears in Zen literature as the dispenser of teachings that lead Zen students astray, "wild fox slobber" also is used as a metaphor for plausible or sham Zen teachings. The story of an old priest who collected the saliva of wild foxes

is told in *Kuang yi chi,* a T'ang dynasty collection of supernatural tales of ghosts and goblin foxes first published at the end of the Ming dynasty. The priest buried a jar filled with the saliva in the earth; after leaving it there for a certain time, he dug it up and made it into a powder that could be used, with powerful effect, for casting magic spells. The term appears in *Miscellaneous Records of Zen Master Ming-pen of Mount T'ien-mu* (*T'ien-mu ming-pen ch'an-shih tsa-lu*), a collection of the Zen records of the Yuan dynasty master Chung-feng Ming-pen (1263–1323), under the title "For the Instruction of Zen people": "Most students around the country today, hoping merely to attain self-emancipation, engage in a plausible, sham Zen. They practice merely to gain a proficiency in elucidating the Zen teachings, never realizing as they try to cut the flow of thoughts in their deluded minds that such thoughts can never completely be extinguished. This is what is called pernicious knowledge, pernicious awakening. The ancients referred to it as 'wild fox slobber.' A single drop finding its way into your mind will drive you completely insane."

In Hakuin's writings the terms "fox slobber" and "wild fox slobber" have a similar meaning referring to a substance of virulent poison, but they invariably appear in a more positive sense. For example, in describing the utterances of the Sung priest Hsi-keng, he describes him "spewing and leaving masses of venomous fox slobber behind in the temples where he served" (*Essential Teachings of Zen Master Hakuin,* p. 9). In other words, the utterances Hsi-keng and other great Zen teachers use in teaching students possess the power to cause sudden death in students, raising the great doubt in their minds that will lead them to the "great death" and the rebirth of satori or enlightenment.

16. A shade tree is a metaphor for an enlightened teacher who provides refreshing shade for sentient beings, i.e., enables them to dispel their illusions and afflicting passions. From the *Nirvana Sutra* and *Record of Lin-chi.*

17. Fa-jung (594–657), a Dharma heir of the Fourth Chinese Zen patriarch Tao-hsin, taught on Mount Niu-t'ou and founded a line of Zen known as the Ox-head (Niu-t'ou; Japanese Gozu) school.

18. Hakuin uses these two terms, "claws and fangs of the Dharma cave" (*hokkutsu no sōge*) and "divine, death-dealing amulets" (also talismans; *datsumyō no shinpu*), to refer to koans and the power they possess to bring students to experience the Great Death. The former alludes to the harsh and rigorous means Zen teachers employ in teaching students, comparing them to the means used by the lion in rearing its cubs. The latter were Taoist charms said to give the possessor great power, including the taking of human life.

19. An allusion to a famous Zen saying about the Five Schools of Chinese Zen that emerged during the ninth and tenth centuries, and developed in the eleventh century into Seven Schools, when koan Zen began to evolve.

20. A Tendai classification of sutras the Buddha preached over his lifetime divides them into five periods (*goji-kyō*). He expounded the *Flower Garland Sutra* three weeks after his enlightenment (the Flower Garland period), but finding his listeners unable to understand its subtleties, over the next twelve years (the Deer Park period) he preached the Hinayana sutras, adapting his teaching to his listeners. Thereafter he preached the various Mahayana sutras. The five principle Mahayana sutras referred to here are the *Flower Garland Sutra, Great Assembly Sutra, Larger Prajnaparamita Sutra, Lotus Sutra,* and *Nirvana Sutra.*

21. Case 96, "Chao-chou's Three Turning Words." A gold Buddha does not pass through a furnace; a wood Buddha does not pass through fire; a mud Buddha does not pass through water.

22. Hakuin's childhood name was Iwajirō. The abbreviated Iwaya (which may possibly be read Iwano) derives from it.

23. According to the account in *Wild Ivy*, this was Shōgen(kyō)-ji, a Nichiren temple near the family home in Hara. The *Chronological Biography* dates these visits to his tenth year; *Wild Ivy,* to his sixth or seventh year. "Teaching Schools" would include all Buddhist schools except Zen, whose transmission of the Buddha-mind is from mind to mind, and apart from the scriptural teachings.

24. According to *Wild Ivy*, this was Asanuma Hachirō, the husband of one of Hakuin's sisters.

25. The sacred grove (*Tenjin no mori*) attached to the Tenjin shrine in Hara was located between Sainen-ji and the post-house run by Hakuin's family.

26. This is a metaphor for the use of expedient means that appears in the *Nirvana Sutra, ch.* 20: "When a young child is crying, its mother will show it some yellow poplar leaves and say, 'Don't cry. Don't cry. Look, I'll give you some gold.' Seeing the leaves the child thinks they are real gold and stops crying. But the yellow leaves are not really gold."

27. The *Tenjin Sutra* (*Tenjin-kyō*) is a brief text of roughly one hundred words that was probably composed around the beginning of the Edo period (1600–1868). It was printed individually and was also inserted at the end of textbooks and copybooks used in *terakoya,* schools in Buddhist temples that taught children reading and writing. The text, incorporating elements of the Tenjin cult and Buddhism, is generally Buddhist in vocabulary but with a meaning that is at times unclear. It closes with the invocation to Tenjin: "Namu Tenman Daijizai Tenjin" ("Homage to Tenjin, deity of great freedom, deity of the Tenmangu Shrine").

28. Both here and in *Wild Ivy* Hakuin reports memorizing the *Kannon Sutra* in only one or two nights, though that would be quite a remarkable feat.

29. Nothing is known about Morioka Kunai. In the *Wild Ivy* account of this episode, Hakuin says he saw the performance at the village of Suwa (probably Ōsuwa, or Kosuwa, located several villages east of Hara). The play in question, whose subject is the evangelist Nichiren priest Nisshin Shōnin (1407–88), known as "Pot-wearing Nisshin," is probably *Nisshin Shōnin*

tokkō ki ("The Virtuous Conduct of Nisshin Shōnin"), a work by Chika-matsu Monzaemon that is said to have been first performed at the begin-ning of the Genroku era (1688–1704). The words about true believers in the *Lotus Sutra* being able to enter a fire without being burned, etc., are found in the *Fumon-bon* chapter of the sutra (the chapter also known as the *Kannon Sutra*). Similar sayings are also found in early, pre-Buddhist Chinese works; see *Records of the Grand Historian, Qin Dynasty* (trans. Burton Watson, Columbia University Press, 1993, p. 57).

30. A collection of Chinese phrases culled from Chinese and Zen literature used in koan study.

31. Sugawara Michizane's (later the deity Tenjin) birthday fell on the twenty-fifth of the month; the twenty-fifth became a special day of observance each month at Tenjin shrines.

32. Cold water ablutions are a traditional regimen for strengthening spiritual resolve and promoting religious attainment.

33. Kan'e-bō was a Nichiren priest who is said to have constructed a small hermitage next to Sainen-ji (the Ji Sect temple near Hakuin's home; see above, note 25) and devoted his time to chanting the *Lotus Sutra*. "He had nothing but the deepest affection for young Hakuin's ability and courage" (from a parenthetical note attached to the manuscript draft of the *Chron-ological Biography*).

34. The ideas that all things in the relative, mundane world are, as such, man-ifestations of ultimate truth and that the *Lotus Sutra* represents the Bud-dha's supreme teaching—the one vehicle—are both preached in the "Expedient Means" chapter of the *Lotus Sutra*.

35. These are classical war chronicles written in the twelfth century.

36. Byakuge-zan is the "mountain" name of Zensō-ji, a Rinzai temple in Shi-mizu. The story occurs in *Praise of the True School* in the biography of Yen-t'ou Chuan-huo: "One day Yen-t'ou told his assembly, 'When I leave you, I will do it after emitting a loud shout.' Later, when bandits came to ransack the temple and found nothing worth stealing, they ended up putting all the monks to the sword. Yen-t'ou remained completely calm and collected to the end. Before he died, he emitted a loud shout that was heard for several leagues." Reference to a great teacher appearing only once every five hundred years appears in the *Blue Cliff Record*, Case 26; its ultimate source is *Mencius*.

37. These, of course, are not suitable pastimes for a Zen monk in training. Yoshizawa Katsuhiro quotes a relevant passage from *Ta-hui's Arsenal*: "Zen Master Yuan-tsung remarked during a snowfall, 'This snow falls on three kinds of monks. The best ones are doing zazen in the training hall, the mediocre ones are dipping their brushes in ink and composing verses on the snowfall, and the inferior ones are sitting around the fire discuss-ing food.'" *Yaemugura, maki no san*, p. 134.

38. The *Chronological Biography* includes a parenthetical note identifying this man, whose dates are unknown, as a son of the famous Neo-Confucian teacher Kumazawa Banzan, 1619–91. In *Wild Ivy* Onbazan is described as

Baō's sole disciple at the time and a poet of some reputation, who would drop over from time to time and help Hakuin with the composition of linked verse. "We would start off our sessions by composing a hundred lines between us, Onbazan doing the first line, I matching it. It never took long to accomplish this—about the time for a couple sticks of incense to burn down."

39. A note in Tōrei's *Draft Biography* (age 22), omitted from the published text, suggests that Baō's trips into Ōgaki were occasioned by an infatuation with a woman named Jukei who lived in the town.

40. "A man who resembles a monk but is not a monk, resembles a layman but is not a layman—the Buddha calls such people 'bat-monks,' or 'shavepate laymen.'" *Admonitions for the Zen School* (*Hsi-men ching-hsun*), a Ming dynasty work on Zen practice.

41. The author of *Spurring Zen Students Through the Barrier,* Yun-ch'i Chuhung, is the subject of severe criticism in Hakuin's writings for his advocacy of "Nembutsu Zen." The work was first published in Japan in 1656.

42. In 1762, when Hakuin was seventy-six, some of his students had *Spurring Zen Students Through the Barrier* reprinted with a preface by Tōrei Enji. Hakuin did not know of the project until he was handed a newly printed copy of the book. He described his feelings in a letter: "I raised the book up in reverence two or three times, unable to stop the tears falling down my cheeks. My joy was extreme. I felt like jumping up and dancing about the room . . . I could have received no greater expression of Dharma gratitude. This book has meant more to me than anything else, even my teachers or my parents . . . During my pilgrimage . . . it never left my side." Quoted in *Shamon Hakuin*, p. 70.

43. These were probably Masaki Ryōkō, Tarumaru Sokai, and Nanzen Keryū of the Hōfuku-ji in Horato, three followers of Bankei Yōtaku's Zen teaching who are also mentioned in the *Chronological Biography* (age 22). The assembly of monks at Hōfuku-ji is also described in *Wild Ivy* (p. 21).

44. According to the *Chronological Biography* (age 22), while Hakuin was at Jōkō-ji, "he chanced to read a line of verse the Chinese priest Yun-chu Hsiao-shun had written upon returning home to resume the abbotship of Ch'i-hsien temple: 'How often I rejoice; how often I grow angry.' The moment he read it his eyes filled with tears. He had experienced something he had never known before."

45. The incumbent at Shōshū-ji was Itsuzen Gijun (d. 1703). According to the *Chronological Biography* (age 22), Itsuzen was lecturing on *Three Teachings of the Buddha-patriarchs*. The councillor is identified in the *Hara-chō shi* ("History of Hara Township," p. 359) as Okudaira Fujizaemon, a vassal of Matsudaira Sadanao, the Daimyo of Matsuyama Castle.

46. Ungo Kiyō (1582–1659), a prominent Myōshin-ji priest who rebuilt Zuigan-ji at Matsushima in northern Honshu. According to both *Wild Ivy* and the *Chronological Biography,* the calligraphy was by Daigu Sōchiku (1584–1669), another prominent Myōshin-ji priest. Ungo is reported to have had some connection with Shōshū-ji, but the calligraphy of both

men is highly idiosyncratic, making it difficult to determine whose calligraphy Hakuin actually saw.

47. In the *Chronological Biography* this is given as Tenju-ji. Tenshō-ji was the family temple of the Okudaira branch of the Matsudaira clan.

48. Daijōshō-ō is the honorific "National Master" (*Kokushi*) title of Kanzan Egen (1277–1360), founder of the Myōshin-ji. This story is probably based on the account in the *Kanzan kokushi betsuden*: "Kanzan was asked by his teacher Daitō Kokushi, 'When you passed through Suruga province did you see Mount Fuji?' 'No, I didn't,' replied Kanzan. 'That's how it is, Egen Zōsu, when a person is utterly devoted to the Way,' said Daitō, praising him." Katō Shōshun, *"Ōzen Fuzen Kanzan kokushi betsuden ni tsuite"* (*Zengaku kenkyū*, 61).

49. Hsien-yang, the capital of the great Ch'in empire.

50. "When they reached the city of Hyōgo, they bought passage on a boat" *Chronological Biography* (age 23). From Hyōgo (incorporated into the present-day city of Kobe) they sailed as far as Osaka.

51. The neighboring temple was probably Tokugen-ji, adjacent to Shōin-ji. According to the account in the *Chronological Biography* (age 23), "Chō Shuso, a disciple of the Ōbaku priest Egoku Dōmyō, was staying at Tokugen-ji accompanied by Kin Shuso, Ryū, and Ei. While they were there, the master [Hakuin] paid Chō a visit." Ryū Jōza (Senior Monk Ryū) seems to have been the incumbent at Tokugen-ji at the time, and Chō [Shuchō] Shuso was visiting him. Nothing else is known of Shuchō Shuso. In his edition of the *Chronological Biography*, Katō Shōshun identifies Ryū as Shōgen Genryū (d. 1765).

52. Eigan-ji was the family temple of Toda Tadazane (1651–1729), head of the Takada clan of Echigo. The head priest at the time was Shōtetsu Soron.

53. Although the term "silent illumination" (*mokushō*) is usually reserved to describe the practices of Sōtō Zen, in contrast to those of the Rinzai sect, with its stress on "introspecting the koan," in Hakuin's writings it indicates any type of Zen practice that does not focus on achieving *kenshō*.

54. Compare the account in the *Chronological Biography*: Chapter Six, p. 165.

55. These words are ones the Sōtō monk Dōgen is said to have spoken on attaining enlightenment while studying in China. Even as Hakuin attacked Sōtō Zen for espousing "silent illumination," he always expressed the highest regard in his writings for its founder, Dōgen, whose practice and enlightenment he considered consonant with his own *kenshō*-centered Zen.

56. These two phrases appear in other of Hakuin's works and were apparently his own.

57. Hakuin gave a very similar description of the enlightenment experience in *Poison Flowers in a Thicket of Thorns*: "If you proceed forward fearlessly without retreating, it will be like a sheet of solid ice suddenly shattering to pieces, like shoving over a jade pavilion. Becoming one with the world in all the ten directions, with heaven and hell, it then all at once will break into tiny pieces, and vanish. This is the occasion when you strike down

into the field of the eighth consciousness and break through beyond it. The world in the ten directions and emptiness as well all cease to exist, not a particle remains of the great earth, and the great and perfect light [of the mirror wisdom] will suddenly shine forth in pure and perfect clarity. There is nothing whatever to which it may be compared."

58. See note 36.

59. Presumably, this was done so that he could grab and wield the staff at an instant's notice.

60. A Bandō accent would imply a harsh provincial ring.

61. This is the most detailed account in Hakuin's records of Dōju Sōkaku (1679–1730), the new arrival who would figure prominently in Hakuin's life. Sōkaku (the name is often abridged to Kaku in Hakuin's writings) was twenty-nine years old at the time.

62. Hakuin introduces himself using the colorful alliterative phrase Suruga-zuru, "Crane from Suruga Province." The character Kaku, from Hakuin's name Ekaku, means "crane," but it can also be read zuru (tsuru), also meaning crane.

63. "Seeking advice about one's own ideas" (teige-mon) is a term that appears in The Eye of Men and Gods, ch. 2, in a passage in which Zen Master Fen-yang classifies the questions posed by Zen monks into eighteen types, grading from simple requests for instruction up to the deepest "silent question." Teige-mon is the second of the classifications, representing a rather elementary level, in which a student merely asks about a viewpoint that has been expressed.

64. Details of Shōju's life are uncertain. He was the son, perhaps adopted, of Matsudaira Tadatomo, Lord of Iiyama Castle, who raised and educated him. He showed an aptitude for religion at an early age and is said to have had an enlightenment experience at the age of fifteen. He was ordained by Shidō Munan, a disciple of the eminent Myōshin-ji priest Gudō Tōshoku, at Tōhoku-in in the Azabu district of Edo. Daien Hōkan is Gudō's honorific "National Master" (Kokushi) title. Gudō was one of the most highly respected Rinzai prelates of the early Edo period. He was a great-grandfather in the Dharma to Hakuin. Hakuin held him in great respect. He wrote a work titled Gudō's Lingering Radiance in which he extols Gudō's virtues and urges his fellow priests to sponsor a printing of Gudō's Zen records.

65. Su-shan's Memorial Tower is Case 40 in the Kattō-shū collection of koans. The head monk came to inform Su-shan Kuang-jen that construction of his memorial tower had been completed. Su-shan asked, "How much will you pay the builder?" "That's for you to decide," the monk replied. The master asked, "Would it be better to give him three cash, two cash, or one cash? If you can answer that, you would build me an even finer memorial tower." The monk was dumbfounded.

A monk visiting Lo-p'u Yuan-an's hermitage on Ta-yu Peak recounted the conversation between Su-shan and the head monk. "Has anyone come up with an answer?" asked Lo. "Not yet," replied the monk. "Then," said

Lo, "go back and tell Su-shan that if he gives the builder three cash he will never get a Memorial Tower; if he gives him two cash, he and the builder will work as a single hand; and if he gives him one cash, they both will lose their eyebrows" (the retribution for preaching false Dharma). The monk returned and gave the message to Su-shan. The master assumed a dignified manner, gazed in the direction of far-off Ta-yu Peak, and after performing a bow, said, "It looked as if no one would be able to come up with an answer, but an old Buddha on Ta-yu Peak has emitted a dazzling shaft of light that reached me even here. He is, nonetheless, as rare as a lotus flower blooming in mid-winter."

Upon learning of Su-shan's words, Lo said, "I would have said, 'The tail hairs of the tortoise have already bushed out several feet.'" Cf. *Zen Dust*, pp. 60–61; *Entangling Vines*, pp. 69–70.

66. The Lin-chi priest Hsu-t'ang Chih-yu reached enlightenment while working on the "Old Sail Not Yet Raised" koan and went to his teacher Yun-an P'u-yen's chambers to inform him of his breakthrough. The moment Hsu-tang entered the door the master could tell he had penetrated the koan, and instead of asking about it, he asked about another koan, "Nan-ch'uan Kills the Cat." Hsu-t'ang replied immediately, "Nowhere on earth you can put it." Yun-an smiled, confirming Hsu-t'ang's understanding. But Hsu-t'ang's mind was still not at peace, and for almost six months after that he still felt hindered when he engaged with others. He left Yun-an and worked for four years on Su-shan's Memorial Tower. One day he suddenly grasped "the point at which the old Buddha on Ta-yu Peak emits a shaft of dazzling light." From then on, he was perfectly free in whatever he did, and the great pride that had made him despise other students vanished. When he looked at koans he had previously penetrated, his understanding of them was altogether different and he realized clearly that this had nothing at all to do with words (*Hsu-t'ang yu-lu, ch.* 4).

The words "his descendents will increase day by day" appear in a verse Hsu-t'ang presented to his Japanese student Nampo Jōmyō (better known as Daiō Kokushi) when the latter was about to return home to Japan:

He visited Zen teachers, practiced with great devotion;
Where the path came to an end, he kept right on going.
[or, His search at an end, he now returns to his homeland;]
It is clear Jōmyō preaches together with old Hsu-t'ang;
My descendents will increase daily beyond the Eastern Seas."

The verse became known in Japanese Zen as "Hsu-t'ang's prophecy" (*Empō dentō-roku*). To Hakuin's mind, the transmission to Japan of authentic Zen (that which stressed attainment of *kenshō*) occurred through this lineage, passing from Nampo Jōmyō to Shūhō Myōchō (Daitō Kokushi) and on to Myōshin-ji founder Kanzan Egen; three hundred years later, it reached Hakuin by way of Gudō Tōshoku, Shidō Munan, and Shōju Rōjin.

67. Hakuin frequently alludes to this statement by the Sung dynasty master Ta-hui Tsung-kao. No source has been found among Ta-hui's voluminous records, and it appears Hakuin got it from *Jottings at the Bamboo Window, Second Series,* by the seventeenth-century Ming priest Yun-chi Chu-hung.

68. This incident is also described in the *Chronological Biography* (age 23). The account in *Wild Ivy* says he was "attacked by the occupant of the house," described by bystanders as "a crazy man." Hakuin's inconsistency on the matter would seem to confirm his self-description as "a lump of blank oblivion" at the time he was assailed.

69. "When you men are able to put a stop to the continuous seeking in your minds, you are no different from the Buddha-patriarchs. You're keen on acquiring an understanding of the Buddha-patriarchs, but the teaching you are hearing this instant, right before your eyes, is the true teaching." *The Record of Lin-chi.*

70. This verse is attributed to Ikkyū Sōjun in *Ikkyū Banashi* ("Tales of Ikkyū"), a series of popular illustrated works that appeared in the seventeenth century.

71. *The Precious Mirror Samadhi,* composed of ninety-four lines of four-character verses, contains the doctrine the Five Stages or Five Ranks (*Go-i*) that was very influential in the Ts'ao-tung (Japanese, Sōtō) line of Zen. A description of the study of the Five Ranks in modern Rinzai Zen, the final step in formal koan training, is found in *Zen Dust,* pp. 62–72, which also provides a translation of Hakuin's commentary on the Five Ranks in *Poison Flowers in a Thicket of Thorns.*

72. Although the Four Vows are traditionally recited in this order, in presenting his understanding of the vows in the following pages Hakuin changes the usual sequence, making them agree with his own program for *kenshō* and post-satori training.

73. In *Admonitions for Buddhists (Hsi-men ching-hsun),* a Zen work of the Yuan dynasty (1271–1368), this statement of the Bodhisattva Vow is attributed to the T'ien-t'ai teacher Chih-i.

74. Hakuin includes a section devoted to Shōju's teachings in *Wild Ivy* as well, although the teachings in both cases seem to be at least in part Hakuin's own.

75. A stick of incense of the customary length burns for about forty minutes, so his evening zazen would have lasted in excess of five hours.

NOTES TO CHAPTER 2

1. *Blue Cliff Record,* Case 60: "Zen Master Yun-men held up his staff before the assembly and said, "This staff has transformed into a dragon. It swallows the entire universe."

2. In *The Tale of My Childhood,* an elderly layman is quoted as saying that during just two relatively brief teaching visits to Edo (in 1759 and 1761) Hakuin awarded Dragon Staff certificates to as many as seventy students.

Similarly large numbers seem to have been given out at other meetings he held in his later years, several to young boys and girls in their early teens. I have heard it suggested that criticism also came from members of his own Zen school, dismayed at the possibility that he was awarding them to students who had not truly earned them. Whether or not this is related to Hakuin's admission in *Tale of Yūkichi* that he awarded the Dragon Staff certificates to lay students as a means of encouraging them to continue their practice in hopes they would eventually reach a deeper understanding is still to be answered. Unfortunately, at this point not much is known about this fraternal criticism.

3. Later in the work Hakuin calls this man Iiyama Kiemon. In the *Draft Biography*, under the year 1760 (not 1759), is the entry: "In autumn the master went at the request of the abbot of Denshū-ji [in Taru village] to lecture on *Ch'uan-lao's Comments on the Diamond Sutra*." Taru village (now incorporated into the city of Mishima) was close to the Mishima post station and thus not far from Hakuin's temple in Hara. Traveling from Edo, Hara was two post stations further west on the Tōkaidō, a distance of five or six miles.

4. The lectures on the *Blue Cliff Record* at Sōyū-ji were said to have been attended by over three hundred people.

5. See the introduction to *The Tale of My Childhood*, p. 5.

6. A hundred *ryō* would have been an extremely large amount of money. Three years earlier, Hakuin had paid that same amount to buy a large tract of land for a new temple (Ryūtaku-ji) he wanted to establish. Apparently Sōsuke's friends were planning to set up a large and ongoing business enterprise of some sort.

7. The deity does not fully explain how post-satori practice would have helped Sōsuke avoid his present troubles. Perhaps it is a question (as he puts it a few pages below) of the gods and Buddhas protecting sincere religious seekers from misfortunes of all kinds.

8. The Yellow Springs: the realm of the dead in the netherworld. The three unfortunate realms of karmic rebirth (*sanzu*) are the realms of Hell, where blazing fires torment the sinner; of Animals, where inmates engage in constant fighting and killing; and of Hungry Spirits, where tortures are inflicted with razor-sharp swords.

9. Present-day Osaka and Hyōgo prefectures.

10. The full title of the work is *Shuang-lin Shu-hsia Tang-lai Chieh-t'o Shan-hui Ta-shih Hsin-wang ming*, in Japanese pronunciation, *Sōrin Juge Tōrai Gedatsu Zenne Daishi Shinnō-mei*: *Treatise on the Mind King by the Bodhisattva Zenne Who Will Attain Liberation Under the Twin Sala Trees* (the trees under which Shakyamuni Buddha Entered Nirvana). Sōrin Juge Tōrai Gedatsu Zenne Daishi is the religious name adopted by Fu Ta-shih (Japanese: Fu Daishi, 497–569), an important, though semi-legendary, layman of early Chinese Buddhism whom the Zen school has regarded as a precursor of their school in China. A brief work made up of eighty-six lines of four-character verse, the *Treatise on the Mind King* is included

in Shan-hui's recorded sayings, *Shan-hui Ta-shih yu-lu (Zenne Daishi goroku)*, *ch.* 3. A Zen commentary on the *Treatise on the Mind King* by Hakuin, *Hakuin Oshō Teishō Shinnō-mei*, was privately published in 1928 by Mubutsu Koji.

11. See note above.

12. Purna, one of the Buddha's ten chief disciples, noted for his eloquence. The rest are roughly contemporary with Hakuin: the Tendai priest Reikū (1652–1739), the Sōtō priest Tenkei Denson (1654–1738), and the Kegon priest Hōtan (1654–1738). Gizui has not been identified.

13. The terms used are self-power (*jiriki*), attaining emancipation through one's own efforts, which is associated with the Zen school, and other-power (*tariki*), attaining emancipation by entrusting oneself completely to the compassion of Amida Buddha, which is characteristic of the Pure Land schools.

14. The proverb "a crow aping a cormorant is soon drowned" (*u no manesuru karasu mizu ni oboreru*): not knowing the limits of your own ability; to bring ruin on yourself by aping your betters.

15. The proverb "the goose takes flight, the tortoise (trying in vain to fly as well) stamps his feet in chagrin" (*gan ga tobeba ishigame mo jitanda*): know your limitations.

16. The proverb "crabs dig holes to the shape of their shells" (*kani wa kō ni nisete ana wo horu*): act and speak in keeping with your ability and station in life.

17. This passage is significant in that it suggests Hakuin's real motive in awarding these certificates was an "expediency" (*hōben*) to inspire students and encourage them to continue their practice.

18. The hells named here are found among the Eight Great Fiery Hells and Eight Great Freezing Hells. The Red Lotus Hells are so called because the tortures cause victims' flesh to burst open like red lotus flowers.

19. Hakuin states throughout his writings that he read this story in *Collection of Sand and Pebbles*. It is not found in any of the surviving texts of that work, although there are several references to priests lacking the Bodhi-mind falling into the evil ways. According to a fundamental Mahayana tenet, when enlightenment is attained, unless Bodhi-mind (Japanese, *Bodai-shin*; Sanskrit, *Bodhi-chitta*)—the desire to save all other beings—arises in the mind, one is destined for Hell. "If what is known as the Bodhi-mind is forgotten and lost, all the good deeds that you may perform become evil karma." *Flower Garland Sutra, ch.* 42.

20. In the *Lotus Sutra* the Buddha preaches four kinds of compassionate acts: dispelling others' suffering, imparting happiness to others, rejoicing in the freedom and happiness they attain, remaining unattached while engaged in the first three compassionate acts.

21. Hakuin omits the fifth and sixth lines of Han-shan's poem: "His golden bridle awes men of high rank; / His banquet table attracts a host of friends."

22. This is one of several slightly different lists that Hakuin gives of the "diffi-cult to pass" (*nantō*) koans.

23. Monju: Manjushri, the Bodhisattva of meditation and wisdom. Fugen: Samantabhadra, the Bodhisattva of teaching and practice. Kannon: Ava-lokiteshvara, the Bodhisattva of Compassion. Seishi: Mahāsthāmaprāpta, a Bodhisattva symbolizing wisdom. Jizō: Ksitigarbha, a Bodhisattva who liberates beings in hell and the other realms of evil.

24. The source of this legend, and the others that follow in this paragraph, is unknown.

25. It is unclear who the speaker is here, and who the person is responding in the next paragraph. As it seems unlikely Hakuin would have a mem-ber of the audience interrupting the deity to ask a question, the exchange would appear to be something Hakuin himself decided to interject into the narrative.

26. These are two metaphors from the *Lotus Sutra* (chapter 27) describing the difficulty of encountering a Buddha in the world (and thus gaining the possibility of release from suffering): like a one-eyed turtle finding a hole in a log floating in the ocean, and witnessing the blossoming of an *udum-bara* flower, which is said to occur only once in 3,000 years.

27. This saying, often cited in Hakuin's works, is probably taken from *Ta-hui's Letters*: "The Buddhist teachers say, 'To create worldly fortune is a curse that will extend for three lives.' What do they mean? In one's first life, one receives worldly fortune without understanding its nature. In one's sec-ond life, unless one receives worldly fortune with a deep sense of humility and strives to perform benevolent deeds, he will simply create bad karma. In the third life, having now received all the good fortune karmically due him, if he does not perform benevolent deeds, when he dies he will go directly to Hell—straight as an arrowshot."

28. When Bodhisattvas reach this stage in their career, they are assured of enlightenment.

29. This refers to ten kinds of evil produced by the body (taking life, theft, unchastity), mouth (lying, duplicity, abusive language, exaggeration), and mind (covetousness, anger or enmity, false views).

30. The three (evil) ways of existence (*sanzu*): Hell (where you are burned by raging fires; the realm of animals; and the realm of hungry ghosts, where even leaves and grasses are sharp-edged swords. The eight diffi-cult rebirths (*hachi-nan*) are places where one cannot encounter either a Buddha or the Dharma teaching, making it impossible to gain deliverance from the suffering of rebirth.

31. The famous saying thought to epitomize Zen teaching and practice: "Attaining Buddhahood by pointing directly to the human mind and see-ing into the true nature of self (*kenshō*)."

32. The Kiso Road (also called the *Nakasendō*, "road through the central mountains") ran between Kyoto and Edo and was sometimes used as an alternate to the Tōkaidō. It consisted of sixty-nine post stations. It was

called the Kiso Road or Kiso Kaidō, because for part of the way it followed the Kiso River.

33. Taro village and Denshū-ji are now incorporated into the city of Mishima. They would have been little more than a long walk from Shōin-ji.

34. The haiku poet Ōshima Ryōta (1718–87). The text gives the name as *Ōshima So-an-so (nanigashi) Sensei*.

35. Akiba Daigongen, a deity who protects against fire, is honored at a large shrine on Mount Akiba (in present-day Shizuoka prefecture) not too far from Shōin-ji. The main Kompira shrine, whose deity is worshipped as the god of travelers and mariners, is on the island of Shikoku. Hakuin inscribed for his lay followers large-character, single-line calligraphies bearing the names of these two deities.

36. Nihonmatsu is in present-day Fukushima prefecture.

37. What follows is presumably the section that Hakuin added in response to Iiyama's appeal, the "missing four or five pages" he wrote while Inryō waited. Thus, from this point until the final paragraphs of the work, it appears that Hakuin himself, not Yūkichi, is the speaker.

38. Mahākāshyapa was foremost among the Buddha's ten great disciples in the ascetic practice of the twelve *dhūtas*: wearing only cast-off rags, only three garments; eating only food received as alms, taking only breakfast and noon meals, taking no food between them, in only small amounts at each sitting; dwelling as a hermit, among tombs, under a tree, under the open sky, dwelling anywhere without preference; sitting without ever lying down.

39. This verse by Ta-mei Fa-ch'ang is recorded in *Compendium of the Five Lamps*, ch. 3: "Clad in lotus leaves from the pond, I never lack for clothing. / Eating pine nuts from the trees, there's always more than enough food." Here Hakuin's source may be the *Gyōji* (Sustained Practice) chapter of Dōgen's *Shōbōgenzō*: "In doing zazen, Master Ta-mei placed a ten-inch pagoda on top of his head like a Dharma crown, thinking that if he was diligent in keeping the pagoda from tumbling to the ground, it would keep him from falling asleep."

40. This story, too, is found in *Shōbōgenzō Gyōji*.

41. Yang-ch'i Fang-hui. Based on a story in *Precious Lessons of the Zen School*.

42. It is said that Master Po-chang Huai-hai was always first in the fields to begin work, and that in his final years (he lived to be ninety-four), his monks hid his tools attempting to dissuade him from working. "I have no virtue," he replied. "How can I ask others to do my work?" As he continued seeking throughout the temple for his tools, forgetting even to eat, the monks were obliged to return them to him. His words "A day without work, a day without food" became a maxim in the Zen world. The story appears in most accounts of Po-chang in the Zen records, and is also found in *Shōbōgenzō Gyōji*.

43. *Compendium of the Five Lamps*, ch. 1.

44. *Records of the Lamp*, ch. 18.

45. Ibid., *ch. 9.*

46. Tz'u-ming is the posthumous Zen Master title of Shih-shuang Ch'u yuan (986–1039). For the importance of this story to Hakuin's religious quest, see Chapter One, pp. 20–21.

47. Pao-shih has not been identified.

48. Hakuin's sources for the stories of Hsueh-feng I-ts'un and National Master Nan-yang Hui-chung are unknown. The "old crock" who lived on baked yams is Ming-ts'an. Completely unfazed when fellow priests criticized him for being indolent, Ming-ts'an came to be known as "Lazy Ts'an." His bizarre lifestyle and utterances attracted the notice of T'ang Emperor Su Tsung, who sent an emissary to visit him. When the emissary entered the cave where Ming-ts'an lived and tried to impress upon him how grateful he should be to receive such a great honor, Ts'an never even rose from his seat, merely poked in his cow-dung fire, took out a yam, and ate it. *Blue Cliff Record,* Case 34.

49. This story, dating from about the fifteenth century, has him maturing his realization for twenty years while living with beggars under the Gojō Bridge in Kyoto.

50. The following passage appears in Bassui's religious biography *Bassui Oshō Gyōjitsu:* "All previous ideas and views completely vanished. When he ate he could not tell the taste. He became like a dead man. Those who saw him said he resembled a corpse and feared that he could not have much longer to live."

51. The story of Shōsai Hosshin (n.d.), a Zen priest of the Kamakura period who founded Zuigan-ji in Matsushima (present Miyagi prefecture), is from *Collection of Sand and Pebbles:* "Senior priest Hosshin-bō of Matsushima in Mutsu province became a monk late in life. Although completely illiterate, he traveled to Sung China and studied with Zen Master Wuchun at the Wan-shou monastery at Mount Ching. Wu-chun assigned him the koan The Chinese Character *Chō* Inside a Circle. He worked on it, practicing zazen for many years, until the skin on his buttocks festered and maggots appeared. Still he refused to stop and continued sitting nine more years."

52. Daien Hōkan Kokushi is the posthumous title of Gudō Tōshoku. The story appears in Gudō's chronological biography, *Daien hōkan kokushi nempu:* "One summer night, Gudō entered the bamboo grove at the back of the temple, determined to work until morning on his koan. All at once, he experienced the great change, attaining Zen's wonderful working and a discernment that was absolute. When he stood up and straightened his robe, thousands of mosquitoes gorged with his blood fell to the ground around him. He trembled all over as he watched them writhing on the ground. When he entered Master Yōzan's chambers and told him what he had experienced, the master was overjoyed."

53. *Treatise on the Great Man (Ta-chang fu lun.)* The text in these next few pages contains passages quoted verbatim from the earlier *Record of Sendai's Comments on the Poems of Cold Mountain.*

54. The text refers to four virtues possessed by Bodhisattvas that enable them to lead sentient beings to perceive and cherish the truth: giving them what they desire, affectionate speech, doing what benefits them, adapting the teaching according to their needs. The Eightfold Noble Path consists of eight types of practice for attaining Nirvana: right views, thoughts, speech, acts, living, effort, mindfulness, and meditation.

55. *Wei-ts'eng-yu ching* (Sanskrit, *Ajatashatrukaukrtyavinodana*). A sutra in which Manjushri, the Bodhisattva of wisdom, demonstrates through his effortless teaching activity the true nature of Buddha wisdom.

56. Hakuin seems to be quoting from Nagarjuna's *Ta-chih-tu-lun* (*Treatise on the Perfection of Great Wisdom*), ch. 22.

57. The realm of desire (*kāmadhātu*) is one of the realms that make up the Three Worlds; it is inhabited by beings whose existence is dominated by desire, especially the desire for food, sleep, and sex.

58. It appears that in his haste to finish the work, Hakuin is interjecting his own thoughts into the narrative (see note 37).

59. Source unknown.

60. A similar statement appears in *Records from the Zen Forest* (*Lin-kuan lu*), a Sung collection of Zen anecdotes, in the section on the poet Po chu-i.

61. Similar words appear in the *Record of Chao-chou* and in *Eye and Treasury of the True Dharma* (*Cheng-fa yen-ts'ang*), a collection of koans with commentary by the Sung master Tai-hui Tsung-kao.

62. Here Hakuin brings Yūkichi back as a device to wrap up his narration (see note 37).

63. Well-known lines from the *Lotus Sutra*, "Phantom City" chapter. Cf. Watson, p. 130.

64. Because this colophon was printed together with the story, the criticism Hakuin refers to must have been made by people who had read the work in manuscript. They were probably students of Hakuin from the Takayama area who had firsthand knowledge of the events described. See p. 5.

65. When written in cursive script, the Chinese characters for *crow*, *here*, and *horse* closely resemble one another, and were thus easily mistaken by scribes.

NOTES TO CHAPTER 3

1. Hakuin had composed another work in 1755 using the same *Idle Talk on a Night Boat* title, but it was never published. Written as a letter to the retainer of a provincial Daimyo, it warns, in the manner of *Snake Strawberries* and *Mutterings to the Wall,* against oppressive taxation and describes the terrible karmic fate that awaits tyrannical rulers.

2. Conflicting theories have been advanced by twentieth-century writers as to what this malady was. Both physical (tuberculosis) and psychological (a neurotic disorder) causes have been proposed, with perhaps the latter being favored owing to the difficulty a person with a disease as

debilitating as tuberculosis would have engaging in the type of itinerant life Hakuin led at this time.

3. *Ki*-energy translates the term *ki* (Chinese *ch'i*), a key concept in traditional Chinese thought and medical theory. It has been rendered in English in various ways (e.g., vital energy, primal energy, vital breath, vital spirit). *Ki*, circulating through the body, is central to the preservation of health and sustenance of life.

4. The major differences are that the initial version is shorter than the others by about one-fourth; the independent version translated here contains a preface absent from the other two texts; and the final, *Wild Ivy* version ends with a few pages of new material reporting the circumstances of the sage Hakuyū's death.

This version is revised from my translation published in 2002 in the *Eastern Buddhist* vol. XXXIV, no. 1. A lightly annotated translation of the *Wild Ivy* version appeared in *Wild Ivy: The Spiritual Autobiography of Zen Master Hakuin*, Shambhala, 1999. In the present translation all significant variations between the three texts are given in the notes, with the exception of two lengthy passages Hakuin added at the end of *Wild Ivy*, which are appended as supplements to this chapter.

5. At the beginning of the preface we are told that Hakuin's followers had pleaded with him to publish the work. His reason for using this device is not readily explained, but he uses it in some form in a number of other works as well. In the *Chronological Biography*, for example, one of his lay followers is accused of making off with the manuscript of *Poison Flowers in a Thicket of Thorns* and having it printed against Hakuin's wishes, although we know from Hakuin's letters that he himself was very actively engaged in arranging for the publication of the work.

6. The saying is based on the story of a countryman who brags to his friends that he had visited Kyoto and seen all its marvelous sights, but when they ask about the scenery he saw along the Shirakawa River (which is in fact a shallow brook), he hedges, saying that night had already fallen when his boat floated down the river.

7. R. D. M. Shaw published a translation of *Idle Talk on a Night Boat* in *The Embossed Tea Kettle* (George Allen & Unwin, 1963); a revised version, done in collaboration with Wilhelm Schiffer, appeared in *Monumenta Nipponica* 13:1–2, 1957. Trevor Leggett also translated the work in *A Second Zen Reader* (Tuttle, 1988).

8. Hakuin uses this same attribution—"Compiled by Hunger and Cold, the Master of Poverty Hermitage" (*kyūbō-anju kitō-sen*) in several other works, including *Poison Words for the Heart*. A few paragraphs below, a student of Hakuin's is mentioned as author of the preface.

9. In the Taoist tradition, "external" alchemy involved the search for a "pill" or "elixir" of immortality, the most important element of which was a mercury compound, *tan*, or cinnabar. Once obtained and taken into the body, it was supposed to assure immortality and ascent to heaven, commonly on the back of a crane. The meditations taught in *Idle Talk on a*

Night Boat are concerned with the internal ramifications of this tradition; the "elixir" is cultivated in the "cinnabar field" (*tanden*), or "ocean of *ki*" (*kikai tanden*), which is the center of breathing or strength located slightly below the navel. Hakuin often uses *tanden* in the combined form *kikai tanden*. "There are *tanden* located at three places in the body. The one to which I refer is the lower *tanden*. The *kikai* and the *tanden*, which are virtually identical, are both located below the navel, the *tanden* is two inches below it, the *kikai* an inch and a half. It is in this area that the true *ki* always accumulates" (*Oradegama*).

10. This describes the dual function of blood and *ki* in preserving health and sustaining life. One theory describes "defensive *ki*" circulating in the subcutaneous layer of the body and functioning as the first line of defense against external pathogens, with "nutritive blood" accompanying it, supplying nutrition obtained from food. There are other explanations of these difficult terms.

11. This refers to a *tenbyō*, a gourd the gods were said to use when ladling beneficial rain down to earth.

12. The text uses the metaphor "tigers" for the attendant monks, based on a well-known anecdote in the *Records of the Transmission of the Lamp, ch. 8*. Instead of the usual monk attendants, Ch'an Master Hua-lin was served by two tigers that he called Ta-k'ung (Big Emptiness) and Shao-k'ung (Little Emptiness). Unaware of this, Prefect P'ei Hsiu visited the master and asked why he saw no attendants. Hua-lin called out their names and the two tigers emerged from behind the hermitage, badly frightening P'ei. Hua-lin then dismissed them, "You can go now," he said. "I have a guest." Excusing themselves with loud roars, they tamely withdrew.

13. "Bowl pouch," a bag in which the begging bowl is carried during pilgrimage. Hanging it up would signify that he was there to stay, his days of seeking instruction over and his practice complete.

14. Among the gravestones in the Shōin-ji cemetery are a great number erected for young monks (*unsui*) and dating from the period of Hakuin's residency, presumably victims of sickness or famine. The famine that struck the Hara area in 1747, for example, was said to have been so severe it forced the brotherhood at Shōin-ji to disperse.

15. Sung Yu and Ho Yen were celebrated for their masculine beauty. The careers of T'ang poets Tu Fu and Chia Tao were marked by periods of extreme privation. The poet and loyal minister Ch'u Yuan committed suicide after being unjustly dismissed from his position and sent into exile. In the *Shih-chi* he is described as "wandering along the river embankment lost in thought, his hair unbound, his face haggard with care, his figure lean and emaciated . . . [finally] he grasped a stone in his arms, cast himself into the Mi-lo river, and drowned." Burton Watson, *Records of Grand Historian of China* (New York: Columbia University Press, 1962), 1:504.

16. "Lowering his cloud." See Chapter One, note 10.

17. In the Taoist tradition, the term *Naikan* is used to refer to methods of inward-focused contemplation designed to cut off thought. It was also

used to describe types of meditation from early Chinese Buddhism (e.g., T'ien-t'ai founder Chih-i's *Great Cessation and Insight, ch. 5,* which Hakuin mentions in his text). In Hakuin's writings, it refers to meditations designed to concentrate *ki* in the *tanden,* below the navel, performed for therapeutic benefit (e.g., the "butter method"; see note 90), but he also uses the term for meditation practices, such as those set forth in the Preface, using koan-like themes. In *Oradegama,* Hakuin states that Shakyamuni and Chih-i both taught the essentials of the *Naikan* method and stressed the importance of keeping *ki* focused in the *tanden.*

18. The five organs—heart, liver, spleen, lungs, and kidneys—that generate and store *ki* vital to life.

19. Pien Ch'ueh, Ts'ang Kung, and Hua T'o are legendary physicians of ancient China. An innkeeper, Pien Ch'ueh one day received a mysterious drug from a stranger that gave him the power to discern the true nature of things and perform miraculous cures. It was said he could see into the vital organs of his patients, and a knowledge of the pulse is still inseparably associated with his name (Giles, *Biographical Dictionary,* #396). Hua T'o is said to have mastered life-nurturing techniques that enabled him to live past the age of one hundred.

20. "Returning the elixir" (*gentan*) refers to the Taoist alchemists' secret method for refining cinnabar to obtain pure elixir. The alchemist Ko Hung's *Pao p'u tzu* ("The Master Who Embraces Purity") states, "If you consume elixir turned nine times, you will in three days become an immortal."

21. "Pure Land of the mind." Whereas the Pure Land sutras state that "Amida Buddha resides to the West, a hundred billion Buddha-lands distant from here," Zen teachers assert that "you yourself are Amida Buddha," that "Amida's Pure Land exists within your own mind." Words to this effect are found in the *Ching-t'u huo-wen* of the Yuan dynasty Zen master T'ienju Wei-tse; in Japanese Zen, they appear in such works as Ikkyū Sōjun's *Amida hadaka monogatari,* Shidō Munan's *Sokushin-ki,* Suzuki Shōsan's *Mōan-jō,* and, in secular literature, Noh plays such as *Sanemori* and *Kashiwazaki.*

22. The point in each of these rhetorical questions is that the Pure Land and Amida Buddha must not be sought outside the self. For example, if the Pure Land is located in the ocean of *ki* below the navel, how could it possess the "splendors" or beautiful adornments (*shōgon*) described in Pure Land sutras? Presumably, the object of all four contemplations outlined here, which are designed to return one's essential being (i.e., "Original Face") to its "native place," is to bring the practicer's *ki* down and focus it in the *tanden.* In *Oradegama,* Hakuin adds one more contemplation to these four: "The *tanden* located in the ocean of *ki*—the lower back and legs, the arches of the feet—it is all Chao-chou's Mu. What principle can this Mu possibly have?"

23. The sense of this image is not entirely clear. One commentary describes

it as a brand new leather kickball: one not yet softened for use by being beaten with a bamboo stick.

24. Any congestion of *ki* in the five organs and six viscera (gall bladder, stomach, small and large intestines, urinary bladder, and the *san chiao*, or "triple heater," described in note 53 below) that restricts its flow will create an imbalance between the organs that will result in disorder and illness. According to *Yasenkanna hyōshaku* (p. 41), the term translated here as "weakening the body" refers to "weakness in the lungs and spleen, a condition we call today tuberculosis."

25. The T'ang Zen master Chao-chou said to a disciple, "Just investigate the Dharma-principle by doing zazen for two or three years. If after that time you are still unable to attain the Way, you can come and cut off my head." *Jōshū-roku*, ed. Akizuki Ryōmin (Chikuma-shobō, 1972), p. 191.

26. In the *Sutra of Forty-two Sections*, section 26, the Buddha refers disparagingly to his body as "this bag of skin, full of every kind of filth!"

27. Hakuyū (also Hakuyūshi), the teacher who appears in the main text below.

28. P'eng Tsu is the Chinese Methuselah. According to the *Lieh-hsien chuan* (*Lives of the Sages*), "P'eng Tsu lived over eight hundred years, ate nothing but the *ling-shih* fungus, and was adept in the yogic practice of controlling *ki.*"

29. "Corpse-guarding spirit" (*shushiki*) alludes to a death-in-life type of existence in which the mind merely keeps watch over the body without making any exertion toward bettering its existence.

30. Taoist figures noted for their extremely long lives: the physician Ko Hung, 283–363; [Li] T'ieh-kuai and Chang Kuo (the text has Chang Hua), both of whom are numbered among the Eight Taoist Immortals; and Fei Chang (Fei Ch'ang-fang), necromancer of the Latter Han.

31. The phrase "imposing comportment of the Bodhisattva" (*Bosatsu no igi*) alludes to the Bodhisattva's practice dedicated to fulfilling the Four Universal Vows.

32. True elixir (*shintan*) is obtained by means of the *Naikan* meditation. When one's *ki* is always replete in the *tanden*, "body and mind remain in constant equanimity; even at the age of one hundred the hair does not turn white, the teeth remain sound, the eyes see more keenly than ever, and the skin acquires a fine luster—the result of nurturing the primal *ki* and bringing the divine elixir to maturity" (*Oradegama*).

33. The formula for nurturing *ki* in this paragraph was a favorite of Hakuin's, and he frequently inscribed it to give to people. Hakuin attributes the passage to at least five different people in his writings, making it likely that he wrote it himself or cobbled it together from assorted texts. In the so-called external alchemy of Taoism, the true elixir for longevity is produced by "turning" or kneading the cinnabar substance nine times. "If you consume elixir turned nine times, you will in three days' time become an immortal" (*Pao p'u tzu*). In the inner alchemy and from Hakuin's Zen

standpoint, it is a matter of concentrating *ki* in its ultimate source in the *tanden*.

34. A line from a poem titled "Reply to Ya Tang" by the T'ang poet Keng Wei, found in the *San-t'i shih* (*Poems in Three Forms*; Japanese, *Santai-shi*), a Sung anthology of T'ang poetry much read and studied in Japanese Zen circles. The full couplet, which Hakuin uses as a "capping verse" in *Dream Words from the Land of Dreams*, is: "The moon reaches the summit, shadows disappear from the wall / The frost hangs heavily, willow branches are sparse."

35. Hakuin was ordained at fourteen and began his Zen pilgrimage at nineteen. The enlightenment referred to here is apparently the one he experienced in his twenty-third year while he was at Eigan-ji in Echigo province. Cf. *Chronological Biography* (Age 23); also *The Tale of My Childhood*, pp. 25–26.

36. A well-known saying from *The Doctrine of the Mean* (*Chung-yung*).

37. It was a commonplace of Chinese medical lore that excessive exercise of one's mental faculties would cause the "heart-fire" or "mind-fire" to overheat, and instead of being concentrated in the lower body, to mount upward, causing symptoms such as those described here. In the *Chronological Biography* (Age 25), twelve morbid symptoms are described that appeared at this time.

38. In the later *Wild Ivy* version, Hakuyū's age is given as three hundred and seventy, and his cave is described as "two or three leagues from human habitation." In the *Record of Sendai's Comments* version, the sentence "In appearance he resembled a simpleton or ignoramus" is inserted here.

39. The samurai Ishikawa Jōzan retired to the hills northeast of Kyoto in 1641. His villa, Shisendō (Hall of Poetry Immortals), is located on a hillside overlooking the northern part of Kyoto. Several caves Hakuyū is said to have inhabited are located in the hills behind the villa. See above, pp. 86–87.

40. 1710. Hakuin was twenty-five.

41. According to the *Chronological Biography*, this was Reishō-in in Mino Province.

42. Both Kurodani ("Black Valley") and Shirakawa ("White River") are located in northeastern Kyoto. After entering Kyoto from the east on the main Tōkaidō road, Hakuin would have turned north and passed Kurodani on his way to Shirakawa, the site of Hakuyū's cave.

43. In the *Wild Ivy* version Hakuin inserts a passage at this point to enhance narrative interest: "Not knowing what else to do, I sat down on a nearby rock, closed my eyes, placed my palms before me in *gasshō* and began chanting a sutra. Presently, as if by magic, I heard in the distance the faint sounds of someone chopping a tree. After pushing my way deeper through the forest in the direction of the sound, I spotted a woodcutter."

44. Among five contemplations (*gojō shinkan*) designed to rectify various disorders of mind outlined in Chih-i's *Ssu-chiao-i* is breath counting, practiced to rein in an unruly mind.

45. The Confucian teacher Fujii Shōsui, who in 1698 (when Hakuin was eight years old) wrote the earliest known account of Hakuyū and his cave, describes his hair as falling down and covering his entire back (Itō Kazuo, *Hakuyūshi: shijitsu no shin-tankyū*, p. 34). Hakuin's description of Hakuyū's cave also suggests the influence of Fujii's account: "The mountain where Hakuyū lives is in the northern part of Shirakawa. There is a giant rock, six or seven feet in height, on the mountainside. In it is a small cave, no more than five feet square. The opening to the cave is covered by a screen made from woven reeds" (ibid.). The three works on Hakuyū's desk exemplify his roots in the three traditions of Confucianism, Taoism, and Buddhism.

46. The wild mountain fruit (*saritsu*) is apparently the *koboke*, which dictionaries describe as being "the size of a Japanese pear, bitter in taste and almost inedible."

47. The pulses are taken at three points on the wrist, with each place being read at three levels: shallow, medium, and deep.

48. Celebrated physicians of ancient China who appeared before; see note 19.

49. In other words, the cause of the illness, and the cure, are the same. The adage, originally from *Ta chuang-yen lun* (*Treatise on the Majestic Adornments*), ch. 2, also appears in the *Records of the Transmission of the Lamp*, ch. 1, section on Upagupta.

50. At this point in the *Record of Sendai's Comments* version of the story, Hakuyū goes on to say: "Be sure that you do not divulge the secret method indiscriminately to others. If you do, not only will it hurt you, it will be very harmful to me as well."

51. Traditional Chinese medical theory describes *ki* as moving constantly among the five internal organs (see note 24). If a full and vital supply of *ki* is not maintained in them, or if the *ki* becomes stagnant, illness results. Defensive energy and nutritive blood (or nourishing energy) are two forms of *ki* (see note 10); the former protects the surface of the body against external pathogenic factors; the latter, produced from food, flows inside the blood vessels, circulating through the body and supplying it with nutrients.

52. According to the traditional Chinese concept known as *wu-hsing* (translated variously as five phases, stages, or elements), which was employed in astrology, medicine, military strategy, and many other areas of Chinese thought, phenomena are classified into five categories—Wood, Fire, Earth, Metal, and Water—as a means of describing their relationships and interaction: e.g., Wood feeds Fire; Fire creates Earth (ash); Earth bears Metal; Metal carries Water; Water nourishes Wood. In traditional medical theory these concepts are used to describe qualities of *ki* within the body in a process of mutual production and overcoming. The five phases serve as the core for a system that, together with the yin and yang, operate in cycles of rising and falling and in a universal pattern, uniting Man and Nature. The five phases are tied to many corresponding

categories of five—such as the five internal organs (lungs, heart, liver, spleen, and kidneys), which correspond to Metal, Fire, Wood, Earth, and Water, respectively. Maintaining the correct balance between them is essential for preserving health. The internal organs are invested with seven marvelous powers: the liver with the ethereal aspect of the soul (*hun*) that leaves the body at the time of physical death and returns to heaven, lungs with the corporeal soul (*p'o*) that returns to earth, heart with the spirit, spleen with thought and knowledge, kidneys with the life essence and will.

53. The description in this paragraph appears in the ancient Chinese medical classic *Huang-ti nei-ching* (*Yellow Emperor's Manual of Corporeal Medicine*).

54. Hakuin uses the terms *go-i* and *roku-zoku* to refer to the five internal organs and the six viscera (*rokufu*)—the large intestine, small intestine, gall bladder, stomach, urinary bladder, and the *san chiao* or "triple heater." The "triple heater" is described as a network of energy conduits that participate in the metabolic functions located in three parts of the body cavity, one below the heart and above the stomach, another in the stomach area, a third above the urinary bladder.

55. The seven "misfortunes" (*shichi-kyō*)—joy, anger, grief, pleasure, love, hate, and desire—are so called because they are the causes of illness. The four "evils" (*shi-ja*) are harmful influences to the body caused by wind, cold, heat, and moisture.

56. Left side and right side refer to diagnostic areas on the left and right wrists where the pulses are taken in reading the five internal organs.

57. The terms translated here as the five senses (the five organs of sense: eyes, ears, nose, tongue, and skin) and six roots (the five senses plus the mind) are subject to different explanations in the commentaries. I follow Yoshizawa here.

58. See *Chuang Tzu*, Burton Watson (Columbia, 1968), p. 78.

59. Hsu Chun has been identified as the Korean physician Ho Chun (n.d.). The "lower heater" (*kashō*) and "upper heater" (*jōshō*) are two elements of the *san chiao* or "triple heater" described in note 54 above. The essential point in all these quotations is to concentrate *ki* in the lower body.

60. Shang-yang tzu is a sobriquet of the Yuan physician Ch'en Chih-hsu, who is described as an adept in the Taoist arts of prolonging life. The source of the quotation is unknown. Here and in the following section various permutations of the divination signs in the *I Ching* (*Book of Changes*) are used in describing the movement of *ki* within the body. This manual on divination, used since ancient times and one of the Five Classics of Confucianism, is based upon five diagrams made up of trigrams—three lines—undivided and divided, which are increased by doubling them into hexagrams to sixty-four. Attached to each hexagram is a short, enigmatic text ascribing a meaning to each line of the hexagram.

61. The twelve conduits or meridians (*jūni no keimyaku*) are reckoned as one for each of the five organs and six viscera and an additional conduit for the

aorta. Pre-modern Japan followed the Chinese method of dividing days into twelve hours.

62. ▤

63. ▤

64. ▤

65. *Enju-sho*. Several works have titles similar to this, but the present quotation itself has not been found in any current editions of them.

66. Neither Wu Ch'i-ch'u nor Master Shih-t'ai has been identified. Although here Hakuin has Shih-t'ai teaching Wu Ch'i-ch'u, when this same passage is quoted in *Wild Ivy*, their roles are reversed, with Wu Ch'i-ch'u teaching Shih-t'ai. Elsewhere in his writings Hakuin attributes this passage to three or four other teachers. A similar dialogue, between Master Kuang Ch'eng and the Yellow Emperor (Huang Ti), appears in the *Chuang Tzu* (Watson, pp. 116–18) and in the *Shen-hsien chuan* (Lives of the Sages), a work attributed to Ko Hung.

67. In *Oradegama*, Hakuin quotes the following teaching by Hakuyū on the state of five "non-leakages" (*go-muro*), attained when afflicting passions disappear from the mind: "People often learn only that the divine elixir is refined by bringing together the five phases—Water, Fire, Wood, Metal, and Earth—without knowing they are also the five sense organs—eyes, ears, nose, tongue, and body. To bring the five organs together and refine the divine elixir, we have the teaching of the five non-leakages: when the eye does not see erroneously, when the ears do not hear erroneously, when the tongue does not taste erroneously, when the body does not feel erroneously, when the consciousness does not think erroneously, then the diffuse primal *ki* accumulates right before your eyes."

68. Neither T'ai-pai Tao-jen nor the source of the quotation has been identified. Mencius describes a "vast, expansive energy" (*hao jan ch'i*) that is "immense and flood-like, unyielding in the highest degree. If man nourishes it with integrity and places no obstacle in its path, it will fill all Heaven and Earth and he will be in the same stream as Heaven itself." D. C. Lau, *Mencius* (Penguin Classics, 1970), p. 77.

69. A student would "overturn" the elixir furnace (originally, the crucible or stove Taoist alchemists used for refining the cinnabar elixir) when he succeeded in refining the elixir within himself. The phrase appears in a verse in the *Wind and Moon Collection of Zen Poetry*: "If you are able to operate the elixir furnace, your *ki* is like a rainbow. / If you overturn the elixir furnace, you arrive at a state of perfect freedom." Crossing this threshold (described here as a kind of satori) the student grasps that the Great Way and the elixir are one, and realizes the futility of seeking it externally.

70. In *Preaching at the Crossroads*, Hakuin explains that "churning the Long River into the finest butter" refers to the Bodhisattva's activity of assisting others to enlightenment. "Transforming the earth into purest gold" would have a similar connotation. Hakuin contrasts these activities with the "superficial feats of magic" attributed to Taoist sages enumerated in the previous sentence.

71. The source of this quotation has not been traced. Nor is Hakuin's reason for citing it here entirely clear.

72. Li Shih-ts'ai was a noted Ming physician who wrote several important medical works. This passage is from his *I-tsung pi-tu*.

73. After Completion and Before Completion are the two final hexagrams in the *Book of Changes*. In the After Completion configuration, descending Fire and ascending Water intermingle; in the Before Completion configuration, they are separated, Water above and Fire below, not intermingling.

74. Tan-hsi: the school of medicine founded by the Yuan physician Chu Tan-hsi.

75. The source of this quotation is unknown.

76. The division of the Fire principle into "princely fire" and "ministerial fire" appears in chapter 71 of the *Su-wen* (Plain Questions), the first part of *Yellow Emperor's Manual of Corporeal Medicine*, the basic medical text in Tokugawa Japan.

77. According to *Yasenkanna hyōshaku* (p. 102), this paragraph is based on Chu Tan-hsi's *Hsiang-huo lun* (*Treatise on Ministerial Fire*). Sea, marsh, and bog are apparently allusions to the area in and around the *tanden* in the lower body.

78. "Diverse meditation" (*takan*) presumably refers to unfocused meditation on koans in which the meditation topic becomes the object of discrimination and *ki* does not gather in the lower body. "No-meditation" (*mukan*) refers to an advanced meditative state similar to *munen* ("no-thought") or *mushin* ("no-mind"), in which discriminations and dichotomies have ceased.

79. Although no source has been found for the words here attributed to the Buddha, *Yasenkanna hyōshaku* (p. 109) cites a similar teaching in Chih-i's *Great Cessation and Insight:* "If the mind is always kept concentrated in the feet, any illness can be cured."

80. Agama sutras: a generic term for Hinayana sutras. No source in the Agama sutras has been found, but see note 90 below.

81. In the eighth volume of Chih-i's *Great Cessation and Insight*, devoted to the therapeutic uses of Buddhist meditation, a method is described for concentrating the mind on the afflicted area of the body. Eight types of breathing are set forth and their use for specific ailments explained.

82. "Concentrate the mind above the navel. Imagine it the size of a bean. Loosen your robe and give yourself to this visualization. . . . By concentrating the mind above the navel, the breath will issue from the navel and enter through the navel. Exhaling and inhaling in this way through the navel, it will not be difficult to realize the [truth of] impermanence" (*Great Cessation and Insight, ch. 8*).

83. The cessations in relation to phenomena (*ke'en-shi*) and to the ultimate truth of emptiness (*taishin-shi*), achieved during samadhi and leading to clear discernment, are two of three kinds of "cessations" or concentrations

set forth in *Great Cessation and Insight*. In the first, the mind remains unaffected by changes in external or internal conditions; in the second, one grasps that illusion is, as such, true reality. Hakuin refers to these terms in some instructions he wrote for the layman Murabayashi Zesan titled *Gambyō no myōyaku* (*A Miracle Medicine for Eye Disease*): "Cessation in relation to phenomena as set forth in the *Great Cessation and Insight* is a matter of quieting the mind and *ki* by concentrating the mind entirely in the *tanden*—the area from the lower back down to the feet—and becoming like a dead man, completely mute and quiescent at all times, oblivious of all external phenomena. It is the ultimate key to nurturing life. Cessation in relation to ultimate truth is a matter of concentrating the mind at all times directly on the ultimate ground of the one vehicle and the basic principle of all Dharmas as aspects of essential truth." (*Complete Works of Priest Hakuin*, vol. 6.)

84. T'ien-t'ung Ju-ching (1163–1228), the Sung dynasty Ts'ao-t'ung (Japanese Sōtō) Zen master best known as the teacher of Dōgen Kigen (1200–52), founder of Japanese Sōtō Zen and of Eihei-ji in Echigo province. This particular teaching is found in Dōgen's practice diary *Hōkyō-ki*, which he kept while he was studying in China. Ju-ching told Dōgen that placing the heart (mind) above the palm of the left hand during zazen was "the method rightly transmitted by the Buddha-patriarchs." For the full passage and context, see my "Dōgen's *Hōkyō-ki*," Part II, *Eastern Buddhist*, vol. XI, no. 1, 1977, p. 81.

85. The *Hsiao chih-kuan* (*Smaller Cessation and Insight*), epitomizing the teachings in the *Great Cessation and Insight*, is said to have been compiled by Chih-i for his sick brother Ch'en Chen. *Yasenkanna hyōshaku* (p. 114) quotes the following story from the biography of Ch'en Chen in the *Fo-tsu t'ung-chi*: "At the age of forty Ch'en Chen, Chih-i's elder brother, encountered a sage who examined his physiognomy and told him that his vital yang energy was exhausted and he had only one month left to live. Chih-i thereupon taught Ch'en the basics of his *chih-kuan* meditation. After Ch'en performed the meditation assiduously day and night for one year, he was cured and went on to live a long life"—and then points out the striking similarities between the illnesses and cures experienced by Ch'en Chen and Hakuin, as well as the roles that Chih-i and Hakuyū played in those cures.

86. Po-yun Ho-shang (Japanese, Hakuun Oshō). In a letter to a lay follower Hakuin attributes this quotation to the eleventh-century Rinzai priest Huang-lung Hui-nan, but its source has not been traced in his records.

87. A similar passage is quoted in a work by Su Tung-p'o (see next note), who ascribes it to the T'ang physician Sun Ssu-miao (d. 682), author of Taoist medical treatises including *Ch'ien-chin yao-fang* (*Prescriptions Worth Thousands in Gold*).

88. Su Nei-han is the noted Sung poet and Zen layman Su Tung-p'o (1037–1110). *Nei-han* was a title given scholars belonging to the Hanlin academy.

Su Tung-p'o was well versed in Taoist medical lore and wrote several works on the subject. Although the present quotation has not been found among them, portions of it appear in one of Su's verses.

89. Ch'u Ch'eng's *Ch'u-shih i-shu* (*Master Ch'u's Posthumous Writings*). *Hakuin Hōgo-shū*, vol. 4, p. 140.

90. Itō Kazuo has found several methods of meditation vaguely similar to this in Buddhist sutras (*New Research into the Historicity of Hakuyū*, pp. 65–66). A "butter" method (*nanso*) appears in a work titled *Chih ch'an-ping pi-yao fa* (*Secrets of an Essential Method for Curing Meditation Sickness*); T15, 333–42 [#620].

91. This is not mentioned in the *Record of Sendai's Commentary* version; a note in the *Chronological Biography* by the editor Taikan Bunshu states that Hakuyū spent a number of years wandering through Tamba, Tajima, Yamashiro, and Wakasa provinces.

92. A reference to the well-known tale "Kantan's Dream," from a T'ang work titled *Chen-chung chi*. A young man named Lu-sheng, on his way to seek a career in the capital, stopped off at a place called Han-tan (Japanese, Kan-tan). While waiting for his lunch to cook, he took a nap and dreamed that he rose through the ranks of officialdom and finally attained the post of prime minister. Awakening, he saw his yellow millet still cooking on the fire, realized that life is an empty dream, and returned home instead of proceeding to the capital.

93. Fujii Shōsui's account of Hakuyū (see above, note 45) mentions him wearing *geta* (pattens), adding that even when Hakuyū was wearing them he "could run like the wind."

94. Here the *Wild Ivy* text has "Again I pressed my palms together and bowed my head low in gratitude."

95. A statement in Chu-hung's *Jottings at the Bamboo Window, Second Series.*

96. Rikugawa Taiun cites this passage from a letter by Hakuin's Dharma heir Reigen Etō: "When he was young, the master [Hakuin] wore three pairs of heavy-soled tabi on his feet. [Later,] after he learned to bring his mind down into the *tanden*, he never went near a brazier, even on the coldest winter days" (*Hyōshaku Yasenkanna*, p. 193).

97. In the *Wild Ivy* version, Hakuin inserts a passage at this point that reports the death of Hakuyū. See *Supplementary Passage A*, p. 112.

98. In the *Wild Ivy* version, Hakuin adds a passage at this point citing examples of people saved from serious illness by practicing *Naikan* meditation. See *Supplementary Passage B*, p. 113.

99. *Yasenkanna hyōshaku* (pp. 145–46) interprets this as appreciative laughter. However, the context of Hakuin's statement—that his intended audience is "mediocre students," not those of superior capacity—suggests that it is derisive, born of failure to appreciate what he has set forth.

100. This is a line from a poem by the Sung poet and Zen layman Huang T'ing-chien titled "Seventeenth Day of the Sixth Month: Noonday Nap": "A straw-hatted, black-booted worldling, amid the world's red dust / My mind on the island of immortal spirits and its dancing white cranes /

The sound of my horse chomping dried bean hulls by my noonday pillow / Became in my dream a tempest that raised great waves on the river" (translation, Burton Watson, in *An Introduction to Sung Poetry* (Harvard-Yenching Monograph, 1967). The poem alludes to a metaphor in the *Leng-yen ching* (*Shuramgama Sutra*), *ch. 4:* "While a man sleeps soundly in his bed, someone in the house is using a rice pounder. . . . In his dreams, he hears the sound as a drum-beat or the booming of a bell." Hakuin's reason for quoting the verse is not totally clear. Yoshizawa suggests this explanation: "Others [i.e., all except superior or mediocre students] will find my idle words a nuisance, like a grating noise distracting them from their midday nap," indicating that it is their somnolent (i.e., unawakened) state that keeps people of limited capacity from understanding the worth of Hakuin's words.

NOTES TO CHAPTER 4

1. A word must be said about a work titled *The Prostitute Otafuku's Tea-Grinding Songs* (*Otafuku jorō kohiki uta*), which in style and content quite closely resembles *Old Granny's Tea-Grinding Songs* and has been considered one of Hakuin's works but which is not by Hakuin. The real author, an unknown nineteenth-century priest, modeled his work (not altogether successfully) on the style of *Old Granny's Tea-Grinding Songs*, and appropriated a few of Hakuin's verses from the opening portion.
2. A detailed discussion of the role Ofuku plays in Hakuin's scheme of things can be found in *The Religious Painting of Zen Master Hakuin*.
3. Nasono Yoichi was a general of the Minamoto clan celebrated for feats of bowmanship he displayed at the Battle of Yashima.
4. "Understanding men" translates the Japanese *chiin*, referring to a person who really understands another's art (*Lieh Tzu*).
5. Reflecting the social codes of behavior promulgated by the Tokugawa shogunate, Hakuin frequently alludes in his works to the Confucian virtues of loyalty to the ruler or master and filial piety toward parents, though putting his own Buddhist twist on them.
6. Based on a passage in the Confucian *Analects*: "Chi K'ang asked Confucius about government. Confucius replied, 'Let the evinced desires of the ruler be for what is good, and the people will be good. The relation between superiors and inferiors is like that between the wind and the grass. The grass must bend when the wind blows across it.'" The words are used as a capping phrase in the *Blue Cliff Record*, Case 56.
7. T'ai Kung is the title of a minister of the ancient Chou dynasty to whom is attributed the military classic *San-lueh* ("Three Strategies"), though the saying quoted here is not found in any known editions of the work.
8. Warriors who distinguished themselves during the Gempei wars of the twelfth century. Hachirō of Chinzei is the popular name of the military leader Minamoto Tametomo (1139–70), who legend says was seven feet tall and possessed Herculean strength. Sanada Yoichi (Munesada),

a warrior in the service of the first Minamoto Shōgun Yoshitomo, was noted for his skill with the lance. Kyūrō is one of the names of the great hero Minamoto Yoshitsune.

9. In *The Three Teachings in Agreement,* Hakuin states that what Zen calls self-nature, the Pure Land schools call Amida Buddha, what Taoism calls the great path of emptiness and what Shinto calls Takamagahara are all fundamentally the same, the timeless principle in them all being "ultimate good" (*shizen*). Hakuin argues that while the great sages of all three religions attain this ultimate principle, its working differs according to the quality of practice employed. Here Hakuin uses a Confucian term (ultimate good) to express this unity.

He elaborated on this in a letter to a lay student in which he equates the attainment of ultimate good with the "Great Death" he experienced in his initial *kenshō,* and the "clarification of Bright Virtue" (another Confucian term, from the *Great Learning*) with the post-satori practice which enabled him to "attain complete mastery of the Great Way": "All wise ones of the ten directions past and present have worked hard to abide in ultimate good, then consummate the Great Way by clarifying Bright Virtue. When I was a young man, I devoted myself to Zen practice so that I too could abide in ultimate good. It was like one man fighting a host of ten thousand. Finally, at the age of twenty-three, I succeeded in becoming one with all things, breaking free of the defilements of thought" (*Complete Works,* vol. 6, p. 388).

10. The idea is that if you have carefully maintained your Mind Master, it will serve you faithfully even in dire emergencies. There is a well-known Chinese proverb: "A soldier fostered and nourished will serve faithfully for a thousand days; a soldier who has been dragooned will vanish before noon."

11. Takamagahara (the high plain of heaven). In Japanese mythology, the dwelling place of the *kami;* in Shinto, the *kami* leave Takamagahara to enter a shrine or other purified place.

Poisons and desires: the text is literally five desires (that arise from the senses of sight, sound, smell, taste, and touch) and three poisons (greed, anger, and stupidity).

12. The Confucian *Ta-hsueh* (*Great Learning*) begins with the words "The Great Learning teaches us to illuminate Bright Virtue, to renovate the people, and to rest in the Ultimate Good."

13. In the tradition of Taoist "external alchemy," cinnabar was refined in crucibles or cauldrons and consumed in hopes of attaining immortality. Here Hakuin speaks to the question of the "inner alchemy," in which *ki* is refined through religious practice by concentrating it in the *tanden* or cinnabar field, producing the "elixir of immortality," i.e., ushering the practicer into the timeless realm of enlightenment. See also Chapter Three, note 9.

14. According to traditional medical theory, the body is composed of the Four Elements of Earth, Water, Fire, and Air, each of which is liable

to one hundred and one ailments, for a total of four hundred and four altogether.

15. Again the identity of Old Granny and (Buddha) Mind, at one with the entire universe, is emphasized. The questioner here (and below as well) is apparently the prostitute Ofuku.

16. That is, loyal to his master.

17. According to the passage from *Oradegama* quoted above (Chapter Three, note 9) the *tanden* or cinnabar field is located three *sun* below the navel, and the ocean of *ki* halfway between them. One *sun* is 3.03 centimeters.

18. When the practicer can concentrate *ki* in the *tanden*, producing the cinnabar elixir (*dai-gentan*), enlightenment is attained. Taoist alchemical texts refer to producing the cinnabar elixir by "turning" or refining it nine times. A well-known Zen interpretation contrasts the void (also translated "empty space"), representing enlightenment, with Mount Sumeru, representing the realm of illusion.

19. "Samsara and Nirvana are like yesterday's dream." *Sutra of Perfect Enlightenment (Engaku-kyō), ch.* 2.

20. From here to the end of the text, Old Granny cautions students against being satisfied with achieving a small attainment, teaching the essential importance of continuing to strive toward full awakening in the practice of post-satori training.

21. Misdeeds: the Five Cardinal Sins and Ten Evil Acts. See Glossary.

22. Hakuin here assails teachings of contemporary priests who deny the need for Buddhist practice, embracing the so-called *danmu* or *danken* heresy that does not recognize the principle of karmic retribution and rebirth or the existence of heaven and hell; hence, these teachers held that death is the end of existence.

23. Because they cease their training upon initial attainment and do not continue on to engage in post-satori training—the practice of the Bodhisattva path.

24. India, China, and Japan.

25. Good friend (*zenchishiki*): a person who acts as a good teacher to you.

26. Hakuin uses expressions throughout this section reminiscent of his descriptions in *Wild Ivy* of the Unborn (*fushō*) Zen practiced by monks in Mino province who were followers of the teachings of Bankei Yōtaku. At one point, a head priest responded to his questions by telling him to "stop meddling," as it would distract him from his practice. (*Wild Ivy*, p. 56.)

27. In *Wild Ivy*, Hakuin uses this image to describe Zen students who meditate in the training hall without showing the spirit of dedication and concentrated effort essential to authentic koan study.

28. Kuruson (Sanskrit Kakusandha) is the fourth of the Seven Ancient Buddhas and the first of the present age. When enlightenment is attained, unless Bodhi-mind, the desire to save other beings, arises in the mind, one is destined to fall into hell. See Chapter Two, note 19.

29. Here "the prostitute Yamamba" is Hyakuma Yamamba, the *tsure* or supporting character in the Nō play *Yamamba*, who speaks the lines "The

peaks of Dharma-nature soaring up represent entering deeper into Bodhi, the attire of the deep valley of ignorance expresses the return to save sentient beings."

30. Hakuin takes this line verbatim from *Yamamba*.

31. The text has "*danken* heretic." For this term see above, note 22.

32. This and the following four challenges are so-called checking questions (*sassho*) that a Zen teacher uses to test whether students have truly grasped a koan.

33. Old Granny is referring to the koan practice of "closed barrier" Zen. Huang-po's words appear in the *Records of the Transmission of the Lamp*, ch. 9.

34. In China, vigorous carp able to scale the great series of falls known as the Dragon Gate, which had been cut open through the Lung-men mountains for the Yellow River, were said to transform into dragons. Likewise, in Japanese folklore, foxes that were able to jump over the high *torii* at the Inari Shinto shrines were destined to become fox deities attached to the Inari Shrine. Elderly people of great experience and sagacity are sometimes praised as having "leapt the Inari torii."

35. Su-shan's Memorial Tower is translated in Chapter One, note 65. Ch'ien-feng's Three Kinds of Light is translated in *Essential Teachings of Zen Master Hakuin*, p. 19. Yuan-chien's Rhinoceros Fan is found in the *Blue Cliff Record*, Case 91; Nan-ch'uan's Death in *Compendium of the Five Gates*, ch. 4; Po-yun's Not Yet There in *Compendium of the Five Gates*, ch. 19; the Old Lady Burns the Hut in *Compendium of the Five Gates*, ch. 6. Ch'ien and Her Spirit Apart in *Gateless Barrier*, Case 35; Wu-tsu Fa-yen's Water Buffalo in *Gateless Barrier*, Case 38.

36. "Your students' differing needs": the reference in the original is to the three kinds of Buddhist students: superior, average, and inferior. There are various schemata by which Zen students have been ranked in ability or promise.

37. Hakuin was seventy-six. At the end of the text he wrote the words "This ends The Tea-Grinding Songs of Old Granny Mind Master," adding the words "Mind Master" to the original title.

NOTES TO CHAPTER 5

1. The text used is that found in volume 12 of the *Hakuin Zenji Hōgo Zenshū*. An Italian translation of the work, *Lo Hōkyōkutsu no ki di Hakuin: Fede di massa e Zen*, by Silvio Vita, was published in 1979 in the journal *Il Giappone*, XIX.

2. "The Dharma all Buddhas preach is manifested such that it fills the entire Dharma universe" (*Flower Garland Sutra, ch.* 3).

3. "Ever since attaining Buddhahood I have dwelled in the human world of suffering, preaching the Dharma and liberating sentient beings . . . always preaching the Dharma and liberating countless millions of sentient beings." *Lotus Sutra*, "Life Span" chapter.

4. Because his work as a fisherman had obliged him to engage in the taking of life.

5. Amida Buddha is sometimes referred to by this name. He and his attendant Bodhisattvas, Kannon and Seishi, are known as the Amida *Sanzon*, or Triad.

6. The *Meditation Sutra*, one of the main sutras of the Pure Land schools, speaks of the body of Amida Buddha being infinitely vast, beyond the comprehension of ordinary mortals.

7. Aspirants for rebirth in Amida's Pure Land are said to be divided according to their differing capacities into three groups, superior, average, and inferior; these are further classified into three sub-groups.

8. Eshin Sōzu. Another name for the Tendai priest Genshin (942–1017), an important figure in early Pure Land teaching in Japan. The statements quoted here, often attributed to him, are originally from the *Daihōdō Daishū-kyō* (*Great Collection Sutra*).

9. Although not explained until later in the text, the speaker here is Hakuin, who is assuming the persona of a *Rokubu-rokujū* (literally a "sixty-sixer"), a pilgrim or beggar priest whose name derives from the fact that he was supposed to travel through all sixty-six provinces of the country visiting temples and other holy sites and donating at each a handwritten text from of the *Lotus Sutra*.

10. The phrase "reach the field of absolute singlemindedness" echoes a well-known passage in the Pure Land schools' *Amida Sutra* descriptive of the moment the mind of the Nembutsu reciter achieves oneness with the Nembutsu.

11. "One vehicle alone." A phrase from the *Lotus Sutra* (Expedient Means chapter) in which the Buddha explains that the sutra he is now preaching is the sole and ultimate teaching, one that can lead all beings to enlightenment.

12. Kannon appearing from a clam, one of the thirty-three ways in which Kannon is traditionally said to manifest himself, has no scriptural source. It is apparently based on stories found in Sung dynasty Zen records. The following appears in the *Records of the Lamp*:

> The T'ang emperor Wen Tsung was extremely fond of clams, so government officials stationed near the seashore vied with one another in providing them for the emperor's table. One day in the 5th year of T'ai-ho (831), a cook in the imperial kitchens was preparing some clams and came upon one that refused to open despite his best efforts. Thinking it unusual, the cook told the emperor about it. He had them place the clam on the altar and when incense and prayers were offered, it suddenly opened and the Bodhisattva Kannon appeared from within the shell. None of the emperor's ministers were able to explain what this apparition meant, so the emperor wrapped the clam in brocade, placed it in a precious sandalwood box, and presented it

to the Hsing-shan temple, with instructions for the brotherhood of monks to perform ceremonies for it. An eminent Zen
priest was summoned to explain the appearance. He told the
emperor that Bodhisattvas did not appear without reason, and
that this one had no doubt manifested itself in hopes of deepening the emperor's faith in the Buddha Dharma. He quoted some
lines from the *Kannon Sutra* to explain how the Bodhisattva
saves people by manifesting himself to them and preaching the
Dharma. The emperor replied that although the Bodhisattva
had appeared, he had still not heard him preach the Dharma.
The priest asked the emperor if he thought what he had seen
was unusual or not and whether or not he believed what he had
seen. The emperor said that it was definitely unusual and that he
deeply believed in it. "Then you have heard his Dharma preaching," replied the priest. With that, the emperor grasped the true
meaning of the incident in a sudden realization. He ordered
images of the Bodhisattva to be enshrined in temples throughout the empire."

It is not known when the figure of the Clam Kannon was introduced to
Japan; it appears in a standard work on Buddhist iconography published
in the Genroku period (1688–1703). Hakuin seems to have been the first
to depict this Bodhisattva in painting. On a painting he did on another
variation of the Kannon theme, showing the Bodhisattva emerging from
a gourd, he inscribed the words, "If he can appear from a clam, then why
not a gourd."

Ma-lang Kannon (Mr. Ma's Wife Kannon), another of the traditional
thirty-three Kannon manifestations, also known as Fish Basket Kannon,
derives from a tale found in several Sung dynasty Zen collections.

In the 12th year of the Yuan-ho era of the T'ang (817), there was a young
girl of great beauty who sold fish at Golden Sand Shoal from a basket
that she carried about. The young men all sought desperately to make her
their wife. Finally she told them that she had a deep interest in reciting
sutras and would become the wife of anyone who could continue reciting
the *Kannon Sutra* all through the night. At dawn on the next day, twenty
men had performed the feat. She said that, being only one woman, she
couldn't marry them all and suggested that they decide between them by
reciting the *Diamond Sutra* in the same way. Several of the men succeeded
in accomplishing this, so she next asked them to recite the *Lotus Sutra*
for a period of three days. This time, only one man, a son of the Ma family, was successful. He was married to the young woman, but no sooner
had she entered his house than she fell ill and died. Her corpse immediately began to decompose and seemed on the point of disappearing completely, so the remains were quickly placed in a casket. The next day a
priest came to perfom the funeral. When they opened the casket, there
was nothing inside but a set of golden bones. The priest said, "Your wife

was a manifestation of Kannon Bodhisattva. Her only desire was for you to gain salvation" (*Pien-nien t'ung-lan, ch.* 22).

Hakuin's version of the story is found in *Poison Flowers in a Thicket of Thorns,* kan 8:

In a village at a place called Golden Sand Shoal, none of the inhabitants had any knowledge of the Buddha Dharma. One day an old woman came to the village accompanied by a beautiful young girl. The girl moved with an extraordinary grace and had a face as fair as a flower. Although no one knew where the old woman had come from, it was rumored that she was interested in finding a husband for the young girl. Immediately the youths of the village began ardently seeking the girl's hand in marriage.

The old women said to them, "Please remain calm. I only have one young girl, and you are many. She could not possibly accept all of your offers unless she could manifest herself in a thousand forms like the Bodhisattva Kannon. Let us do this. I have a Buddhist scripture called the *Kannon Sutra.* If someone is able to memorize this sutra by tomorrow morning, that person will have my consent to marry the girl." She gave the men copies of the sutra, and that night she taught them how to read it. They strove with all the effort they could command to memorize the sutra and by the next morning about ten of them had succeeded in doing it. The old woman then distributed copies of the *Diamond Sutra* to them, with the same conditions as before. Overnight, seven or eight of the ten were able to memorize it. She next gave them the *Lotus Sutra,* which they found extremely difficult to memorize, it being a much longer text. One by one they reluctantly gave up. The only young man able to accomplish the difficult task was a son of the Ma family, and he took the young girl as his wife.

No sooner were they married than the young woman fell ill and died. The villagers, all deeply saddened by her death, were brought to understand the transience of human life, and took up the practice of reciting Buddhist sutras.

One day, an Indian priest carrying a long staff descended from the sky and proceeded to the young woman's grave. Poking in the earth with the staff, he unearthed a set of bones glittering with a golden light that illuminated everything around it. "These are the sacred bones of the Bodhisattva Kannon," he pronounced in a loud voice. "You must revere them and strive to free yourselves from the karmic obstacles now hindering you." He then vanished into the sky.

13. This story appears in a Pure Land work of the T'ang dynasty titled *San-pao kan-ying yao-lueh*:

There was an isolated island country in the southern seas named Chih Shih-tzu. It consisted of only about five hundred houses, and the people lived by catching birds and eating them. None of them had even heard of the Buddha's Dharma. From time to time schools of large fish, several thousand in number, would approach the shore. The fish were all fluent in the language of the islanders and they constantly repeated words that sounded like "Namu Amida Butsu" or "Nembutsu." Although the islanders did not understand the meaning of these words, they named the fish the Nembutsu fish after the sound of words they kept repeating. One of the fishermen discovered that by reciting the word Amida, he could get the fish gradually to approach the shore, and if he continued reciting the word, the fish would remain close to shore even while he continued to catch them. Their flesh was delicious, although in time the people found that they tasted best if before catching them they would engage in long recitations of Amida's name. People who recited the name for only a short time had trouble catching any fish at all. As the fishermen grew very fond of eating the fish, repeating the name of Amida Buddha became one of their principal occupations.

One day a villager, one who had been among the first to eat the fish, passed away. Three months later, people saw him return to the island beach riding on a purple cloud and emitting a splendidly radiant light. "I was a leader of the fishermen here," he told the islanders. "When I died, I was reborn into the Land of Bliss. Those great fish are manifestations of the Buddha Amida. Pitying our ignorance he took this form in order to guide us to the Nembutsu samadhi. If you don't believe me, take a look at the bones of the fish you have been eating. You will find that they are lotus flowers." The islanders were overjoyed, and after examining the bones and finding that he was speaking the truth, they all became firmly convinced of the truth of the Buddha's teaching. Although they continued to repeat the Buddha's name, they ceased their former practice of taking life and were all reborn in Amida's Pure Land.

14. Here for the first time Hakuin reveals that the narrator belongs to the class of pilgrims known as *Rokubu-rokujū*. They normally traveled in groups of three or four.

15. Records indicate that at some time in the eighteenth or early nineteenth century, there was such a hut on the hill above the cave.

16. Hakuin ends by stressing that the Amida he refers to exists in the mind alone, not in some Pure Land far removed from this world, as is stated in the Pure Land sutras and believed by many devotees of the Pure Land schools. Formulations such as "the Pure Land existing in the mind alone" and "Amida in my own mind" were common in Japanese Zen, deriving originally from Sung and Yuan dynasty Chinese sources.

NOTES TO CHAPTER 6

1. The full title is *The Chronological Biography of Zen Master Shinki Dokumyō, Founder of Ryūtaku-ji* (*Ryūtaku-kaiso Shinki Dokumyō Zenshi nempu*), Shinki Dokumyō being Hakuin's posthumous Zen master title.

2. There were also biographical records of priests' lives known as *gyōjitsu* or *anroku*, which were similar in nature to the *nempu* but generally shorter.

3. The samurai of Kumano were known for their exploits at sea. They fought with distinction on the winning Minamoto side at the Battle of Dannoura (1185).

4. According to custom, when Hakuin's father was adopted into his wife's family, he assumed the Nagasawa surname.

5. The chapter teaches that all beings, even the evil Devadatta, can attain Buddhahood through the power of the *Lotus Sutra*.

6. In a story titled "Kyūshinbō Experiences a Dangerous Fire" in Hakuin's *Kana Inga Hōgo* (*Dharma Words on Cause and Effect in Kana Script*) Kyū-shinbō is described quite differently.

7. Shakyamuni Buddha is said to have engaged in ascetic practice for six years in the Himalayas. Bodhidharma is said to have sat facing a cliff wall for nine years at Shao-lin monastery.

8. In *Wild Ivy*, Hakuin says Nichigon's text was the letters of instruction Nichiren wrote to his followers.

9. The Tenmangu Shrine, enshrining Tenjin, the deified form of the states-man and poet Sugawara Michizane, was in Kyoto. Countless smaller shrines were found throughout the country. This one was attached to Sainen-ji just behind the Nagasawa home.

10. In his autobiographical accounts Hakuin says that the play was performed by a group of traveling Jōruri players.

11. These are the three pats a priest gives his shaven head three times each day as he reflects: Why have I shaved this head? What must I be doing? What is my ultimate goal?

12. A Nichiren priest about which nothing is known except that he lived in a hermitage adjacent to Sainen-ji temple.

13. "Ordinary, everyday (*heijitsu*) Zen" no doubt refers to Bankei Yōtaku's teaching of "Unborn" (*fushō*) Zen, which had won many adherents in this area of central Honshu in the previous century. Tarumaru Sokai had stud-ied with Bankei, and Masaki Ryōkō was a student of Bankei's heir Setsugai Sotei. For Bankei's life and teaching, see *Unborn: The Life and Teachings of Zen Master Bankei*.

14. Yun-chu Hsiao-shun, of the Northern Sung, incurred the displeasure of the local governor, was stripped of the abbotship of the Ch'i-hsien tem-ple on Mount Lu, and returned to lay status. Later, when pardoned and allowed to return to his temple, he read a verse to the brotherhood that ended with the lines "For over half a year I lived without my monk's robe; today, back in my temple again, how often I rejoice, how often I am angry."

15. Shō Zōsu (later Kairyū Ishō) was senior to Hakuin, his brother disciple under Sokudō Fueki, and accompanied him on many of his early travels. Recognizing Hakuin's uncommon ability, Shō became Hakuin's student and was eventually sanctioned as one of his first Dharma heirs.

16. Daigu Sōchiku was a prominent Rinzai priest active during the previous century. Hakuin elsewhere says the calligraphy was by Ungo Kiyō.

17. The Mu koan.

18. This was the Hōei Eruption, the last time that Mount Fuji has erupted. It began with a series of earthquakes on the night of the 22nd in the eleventh

month. The next morning the volcano erupted in violent explosions that continued for four days, until the evening of the 26th.

19. (Gempō) Kokan, one of Hakuin's elder brothers, is known only by this posthumous name.

20. As a boy Sōkaku had served Matsudaira Tadatomo, the lord of Iiyama castle, as a tea attendant. Lord Matsudaira later arranged for him to be ordained by Shōju Rōjin, whom he eventually succeeded at Shōju-an. Sōkaku is known almost entirely through the accounts in Hakuin's auto-biographical writings.

21. Prajnatara, the twenty-seventh of the twenty-eight Indian Zen patriarchs listed in the *Records of the Lamp*.

22. The koan Secretary Ch'en Climbs the Pavilion.

23. The verse appears in *Ta-hui's General Talks (Ta-hui P'u-shuo), ch. 3*, as Ta-hui's comment on the Mu koan: "Lotus leaves, perfect discs, rounder than mirrors. Water chestnuts, needle-sharp, sharper than gimlets."

24. Myōjun is the posthumous name of Hakuin's mother. Maitreya is the Buddha of the Future, said to be dwelling in the "inner palace" in the Tushita Heaven whence, ages in the future, he will be reborn into the human world to lead sentient beings to salvation. Departed souls are thought to remain in the realm of the dead from the seventh day after death until the second death anniversary. During this period, the Ten Kings of Hell, one of which is the King of the Northern Quarter, hold judgment on sins the deceased has committed. The Tushita Heaven would be a favorable rebirth.

25. The formless Mind precepts (*musō shinchi kai*). The principle is, until the true (Buddha-) mind is attained, it is not possible to uphold the individual precepts; once it is attained, they are all upheld as a matter of course, without conscious effort. Hakuin's comments on the Mind precepts are found in the *Supplement* to *Poison Flowers*.

26. These are lines from the *Precious Mirror Samadhi*, which uses hexagrams in the *Book of Changes* to illustrate the teaching of the Five Ranks. The double *Li* hexagram consists of two identical *Li* trigrams (unbroken line, broken line, unbroken line), one on top the other. See *Zen Dust*, pp. 67–72.

27. The World-Honored One Holds Up a Flower. *Gateless Gate*, Case 6.

28. The lay Buddhist name of Nakano Shichirōemon (d. 1730), a wealthy sake brewer of Iiyama. Apparently Hakuin befriended him while he was study-ing at Shōju-an.

29. The episode Hakuin describes here is not found in this work.

30. This was a verse Hsu-t'ang wrote to send off three of his monks (*Hsu-t'ang ho-shang yu-lu, ch. 7*).

31. Kogetsu was abbot of Daikō-ji in Hyūga province on the island of Kyushu. Later it would be said that "Hakuin in the east and Kogetsu in the west divided the Zen world between them." Some of Hakuin's finest disciples, among them Tōrei and Gasan Jitō, began their practice with Kogetsu.

32. That is, Kogetsu was conversing with a priest who was long dead.

33. This is thought to be Sefuku-ji, a large Tendai temple on Mount Makino-o, where Egoku had secluded himself as a young monk. Hakuin may have gone there at Egoku's suggestion.

34. Tesshin Dōin (1593–1690, Sōtō sect) and Egoku Dōmyō (1632–1721; Ōbaku sect). Both of these men, like their great contemporary Bankei Yōtaku (1622–93), had been strongly influenced by the Chinese priest Tao-che Chao-yuan (Dōsha Chōgen; 1600–61?) whom they studied under together in their youth in Nagasaki. Perhaps this was the reason for Hakuin's interest in their Zen teaching.

35. It was also during this period at Inryō-ji that Hakuin's earliest known literary work, *Nuno-tsuzumi* (*Cloth Drum*) was apparently written, a brief collection of stories of the cause-and-effect type that he would continue to write throughout his career. *Nuno-tsuzumi* was later republished with a new collection of tales in 1753 under the title *Saiben Nuno-tsuzumi* (A New Drumhead for the Cloth Drum).

36. The verse alludes to an anecdote about the Sung master Yang-ch'i Fang-hui found in *Precious Lessons of the Zen School*.

37. "Half a persimmon twice a day" alludes to an austere solitary retreat engaged in by Musō Soseki in Kai province (Hakuin tells the story in *Wild Ivy*, pp. 57–60). The eccentric T'ang monk Lan-tsan lived in the mountains shunning the world his entire life, living on mountain yams and bracken (*Blue Cliff Record*, Case 34).

38. Kanzan Egen was living in the mountains of Ibuka (not far from Iwataki where Hakuin was practicing) when he was summoned by Emperor Hanazono to return to Kyoto and become founder of Myōshin-ji.

39. Located at the Okitsu post station west of Hara, Seiken-ji was the most important Myōshin-ji branch temple in Suruga province. Shōin-ji was under its jurisdiction.

40. According to Katō(*Hakuin Oshō Nempu*, p. 160) it was the twenty-first of the 10th month.

41. *P'o-hsiang lun*. One of the works in *Bodhidharma's Six Gates*.

42. Unzan Sotai (1685–1747) originally studied under Kogetsu Zenzai in Kyushu.

43. An unpublished holograph manuscript of *The Tale of My Childhood* contains the following description of this experience. "When I was forty-one years old, an old layman whom I had known intimately and associated with for years came to me and said, 'Recently my late mother appeared to me in a dream. "Ask the master to read the *Lotus Sutra* for the sake of my soul." Please, Master Hakuin, in your great compassion, grant my mother this request.' I had no choice but to agree, so one autumn night, hanging up a solitary lamp in my room, I quietly began to read the sutra. When I came to the Chapter on Parables, I heard the shrilling of a cricket from somewhere by the temple wall. At the same instant I entered the Lotus Samadhi. I attained for the first time the eye for reading sutras. All the doubts and concerns that had plagued me from the age of fifteen, fully twenty-seven years, instantly ceased to exist—like

ice that had melted away. As I thought back over the past, examining the attainments I had experienced in various places over the last forty years, and the ecstatic joy that had accompanied them, I realized that their value was not worth even half a *sen*. I began sobbing loudly, beside myself with joy. After that, I was able to understand the full extent of all the mistakes I had made when I had lectured on sutras and Zen records. This I humbly declare to you all. It is essential for you to know that the practice of Zen (*sanzen*) is no easy matter. If in my fifteenth year doubts about the *Lotus Sutra* had not arisen in my mind, how would the over-whelming joy I then felt ever have been achieved? Is it not a case of "a single wisdom gained by means of one experience"? This all took place on the night of the fifteenth of the seventh month in the twelfth year of Kyōhō.

In *Sentinel at the Gates*, Hakuin states that this experience in his forty-first year confirmed once and for all that the Bodhi-mind was a matter of turning the wheel of the Four Great Bodhisattva Vows, that is, striving to further one's own enlightenment while working to help others still suffering in illusion.

44. Shōji Rokubei, style Yūsai (d. 1750). An influential citizen of Hara who was related to Hakuin's family. Although a patron of Shōgen-ji, a Nichiren temple, both he and his brother Yūtetsu studied with Hakuin.

Satsu (1714–89) married Watanabe Kenzaemon, whose family were proprietors of the Sanken-ya, a *honjin*-type inn, catering to the highest clientele, at the Hara station. She was widowed at forty-four. She is listed in *Goose Grass* among those who passed Hakuin's twofold One Hand koan and received his Dragon Staff certificate. At this time she would have been thirteen years old.

45. A Zen saying cautions against abiding either where there is Buddha or where there is no Buddha. Hakuin's anecdotal collection *Stories from a Thicket of Thorn and Briar* relates what is essentially the same story, then goes on to tell another lengthy tale about Satsu. See Appendix A.

46. Rimpen appears in the *Chuang Tzu* as the name of "Wheelwright P'ien," a wheelwright who embodies the wisdom of the Taoist sages (Watson, pp. 152–53). Apparently this person had adopted the name as a sobriquet.

47. This saying, provenance unknown, was used by Hakuin for calligraphy inscriptions, one of which, written on a painting of Manjushri (Monju) Bodhisattva, reads: "Breaking up white rock inside a poppy seed. Culling frost on the ocean floor."

48. Both these men were from Hina village, near Hara. Ishii Gentoku, 1671–1751, was a physician. There are no dates for Sugisawa Sōshin (Sōzaemon).

49. Furugōri Kentsū (1695–1746) was a physician who on occasion attended Hakuin.

50. *Kanrin Ihō*. This collection of short texts from Zen and other Buddhist writings for instructing and encouraging Zen students was first published in 1769, after Hakuin's death, by Tōrei Enji.

51. Dōju Sōkaku. *Shuso*: senior priest.

52. Nothing else is known of Masa. Unzan, a childhood friend of Hakuin, first appears in the entry for Age 34.

53. *Honchō Jinja-kō*, by the anti-Buddhist Neo-Confucian teacher Hayashi Razan (1583–1657). Hakuin criticized the work in *Supplement to Poison Flowers in a Thicket of Thorns*.

54. See *Poison Flowers, kan 9*.

55. The sense here seems to be that new buildings will not necessarily produce good monks. Master Fen-yang, living in a bitterly cold region "north of the river," was urged by an Indian priest to increase his monks' practice, and before three years were out, six men in his assembly had attained great enlightenment (*Precious Lessons of the Zen School*). Five fords and five bridges refer to the Five Chinese Zen Schools, all deriving from Bodhidharma at Mount Shao-lin.

56. Uematsu Suetsuna (1701–71), head of one of the wealthiest Hara families. Uematsu's residence was almost adjacent to Shōin-ji.

57. They were included in *Poison Flowers in a Thicket of Thorns, kan 7*.

58. All that is known of this monk is that he was from Inryō-ji in Bizen and later resided in Sōrin-an in Yahata south of Kyoto. Yet a note in the *Draft Biography* states: "he served Hakuin for many years, and . . . it was through his efforts alone that Hakuin became widely known throughout the land."

59. Akiyama Michitomo (1682–1740), a wealthy farmer from the Mishima area and lay student of Hakuin.

60. Preparations for this large practice session are described in the preface to *Dharma Talks Introductory to Lectures on the Record of Hsi-keng*. See my *Essentials Teachings of Zen Master Hakuin*.

61. Hsi-keng (Sokkō) was a sobriquet used by Hsu-t'ang. His Zen records are divided into ten sections, each section containing teachings he gave at the ten temples he served at during his career.

62. "Where do you come from when you're born? Where do you go after you die? If you can know the place of this coming and going, you can be called a person who has truly acquired Buddhahood." *Record of Ta-hui*.

63. *Gateless Barrier*, Case 41.

64. *Gateless Barrier*, Case 38.

65. Nothing is known of Reigaku other than the fact that he was elderly. Hakuin's verse appears in *Stories from a Thicket of Thorn and Briar*: "Lamenting a wasted life, withering away, / Sitting silently, desolately, how many years? / Don't say Buddha's Dharma can't turn things around, / It opens up for the first time with a bald head and wriggly teeth."

66. The phrases quoted by the monk, from the *Blue Cliff Record*, Case 16, concern the pecking that occurs when a baby chick about to emerge from its egg pecks at the inside of the shell and the mother hen simultaneously pecks at it from without. Descriptive of the Zen teacher's insight in knowing precisely when a student is on the threshold of enlightenment and at just the right moment uses appropriate means to bring it about.

67. This talk is included in *Poison Flowers, kan* 2.

68. A barrier guarded by nine tigers, thus very difficult to pass through.

69. The story is about the son of a wealthy Edo family who was disowned for his profligate ways and thrown out of the family house. Spurned by his friends, without a cent to his name, and dressed in a ragged robe, he started along the Tōkaidō in the direction of Kyoto. Ravenously hungry, when he saw a teashop selling fried buns, he ordered twenty or thirty of them, gobbled them up, and then ran off without paying. Townspeople soon caught up with him, and when they found he had no money, they gave him a severe beating. He tearfully related his life story to the young men surrounding him, telling them he had been without food for three days and had suddenly decided to eat and run, knowing he would probably be caught and beaten to death. After hearing the story, the young men left him where he was, "crying in the dust." Describing the difficulties the man had undergone in order to prolong his life, Hakuin compares them with the adversities that young monks must undergo in their search for enlightenment, pointing out that both of them endure suffering, but that the end result is as different "as the moon is from a turtle." *Poison Flowers, kan* 2.

70. Amra is the site where the *Vimalakirti Sutra* was preached. "Hanging up the poison drum" is perhaps an allusion to Vimalakirti's celebrated "thundering silence."

71. Nothing more is known about Inoue Hyōma. One section of *Goose Grass* is made up of accounts of people who were miraculously saved from Hell thanks to recitations of the brief *Ten Phrase Kannon Sutra for Prolonging Life*.

72. *Poison Flowers, kan* 2.

73. Ōmi waters: Lake Biwa, in Ōmi, Tōrei's home province. According to Chinese legend, carp that could scale the three-tiered waterfall at the Dragon Gate would transform into dragons.

74. Hakuin did at least two paintings of this subject. Takeuchi Naotsugi, *Hakuin* (Chikuma, 1964), plate 91.

75. Yamanashi Harushige (1707–63) was the son of a prominent family of sake brewers.

76. A key concept in the doctrine of the Five Ranks set forth in the *Precious Mirror Samadhi*.

77. Honkō Kokushi is the honorific title of the Myōshin-ji priest Daikyū Sōkyū (1468–1549). Kanjū Sōtetsu's temple Rinzai-ji in Suruga province was founded by a disciple of Daikyū.

78. The "Three Dark Gates" (*Sangen*) and "Three Essentials" (*Sanyō*) appear in the *Record of Lin-chi*. Their meaning is uncertain.

79. A work in Japanese by the Rinzai monk Takusui Chōmo (d. 1740).

80. Hakuin uses Heishirō's story in his *Rōhatsu Jishu* (Instructions for Rōhatsu), which is read to students on the fifth night of the December *rōhatsu sesshin* (training session) in Rinzai temples. It is also found in a

letter of religious instruction addressed to "A Certain Layman" (*Complete Works*, vol. 6).

81. *Sanshō gōyō*, the title of *kan* 3 of Daitō's *Records*, consists of Daitō's lectures and comments on the *Record of Hsueh-tou*.

82. Kakujū Jōchō became head abbot of Mampuku-ji in 1786.

83. Yotsugi Hachirōbei Masayuki was a wealthy Kyoto merchant; by this time he had passed Hakuin's twofold koan on the sound of one hand (*Poison Flowers*). Ike Taiga (1723–76) is one of the great *bunjin* painters of the Edo period; he also seems to have passed the One Hand koan.

84. The Myōshin-ji temple to which Shōin-ji was affiliated.

85. The records of the Sung priest Wu-hsueh Tsu-yuan (1226–86), founder of the Engaku-ji in Kamakura, which were published in Japan.

86. In spring of 1752, Kyoto experienced an unusually heavy snowfall that reached levels of up to thirty feet in the mountainous districts north of the city.

87. See my translation, *Poison Words for the Heart*.

88. Lord Matsudaira Shigenobu (1728–71).

89. These instructions (*jishū*) are found in *Poison Flowers, kan* 1.

90. The story about Kida making off with the manuscript is apparently a fiction. Other sources show that Hakuin himself was anxiously involved in getting the manuscript published.

91. Gudō's records, *Hōkan-roku*, were published in 1797, after Hakuin's death.

92. *Pao-tsang lun*, a work attributed to Seng-chao (374–414), an early Chinese master of Mahayana philosophy.

93. "Ensnared" (*hikikomi*) is a play on Hikikomi-chō, Rinsen-ji's address in Edo. The final two lines—*yabu nimo kō mono kana*—were a popular saying, to the effect that wonderful things sometimes appear where you least expect them. Hakuin was priest of a tiny rural temple.

94. *Hsueh-feng t'a-ming*. The text is given in *Hakuin Oshō Shōden*, pp. 341–43.

95. Bishamonten: one of the Four Heavenly Kings entrusted with protecting the northern quarter. Idaten is a guardian deity enshrined in Zen temples as protector of the kitchen. The "two wheels" (*ni-rin*) are the Dharma Wheel and the Food Wheel. When a person turns the Dharma Wheel, spreading the Buddha's teachings, he is at the same time turning the Food Wheel, that is, working to receive his own sustenance.

96. Upon receiving Dharma sanction from Hsu-t'ang, Daiō transmitted the Zen of the Yang-ch'i lineage to Japan. These words, known in Japanese Rinzai Zen as "Hsu-t'ang's prophecy," appear in a farewell verse Hsu-t'ang presented to Daiō as the latter was setting out to return to Japan.

97. Myōshin-ji priests were required to obtain the rank of *Dai-ichiza* in order to become temple abbots.

98. A ceremony to enshrine *shari* or relics of the Buddha in the new temple.

99. According to an old Zen story (*Gateless Barrier*, Case 23), after the Sixth Zen Patriarch Hui-neng received the Fifth Patriarch's robe and bowl

symbolizing the Zen transmission, he was obliged to leave the temple in secret in order to avoid the jealous wrath of the other monks. A senior monk named Ming pursued him determined to take back the articles, catching up with him on Mount Ta-yu.

100. Sekkō (1408–86) and Toyō (1428–1504) were important priests of the Shōtaku line of Myōshin-ji to which Hakuin belonged.

101. Mr. Ōmura, said to have been a relative of Zen master Shidō Munan, was proprietor of the Shirokiya, a well-known dry goods store in Nihonbashi, Edo. Nothing is known of the other person.

102. Based on the idea that although the three groups of Buddhist disciple— superior, intermediate, and inferior—will grasp Shakyamuni's preaching of the *Lotus Sutra* in different ways according to their capacities, all will nonetheless eventually attain Buddhahood as prophesied in the sutra.

103. Yōsen (d. 1799). Yōsen and his wife were longtime Hakuin students from Mishima; both had received his Dragon Staff certificates of *kenshō*.

104. Emperor Reigen (1654–1732).

105. According to Katō (p. 291) the attending physician was named Kokei.

106. The Chinese character Tōrei uses to replicate this sound, made of the mouth radical and the character for cow, is used in Buddhist literature to represent the lowing of cattle. Hakuin's deep affinity with the deity Tenjin, whose messenger is a bull, was known to Tōrei (he has described Hakuin as moving like a bull). Un (Sanskrit Om or Aum) is also the final word in the Sanskrit alphabet, and is regarded in esoteric Buddhism as the essence of Bodhi, from which all virtues are derived.

107. Yen-t'ou's death cry was said to have been audible for three leagues. His story is told in Part One, p. 157.

108. Presumably these four priests are singled out from among Hakuin's other Dharma heirs because they were also abbots at temples he had founded, making them also heirs in the *garan-hō* or "temple-succession" Dharma transmission, whereby a teacher appoints a disciple abbot of a temple he has founded or has direct jurisdiction over. While this is obviously the case for Kairyū (Muryō-ji), Tōrei (Ryūtaku-ji), and Suiō (Shōin-ji), it can only be inferred in the case of Tōgan Gen from the Ryūkyū Islands, about whom almost nothing is known. It has been suggested that he may have established a temple in the Ryūkyūs and made Hakuin its honorary founder.

Glossary

Amida Buddha. The central Buddha in Chinese and Japanese Pure Land Buddhism

Arhat. A practicer who has attained the highest rank in the Hinayana tradition

Bandō. The region of east-central Honshū centered on the city of Edo

Bodhi-mind (Sanskrit *Bodhichitta*). "Mind of enlightenment"; the aspiration to carry out the Four Great Vows (deepening self-awakening while working to help others reach liberation) that arises in the mind after attainment of *kenshō;* the source of post-satori practice

Bodhidharma. The First Patriarch of Chinese Zen, who brought Zen's mind-to-mind transmission to China from India

Bodhisatttva. A being who aspires to attain Buddhahood and carries out various practices to achieve that goal. Compassion is the outstanding character-istic of the Bodhisattva, who postpones his or her own entry into nirvana in order to assist others.

Chao-chou's Mu (koan). *Gateless Barrier,* Case 1. See *Glossary: Mu Koan*

Chao-chou's Mud Buddha (koan). *Blue Cliff Record,* Case 96. See *p. 245, note 21*

Chien-feng's Three Infirmities (koan). See *Essential Teachings of Zen Master Hakuin,* pp. 19–20

Ch'ien and Her Spirit Apart (koan). See *Gateless Barrier,* Case 35

Chronological Biography. The Chronological Biography of Zen Master Shinki Dokumyō Founder of Ryūtaku-ji, by Tōrei Enji. Translated in Chapter Six

Cinnabar field *(tanden)*. The center of breathing located slightly below the navel; often used in the combined form *kikai tanden*, "cinnabar field located in the ocean of *ki*"

Claws and fangs of the Dharma cave *(hokkutsu no sōge)*. An expression, originally from the *Records from the Groves of Zen (Lin-kuan lu)*, used for koans, descriptive of the power they possess to bring students to the experience of the "great death" *(taishi ichiban)*, or satori. Used together with divine death-dealing amulets. See Chapter One, note 18

Closed barrier Zen *(kansa Zen)*. Hakuin's term for koan practice, in which students must pass numerous koan "barriers"

Dai-ichiza (lit. "First Seat"). Nominal rank awarded in the Myōshin-ji lineage enabling recipient priests to become temple abbots

Deva realms. Highest of the six realms of unenlightened existence; in the ten realms they are below the four enlightened realms of Shravaka, Pratyeka-buddha, Bodhisattva, and Buddha

Difficult-to-pass koans. See hard-to-pass *(nantō)* koans

Divine death-dealing amulets. *(datsumyō no shimpu;* also life-destroying charms). Originally, Taoist charms said to give the possessor life-destroying powers. Used similarly to "claws and fangs of the Dharma cave," with which it is generally paired, in Hakuin's works

Draft Biography. Tōrei's original draft of Hakuin's *Chronological Biography* (Chapter Six)

Dragon Staff certificate. A certificate that included a painting of a priest's staff transforming into a dragon which Hakuin awarded to students who attained *kenshō*

Eighth "Storehouse" Consciousness (Sanskrit *ālaya-vijnāna*). The fundamental consciousness in which all karma of past and present existence is stored. In Hakuin's writings it is often described as a pitch-blackness or a pitch-dark cave; when broken through or inverted in the attainment of enlightenment, it suddenly transforms into the all-illuminating Great Perfect Mirror Wisdom

Evil paths (of existence). The three lowest of the six paths or worlds in which unenlightened beings transmigrate: the realms of hell, of hungry spirits, and of beasts.

Five Cardinal Sins. Patricide, matricide, killing an enlightened being, creating a schism within the Sangha, shedding the blood of a Buddha

Five Chinese Zen Schools. Schools or lineages of teaching, named after their founders, that developed in Chinese Zen between the T'ang and Sung dynasties: Kuei-shan, Lin-chi, Ts'ao-tung, Yun-men, Fa-yen

Five Ranks (*Go-i*). A teaching device attributed to the T'ang priest Tung-shan used in Japanese Sōtō Zen but generally ignored in the Rinzai school. Hakuin made use of it in his program of post-satori training

Fivefold Eye. The human eye, the eye of the gods that sees all things at all times, the eye of wisdom that discerns the true forms of all things, the Dharma eye that is able to save others using skillful means, and the Buddha eye that knows all things, reflecting them as they are in themselves

Four Great (also Universal; Bodhisattva) Vows (*shigu seigan*). Vows Maha-yana Buddhists take upon their entrance into religious life: to save all sentient beings, to end the inexhaustible delusive passions, to study all the infinite Dharma teaching, to master the unsurpassable Buddha Way

Four Wisdoms. Attained in enlightenment: the Great Perfect Mirror Wisdom, that reflects all things in their suchness; the wisdom that discerns the ultimate sameness of all things; the wisdom that discerns the distinctive features of all phenomena; the wisdom that promotes the work of Buddhahood

Gasshō. Pressing the palms of the hands together, fingers pointing upwards, in an expression of thankfulness, reverence, or prayer

Great Perfect Mirror Wisdom. See Four Wisdoms

Hard-to-pass (*nantō*; literally, "hard to pass through") koans. Koans Hakuin assigned to students after they achieved an initial *kenshō*. He gives a number of different lists for these koans

Hell of Incessant Suffering (Sanskrit, *Avichi*). The lowest level in the realm of hell, reserved for those who have committed one of the Five Cardinal Sins

Inka (*-shōmei*). The certification or sanction of *kenshō* awarded to students by a Rinzai teacher

Jōza. A title given to the head monk of a temple or training hall

Kalpa. An incalculably long period of time; an aeon

Kami. Deities that are the central objects of worship in Japanese Shinto

Kenshō. "Seeing into one's own self-nature"; approximate synonym for satori, but it is normally limited to the initial breakthrough experience

Ki. The vital "breath" or energy present in all living things; in humans, *ki* circulates through the body and is central to the preservation of health and sustenance of life

Kinhin. The "walking meditation" practiced between long periods of zazen

Kokurin ("Crane Grove"). The *sangō* or "mountain name" of Hakuin's temple Shōin-ji; also used by Hakuin as a sobriquet

Latter-Day Dharma. The age of the Dharma's destruction, the last of three periods a Buddha's teaching passes through after his death as it gradually loses its power to lead people to enlightenment

Mind Master (*Shushin*). Hakuin's term for the self in its true and original state; the ultimate principle of Mind; the intrinsic Buddha-mind or Buddha-nature

Mu koan (*Gateless Barrier*, Case 1). Famous koan traditionally assigned to beginning students: A monk asked Master Chao-chou, "Does a dog have a Buddha-nature, or not?" Chao-chou answered, "Mu" [literally, "Nothing" or "Not"]

Naikan meditation ("introspective meditation"). See Chapter Three, note 17

Nan-ch'uan Kills the Cat (koan). See *Gateless Barrier*, Case 14

Nan-ch'uan's Death (koan). See *Essential Teachings of Zen Master Hakuin*, p. 126

Nembutsu. The practice used in the Pure Land schools of repeating the name of Amida Buddha in the formula "Namu Amida Butsu" (I entrust myself to Amida Buddha)

"Old Granny Mind Master" (*Shushin obaba*). The personification of Buddha-mind; main speaker in *Old Granny's Tea-Grinding Songs*

Old Sail Not Yet Raised (koan). See *Essential Teachings of Zen Master Hakuin*, p. 130

Old Woman Burns the Hut (koan). See *Entangling Vines*, Case 162

One Hand, the Sound of (*sekishu no onjō*): Sound of One Hand koans

Oshō (Priest). A term of respect for a senior priest who generally is, or has been, a temple abbot

Po-yun's Not Yet There (koan). See *Essential Teachings of Zen Master Hakuin*, p. 89

Post-satori training (*gogo no shūgyō*). The practice that begins after attainment of *kenshō*, defined by Hakuin as working for deeper self-awakening while helping others reach liberation

Pratyeka-buddha ("Private" Buddha). See Two Vehicles

Ri. The Japanese mile, about 4 kilometers (2.44 miles)

Rōhatsu training session (*rōhatsu sesshin*). The period of concentrated zazen practice held in Japanese Rinzai monasteries from the first day of the twelfth month and ending on the morning of the eighth day

Rokubu-rokujū (lit. "Sixty-sixers"). Beggar-priests of Edo Japan who spent their lives traveling the pilgrim circuits

Ryō. A standard gold piece in use in Edo Japan weighing about 18 grams

Sanzen. Literally, to study Zen. In Hakuin's works it normally refers to koan study and to the Zen teacher's private interview with his students

Satori. Enlightenment

Second Patriarch's Pacification of Mind (koan). See *Gateless Barrier*, Case 41

Secretary Ch'en Climbs the Pavilion (koan). See Chapter Six, pp. 169–70

Shravaka. See Two Vehicles

Shuso. A title given to the lead or head monk in a training hall or temple; next in rank to the abbot

Silent illumination (*mokushō*) Zen. A term usually associated with practices of Sōtō Zen, contrasting them with the koan Zen of the Rinzai school; Hakuin applied it to all types of Zen practice that do not make the student focus on the breakthrough into *kenshō*

Six Paths. The six ways of unenlightened existence: (1) hell, (2) the realm of hungry spirits, (3) beasts, (4) asuras, (5) human beings, and (6) devas (heavenly beings)

Sound of One Hand koans. A two-part koan for beginning students that Hakuin devised in his mid-sixties: Hear the Sound of One Hand Clapping, and Put a Stop to All Sounds

Storehouse Consciousness: See Eighth "Storehouse" Consciousness

Su-shan's Memorial Tower. (koan). See Chapter One, note 65

Talisman, life-destroying: See divine death-dealing amulets

Tanden: See cinnabar field

Ten Evil Acts (*jū-aku*; also Transgressions). They are taking life, stealing, illicit sexual conduct, lying, harsh words, defaming, duplicity, greed, anger, and the holding of mistaken views

Tenjin. Deified form of the court scholar, statesman, and poet Sugawara Michizane (845–903) enshrined at the Kitano Tenmangu in Kyoto

Three Buddha bodies. The three kinds of body a Buddha may possess: the eternal and absolute Dharma-body, indescribable and inconceivable; the Reward- or Recompense-body, obtained as a result of practicing the Bodhisattva way, in which the Buddha preached to the great assemblies described in the sutras; and the Transformation-body, the body he manifests to human beings

Three Poisons. The major evil passions: greed, anger, stupidity.

Three Worlds (also known as Triple World; Threefold World). The realms of desire, form, and formlessness, composing the world inhabited by unenlightened beings in the Six Paths of existence

Two Vehicles. The Shravaka, a disciple who achieves liberation upon listening to the Buddhist teachings, and the *Pratyeka*-buddha, who achieves liberation but does not undertake to teach others. Hakuin regarded them as inferior to the Bodhisattva, whose life is devoted to saving other beings as well

Udumbara. A plant said to bloom only once in three thousand years; in Buddhist literature, a symbol of the difficulty of encountering a Buddha

Unborn Zen. The Zen teaching of the seventeenth-century Zen master Bankei Yōtaku that retained considerable popularity into the eighteenth century. Hakuin uses the term, as he also does Silent Illumination Zen, do-nothing Zen, and dead- [withered-] sitting Zen, in a general sense to indicate a type of Zen practice that does not focus on the breakthrough into *kenshō*

Vimalakirti. The central figure of the *Vimalakirti Sutra*; regarded in Zen as the ideal of the lay practicer

World-Honored One Holds Up a Flower (koan). See *Gateless Barrier*, Case 6

Wu-tsu's Water Buffalo Through the Window (koan). See *Gateless Barrier*, Case 38

Young Woman Comes Out of Samadhi (koan). See *Gateless Barrier*, Case 42

Yuan-chien's Rhinoceros Fan (koan). See *Blue Cliff Record*, Case 91

Zogen. A title given to the head monk or senior priest of a training hall or temple

Zōsu. A title given to the monk in charge of the temple library

Selected Bibliography

Blue Cliff Record. Translation of *Pi-yen lu* by Thomas and J. C. Cleary. Shambhala, 1977.

Ch'an-kuan ts'e-chin (*Spurring Zen Students Through the Barrier*). Compiled by Yun-ch'i Chu-hung. T. 48.

Ch'an-lin pao-tsun (*Precious Lessons of the Zen School*). T. 48.

Cheng-tsung tsan (*Praise of the True School*). Full title *Wu-chia cheng-tsung-tsa* (*Praise of the Five Houses of the True School*). Zokuzō 2B-8.

Chiang-hu feng-yueh chi (*Wind and Moon Collection of Zen Poetry*). Sung-p'o tsung-ch'i. See *Gōkofūgetsu-shū yakuchū.* Ed. Yoshizawa Katsuhiro, Zenbunka Kenkyūsho, 2004.

Ching-te ch'uan-teng lu (*Records of the Transmission of the Lamp of the Ching-te Era*). Compiled by Tao-yuan. T. 51.

Ch'uan-lao Chin-kang ching (*Ch'uan-lao's Comments on the Diamond Sutra*). Zokuzō 38-4.

Chu-ch'uang erh-pi (*Jottings at the Bamboo Window, Second Series*). Yun-chi Chu-hung. Kyoto, 1653.

Daitō-roku (*Record of Daitō*). T. 81.

Dokugo Shingyō (*Poison Words for the Heart*). Hakuin commentary on the *Heart Sutra. Hakuin Oshō Zenshū,* Vol. 2.

Draft Biography. Tōrei's manuscript version of the *Ryūtaku-kaiso Jinki Dokumyō Zenji Nempu.* Unpublished manuscript. (A nearly complete version is found in *Hakuin Oshō Shōden.*)

Embossed Tea Kettle. R. D. M. Shaw. Allen & Unwin, 1963. English translations of *Orategama, Yasenkanna,* and other works by Hakuin.

Emmei Jikku Kannon-gyō Reigen-ki (*Accounts of the Miraculous Effects of the Ten Phrase Kannon Sutra for Prolonging Life*). *Hakuin Zenji Hōgo Zenshū,* Vol. 6.

Essential Teachings of Zen Master Hakuin. Translation of Hakuin's *Sokkō-roku kaien-fusetsu* by Norman Waddell. Shambhala, 1994.

Fo-tsu san-ching (Three Teachings of Buddha-patriarchs). Consisting of *Kuei-shan ching-ts'e, Ssu-shih-erh chang ching,* and the *I-chueh ching.* Zokuzō 59–61.

Fumon-bon (Universal Gate chapter). Japanese title of the twenty-fifth chapter of the *Lotus Sutra;* known separately as the *Kannon Sutra.*

Hakuin Oshō Shōden (Detailed Biography of Hakuin Oshō). Rikugawa Taiun. Sankibō, 1965.

Hakuin Oshō Zenshū (Complete Works of Zen Priest Hakuin), 8 vols. Tokyo, 1934.

Hakuin Zenji Hōgo Zenshū (Zen Master Hakuin's Complete Dharma Writings [in Japanese]). 14 vols. Ed. Yoshizawa Katsuhiro. Kyoto, 2002–2006.

Hakuin Zenji Shū. Ed. Tokiwa Daijō. Dainihon bunko, 1938.

Hakuyūshi: shijitsu no shin-tankyū (New Research into the Historicity of Hakuyū). Itō Kazuō. Kyoto, 1960.

Hebiichigo (Snake Strawberries). Hakuin Zenji Hōgo Zenshū, Vol. 1.

Hōkan-ishō (Gudō's Lingering Radiance). Hakuin Oshō Zenshū, Vol. 1.

Hōkyōkutsu no ki (Record of Precious Mirror Cave). Hakuin Zenji Hōgo Zenshū, Vol. 12.

Hsi-keng lu (Record of Hsi-keng). See *Hsu-t'ang yu-lu.*

Hsi-men ching-hsun (Admonitions for Buddhists). T. 48.

Hsin-wang ming (Treatise on the Mind King). Fu Ta-shih. T. 51.

Hsu-t'ang yu-lu (Record of Hsu-t'ang). T. 47.

Itsumadegusa (Wild Ivy). Hakuin Zenji Hōgo Zenshū, Vol. 3.

Jen-t'ien yen-mu (Eye of Men and Gods). T. 48.

Kabe Sōsho (Mutterings to the Wall). Hakuin Zenji Hōgo Zenshū, Vol. 1.

Kaian-kokugo (Dream Words from the Land of Dreams). Ed. Dōmae Sōkan. Zen-bunka Kenkyūsho, 2003.

Kanrin Ihō (Redolence from the Cold Forest). A collection of short texts compiled by Hakuin from Zen and other Buddhist writings to instruct and encourage Zen students. *Hakuin Oshō Zenshū,* Vol. 4.

Kanzan-shi sendai-kimon (Record of Sendai's Comments on the Poems of Cold Mountain). Hakuin Oshō Zenshū, Vol. 4.

Keikyoku sōdan (Stories from a Thicket of Thorn and Briar). Myōki Sōseki. *Hakuin Oshō Zenshū,* Vol. 1.

Keisō Dokuzui (Poison Flowers in a Thicket of Thorns). Hakuin's Zen records in Chinese. *Hakuin Oshō Zenshū,* Vol. 2.

Kinsei kijin-den (Lives of Eccentrics of Recent Times). Ban Kōkei. Tōyō bunko 202. Ed. Munemasa Isoo. Heibonsha, 1972.

Lotus Sutra. Translated by Burton Watson. Columbia University Press, 1993.

Mo-ho chih-kuan (Great Cessation and Insight). Chih-i. T. 46.

Obaba-dono no Kohiki Uta (Old Granny's Tea-Grinding Songs). Hakuin Zenji Hōgo Zenshū, Vol. 13.

Ongakimori (Sentinel at the Gates). Hakuin Zenji Hōgo Zenshū, Vol. 8.

Oniazami (Horse Thistles). Hakuin Zenji Hōgo Zenshū, Vol. 2.

Oradegama. Hakuin Zenji Hōgo Zenshū, Vol. 9.

Pao-ching san-mei (Precious Mirror Samadhi). Tung-shan Liang-chieh. T. 47.

Pi-yen lu (Blue Cliff Record). Yuan-wu K'o-ch'in. T.80.

Po-shan ching-yu (Cautionary Words of Po-shan). Instructions for koan study by the Ming priest Wu-i Yun-lai. Zokuzō 2–17.

Religious Art of Zen Master Hakuin. Yoshizawa Katsuhiro, with Norman Waddell. Counterpoint, 2009.

Ryūtaku-kaiso Jinki Dokumyō Zenji Nempu (Chronological Biography of Zen Master Jinki Dokumyō, Founder of Ryūtaku-ji). Complete Works of Zen Priest Hakuin, Vol. 1.

Sakushin Osana Monogatari (The Tale of My Childhood; full title, Tales of How I Spurred Myself in My Practice). Hakuin Zenji Hōgo Zenshū, Vol. 7.

Sankyō Itchi (Three Teachings In Agreement). Hakuin Zenji Hōgo Zenshū, Vol. 12.

Sashi-mogusa (Moxa). Hakuin Zenji Hōgo Zenshū, Vol. 8.

Sekishu no Onjō (Sound of One Hand; also titled Yabukōji). Hakuin Zenji Hōgo Zenshū, Vol. 12.

Shamon Hakuin (Buddhist Monk Hakuin). Akiyama Kanji. Issued privately, Shizuoka, 1983.

Shao-shih liu-men (Bodhidharma's Six Gates). A collection of six short treatises attributed to Bodhidharma. T. 48.

Shaseki-shū (Collection of Sand and Pebbles). Iwanami bunko, 1943.

Shibu-roku (Four Part Collection). A Japanese compilation of *Hsinhsinming, Chengtao-ko, Tso-ch'an i*, and *Jūgyū-zu*. T. 48.

Sokkō-roku kaien-fusetsu (Dharma Talks Introductory to Lectures on the Record of Hsi-keng). Hakuin Oshō Zenshū, Vol. 2.

Ta-hui shu (Ta-hui's Letters). T. 47.

Ta-hui wu-k'u (Ta-hui's Arsenal). Ta-hui Tsung-kao. *Ta-hui Tsung-kao* T. 47.

Takayama Yūkichi Monogatari (Tale of Yūkichi of Takayama). Hakuin Zenji Hōgo Zenshū, Vol. 7.

Tōrei Oshō Nempu (Chronological Biography of Zen Priest Tōrei). Ed. Nishimura Eshin. Shibunkaku, 1982.

Tsuji dangi (Preaching at the Crossroads). Hakuin Zenji Hōgo Zenshū, Vol. 10.

Unborn: The Life and Teachings of Zen Master Bankei. Translated by Norman Waddell. New York: Farrar, Strauss & Giroux, 2000.

Vimalakirti Sutra. Translated by Burton Watson. Columbia University Press, 1997.

Wild Ivy. Translation of *Itsumadegusa* by Norman Waddell. Shambhala, 1999.

Wu-men kuan (Gateless Barrier). T. 48.

Wu-teng hui-yuan (Compendium of the Five Lamps). Zokuzō 2B:13.

Yabukōji (Spear Grass). Sekishu no Onjō.

Yaemugura (Goose Grass). A composite work made up of *A Story of Four Filial Sisters of Takatsuka, Accounts of the Miraculous Effects of the Ten Phrase Kannon Sutra for Prolonging Life, The Tale of My Childhood*, and *The Tale of Yūkichi of Takayama*. Hakuin Zenji Hōgo Zenshū, Vols. 5, 6, 7.

Yasenkanna (Idle Talk on a Night Boat). Hakuin Zenji Hōgo Zenshū, Vol. 4.

Yun-jen lun (Treatise on the Original Man). Kuei-feng Tsung-mi. T. 45.

Zen Dust. Miura Isshu and Ruth Sasaki. Kyoto, 1965.

Zen Master Hakuin: Selected Writings. Translated by Philip Yampolsky. Columbia. 1971. Includes translations of *Oradegama, Yabukōji,* and *Hebiichigo.*

Zen Teachings of Master Lin-chi. Translated by Burton Watson. Shambhala, 1993.

Zen Words for the Heart. Translation of *Dokugo Shingyō* by Norman Waddell. Shambhala, 1996.

Index

Printed in the United States
by Baker & Taylor Publisher Services